Palgrave Debates in Business and Management

Series Editor
Anders Örtenblad, Department of Working Life and Innovation, School of Business and Law, University of Agder, Grimstad, Norway

This series will take a refreshing and creative approach to business management research, consisting of a number of edited collections that showcase a current academic debate. Each title will examine one specific topic and shall include a number of chapters from authors around the world, presenting their differing points of view on the question in hand. The intention of this series is to take stock of controversial and complicated topics of debate within business and management, and to clearly present the variety of positions within it.

Frederik Hertel · Anders Örtenblad ·
Kenneth Mølbjerg Jørgensen
Editors

Debating Leaderless Management

Can Employees Do Without Leaders?

Editors
Frederik Hertel
Aalborg University Business School
Aalborg East, Denmark

Anders Örtenblad
School of Business and Law
University of Agder
Grimstad, Norway

Kenneth Mølbjerg Jørgensen
Department of Urban Studies
Malmö University
Malmö, Sweden

ISSN 2524-5082   ISSN 2524-5090 (electronic)
Palgrave Debates in Business and Management
ISBN 978-3-031-04592-9   ISBN 978-3-031-04593-6 (eBook)
https://doi.org/10.1007/978-3-031-04593-6

This Palgrave Macmillan imprint is published by the registered company Springer Nature Switzerland AG
The registered company address is: Gewerbestrasse 11, 6330 Cham, Switzerland

Foreword

The dream of workers prospering without bosses has long intrigued academics, practitioners, and politicians, particularly on the political left. Anarchists have always believed that it's not just the state but all forms of authority that are coercive and pernicious, and that a libertarian alternative would free workers and create a fundamentally better form of society. Although we can trace the origins of such leaderless forms of existence back to both ancient Chinese and Greek philosophers, they are more usually related to the works of William Godwin, Max Stirner, Proudhon, Bakunin, Kropotkin, Makhno, and the like. In terms of practice, their presence is less obvious, but they were important influencers on the 1871 Paris Commune, the mutiny at Kronstadt in 1921, and of course, in the Spanish Civil War (1936–1939). But our understanding of how we could organize work without managers is rather less colored by such events and often colored by other forms of romantic nostalgia.

So, while the theoretical attempt to distance organizational forms from the moral and ethical dilemmas of conventional hierarchies have continued over time, there are few substantive and scholarly accounts of what these forms might be—or why they might not prove viable. This collection is an attempt to address this lacuna and to establish whether peer-based alternatives to leader–follower hierarchies can work—the first part of the collection; or why they might or might not—the second part; or why they won't work—the third part. A final chapter considers looking beyond all these debates.

Nielsen's opening chapter in the "For Leaderless Management" half (Chapter 2 in this volume) considers the "moral necessity of leaderless organizations," which of course implies that all conventional leader–follower relations in "leader-based organizations" are immoral or unethical in some way. That includes so-called transformational or servant leaders, since the purpose of these leaders is to redirect the activities of their followers toward the goals set by the leaders, not goals mutually agreed, and inegalitarian power is used to ensure this. That power—inevitably in the eyes of many of the writers in this section—implies not just that a leader generates followers but that the leader will be stained by that very same power and discourage the followers from the honest, moral truth that Habermas and Lukes (1986) regarded as necessary for ethical power. Nielsen's alternative to this, a "leaderless organization", requires a network of temporary peers to coordinate activities but not to lead in a formal sense. Jo Freeman's (1972) paper on what happens when procedural structures are removed to overturn patriarchy—the same old tyrants return to power—suggests that leaderless organizations might require a significant level of administrative control for there to be any non-coercive forms of leadership and Nielsen suggests that peer councils, rotational stewardships, and mentoring would work to this end. Possibly, though the number of organizations that use something like these procedures—and survive—are desperately small, Nielsen's opening chapter is followed by Bob Garvey and Pauline Fatien Diochon's conceptual work on "Eco-Friendly Coaching Practices" (Chapter 3 in this volume) designed to reverse the usual ego-massaging coaching that normally transpires, and to support this with Wenger-inspired "Communities of Discovery" practices, that place situated-learning at the center of social activities. Next, Thomas Borchmann and Bendt Torpegaard Pedersen (Chapter 4 in this volume) pose a more general suggestion—that democratic control is inherently superior to traditional managerial control, and it is worth highlighting here the democratic proclivities of the Scandinavian countries to which many of the authors in the first part of the book belong which would facilitate this kind of argument; one that would probably not emerge spontaneously from British or American sources. Intriguingly, Garvey and Fatien Diochon (Chapter 3 in this volume) conclude that enacting procedures to minimize the damage of conventional management-led organizations by increasing democratic controls, rather than replacing management with democratic control, might actually weaken worker-representation through trade unions, etc., and this is an unintended consequence to be wary of.

Rebecca Selberg and Paula Mulinari (Chapter 5 in this volume) take health care as their empirical focus and suggest that nurses and nursing could be the real focus of interest in establishing the importance of leaderless management since nurses, generally speaking, do not need "leading" by managers because the former are the "knowledge-bearers" of health care. This, of course, is exactly why F. W. Taylor wanted to deskill all employees and deposit all that know-how into the minds of management, so they could control the workforce better. Taylor's schema was intended—according to Taylor—not to exploit the workforce more but to secure greater productivity from them to the benefit of all. Understandably, Taylor's Moral Revolution that he thought should accompany his Scientific Revolution never quite took off in capitalist America but formed the frame for Lenin's assumption that Bolshevism + Taylorism would inaugurate the communist utopia. But this was not for Lenin the leaderless management that actually formed the mainstay of the original "All Power to the Soviets" claim and the Workers' Control that challenged the power of the Bolshevik Party, and it was never going to be tolerated once the Bolsheviks had consolidated their power. And therein lies another warning for proponents of leaderless management—what is the political context within which these alternative models are designed to work within? In effect, could we organize the kind of health system envisaged by Selberg and Mulinari (Chapter 5 in this volume) in a political context that was hostile to it and controlled the resources necessary to run it?

Shih-wei Hsu and Yafei Sun (Chapter 6 in this volume) shift the focus from health to gaming in their chapter and pose "Autonomist Leadership" as an alternative which removes the permanent "leader–follower" binary without discarding leaders, but also alerts us to the "dark side" of this arena because leaderless groups have long operated in terrorist organizations of the extreme right, as well as the left. In their empirical work on the World of Warcraft (WOW) online game, leadership is often temporary and spontaneous and embodies much of the decentering of leadership which they regard as essential to autonomist leadership. But does gaming replicate life?

Ana Martins and Isabel Martins (Chapter 7 in this volume) use the conceptual work of Mary Parker Follett (once called "the Mother of Modern Management" by Morgen Witzel, 2005, p. 167) to promote leaderless management by suggesting that relational activities and non-coercive power sharing ("power-with," not "power-over") are the key to successful organizations. Another conceptual piece, this time by Kenneth Mølbjerg Jørgensen and Sissi Ingman (Chapter 8 in this volume), takes Hannah Arendt's work of Action and the construction of common spaces in the symbolic "agora" as the starting point for their critique of work that inhibits political agency. In short, that small-scale organizing and informal leadership are the bedrocks of leaderless management, and the metaphor of the library is a way of capturing such a place of collective debate, learning, and leadership. Alas, and certainly in England, libraries have been decimated by a decade of government-inspired austerity and again this highlights the importance of political and economic context.

The final chapter in the first section of the book is another conceptual piece, this time by Frederik Hertel and Mogens Sparre (Chapter 9 in this volume), and it is the most radical, suggesting that merely replacing permanent leaders with temporary leaders does not do away with leadership nor does constructing a "leaderless" organization—since this implies that something is missing from the now incomplete organization. Taking Kant's idea that humans should be ends in themselves not a means for something else, the authors argue that conventional Marxism has operated to sustain belief in leaders and leadership while anarchism holds out for a different possibility and invoked what they call a "fluid leadership" that changes with the task required, or what traditional anarchists associate with the "end of the state" rather than the change in who controls the state.

Part II of the book—"In Between For and Against Leaderless Management"—has three chapters. The first, by Jessica Flanagan (Chapter 10 in this volume), warns proponents of the leaderless management movement that some practices—greater workplace democracy for instance—are already in existence in many areas but that even these might have deleterious consequences since they encourage workers to become even more dependent upon their leaders, rather than more independent. Or they might be less efficient than hierarchal organizations thereby asking employees to trade income for influence—something not everyone is willing to do. Furthermore, since many workplace organizations are actually closer to tyrannies than democracies, employees might be rightly skeptical of anything which induces them to take greater responsibility for what goes on at work. Indeed, some of the more egalitarian organizations—trade unions for instance—have historically been as discriminatory as conventional hierarchical employers and are not, therefore, necessarily ethically superior. Or, as Flanagan warns, trading one boss for a thousand bosses does not necessarily resolve the problems of hierarchy and morality at work. The second chapter in this section is by Marjo Siltaoja and Suvi Heikkinen (Chapter 11 in this volume) and they criticize the very idea that passionate individuals—or groups—(often related to charismatics) are somehow necessary for organizational success—whether in leaderless organizations or leader-centric organizations. In one of the few empirical chapters in the collection, they look at sports leadership where success, not ethics, is often the primary color of the those "in charge." The third chapter in the section, authored by Camille A. McKayle (Chapter 12 in this volume), uses the conventions around VUCA to suggest we need to apply creative leadership rather than leaderless leadership to address the problems created by the alleged instability that pervades the world.

Part III of the book switches from pro- to anti-leaderless organizations and has much more of an American flavor, in contrast to the Scandinavian flavor of the first half, in the sense that it both promotes leaders and leadership as essentially good in and of themselves. It starts with a piece by Yusuf M. Sidani and Yasmeen Kaissi (Chapter 13 in this volume) who promote the opposite thesis to that developed by most authors in the first part of the book: Leaders are necessary and functional, and, they suggest, to argue the opposite runs in the face of empirical reality. Thus, without leaders' organizations cannot be inspired, not keep to their values, nor run efficiently and effectively. That most traditional of arguments is tempered by the second chapter by Tommi Auvinen, Pasi Sajasalo, Teppo Sintonen, and Tuomo Takala (Chapter 14 in this volume) whose approach, rooted in an empirical chapter on a Finnish company, suggests that where leaders are missing, followers construct replacements—ghost leaders—to fill the void. Jenika Gobind (Chapter 15 in this volume) looks at leaderless organizations in South Africa and suggests that, given the history of the country and the embedded nature of racial hierarchies at the top of organizational hierarchies, the country needs ethical leaders far more than it needs leaderless organizations because in the absence of ethical leaders' corruption prevails. As the author asks, "How can people in the township who are suffering from a devastating healthcare system, lack of nutrition and poor education find the resources to engage in endless discussions on leaderless management?" Warren Blank (Chapter 16 in this volume) follows Gobind and suggests, in the most conventional practitioner chapter, that organizations need leadership-full not leaderless organizations, and that requires us to differentiate between management and leadership, though again the impact of coercive leadership on followers is considered as a redundant problem in the world envisaged by Blank. And Sharon E. Kenny-Blanchard (Chapter 17 in this volume) suggests that the real issue is ensuring we have "principled" leaders rather than replacing them with leaderless organizations because people need to be led and leaderlessness would lead to the status quo (which rather begs the question about how we got to the status quo without leaderlessness in the first place). Cecile Gerwel Proches (Chapter 18 in this volume) continues in this direction with another VUCA-based address that apparently requires "strong leadership" on the assumption that the turmoil represented by COVID is here to stay. Quite what people in previous centuries of disruption would have to say about our apparently uniquely destabilizing world is anyone's guess but it looks like we are, alas, back to requiring our (individual) leaders to be paragons of virtue.

The final chapter, by Jennifer Chandler and Emily Mertz (Chapter 19 in this volume), tries to take the reader beyond the theoretical purity of the first section and the reconstructed heroism of the third section, to consider what else we might consider. They go back to the origins of the leaderless debate to Bion's work with the British Army selection board, where ambiguous situations required individuals to take up leadership acts, and then consider animal leadership to reflect on human leadership, suggesting that group coordination and collective decision-making are undertaken by large numbers of individuals in terms of how they influence each other. In effect, and reflecting what we know about humans, leadership is not the act of particular individuals but the results of shared experiences and influences.

In sum this is a diverse and worthy collection of pro and anti-leadership accounts; some are grounded in utopian visions, others are flights of tradition, but if the reader is looking for a volume that covers the whole gamut of approaches to a remarkably important topic, then this is that volume.

Keith Grint
Emeritus Professor at Warwick
Business School
The University of Warwick
Coventry, UK

References

Freeman, J. (1972). The tyranny of structurelessness. *Berkeley Journal of Sociology, 17*, 151–165.

Habermas, J. (1986). Hannah Arendt's communications concept of power. In S. Lukes (Ed.), *Power* (pp. 75–92). New York: New York University Press.

Witzel, M. (2005). *The encyclopedia of the history of American management.* London: Continuum International.

Keith Grint is Emeritus Professor at Warwick Business School, the University of Warwick. He has also taught at Brunel, Oxford, Lancaster, and Cranfield Universities. His books include *Leadership: Limits & Possibilities* (2005); *Leadership: A Very Short Introduction* (2010); *The Arts of Leadership* (2000); *Leadership, Management & Command: Rethinking D-Day* (2008); and *Mutiny and Leadership* (2021).

Contents

Notes on Contributors

Tommi Auvinen, Ph.D. is Senior Lecturer at the Jyväskylä University School of Business and Economics (JSBE), Finland, and a docent in narrative leadership research at the University of Lapland focuses on leadership themes, such as storytelling and discursive power, and strategy-as-practice in his research. He has published over 30 refereed articles in national and international journals and book chapters in edited volumes by such esteemed institutions as Routledge and Springer.

Warren Blank is President of The Leadership Group with offices in Vero Beach, FL, Bainbridge Island, WA, and Fairfield, IA, and provides leadership and organizational development training, consulting, speaking, and coaching. Since 1986, he has worked with hundreds of public and private organizations in 30 countries throughout the world. He is the author of seven books on leadership and numerous articles published in professional journals.

Thomas Borchmann is Associate Professor of Work and Organizational Psychology at the Department of Psychology and Communication at the

University of Aalborg, Denmark. His main research interest is in Occupational Health Psychology and Critical Management Studies. He has authored the book *Intimideringskommunikation* with Bendt Torpegaard Pedersen. He has also authored a variety of book contributions, research reports, and articles.

Jennifer L. S. Chandler, Ph.D. is Senior Lecturer at Arizona State University and is the Assistant Director for Diversity and Leadership for the Center for Bio-mediated and Bio-inspired Geotechnics both in Arizona, United States. Her research focuses on revealing and disrupting dominant normative behaviors that are embedded in organizational leadership practices, procedures, and structures that perpetuate systemic oppression.

Pauline Fatien Diochon is Associate Professor of Management at Grenoble Ecole de Management (France) with an international career in Europe, North and South America. Her research explores the ethical, spatial, and political dimensions of leadership development (especially coaching and mentoring). She holds a Ph.D. in Management from HEC School of Management (Paris, France) and a Research Master in Sociology of Power from Université de Paris (France).

Jessica Flanigan is the Richard L. Morrill Chair in Ethics and Democratic Values and an Associate Professor of Leadership Studies and Philosophy, Politics, Economics, and Law in the Jepson School of Leadership Studies at the University of Richmond. Her research addresses the ethics of public policy, medicine, and business. She published in journals such as the *Journal of Business Ethics, Leadership*, and the *Journal of Political Philosophy*.

Bob Garvey is Emeritus Professor at Sheffield Business School (UK). He is one of Europe's leading academic practitioners of mentoring and coaching. He has extensive experience in working internationally and across many sectors of social and economic activity. He is in demand as a keynote speaker at international conferences where he is known for his engaging and challenging style.

Cecile Gerwel Proches is Associate Professor in the Graduate School of Business and Leadership at the University of KwaZulu-Natal (UKZN), Durban, South Africa. She holds a Ph.D. in Leadership Studies. She has successfully supervised several Master's students (M.B.A., M.Com. in Leadership Studies) and also supervises Doctoral students (D.B.A., Ph.D.). Her research, teaching, and consulting interests include leadership, organizational behavior, systems thinking, and complexity theory.

Jenika Gobind, Ph.D. is Senior Lecturer Human Resources at the University of Witwatersrand Business School in Johannesburg South Africa, Wits Business School (WBS). She has extensive experience in the private sector, chairing multiple disciplinary hearings and consulting in labor relations and human resource issues. Her research areas include Human Resource Management, Leadership, and Labor Law.

Suvi Heikkinen is Postdoctoral Researcher at Jyväskylä University School of Business and Economics (JSBE). Her research interest includes ethics in working life, particularly social sustainability and equality in HR, and management and leadership in different contexts. Her work has been published in journals such as *Gender, Work and Organization, Journal of Business Ethics, International Journal of Human Resource Management*, and *Scandinavian Journal of Management*.

Frederik Hertel, Ph.D. is Associate Professor at the Business school of Aalborg University, Denmark. For more than a decade, he worked as project manager, Head development, etc. in regional offices and institutions of higher educations. He is a former head of the study board for the undergraduate programs at the Business school, Aalborg University. His research interests are organizational sociology, creativity, philosophy of management, creativity, and philosophy of science.

Shih-wei Hsu teaches Organizational Behavior at the University of Nottingham Ningbo China. He is Associate Editor of *The Learning Organization*. His primary research interests are in business ethics, social movement organizations, learning organizations, poststructuralism, and critical leadership studies. His recent research interests include management education, paideia, and the concept of "democracy to come."

Sissi Ingman is Assistant Professor at the Department of Urban Studies at Malmö University, Sweden. She teaches leadership, organization, and informatics. Her research interests focus upon Hannah Arendt as a theorist of human organizing, and practices of public organizing between and beyond existing organizations. Her current research focuses on local organizing processes in the city.

Kenneth Mølbjerg Jørgensen, Ph.D. is Professor of Organization Studies at the Department of Urban Studies, Malmö University, Sweden. He teaches leadership and organization regarding societal challenges of sustainability, inclusion, and technology. He researches storytelling, ethics, and power in organizations. His current research focuses upon how to combine storytelling and Gaia into a concept for sustainable leadership. Furthermore, he researches the relations between entrepreneurial stories and urban spaces.

Yasmeen Kaissi received an M.Sc. in Human Resources & Organizational Analysis from King's College London and a B.B.A. from the American University of Beirut. Her career included working at Unilever in both the HR & Marketing functions, and currently as the person responsible for Market Research & Business Development at *Riyada for Social Innovation*, a women-led social enterprise. Her research interests include Human Resources Management, Leadership, and Entrepreneurship.

Sharon E. Kenny-Blanchard, Ed.D., M.Ed., B.Sc. has worked for over 30 years in academic and senior leadership roles encompassing internationalization, enrollment management, institutional communications, governance, innovation, and entrepreneurship. She resides in New Zealand continuing to participate in leadership development research within the Canadian and New Zealand context. She has a long history of governance experience and continues to collaborate with leaders and organizations affiliated with the Principled Leadership Institute.

Gabriele Lakomski is Professor Emeritus in the Melbourne Centre for the Study of Higher Education at the University of Melbourne. Her research interests are in the areas of leadership, organizational and administrative theory, organizational learning and culture, and decision-making. Her naturalistic research program focuses on what affective, cognitive, and cultural neuroscience can tell us about a range of phenomena in organizational behavior including leadership.

Ana Martins, Ph.D. is Associate Professor in Leadership at the University of KwaZulu-Natal, Graduate School of Business & Leadership, South Africa. Her scholarship encompasses diverse countries, namely UK, South Africa, Hong Kong, China, Germany, Portugal, including the Middle East. Her research is indexed in international peer-reviewed academic journals and book chapters with Springer, SAGE. Her key research topics embrace Emerging Concerns Related to Humanizing Leadership and Organizations.

Isabel Martins, Ph.D. is Associate Professor in Organizational Behavior at the University of KwaZulu-Natal, School of Management, IT & Governance, South Africa. Her scholarship spans across Europe, the Middle East, and Africa. Her research is indexed in international peer-reviewed academic journals and book chapters with Springer, Taylor & Francis. Her predominant research includes Organizational Learning, Unlearning, Learning Organisation, Intellectual Capital, Innovation, and Creativity.

Camille A. McKayle, Ph.D. is Provost and Professor of Mathematics at University of the Virgin Islands (US). Her research focuses on organizational creativity, creativity in higher education, creativity and self-efficacy in students, and higher education leadership focusing on Historically Black Colleges/Universities that successfully produce disproportionately number of graduates who are successful in STEM. She is a lead Investigator for the National Science Foundation-funded Center for the Advancement of STEM Leadership.

Emily Mertz, Ph.D. is Lecturer in the Leadership and Integrative Studies Department, College of Integrative Sciences and Arts, Arizona State University in Tempe, AZ, United States. Her research focuses on environmental leadership and the interdisciplinarity of conservation and development. She, e.g., examines how environmental leadership can create solutions that align conservation, sustainability, and social justice.

Paula Mulinari is Associate Professor at the Department of Social Work, Malmö University. She focuses on gender, race, class, and economy. She has done extensive work analyzing intersectionality and everyday resistance in work. Mulinari also studies trade unions, strikes, and individual and collective mobilization. A recent problem addressed is conflicting identities and fractured solidarities—through the lens of class, masculinities, and whiteness—in three male–dominated trade unions in Sweden.

Jeffrey S. Nielsen is Lecturer in philosophy at Utah Valley University specializing in applied ethics and moral decision-making, where he also is a fellow at the Center for the Study of Ethics. He has taught ethical leadership and governance at the Bill and Vieve Gore School of Business at Westminster College in Salt Lake City, Utah and traveled internationally mentoring organizations in ethical management practices.

Anders Örtenblad is Professor of Working Life Science at the School of Business and Law, University of Agder, Norway. He has edited books that have been published by Edward Elgar Publishing, Oxford University Press, Palgrave Macmillan, Routledge, Sage, and Springer. He is a big fan of research as open, academic debate, and is the editing founder of the book series *Palgrave Debates in Business and Management*.

Bendt Torpegaard Pedersen is Associate Professor of Work and Organizational Psychology at the Department of Psychology and Communication at the University of Aalborg, Denmark. His main research interest is in Occupational Health Psychology and Critical Management Studies. He has authored several books including *Klinisk Social Psykologi* and *Intimideringskommunikation* with Thomas Borchmann. He has also authored a variety of book contributions, research reports, and articles.

Pasi Sajasalo, Ph.D. is Lecturer in Management and Leadership at the Jyväskylä University School of Business and Economics, Finland, and focuses on strategy work in varying contexts on his research. Most recently on strategy-as-practice inspired work, including cognitive aspects of strategy, such as strategy-related sensemaking and sensegiving. His work appears in national and international journals as well as in book chapters of volumes published by renowned international publishers.

Rebecca Selberg is Senior Lecturer in Gender Studies at the Department of Gender Studies, Lund University. She is Ph.D. in Sociology from Linnaeus University. Her research revolves around political economy, public sector work, care work and nursing, and relations of gender, power, and race in organizations. Between 2021 and 2022, Selberg has been employed as a researcher at Skåne University Hospital and its intensive care units, evaluating their COVID-19-crisis response.

Yusuf M. Sidani, Ph.D. is Professor of Leadership and Business Ethics at the Suliman S. Olayan School of Business, American University of Beirut (AUB). His research focuses on business and employee ethics, gender, and diversity in organizations, and international human resource management with special interest in the Middle East region. His research appeared in leading international peer-reviewed academic journals.

Marjo Siltaoja is Associate Professor of management and leadership at Jyväskylä University School of Business and Economics (JSBE). Her research interests include moral struggles in business and society relations such as (de)legitimation and stigmatization efforts, and corporate sustainability and ethics. Her work has been published, among others, in the *Academy of Management Learning and Education, Journal of Business Ethics, Organization, Organization Studies*, and *Organization Theory*.

Teppo Sintonen, Ph.D. (Management and Leadership), Ph.D. (Sociology) is Senior Lecturer in Management and Leadership at the Jyväskylä University School of Business and Economics, Finland. His research focuses on diversity, identity, and storytelling in organizations. He specializes in qualitative research methods, especially narrative methods. His research focuses on leadership themes, such as organizational storytelling, discursive power, diversity, and gender issues.

Mogens Sparre, Ph.D. is Associate Professor at the faculty of Humanities at Aalborg University, Denmark. With more than 20 years of leadership and consulting experience from large Danish and international organizations, he started his Ph.D. in 2013, which he defended in 2016. His research areas are leadership, organizational development, and culture bound together by participatory action research. Cooperatives and Storytelling are important issues in his work.

Yafei Sun graduated from the University of Liverpool with a major in Human Resource Management. She is an Office Administration Specialist and a music teacher at the Anyang Preschool Education College. She teaches vocal music, piano, music theory, and solfeggio. Her research interests include game studies, critical leadership studies, human resource management, and organization behavior.

Tuomo Takala is Professor of Management and Leadership at the Jyväskylä University School of Business and Economics, Finland, and does research by using qualitative research methods. One of his current projects is "Charisma in various contexts" dealing with questions such as what is charisma, who are charismatic people, and does charisma lead to redemption or ruin? He also studies business ethics and CSR themes.

List of Tables

1

Introducing the Debate on Leaderless Management

Frederik Hertel, Anders Örtenblad,
and Kenneth Mølbjerg Jørgensen

Introduction

Most employees occasionally doubt that their leaders do a good job, and some even wonder whether their job and life would be easier and better without leaders. In fact, there is even a relatively recent stream of the

F. Hertel (✉)
Aalborg University Business School, Aalborg University, Aalborg, Denmark
e-mail: fhl@business.aau.dk

A. Örtenblad
Department of Working Life and Innovation, School of Business and Law, University of Agder, Grimstad, Norway
e-mail: anders.ortenblad@uia.no

K. M. Jørgensen
Department of Urban Studies, Malmö University, Malmö, Sweden
e-mail: Kenneth.molbjerg-jorgensen@mau.se

leadership literature that has started to heavily criticize the leadership that some (too many, according to the critics) leaders perform (Aasland et al. 2010; Kellerman 2004; Lipman-Blumen 2005a, 2005b; Morris and Edmonds 2021; Örtenblad 2021; Schyns and Schilling 2013; Tepper 2000). However, even this stream of literature seems, to us, to put a lot of focus on "leaders", thereby legitimizing and underlining the existence of leaders, rather than questioning it, even though the perspective taken is a much more critical one than within the mainstream leadership literature.

One corner stone behind the present book is the tendency of overestimating the importance of leadership and leaders that is prevalent in much leadership literature. In fact, hardly anyone questions their legitimacy. In this literature, as well as among many people in general, there is an assumption that leaders are necessary (Mintzberg 1989; Parker et al. 2020, p. 111; Pfeffer 1994). Leaderless management was unthinkable for scholars such as Drucker (1974), who argued that managers were those that held an organization—the smallest as well as the biggest—together and made it work. Much of the literature could be said to—more or less implicitly—embed their argument in the *great man theory* (see Jørgensen and Ingman, Chapter 8 in this volume), which sometimes comes under the notion of the *leader-centric approach* (see Lakomski, Epilogue in this volume). An implication for practice from such a theory/approach is that leaders—consciously or unconsciously—attempt to upgrade their importance and legitimize the demand for themselves, while downgrading the importance of employees. These iconic (Peirce 1998), self-referential (Luhmann 2000), and hyperbole (Aristoteles 2007, p. 230) aspects of daily leadership are embedded in and expressed in leaders' communication, behavior, and action. They can also be noticed when leaders conduct micromanagement and act as "commanders" (Alvesson and Spicer 2011, p. 118).

We strongly believe that basic assumptions such as this one—that leaders self-evidently are needed—should be questioned. Inspired by Ohlsson and Rombach's (2015) "art of constructive criticism"—where they suggest that one reflects on "could it be the other way around?"—we dare to think the apparently unthinkable and ask questions such as: What would happen if there were no leaders? Will organizations be able to exist without formal as well as informal leadership and will employees be able to find new ways to handle production and the exchange of production? These are the questions we asked the contributors to consider in their chapters. Two sub-questions are of special interest: the *realizability* and the *desirability* of management without both any formal and informal leaders. The debate is, thus, focusing on if organizations (in its broadest term, thus inclusive of private, public and voluntary organizations) can be managed by the employees themselves ad-hoc (De Geus 2014), as well as whether or not it is an idea worth striving for.

For some rarely questioned assumptions, there is a need to put counterarguments only, something which would result in an "against book" (Örtenblad 2020; Parker 2002). In other cases—such as this one—we believe that an open debate, with room for contributors taking any position of their own choice (thus, including both contributions from those who argue "for" and from those arguing "against"), is the most relevant form for critical examination. We dedicate the present book to such examination and invite the readers to reflect upon the necessity of leaders while reading the debate on whether employees can do without leaders that the book contains.

Thus, we do not wish to prescribe which position the reader should take. Instead, we encourage the reader to critically examine the arguments that are put forward in the book and make up their own mind. Even if the individual chapters can be regarded as normative—in the sense that its authors take a clear and explicit standpoint to "leaderless management" (something which in our opinion is too rarely seen in leadership literature, but see Kirkeby [2010] for an exception, who also underlines that all approaches to management and leadership should be normative)—the total collection of chapters, the present book per se, is not normative. It does not prescribe whether management should be leaderless or not (or anywhere in between). Instead, the very idea about this book is to let the reader judge for her- or himself. We strongly believe in "debating" as a format for pedagogics as well as for communicating research outcomes. Our effort has been to offer a broad variety of positions and arguments, thereby inviting readers to make up their own minds of whether they have faith in leaderless management or not.

In the remainder of this chapter, we first share with the readers how we, the editors, position ourselves within the debate on leaderless management. Thereafter, we present our own definitions of the term "leaderless management" as well as of its constituent elements. The chapter continues with a presentation of the book and its structure and content, that is, the book's four parts (plus an epilogue), and a brief presentation of each of the chapters in the book (see Appendix for an overview of the book content and structure). Finally, we present some observations regarding the chapters' orientation to either arguing for/against that leaderless management is *realizable* or that it is *desirable*.

The Position(s) Taken by the Editors

It is, of course, difficult not to let one's own position in the debate color the editing of a book such as this one. We have nevertheless tried hard to respect the authors' line of argumentation in our editing of the book's chapters. Our efforts have been targeted toward putting together a nuanced book mirroring many different positions and arguments. It is nevertheless a good idea to share the positions taken by the editors. Two of the three editors have themselves contributed to the debate, with one co-authored chapter each. Both of these chapters appear in Part I of the book and argue, thus, *for* leaderless management. The one of the editors who has not contributed with any chapter of his own to the very debate is somewhat of a "leaderlessness realist/pessimist/doubter"—he thinks it is a beautiful ideal and has high hopes, but he doubts it would be realizable in practice, at least in the near future (this is at least his current position).

The editors who are for leaderless management are critical about much of the debates concerning curriculums for leadership education, which focus on the traits and capabilities of leaders as persons—debates which have been ongoing since ancient times (Cleary 2004; Quintilian 1996). This position is born from the conviction that the challenge of leadership is less a question of who should be in charge than it is a question of whether some people are in charge (Kinna 2005). From here, the questions developed, and they soon found themselves asking: "Can employees do without leaders?". Their immediate answer is "yes" since people in organizations in any case manage without a leader being physically present. In fact, organizations cannot function without such self-management. Intuitively, this suggests that the importance of centrally positioned leaders are exaggerated. Leaders are always only temporary present and cannot monitor, control, and manage all activities in everyday organizational life.

Leaders are forced to leave room for what Johnsen (2002, p. 600) calls co-leadership conducted by employees. It is a result of a leadership vacuum left to be filled by employees to ensure that the organization obtains its aims. Formally or informally appointed leaders always rely on co-leadership. Leader-centric organizations are always continually passing between leadership and the absence of leadership (see Auvinen et al., Chapter 14 in this volume). The temporary presence/absence of leaders is a distinctive mark of leadership.

Defining "Leader", "Leaderless", "Management", and "Leaderless Management"

We stumbled in our attempts to find a proper expression for organizations functioning without leaders. The first and probably most obvious attempt is the expression "leaderless organizations" (Kinna 2014; Parker et al. 2020; Ward 1966). We soon realized that this expression may connotate "headless organizations" and thereby refers to organizations where employees might suffer from or enjoy their leaders being mentally or physically absent. Our interest, though, was not to debate headless organizations (Groat 1997). Nor was our interest to debate the idea of "co-leadership", by which Johnsen (2002) referred to employees handling leader tasks and thereby conducting co-leadership. Instead, we came up with the term "leaderless management", a term that others before us also have used (e.g., Ropo et al. 2020)—not necessarily, though, do we define the term in the exact way as those who previously have used it.

The term "management" etymologically implies "handling" (The Online Etymology Dictionary 2022). Hence, in the original sense of the term, "management" referred to people (in plural) "handling everyday practices", like, for example, a household. It was only later that it became associated with one person, the *manager*, being formally responsible for managing and coordinating people. Thus, the term "management" has today a different meaning from its etymological origin.

We have for this book chosen the term "leader" (as in "leaderless") instead of the term "manager". While we did not want to re-start the mainstream discussion about the possible differences between leaders and managers (Kotter 1999), we chose "leader" merely to emphasize that even if an organization is free from *formal* leaders—that is, managers—*informal* leaders may take over. Thus, what we had in mind when inviting scholars to take part in the debate on "leaderless management", was organizations that could run without even informal leaders.

While not all combined concepts mean the sum of the meanings of its constituent elements (Wisniewski 1997), a fair interpretation of what we mean by "leaderless management" is, in fact, the sum of our above definitions of "management" and (the lack of) "leaders", respectively. Hence, by this term we refer to a state where the employees themselves take care of the running of a business, with no individual having been formally assigned any more responsibility or power than any other individual, and where no individual through informal power can take on a leading position in the management on a continuous, informal basis. It refers to situations where employees in everyday life manage without leaders. Thus, when inviting scholars to contribute to the present book, we took the initiative to a debate on whether or not employees permanently *can* do without leaders whatsoever and whether or not that is *desirable*.

Nonetheless, it is true—we must confess—that we were not fully clear on what we meant by the term "leaderless management" in our invitation to the contributions. In any case, what we explained above was (we now think) what we meant when inviting scholars around the world to contribute to the debate on "leaderless management". We do not believe that the lack of preciseness at our end has had any devastating impact on the outcome; on the contrary, we believe that the lack of clarity in this respect opened up for arguments and contributions we may otherwise had not received.

The Content of the Book

The book is divided into four parts (see Appendix for an overview of the parts, chapters, and—especially—their main arguments and contributions related to leaderless management). We prefer to start the book off by those chapters representing the "anti-thesis", that is, those arguing that leaderless management in fact is desirable (and practicable), while those who defend status quo—thus representing the "thesis"—get the final word. Well, not the very final word, since we have put the chapter arguing *beyond* leaderless management as the final part of the book (Part IV). Then again, there is also an Epilogue, at the very end of the book. Between the first two parts, that is, between Part I containing the chapters arguing *for* leaderless management and Part III where the chapters arguing *against* leaderless management are put, there are a few chapters that argue *in between* for and against leaderless management, which thus appear in Part II.

Below we present the chapters and go through how they approach the question of leaderless management.

Part I. *For* Leaderless Management

Part I of the book contains contributions from authors arguing for leaderless management. They are very different, but a common thread is that they define "leaderless management" as that employees make the decisions, instead of leaders. Several authors refer to anarchism as a source of inspiration to leaderless management. They furthermore express a strong conviction about collaboration (collectivism), where members of the organization share purposes and act collectively based on equality (democratic participation in decision-making). Leaderless management is thus perceived as non-hierarchical, peer-based, self-led, and self-organized democratic communities, but it could, according to some authors, also be a system of rotational stewardship positions and mentors.

Chapter 2, "The Moral Necessity of Leaderless Organizations", written by Jeffrey S. Nielsen, argues that leaderless management ensures basic human dignity and autonomy. It furthermore empowers people to involve in decision-making affecting their own life. It is an ethical belief in humans having a mutual, equal, and reciprocal obligation to speak and listen to each other. Chapter 3, "Developing for Leaderless Organizations: Two Eco-Friendly Coaching Practices", written by Bob Garvey and Pauline Fatien Diochon, argues for leaderless management to impose collaboration in communities based on self-organization. Garvey and Fatien Diochon furthermore argue for self-led democratic communities weaving people together around a common horizon.

Chapter 4, "When Matters Are Too Important to be Left to Leaders and Better Left to Democratic Control", is written by Thomas Borchmann and Bendt Torpegaard Pedersen. They argue for leaderless management to obtain democratic practice in organizations. They argue, as evident in the chapter title, that issues about the work environment are too important to be left to leaders to handle. Chapter 5, "Leaderless Management as the Solution to Struggles Over the Moral Center of Healthcare? Ward Nurses' Critique of Management as 'Real Utopias' in the Public Sector", is written by Rebecca Selberg and Paula Mulinari. It is one of few chapters that is based on empirical studies, in this case conducted in the healthcare sector. By indicating that employees may need some people to handle managerial tasks, but since employees rely on their professions, they do not need leaders to manage.

Chapter 6, "Dissolving the Leader–Follower Schism: Autonomist Leadership and the Case of World of WarCraft", written by Shih-wei Hsu and Yafei Sun, introduces autonomist leadership to solve what they call the leader–follower schism. Hsu and Sun are thereby among authors who refer to an anarchist approach in the debate on leaderless management. They apply a semi-empirical approach by including examples from computer games (World of WarCraft) to illustrate how players interact and act in the frame of leaderlessness. They argue for organizing without a fixed leadership in the center. Chapter 7, "In Favor of Leader*less* Management: Follettian Perspective of Co-leadership", written by Ana Martins and Isabel Martins, argues that leaderless management is inherent in and shared by the group. Mary Parker Follett (1868–1933) inspires them, and as a result, the authors argue that leaderless management promotes an auspicious learning culture in organizations. Chapter 8, "Leaderless Leadership: Implications of the 'Agora' and the 'Public Library'", is written by Kenneth Mølbjerg Jørgensen and Sissi Ingman. Using Hannah Arendt's (1998) distinction between *action* and *work*, they develop a variant of leaderless management that they call *leaderless leadership*. They use the metaphor "agora" to denote how organizations can be led leaderlessly through democratic participation. They combine this with the metaphor of "public library" to denote a space of generosity, which is necessary for preservation of a common space among people. Chapter 9, "Beyond Leaderlessness: Even Less Than Nothing Is Way Too Much" written by Frederik Hertel and Mogens Sparre, completes Part I. This chapter is one of the most radical contributions to leaderless management in arguing for an anarchistic organization. The principal argument is that we need to break away not only from the leadership approach but also from the interconnected idea about leaderless management to fulfill Proudhon's watchword: "the government of the none".

Part II. *In Between* For and Against Leaderless Management

The contributions located in Part II, "*In between* for and against leaderless management", contain definitions of leaderless management that are similar to or at least comparable with the definitions included in Part I, "*For* leaderless management". One of these contributions is Chapter 10, "Leaderless Work and Workplace Participation" authored by Jessica Flanigan. The author questions both leader-centric and collective leadership approaches in favor of organizational frameworks that emphasize individual freedom and reward individual performance. Central to her argument is the idea that employee participation does not lead to better leadership, nor to democratic leadership.

In their Chapter 11, "Who Sustains Whose Passion?", Marjo Siltaoja and Suvi Heikkinen ask critical questions both about leadership practice and about leaderless management. By taking the in-between position, they invite us to ponder upon the ethical tensions arising from leaderless organization and also speculate why such organization can be misaligned with collectively shared and negotiated ethical practice. They discuss whether shared leadership could help solve some of the ethical tensions. The third chapter in Part II, Chapter 12, "Leaderless Organization Versus Leading for Creativity: The Case for Creative Leadership", is authored by Camille A. McKayle, who sees advantages with leaderless management. However, when organizations exist in a VUCA (volatile, uncertain, complex, and ambiguous) world, such leaderless organization is less effective—under such circumstances there is a need for creative leadership to ensure that employees produce innovative outcomes.

Part III. *Against* Leaderless Management

Part III contains contributions arguing against leaderless management. Some of the contributions argue that leaders are necessary because otherwise organizations will suffer from losing values, identity, and direction. This theme is common, in Part III, and represents an underlying assumption that chaos arises if there are no leaders. But there is also one chapter arguing that even in organizations without leaders, employees will tend to construct an image of them anyway—leaders will always be created narratively, even when they are absent.

In Chapter 13, "Why Leaders Are Necessary" written by Yusuf M. Sidani and Yasmeen Kaissi, the argument is that organizations in trying to include leaderless management will suffer from losing values, identity, and direction. The only way to get this is to reject leaderlessness and ensure that organizations are leaderful. Chapter 14, "Ghostbusters! On the Narrative Creation of (Absent) Leader Characters", is written by Tommi Auvinen, Pasi Sajasalo, Teppo Sintonen, and Tuomo Takala. They argue that leaderlessness is a Fata Morgana (i.e., a mirage) since leadership always is present even when the formal leader is physically absent.

Chapter 15, "Against Leaderless Management: What Leaderless Means in South Africa", is written by Jenika Gobind. Here, the context is South Africa. The author argues that leadership and, more precisely, ethical leadership, is required to avoid waste of resources. South African society is caught in several problems, making it impossible to experiment with leaderless management. Therefore, Gobind argues for the need for ethical leadership. Chapter 16, "Leaderless Management: No! Leaders at All Levels: Yes!", is written by Warren Blank. The author argues that the expression "leaderless management" is a misnomer. It is wrong and somehow an inaccurate use of an expression. Blank explains that information technology already reduces the organizational hierarchies and that organizations need leadership on all levels to function.

Chapter 17, "Principled Leadership: The Antidote to Leaderless Management", is written by Sharon E. Kenny-Blanchard. The argument is that leaderless management leads to status quo, and that leadership is required to ensure that organizations follow the right direction and to avoid chaos. Employees need support, which is ensured by principled leadership. Chapter 18, "The Enabling Role of Leadership in Realizing the Future", is written by Cecile Gerwel Proches. She argues against leaderless management on the backdrop of the present state produced by the pandemic but also other challenges, namely what is called VUCA (volatility, uncertainty, complexity, and ambiguity). For Gerwel Proches, VUCA characterizes contemporary organizations, and it requires leaders with a great spirit and courage, who take the lead instead of poor leadership practices affected by corruption, nepotism, and incompetence.

Part IV. *Beyond* Leaderless Management

Part IV contains a contribution arguing, kind of, "beyond" leaderless management. Here we find a chapter that is significantly different from the other chapters in the authors' approach to the phenomenon. Chapter 19, "Organizational Management Is Paradoxically Both Leaderless and Leaderful", is authored by Jennifer Chandler and Emily Mertz. The key argument is that leaderless management originally was a scenario produced by psychologists during World War II to access leader potentials among soldiers. Leadership is not a person but a process, which means that all members of an organization somehow collaborate or participate in generating leadership—therefore, all or none can already be considered "leaders". Organizations are, therefore, simultaneously leaderless and leaderful.

Epilogue

In the epilogue, Gabriele Lakomski presents an "Afterword", where she offers a context for the debate on leaderless management and highlights some important learning points.

A Note on Arguments on Realizability and Desirability

It is not that easy to comment on the content of a book that is supposed to offer a variety of standpoints and for which no unified conclusion is supposed to be offered. Any commentary from the editors runs the risk of being regarded as a way to manipulate the readers, by discretely convincing them of the grandiosity of the position(s) taken by the editors. We have for this reason chosen to keep our commentaries to a minimum. The one theme we have decided to comment on is one which we regard to be very basic for the debate on leaderless management, namely whether the authors mainly have focused on realizability or desirability (or both) in their argumentations. To further avoid editor-bias, we avoid making evaluative statements—instead, we merely present the various focuses and suggest how these offer space for further contributions to the debate, beyond the present book.

One of the characteristics of chapters in Part III—"*Against* leaderless management"—is that their approach to leaderless management focuses on (the lack of) "realizability" rather than (the lack of) "desirability". Several of the chapters claim that leaderless management would not function in reality since employees need leaders, e.g., leaders are needed to impose values, to direct, and to guide. Appendix indicates that only one of the chapters (by Gobind, Chapter 15 in this volume) arguing against leaderless management includes ethical arguments. The fact that these chapters generally leave out arguments connected to "desirability" (or the lack thereof) leaves room for others—who may want to add to the debate on "leaderless management"—to put forward arguments supporting the undesirable effects that leaderless management may have. Simultaneously, it gives reason for supporters of leaderless management to strengthen their arguments of the realizability of leaderless management. Alternatively, they may want to criticize their opponents for not having any strong arguments against the desirability of leaderless management, and that it, therefore, not is a that bad idea after all—that which is desirable but difficult to practice could always be realized in the long run.

Let us now take a closer look at the line of argumentation in the chapters in Part I—"*For* leaderless management". Despite the variety in the authors' arguments, they all consider leaderless management possible and several of them, furthermore, considers it being desirable from an ethical perspective (e.g., Nielsen, Chapter 2, in this volume; Selberg and Mulinari, Chapter 5 in this volume). Here, some contributors argue against treating others as means, while others consider contemporary leadership as unethical (Nielsen, Chapter 2 in this volume) and that it should be replaced by leaderless management. The authors base their arguments on ideals about equality (in connection to gender, economy, decision-making, etc.), justice, the realization of human potential, etc. Several authors (e.g., Hertel and Sparre, Chapter 9 in this volume; Hsu and Sun, Chapter 6 in this volume) refer to anarchism as a means to understand leaderless management, but only two contributions include a discussion about the contemporary fight for increasing the production of surplus-value (Hertel and Sparre, Chapter 9 in this volume; Martins and Martins, Chapter 7 in this volume). Thus, opponents to leaderless management may want to develop counterarguments to, especially, the idea that leaderless management is a more ethical form of management than leaderful management, but also to the idea that leaderless management better than leaderful management actually may be a successful form of management in economic terms.

References

Aasland, M. S., Skogstad, A., Notelaers, G., Nielsen, M. B., & Einarsen, S. (2010). The prevalence of destructive leadership behavior. *British Journal of Management, 21*(2), 438–452.

Alvesson, M., & Spicer, A. (Eds.). (2011). *Metaphors we lead by*. Oxon, UK: Routledge.

Arendt, H. (1998). *The human condition* (2nd ed.). Chicago: University of Chicago Press.

Aristoteles. (2007). *Retorik*. Viborg, Denmark: Museum Tuscalanums forlag.

Cleary, T. (2004). *Zen lessons: The art of leadership*. Boston: Shambhala Publications, Inc.

Drucker, P. (1974). *Management: Tasks, responsibilities, practices*. London: Routledge.

De Geus, M. (2014). Peter Kropotkin's anarchist vision of the organization. *Ephemera—Theory & Politics in Organization, 14*(4), 853–871.

Groat, M. (1997). The informal organisation: Ride the headless monster. *Management Accounting, 75*(4), 40–42.

Johnsen, E. (2002). *Managing the managerial process*. Gentofte, Denmark: Djøf Publishing.

Kellerman, B. (2004). *Bad leadership: What it is, how it happens, why it matters*. Boston: Harvard Business Publishing.

Kinna, R. (2005). *Anarchism: A beginner's guide*. Oxford: Oneworld Publications.

Kinna, R. (2014). Anarchism and critical management studies. *Ephemera— Theory & Politics in Organization, 14*(4), 639–658.

Kirkeby, O. F. (2010). *Management philosophy*. Heidelberg: Springer-Verlag.

Kotter, J. P. (1999). *I spidsen for forandringer*. København, Denmark: Peter Asschenfeldts nye forlag.

Lipman-Blumen, J. (2005a). *The allure of toxic leaders: Why we follow destructive bosses and corrupt politicians—And how we can survive them*. New York: Oxford University Press.

Lipman-Blumen, J. (2005b). The allure of toxic leaders: Why followers rarely escape their clutches. *Ivey Business Journal*, *69*(3), 1–8.

Luhmann, N. (2000). *Sociale systemer*. Copenhagen: Hans Reitzels forlag.

Mintzberg, H. (1989). *Mintzberg on management*. New York: The Free Press.

Morris, L. R., Jr., & Edmonds, W. M. (2021). *When leadership fails: Individual, group and organizational lessons from the worst workplace experiences*. Bingley, UK: Emerald Group Publishing.

Ohlsson, Ö., & Rombach, B. (2015). The art of constructive criticism. In A. Örtenblad (Ed.), *Handbook of research on management ideas and panaceas: Adaptation and context* (pp. 149–170). Cheltenham, UK and Northampton, MA, USA: Edward Elgar Publishing.

Örtenblad, A. (Ed.). (2020). *Against entrepreneurship: A critical examination*. Cham, Switzerland: Palgrave Macmillan.

Örtenblad, A. (Ed.). (2021). *Debating bad leadership: Reasons and remedies*. Cham, Switzerland: Palgrave Macmillan.

Parker, M. (2002). *Against management: Organization in the age of managerialism*. Oxford: Polity.

Parker, M., Stoborod, K., & Swann, T. (Eds.). (2020). *Anarchism, organization, and management: Critical perspectives for students*. New York: Routledge.

Peirce, C. S. (1998). The essential Peirce (Vol. 2, N. Houser, J. R. Eller, A. L. Lewis, de Tienne, A. C. L. Clark, & D. B. Davis, Eds.). Bloomington, IN: Indiana University Press.

Pfeffer, J. (1994). *Managing with power*. Boston: Harvard Business School Press.

Ropo, A., Mäkinen, E. I., & Seppä, I. (2020). Online company blogs as narrations of plural leadership. *Journal of Organizational Change Management*, *33*(4), 609–621.

Quintilian, M. F. (1996). *Kritik og retorik*. Aarhus, Denmark: Aarhus University Press.

Schyns, B., & Schilling, J. (2013). How bad are the effects of bad leaders? A meta-analysis of destructive leadership and its outcomes. *Leadership Quarterly*, *24*(1), 138–158.

Tepper, B. J. (2000). Consequences of abusive supervision. *Academy of Management Journal*, *43*(2), 178–190.

The Online Etymology Dictionary. (2022). Manage. https://www.etymonline.com/word/manage. Accessed 18 Feb 2022.

Ward, C. (1966). The organization of anarchy. In L. I. Krimerman & L. Perry (Eds.), *Patterns of anarchy* (pp. 386–396). New York: Anchor Books.

Wisniewski, E. J. (1997). When concepts combine. *Psychonomic Bulletin & Review, 4*(2), 167–183.

Part I

For Leaderless Management

2

The Moral Necessity of Leaderless Organizations

Jeffrey S. Nielsen

Introduction

In this chapter, I will argue for the moral necessity of leaderless organizations. This position rests on two supporting arguments. One, leader-based organizations inevitably create unethical relationships between leaders and followers. Two, leaderless organizations are an ethical and effective alternative to leader-based organizations. By leaderless organizations, I mean the absence of permanent and professional leader and manager positions and the presence of a peer-based management system, where the language of "leader" (or manager) and "follower" is replaced by the language of councils, rotational stewardship positions, and mentors (Nielsen 2004). The governing principles of a leaderless organization are

J. S. Nielsen (✉)
The UVU Department of Philosophy and Humanities, Utah Valley
University, Orem, UT, USA
e-mail: nielsjef@uvu.edu

© The Author(s), under exclusive license to Springer Nature
Switzerland AG 2022
F. Hertel et al. (eds.), *Debating Leaderless Management*,
Palgrave Debates in Business and Management,
https://doi.org/10.1007/978-3-031-04593-6_2

the ethical imperatives that no one should be denied the opportunity to participate in the decision-making affecting their own lives and that each person possesses the equal privilege to speak, and each person shares an equal and reciprocal obligation to listen. Respect for our basic human dignity and autonomy requires nothing less.

Of course, the prevailing management theory assumes that all organizations must be leader-based in order to perform effectively the required management functions such as planning, organizing, coordinating, and motivating employees (Greenleaf 1977; Mintzberg 2009). Further, it is argued that previous attempts at creating leaderless organizations, or substitutes for leadership, have been ineffective, thus proving the necessity of leaders (Podsakoff et al. 1993). At most, it may be conceded that only in very limited contexts can groups or teams within organizations function without leaders (Dionne et al. 2005). I disagree and will argue that not only do leader-based organizations create an unethical power relationship between leaders and followers, which these arguments overlook, but that a peer-based management system in a leaderless organization can effectively perform the necessary management functions, and most importantly, do so by respecting the dignity and autonomy of all organizational members.

This argument for leaderless organizations in this chapter is structured as follows. I begin by presenting the ethical problem inherent in all leader-based organizations. I will define what is meant by "leader" and look at the evolution in our concept of leader. Then, I will show how every conception of leader produces an unethical power relationship between leaders and followers. I will address why we think we need leaders and then argue that if there is an ethical and effective alternative to leader-based organizations, then we are morally obligated to replace leader-based organizations with this alternative. I will conclude by showing why a peer-based management system in a leaderless organization is this ethical and effective alternative.

The Ethical Problem Inherent in Leader-Based Organizations

Of course, my argument for leaderless organizations is not an indictment of the individuals who hold leadership positions. This is an argument against the context of leader–follower relationships and the unethical effects on leaders and followers alike. As Robert Greenleaf (1977) and Vaclav Havel (1997) have pointed out, the burdens and privileges of rank-based leadership positions have isolating and corrupting influences on the well-being and happiness of the leaders themselves. Ultimately, however, the argument is that a leaderless organization will be both ethical and strategically more competitive and successful than its leader-based counterparts. Further, good leaders will be even more effective as good mentors and coaches to the peer councils in leaderless organizations. But first things first. I will explore what is meant by leader and the unethical power dynamic that follows.

A Definition of Leader in Leader-Based Organizations

Of course, there are many different definitions and uses of the word, "leader." We might think of a leader on a team, who motivates her teammates to greater effort, or we might call someone a leader who in any context inspires others and lives a morally excellent life. However, in this chapter, we are interested in leaders in the sense of professional leaders in management positions: leaders in leader-based organizations. In this context, we are referring to an individual in a position of high power (the leader), who influences a group of individuals in low power positions (the followers) to act toward some goal or objective decided by the leader and in a manner chosen by the leader (Ciulla 2003). A leader in a leader-based organization is the person privileged to monopolize information, control resources and decision-making, and command compliance from the followers. In other words, in leader-based organizations, only the leader has a privilege to speak, and the follower possesses the unreciprocated obligation to listen and obey. Of course, the leader may decide not to exercise his or her privilege to monopolize, command, and control, and even sincerely invite greater participation from the followers. Yet, as we will see, the unequal power relationship remains. Everyone knows that the prerogatives of unequal power may be invoked at any time, *ex cathedra*, simply by whim of the leader, without the need for any further justification than an appeal to the leadership position.

Evolution of the Definition of Leader

There has been a gradual emergence of three different types of leadership models over time: namely, Traditional, Transactional, and Transformational leadership (Burns 2010). Traditional leadership, though still alive and well today in many business organizations, dominated until the early decades of the twentieth century. It rested on the leader's ability to impress their will on the followers and to produce a blind obedience through the coercive exercise of power over their followers, who cooperated primarily out of fear. This style of autocratic leadership was superseded by the transactional leadership found in the works of persons like Frederick Taylor and Henri Fayol (Fayol 1949; Taylor [1911]2006).

Transactional or bureaucratic leadership rests on the ability of the leader to motivate the followers to do what the leader wanted them to do by exchanging with the followers something they wanted. Fredrick Taylor was the great architect of this first formally thought-out leadership theory presented in his 1911 book, *The Principles of Scientific Management* (Taylor [1911]2006). In transactional leadership, the interests of the followers were recognized but then manipulated through threats of loss or offers of gain. Of course, because the leader always held all the power, there was no fair transaction going on, but it was essentially a ruse to trick the will of the followers, who were manipulated out of ignorance and to a lesser extent fear (Sejersted 1996). Because it was believed by transactional leaders like Taylor, that the followers were by nature lazy, selfish, and greedy, some form of manipulation was often called for. Transactional leadership was replaced by transformational leadership models beginning in the 1950s, with the rise of the organizational development theories of social scientists like Kurt Lewin and Douglas

McGregor. An insightful account of the emergence of this more human-istic leadership theory can be found in Art Kleiner's *The Age of Heretics: Outlaws and the Forerunners of Corporate Change* (1996).

Transformational or character leadership models come in a variety of different flavors, such as *authentic leadership, participative leadership, servant leadership*, etc. Transformational leadership recognizes that people are motivated by more than just selfish concerns. The interests of the followers are recognized, and to a degree respected, but the followers are told they must transcend their own selfish interests to pursue some common good as decided upon by the selfless leader. (Note the implicit assumptions of the superiority of leaders.) The selfless leader inspires the selfish followers to sacrifice their own interest to achieve something larger as identified by the leader (Bass and Riggio 2006; Hunter et al. 2013). Most of the leadership books, programs, training, and centers of leadership around the world today are based in transformational leadership.

In the end, however, I believe transformational leadership ends up being manipulative. Followers are told their dignity and interests are valued and that they are equal partners with the leader, but when it comes to information, decision-making, and rewards, they quickly realize they are not! The transformational leader still sees followers as weak and incapable of leading themselves, so they need the leader's wisdom and beneficence to take charge of their own lives. Additionally, trans-formational leadership is marketed as a position of character strength requiring a moral and intellectual superiority, so not being a leader is considered, at least implicitly, a moral failure. Power is being ultimately exercised manipulatively. It relies on the illusion of persuasion for, if the followers don't comply, the transformational, but still rank-based leader, can punish them, for their own good. The apparent selfless devotion of the leader turns out to be in practice nothing but the leader's own pride and egoism. Further, transformational leadership is caught in a perfor-mative contradiction. It requires that followers become more responsible, but it gives them no authority to do so. It is rather like trying to accel-erate your car by stepping on the gas and brake at the same time. And no amount of transformational leadership workshops will change this power dynamic. It is time to examine the unethical power relationship between leaders and followers that every model of leadership creates.

The Unethical and Unequal Power Relationship in Leader-Based Organizations

Leader-based organizations create unequal power relationships. You cannot have a leader without a follower and the necessary relationship between them is of unequal power. The leader is in a high power position and the followers are in a low power position. It is as simple as that. These relationships of unequal power create unhealthy and unethical power dynamics, which produce fewer constraints on dishonesty, promise breaking, cheating and harming others. We tell the person above us what we think they want to hear, and we tell the person below us only what we think they need to know. This behavior distorts communication and creates the context for secrecy, dishonesty, and the rationalization for unethical behavior. This is one of the crucial observations I made in my book, *The Myth of Leadership: Creating Leaderless Organizations* (Nielsen 2004):

> In the absence of equality, you'll seldom have honest, open communication…. This creates not only low levels of trust between individuals, but a growing gap between business reality and the world of the top executives, a gap that is endemic in almost every corporation today.
>
> Similarly, with the lack of genuine communication, organizations become obsessive about controlling access to information, and secrecy comes to dominate corporate life. With secrecy, positions of [unequal] power seduce even good people into taking undue advantage and abusing their privileges. This is important to remember—even good, decent people can get caught in this dynamic. It's not a character problem as much as a context [environment] problem. And the context [environment] as I have come to discover, is that of rank-based power and authority [i.e., unequal power relationship]. (Nielsen 2004, pp. 4–5)

Several studies in the last ten years have examined how a person's position in an unequal power relationship will affect their behavior (Carney et al. 2009; Lammers et al. 2010, 2011). The conclusions, in part, are that the presence of unequal power relationships leads to poor communication, the justification of the coercion and manipulation in the exercise of power, along with the felt obligation to cooperate with the unethical uses of power, the dynamic of hypocrisy, loss of empathy, fewer psychological constraints on lying and cheating, and the feeling of entitlement to the perks and privileges of power, because people with power enjoy positive emotions, increases in cognitive function, and physiological resilience such as lower levels of the stress hormone cortisol (Carney et al. 2009). These studies and others like them lead to the conclusion that the biochemistry of unequal power relationships overcomes any good intentions on the part of both powerful and powerless people (Lammers et al. 2011). These studies, and others like them, are not simply uncovering a correlation between high power positions and unethical behavior, but a causal link between holding a high power position and becoming a less ethical person.

Given the nature of the unequal power relationships, the first and primary objective of any leader-based organization becomes preserving the power position of the leaders. Everything else is sacrificed to that end: the employees, society, and the environment. The German sociologist, Robert Michels, discovered this organizational fact in his 1915 masterpiece, *Political Parties*. He named it the "Iron Law of Oligarchy." In over 400 pages of detailed analysis, he demonstrated how any leader-based organization, regardless of the egalitarian, noble, or even sacred goals it began with, would eventually come to serve primarily the well-being of the leaders, to maintain their power and privilege, with the acquiescence of the followers. The Iron Law of Oligarchy is the inherent tendency of all leader-based organizations to develop a governing mentality, where the interests of the leaders, not the well-being of the organization, becomes the main objective. In a stunning claim, he says, "Who says organization, says oligarchy" (Michels [1915]1962, pp. 364–365). Of course, he was focused on political leadership, but his arguments are equally valid for all organizations. Sadly, Michels, and most everyone else, believed, *faute de mieux*, there was no other way to organize, design, and manage our organizations except through leader-based hierarchies. I disagree.

The very chemical make-up of our brain creates ethically problematic behaviors and damaging habits in every organization organized with unequal power relationships. Persons in high power positions are prone to a superiority complex, which tickles their egos and makes them more likely to behave in selfish ways at the expense of the group. While those persons in low power positions suffer from an inferiority complex, which sabotages their sense of self-respect and makes them more prone to self-defeating submission to coercion or manipulation (Lammers et al. 2010). So, we see that every type of leadership creates unequal power relationships, and, in the end, all leadership becomes coercive and manipulative.

Unequal power relationships socialize people into believing that coercion and manipulation are perfectly acceptable ways to motivate people in our organizations. This is the ethical problem with leader-based organizations; they support and sustain the nearly universal assumption that when you go work for a person or organization, you agree to surrender your agency to some boss, leader, or manager, and they are entitled to coerce and manipulate you in return for a paycheck. If we want to design organizations that will avoid the unethical practices of coercion and manipulation, then we will need to find a way to create a governance system that manages through equal power relationships. In other words, we must find a replacement for leader-based organizations.

Why We Think We Need Leaders

Our belief in the need for leaders has so completely captured our imagination that we have a difficult time thinking organizationally without it. Our concept of leader is so stubbornly embedded in our organizational discourse that it is taken to be an absolute necessity. We become so neurologically hardwired to believe organizations require leaders that most people would have a difficult time even imagining an organization without leaders (Nielsen 2004, p. 41). The positive intent behind our belief in the necessity of leaders is the realization that a management system is required. Obviously, there are certain management functions that need to be performed in our organizations. Things like setting goals and objectives, scheduling work, marshaling resources, solving problems, and making strategic decisions. Further organizations need vision, wisdom, competence, teamwork, communication, and similar attributes to be successful. We are conditioned to believe that only with leaders can these functions be effectively performed, and these attributes developed.

At the heart of our belief in organizational leadership, is the belief that the true leader makes the hard choices, because most people are unable to. The true leader inspires followers to transcend their selfish limitations, something they are unable to do themselves. The true leader understands the followers better than they understand themselves, because the leader possesses greater empathy than the followers. Putting aside for the moment, the research that indicates that those in high power positions generally have less empathy than those beneath them in status, and also putting aside the false assumptions of the concept of leadership that followers are less capable of intrinsic motivation, we acknowledge that leaders often make hard choices, but the question is do they make the right ones? As Michels ([1915]1962) has shown, leaders often put aside what's best for the organization in the long run—in order to preserve their well-being in the short run.

Most people are capable of making hard choices, of sacrificing their personal interests to serve some larger good, and most persons are capable of empathy. Yet, in our organizational life, we treat people as incapable of these things and so needing to be inspired by the leaders. Should we be surprised that so many live down to these deleterious expectations? One could think of the work by Argyris and Schön (1974) on the difference between espoused beliefs (espoused theories) and lived beliefs (theories-in-use). Regardless of the espoused belief of the leader, whatever particular leadership book they just read or leadership seminar they just attended, in the boardroom, the executive suites, and management offices, where decisions are made, the lived belief is the concept of leader, with the unethical dynamic of unequal power relationships.

If there is an ethical and effective alternative to leader-based organizations, then we are morally obligated to replace them with this alternative way of managing. In the final section of this chapter, I will outline just such an effective and ethical alternative to leader-based organizations. To quote the physicist and social thinker David Bohm, "the whole of society has been organized to believe that we can't function without leaders. But maybe we can" (Bohm 1996, p. 41).

Leading Without Leaders

I define a "leaderless organization" as an organization of peers. Peers are persons in equal power relationships who are free to choose for themselves how they want to participate in performing the functions of management, whether in councils, in rotational stewardship positions, or as mentors. Such freedom evokes the talents and diverse abilities of everyone in the organization.

Some may object, "Aren't you exaggerating, or overestimating, the ability of the vast majority of people?" I believe in our common human capacity for goodness. I believe that each of us possesses remarkable talents to contribute toward the success of our organizations, and we are naturally motivated to use our talents for something larger than ourselves. Leader-based organizations prohibit many from making genuine contributions. I am not saying we are all equal—there is great diversity. What I am saying is that we have historically organized ourselves in rank-based ways that privilege the few over the many. So, the many never have the opportunity to fully develop their skills and abilities, but live less than meaningful and satisfying organizational lives. This time has passed. Leaderless organizations give everyone equal standing in information sharing and participation in decision-making. We will take on different roles and responsibilities. We will have different ambitions, but there will be no artificial barriers that keep anyone from fully contributing to the success of their organizations. To do this, we need access to information and participation in decision-making.

Others may object, "So why call them leaderless organizations? Can't we just redefine leaders as something like 'peer leaders' and keep the idea of leaders and leadership?" My response is that any conception of leadership that we could come up with will create a dualistic organization of unequal power relationships. You cannot name someone a leader without simultaneously naming someone a follower, and the necessary relationship between them is one of unequal power. It produces a privileged elite who, no matter how sincere they are, will eventually be seduced by their power position (Michels [1915]1962). I have experienced this in every organization I have consulted. So, you will inevitably get secrecy, distrust, overindulgence, and the inevitable sacrifice of those below for the benefit of those above. That's why I have argued for creating leaderless organizations, and the wording here is terribly important. Language acts upon the world (Austin 1975; Foucault 1980). Language tends to structure our thinking, even in subconscious ways (Deleuze and Guattari [1972]2009; Lacan 2017). When we use the word "leader" in organizational management, we immediately create a ranked division of people in ways that do not serve healthy organizational relationships.

The Ethical Use of Power and Equal Power Relationships in Leaderless Organizations

Power is the ability to influence and affect the mental and physical behavior of others. The person who exercises power will only be successful if the person the power is exercised upon cooperates. Even a tyrant requires the cooperation of the people they tyrannize (Brecht 2013). If the people refuse to cooperate with the tyrant, they lose their power. So, we must ask two questions: how do we exercise power, and why do we cooperate with the exercise of power? Perhaps the most common understanding of power is one expressed by the philosopher, Thomas Hobbes. He understood power as exercising influence to get what you want; in a sense, to use other people to get what you desire (Dahl 1957). There have been several great thinkers who have made contributions to the topic of power. Philosophers such as Max Weber and Bertrand de Jouvenal, who both saw power as the imposition of one's will upon the will of others, regardless of their wishes (Arendt 1970; Weber [1922]1947). Hannah Arendt believed that both Weber and de Jouvenal were failing to distinguish power from merely coercion or even violence. She saw power as a property of shared minds reaching a common will through consensual means.

Arendt's more generous view of power was picked up and elaborated upon by Jürgen Habermas, who summarized Arendt's view as a theory of communicative power, which is to be ethical and effective, he added, must satisfy his three rational validity claims to truth, rightness, and truthfulness (Habermas 1986). In other words, ethical power is exercised within a dialogical context where each person implicitly promises to speak the truth, to speak what is morally correct, and to speak honestly. I have already shown that the presence of a leader in an organization will violate these ethical requirements of power by the very nature of the unequal power relationships in leader-based organizations.

Robert Greenleaf, the originator of the concept of the "servant-leader," speaks of power in terms of coercion and persuasion (Greenleaf 1977). Coercion leads to dominating and manipulating people, and we cooperate with coercion out of fear or ignorance. The manipulative effect of coercive power serves to impose one's will on the will of the other in a win-lose or lose-lose fashion (in the manner of power discussed by both Hobbes, Weber, and de Jouvenal). Greenleaf goes on to say, "The trouble with coercive power is that it only strengthens resistance. And, if successful, its controlling effect lasts only as the force is strong" (Greenleaf 1977, pp. 55–56). Unfortunately, in leader-based organizations, coercion is unavoidable. Even Greenleaf confesses, "Part of our dilemma is that all leadership is, to some extent, manipulative" (Greenleaf 1977, p. 55). Greenleaf does favor persuasion, an ethical manner of exercising power more in line with the communicative power of Arendt and Habermas. We cooperate with persuasion out of respect for the person seeking to influence us. With persuasion, we seek to create a mutual will, a shared sense of purpose with the other person or persons in a win–win fashion. Greenleaf (1977, p. 55) says that persuasion creates opportunities and builds the autonomy of individuals. He realizes that genuine persuasion is unlikely to occur in a leader-based organization, due to what I have called unequal power relationships.

However, in a leaderless organization, there are no fixed or permanent leaders and followers, and so no unequal power relationships. There are only peers, who cooperate together in both leading and following as necessary. Thus, fostering and maintaining an environment of equal power relationships, giving people the opportunity to contribute to and participate in decision-making, as they choose. The barriers to persuasion are removed as each person possesses the equal privilege to speak and shares in the equal and reciprocal obligation to listen. When a person feels valued and respected as an equal partner with others, their cooperation does not need to be coerced or manipulated but is given freely (Deleuze and Guattari [1972]2009; Ehrenfeld 1993; Freire 2006). In equal power relationships, the conditions for the exercise of ethical power are in place; namely, the three commitments to truth, rightness, and truthfulness (Habermas 1986). Nevertheless, even if leaderless organizations are more ethical than leader-based organizations, if they are also not effective in performing the required management functions, then we ought not pursue them. In the next section, I will show how leaderless organizations would be as effective, if not more so, than leader-based organizations.

Effectively Performing Management Functions in Leaderless Organizations

Our organizations need governance. We need to exercise power and organize cooperation, so people in our organizations can do the work to accomplish agreed upon ends. Anarchy is not an option, and leader-based organizations demean the value of most persons working in them. To work together in our organizations, we have to be willing to limit our own freedom to cooperate with others. We must be willing to sacrifice some of our own desires for the sake of accomplishing a common goal. We have to get autonomous individuals to limit their own freedom in order to cooperate with others. This creates a tension between individual freedom and cooperation, and in our organizations, we have to balance the tension between them. Anarchy leads to chaos, as no constraints are placed on individual freedoms. Leader-based organizations lead to authoritarianism, as individual freedoms are denied, and cooperation coerced through leadership practices. We must liberate cooperation from the constraints of hierarchical control, while avoiding the pitfalls of no constraints as all. A peer-based model of leaderless organizations points to the belief that leading is not a permanent and fixed position but should be a competence developed and shared by everyone in the organization. In a leaderless organization, the necessary management functions are carried out through councils, rotational stewardship positions, and mentors.

Peer Councils

When an organization charters peer councils, composed of individuals from all levels of expertise and all areas of the organization, employees get out of their hierarchic roles and are able to see things differently. People from all over the organization get to know one another and learn how to communicate genuinely. People productively work together and cooperate when they share common goals, receive accurate information, have the skill sets, and are able to recognize, utilize, and balance each other's strengths and weaknesses. Many of these necessary elements are missing in the traditional leader-based organization with its centralized authority and top-down command structure. With peer councils, a greater sense of community is developed that fosters increased competency in all members of the organization. Councils provide the vehicle for this development by creating a space for genuine dialogue and collaborative decision-making. Councils are responsible to make the strategic, operational, and resource decisions affecting the entire organization.

Rotational Stewardship Roles

Obviously, not every decision can or should be brought before the entire council. Peer councils make the major decisions, but persons and teams in rotational stewardship roles perform and carry out these decisions. Day-to-day and routine decision-making can be delegated to administrative positions within each council. The essence of rotational stewardship roles is those in administrative positions within the councils have definite term limits to fill their management assignment. These administrative positions are responsible to the council out of which they were selected. These stewardship positions are for individuals, teams, or task forces. After their time is up, other individuals will be chosen, and the rotation continues. This will keep the energy flow through the organization generative. Rotating who has important positions on a regular basis is a very effective way to begin fostering and maintaining an environment of equal power relationships. Rotating stewardship positions on a regular basis will give people a greater chance at participation and contribution. Also, the fact that people share in the ownership of governing means that they also share in the burden of communicating knowledge and information to others. This improves trust and knowledge sharing in a manner that makes organizations self-correcting. There must also be clear rules for rotational stewardship positions, so they don't become permanent leadership positions.

Mentoring

Mentoring is a crucial role in a leaderless or peer-based organization. Mentoring is a position of teaching, coaching, advising without decision-making authority. Mentors play the crucial role of linking the various peer councils with one another. They create the network. In many ways, mentoring replaces leading, and mentors replace leaders in peer-based, leaderless organizations. A leader leads followers, and the implication, given the understanding of leadership, is that this leadership is "over" others. It is the command and control of others using rank-based authority. A mentor advises and counsels others. A mentor possesses greater expertise, knowledge, and experience and shares this with members of the organization who are lacking in these areas. It is a relationship, not of rank, but alongside of the one being mentored. The difference in symbolism is very important. A mentor is a person committed to the improvement of self and others.

Examples of the Competitive Strength of Leaderless Organizations

Leading without leaders is the idea that we each share in the competency and responsibility of leading and following as we cooperate and make decisions together on peer councils, as we take turns functioning as rotational stewards for specific periods of time or on specific assignments, and as we serve as mentors teaching and developing others to reach their full potential in our organizational life. One could point to several organizations, which exemplify many of the elements of the leaderless organization, to reasonably defend the position that leaderless organizations could not only be as effective as leader-based organizations, but perhaps even more competitive. One of these is the Brazilian company, Semco, mentored by their maverick owner, Ricardo Semler (1995). They have been consistently profitable in one of the most unstable and highly inflationary countries and economies in the world. A second is the internationally recognized and Grammy nominated, Orpheus Chamber Orchestra, in Manhattan. Since its inception in 1970, Orpheus has been a world-class, but conductorless orchestra (Seifter and Economy 2002). The third is W. L. Gore & Associates, a chemical engineering and product manufacturing company, famous for its lack of assigned leaders and managers (Van Dyk 2019).

Conclusion

Leaderless organizations will not be perfect, nothing is, but they will respect the dignity and honor the autonomy of everyone in the organization. So, they satisfy the ethical demands of living and working together as we should. However, if leaderless organizations are ineffective and unable to perform the necessary management functions, as some believe, then they would not be worth pursuing. I can sympathize with those who think that. Yet, I hope I have shown how a leaderless organization through the peer management vehicles of councils, rotational stewardship positions, and mentors can effectively perform the required tasks of planning, organizing, coordinating, and motivating people. Certainly, leaderless organizations require trust in people—in humanity's potential for goodness. I believe that when people feel trusted, they will live up to that trust. They require that we aspire to the greatness of goodness, and that we see the objective of human organization is not only profit, but the ultimate aim is the development of human potential and the flourishing of everyone in our business organizations. In the introduction of this chapter, I argued that if there is an ethical and effective alternative to leader-based organizations, then we are morally obligated to replace leader-based organizations with this alternative. I will conclude by stating that a leaderless organization is this ethical and effective alternative. We have a moral responsibility to begin creating leaderless organizations.

References

Arendt, H. (1970). *On violence*. New York: Harcourt Brace Javanovich.

Argyris, C., & Schön, D. (1974). *Theory in practice: Increasing professional effectiveness*. San Francisco: Jossey-Bass.

Austin, J. L. (1975). *How to do things with words* (2nd ed.). Cambridge, MA: Harvard University Press.

Bass, B. M., & Riggio, R. E. (2006). *Transformational leadership*. New York: Psychology Press.

Bohm, D. (1996). *On dialogue*. New York: Routledge.

Brecht, B. (2013). *The resistible rise of Arturo Ui* (trans: Wise, J.). New York: Methuen Drama.

Burns, J. (2010). *Leadership*. New York: Harper Perennial Political Classics.

Carney, D., Yap, A., Lucas, B., & Mehta, P. (2009). *People with power are better liars* (Working Paper). New York: Columbia Business School.

Ciulla, J. (2003). *The ethics of leadership*. Belmont: Wadsworth.

Dahl, R. A. (1957). The concept of power. *Behavioral Science, 2*(3), 201–215. doi:10.1002/bs.3830020303.

Deleuze, G., & Guattari, F. (1972). *L'Anti-Oedipe*. Paris: Les Editions de Minuit. English edition: Deleuze, G., & Guattari, F. (2009). *Anti-Oedipus: Capitalism and schizophrenia* (trans: Hurley, R., Seem, M., & Lane, H.). New York: Penguin Classics.

Dionne, S. D., Yammarino, F. J., Howell, J. P., & Villa, J. (2005). Substitutes for leadership, or not. *The Leadership Quarterly, 16*(1), 169–193.

Ehrenfeld, D. (1993). *Beginning again: People & nature in the new millennium*. New York: Oxford University Press.

Fayol, H. (1949). *General and industrial management*. New York: Martino Fine Books.

Foucault, M. (1980). *Power/knowledge: Selected interviews and other writings* (C. Gordon, Ed.). London: Harvester.

Freire, P. (2006). *Pedagogy of the oppressed*. New York: Continuum Press.

Greenleaf, R. (1977). *Servant leadership: A journey into the nature of legitimate power and greatness.* New York: Paulist Press.

Habermas, J. (1986). Hannah Arendt's communications concept of power. In S. Lukes (Ed.), *Power* (pp. 75–92). New York: New York University Press.

Havel, V. (1997). *The art of the impossible: Politics as morality in practice.* New York: Alfred A. Knopf.

Hunter, E., Neubert, M., Perry, S., Witt, L., & Weinberger, E. (2013). Servant leaders inspire servant followers: Antecedents and outcomes for employees and the organization. *The Leadership Quarterly, 24*(2), 316–331.

Kleiner, A. (1996). *The age of heretics and the forerunners of corporate change.* New York: Currency Doubleday.

Lacan, J. (2017). *Formations of the unconscious: The seminar of Jacques Lacan* (trans: Grigg, R.). New York: Polity.

Lammers, J., Stapel, D. A., & Galinsky, A. D. (2010). Power increases hypocrisy: Moralizing in reasoning, immorality in behavior. *Psychological Science, 21*(5), 737–744.

Lammers, J., Stoker, J., Jordan, J., Pollmann, M., & Stapel, D. (2011). Power increases infidelity among men and women. *Psychological Science, 22*(9), 1191–1197.

Michels, R. (1915). *Zur soziologie des parteiwesens in der modernen demomokratie.* Leipzg: Verlag von Werner Klinkhadt. English edition: Michels, R. (1962). *Political parties: A sociological study of the oligarchical tendencies of modern democracy* (trans: Paul, C., & Paul, E.). New York: The Free Press.

Mintzberg, H. (2009). *Managing.* San Francisco, CA: Berrett-Koehler Publishers.

Nielsen, J. S. (2004). *The myth of leadership: Creating leaderless organizations.* Palo Alto, CA: Davies-Black Publishing.

Podsakoff, P. M., MacKenzie, S. B., & Fetter, R. (1993). Substitutes for leadership and the management of professionals. *The Leadership Quarterly, 4*(1), 1–44.

Seifter, H., & Economy, P. (2002). *Leadership ensemble: Lessons in collaborative management from the world-famous conductorless orchestra.* New York: Holt Paperbacks.

Sejersted, F. (1996). Managers and consultants as manipulators: Reflections on the suspension of ethics. *Business Ethics Quarterly, 6*(1), 67–86. doi:10.2307/3857241.

Semler, R. (1995). *Maverick: The success story behind the world's most unusual workplace.* New York: Grand Central Publishing.

Taylor, F. ([1911]2006). *The principles of scientific management*. Middlesex, UK: The Echo Library.

Van Dyk, D. (2019, May). Imagine a company where peers determine your salary and there are no leaders. It exists and it's been around for 61 years. *Inc Magazine*. https://www.inc.com/magazine/201905/deirdre-van-dyk/w-l-gore-goretex-eptfe-waterproof-material-medical-device-technology.html. Accessed 25 Nov 2020.

Weber, M. (1922). *Wirtschaft und Gesellschaft*. Tuebingen, Germany: Mohr. English edition: Weber, M. (1947). *The theory of social and economic organization* (trans: Henderson, A., & Parsons, T.). New York: The Free Press.

3

Developing for Leaderless Organizations: Two Eco-Friendly Coaching Practices

Bob Garvey and Pauline Fatien Diochon

This chapter argues *for* leaderless organizations as offering a sound alternative to the dominant hubristic leadership model. But more than preaching for the desirability of leaderless organizations, this chapter outlines their practicability; in that perspective, it suggests that such community-based organizations require different forms of learning and development (see Martins and Martins, Chapter 7 in this volume), and we present two specific coaching practices.

We indeed argue for alternatives to the leader-centric organizations because those latter embrace a "powerful and greedy model" (Gray et al.

B. Garvey (✉)
Leeds Business School, Leeds, UK
e-mail: bob@coachmentoring.co.uk

P. Fatien Diochon
Grenoble Ecole de Management, Grenoble, France

© The Author(s), under exclusive license to Springer Nature
Switzerland AG 2022
F. Hertel et al. (eds.), *Debating Leaderless Management*,
Palgrave Debates in Business and Management,
https://doi.org/10.1007/978-3-031-04593-6_3

2016, p. 171) of leadership that celebrates the leader as a lonely super-hero (see Nielsen, Chapter 2 in this volume). Such leadership practices work within a larger globalized context, which Shearing (2001) has called "neofeudalism", a wider society where power is concentrated in the hands of the selected few. Leaders are elevated to leadership positions, often on the basis of wealth or because they are in the right network. These are expected to rule whereas employees are expected to follow in an artificially constructed hierarchy (see Martins and Martins, Chapter 7 in this volume) aimed at control.

This leadership edifice relies on a panoply of mechanisms that play a particular role in such leadership processes. This is the case of certain practices of leadership development (see Gerwel Proches, Chapter 18 in this volume for a contrary view on leadership development) that are principally concerned with the maintenance and perpetuation of leadership power and domination, such as dominant forms of coaching. With an exaggerated preoccupation of the ego and the reproduction of an established position, coaching for leadership development in such contexts contributes to "massaging egos" rather than to any substantial organizational development. Often, the results are that coaching for leadership supports leaders who abdicate their social responsibilities, develop dubious loyalties as they temporarily commit to the highest bidder (see Nielsen, Chapter 2 in this volume). The COVID-19 pandemic has exposed many of these elites to be morally bankrupt (see Grint 2020). This version of coaching for leadership based on hierarchy fails to develop leaders' intrinsic ability to cooperate and instead discriminates and separates.

In contrast, we argue that leaderlessness offers a genuine and ethically sound alternative that can weave people together around a common horizon (see Nielsen, Chapter 2 in this volume). Such community-based organizations also, however, require different forms of learning and development. Arguing for this practicability is required because one common argument *against* leaderless organization is that such organizations are not realistic (Buechler 1990; Cornell 2011). In this chapter, we argue rather for the realization of "leaderlessness organizations" and we do this by outlining ways as to which leaderless management could be developed and put into practice.

Table 3.1 Contrasting two approaches to coaching in leadership development

Type of coaching	Ego-massaging	Eco-friendly
Approach to leadership	Leader-centric Heroic leadership	Community-centric Collective leadership
Types of organizations	Leader-based organizations	Leaderless organizations
Type of coaching	Individual and performance-oriented	Self-sustaining ecosystem

We define a leaderless organization as one that works on the basis of collective collaboration in communities in which all people can participate and are responsible to the whole. Such communities require fundamentally different organizational technologies in order to work. We propose and discuss in this chapter specific coaching programs for self-organization and self-led democratic communities that support collaboration. We argue that coaching for leaderless organizations presents a substantial move away from the dominant coaching practices that are neofeudalistic, individualistic performance-oriented, and, instead, employ an eco-friendly coaching approach. An eco-friendly approach takes into account the whole system of the organization and views this as a self-sustaining, self-organizing ecosystem. It facilitates the growth of a democratic organization, which is focused on using profits to support the social and economic life of the wider population. The contrast between the two approaches is outlined in Table 3.1.

In this chapter, we therefore discuss two kinds of "eco-friendly" humanistic informed practices that can sustain and develop leaderless organizations and we explain why and how they equip individuals for leaderless organizations.

The first approach is a *learning theory informed type of coaching*, where the coach becomes far more coachee-centered and flexible in their approach than in traditional coaching. This is important for leaderless organizations because this enables someone to learn about operating in a network or ecosystem where values of cooperation, trust and collaboration become important. Such a bottom-up form of coaching targets a holistic development of coachees likely to support genuine cooperation required within leaderless organizations.

The second coaching approach that we propose for leaderless organizations is *community of discoveries* (to distinguish from "community of practice") where the coach facilitates learning through diversity. This is a form of team coaching (Clutterbuck 2007). It supports the exploration of multiple worldviews, social positions and ways of knowing within a community to understand how we think differently within the frameworks of different cultures, social settings and the complexities of work. A community of discovery celebrates diversity and recognizes that "break-through" discoveries come from interactions of difference in regard to cultures, identities and knowledge. We argue that a community of discovery philosophy may play a central part in leaderless organizations in sustaining and building communities. In fact, the presence of a single individual leader will destroy the community and the values of trust, tolerance and the celebration of difference within a network of relationships.

This chapter continues by, first discussing the underlying dominant discourses of coaching found in some of the literature, and we argue that it needs to change to facilitate the leaderless organization. It then goes on to discuss a learning informed framework and a community of discovery approach to coaching more suitable for leaderlessness. The chapter concludes with a table that summarizes the main characteristics of eco-friendly coaching practices aimed at enabling the kind of self-organization necessary for leaderlessness.

Beyond "Ego-Massaging" Coaching Discourses and Practices

As raised in our introduction, much of the current discourse found in the coaching literature is, broadly speaking, positioned as a helping practice designed to support individuals, teams and organizations change, with often an expected outcome of increased performance. Discourses are important in shaping social behavior and in this section, we argue that the dominant discourse which currently surrounds coaching needs to change to facilitate the leaderless organization.

This burgeoning practice emerged in the late 1990s, often as a substitute to established practices, perceived too directive (such as consulting), too generic (such as training), too something-to-fix (therapy). Rather, coaching offers an optimistic and customized service for those who want to do even better. A dominant sub-segment of the umbrella coaching practice is executive coaching designed for the "so-called responsible" leaders (see Borchmann and Pedersen, Chapter 4 in this volume) (Amado 2004, p. 51).

With roots in sports, many current coaching practices are designed for powerful individuals, champions and even heroic characters (see Borchmann and Pedersen, Chapter 4 in this volume). Western (2012) argues that modern coaching is essentially for the "Celebrated Self" that perfectly fits with the leader-led organization. The "Celebrated Self" is based on individualism and focuses on building high performance. Individual happiness based on material wealth and consumerism is a key driver of the "Celebrated Self". It is about the "new" managerialism at work where success in work means the leader has to be passionate, motivated, positive and authentic and emotionally intelligent (see Western 2012). The Executive coaching discourse speaks to the "Celebrated Self", massages the ego and celebrates individual performance. However, Western (2012) also argues that despite the celebrated self-discourse, the "wounded self" always appears with the coaching conversation. It is here that the weaknesses, human frailties and incompetent selves appear. The heroic leader is a flawed human like the rest of us! (see Martins and Martins, Chapter 7 in this volume) This is a further argument against the current dominant models of leadership and for the concept of leaderlessness. Too much is invested in lonely, wounded individuals that are propped up by the executive coach.

The "Celebrated" and "Wounded self" discourses take place within larger discourses that inform coaching practice. Western (2012) distinguishes four and these include:

- The Managerialist, drawing on scientific rationality, with a focus on maximizing efficiency and increasing productivity;
- The Psy Expert, where the coach as a technician of the psyche, will modify coachees' thinking and behavior to support their success;

- The Soul Guide with the coach acting as a mirror of the soul, creates a space for coachees to discover their desire, face their dilemmas and reflect on their values;
- The Network-Coach helps coaches see the big picture and take a connective stance to see patterns and power in their networks.

These relate to both the "Celebrated Self" and the "Wounded Self" depending on the context in which they appear. In a strong managerially led context, the performative element is accentuated and the "Celebrated Self" is at the heart in a striving for "squeezing" a bit more out of people. The Psy Expert discourse may work with both the "Celebrated Self", to massage the ego or equally it may pick up the pieces from the wounded self in order to move the individual toward improved performance. Both the Soul Guide and the Network may also work with either the Celebrated or Wounded self depending on either, the coachee's perceptions on their situation or the coach's agenda as the agent of the leader. We humans are complex and paradoxical!

Garvey et al. (2018) argue that a combination of the Managerialist and the Psy Expert discourses currently dominate in coaching practice, education and professional bodies. As a result, much of the overall discussion centers on business impact, return on investment to demonstrate coaching monetary value, with a purpose to enhance the utilization of coaching throughout the firm (Garvey et al. 2018). A reason for this dominance, we argue, is that these coaching discourses serve well the leader as savior leadership discourse. Coaching reproduces power dynamics of the leader-led organization. In these mainstream coaching interventions, the coach is the knowledgeable person, as in the organization the leader is portrayed to be. By reducing the coachee to a recipient of their know-how, coaches reproduce and perpetuate a relationship model that maintains followers as passive recipients of someone's else expertise (see Hsu and Sun, Chapter 6 in this volume). Resulting in coaching, the mention of the coachee appears in fact anecdotal, only as the recipient of the coach's expertise or organizational investment. Much like in the dominant leadership discourse, the coachee (or follower) is objectified, a "lucky" beneficiary of the coach (or leader)'s benevolence. Such coach (and leader)-centric discourses celebrate the coach's skills employed to achieve the expected results. Coaching approaches offered by Downey (2014), Whitmore (2009), Rogers (2012), and Starr (2008) mainly focus on the skills of the coach. Despite the rhetoric being about coachee-centeredness, much of this literature assumes that the coach is the driver of the process rather than the coachee (see Garvey et al. 2018).

A further concern, with such coaching approaches is that the coachee is just a means of a performance equation, that of the coach or the organization. The concern for the client is only superficial and reduced to an instrument to change. For leaderless organizations, we need coaching practices that genuinely focus on the coachee's issues without the overlay of organizational power.

Despite the potential for Western's (2012) Soul Guide and Network to relate to either the "Celebrated" or the "Wounded Selves", these discourses do provide an alternative and more humanistic perspective that we see more suitable for leaderless organizations (see Martins and Martins, Chapter 7 in this volume). The Soul Guide discourse is about:

> ...spiritual concerns, identity and relationships, the unconscious, the conscience, the human spirit, values and beliefs and the human and existential concerns such as how to live with meaning, what is the good life for this individual and how to journey towards it and how to face loss and ultimately how to face death. (Western 2012, p. 132)

This discourse is aligned with the many voices (Connor and Pokora 2012; Cox et al. 2014; du Toit 2014; Parsloe and Leedham 2009; Rogers 2012; Rosinski 2004; Western 2012; Whitmore 2009) that argue that coaching is rooted in humanism. This is an ethical and democratic way of thinking and behaving. Within a humanist philosophy, individuals give meaning and shape to their own lives. Humanism celebrates the human potential to act in an ethical way and seeks to build a more humane society. This is achieved through free inquiry, critical discussion and interaction. It is an inclusive philosophy that celebrates diversity.

The Network discourse recognizes that an individual in an organization is in an often complex "system" where complexity is embraced and reductionism is inappropriate. Western (2012) argues that this is creating new forms of organization, which employ technology and strive to contribute to society through sustainable and ethical means. A Network discourse acknowledges the ecosystem to which members of the network subscribe.

There are some signs that such coaching approaches are emerging with a more authentic focus on the coachee. Stelter (2019), for example, repositions coaching as more like mentoring and refers to a coach as a facilitator of dialogue. Additionally, in Stokes et al. (2021), there are new set of dimensions of coaching and mentoring which emphasize context, time and purpose and in Nadeem and Garvey (2020), we see the learning experiences of the coachee coming to the fore as a way of assisting the coach to adapt and develop a repertoire of skills and processes to facilitate the coachee. Further, Rajasinghe's (2018) unpublished PhD focusses on how executives experience executive coaching and this is another piece of work that is exploring coaching from the coachee's perspective.

It is with these discourses that combine a focus on the coachee and learning that we see a new vision for coaching within leaderless organizations.

Learning Informed Coaching

In a leaderless organization, a new type of learning is required. The neofeudalistic model of leader and followers emphasizes the need to comply, often misrepresented as "cooperation". Learning is often positioned as content based rather than process-based to enable people to perform better, this is often presented as "training". The training model places the control of what is learned in the hands of the trainer (Garvey and Williamson 2002), the organization or an individual manager; a model contrary to what is known about adult learners and a model designed to extract compliance and exercise control. It is also a model that specifies the learning outcomes, as if learning happens in a straight-line (see Self et al. 2019).

In a leaderless organization, genuine cooperation is required, genuine questioning and challenging of ideas is necessary in the spirit of enquiry and open debate. Learning *is* the work (Alred and Garvey 2000) rather than something to do on a training course with a content imposed and decided by the hierarchy.

There are a number of researchers who have explored adult learning over the years. For example, Knowles et al. (1998), Schön (1983), Kolb (1984), Maslow et al. (1987), and Rogers (1989) contribute to understanding adult learning. These also resonate with what is said about coaching. Knowles et al. (1998) present six assumptions about adult learners that are relevant to coaching within leaderless organizations:

1. Adults are self-directed in their learning;
2. Adults are goal-oriented in learning;
3. Adults have reservoir of life experiences to learn from;
4. Adults are interested to learn to solve real-life problems;
5. Adults have practical orientation—they learn to apply knowledge;
6. Adults respond more to intrinsic motivators than extrinsic.

Kolb (1984) argues that adults learn from experience and that different people have different learning preferences. Rogers (1989), in his core conditions of learning, provides some underpinning to the humanistic values found within some of the coaching literature (Peltier 2001; Zeus and Skiffington 2000). These assumptions in Kolb (1984), Rogers (1989), and Knowles et al. (1998) resonate strongly with the idea of leaderlessness. For example, self-direction, learning goals, being able to draw on experience to inform activity, working with real everyday issues in a practical way and being motivated by intrinsic motivations are the hallmarks of an individual capable of working in a leaderless context—why would such an individual require leading?

Nadeem and Garvey (2020) offer a heuristic framework that explores the complexities of coaching if the learning needs of the coachee are taken into account. Their study identified eight elements that need to be considered when working in a learning theory informed way in coaching. These include:

1. Working from an understanding of what the coachee may feel they can influence and what they think they can directly control in their context;

2. Being aware of and adjusting the coaching approach to suit the learning style of the coachee;
3. Being aware that certain disciplines prefer the technical over the social and interpersonal;
4. Being prepared to "work in the moment" and adjust;
5. Being aware that coaching is primarily a dialectic process and that some coaches may prefer the opportunity to visualize through diagrams, visualization techniques or practical examples;
6. Being aware that the technical mindset may prefer the coach to use tools such as questionnaires, 360, numerical data and diagrams in order to provide "objective data";
7. Being aware of the use of and the difference between specific goals and learning goals and enabling the coachee to develop strategic critical thinking;
8. Helping to create a calm reflective space to enable the coachee to relax and reflect.

This approach to coaching also takes into account the wider perspective of the context or the ecosystem in which the coaching is taking place.

Taking these relatively new ideas into account, developing people to work within a leaderless organization requires an understanding of the learning preferences of the coachees in order to really meet their needs as well as the ecosystem that they are associated with. It requires a movement away from the ego massaging and individualistic and imposed performative goals, where the goal is often part of the organizational agenda and not of the coachee's, toward a developmental approach which enables people to self-direct and interact with each other because they are intrinsically motivated to do so. Coaching in this sense returns people the democratic humanistic values which gave it life.

Communities of Discovery-Based Coaching

While a learning informed approach to coaching can enable individuals to work with the complexities of leaderlessness, what is going to assist groups of people to work together to develop their organizations? This is an issue of collective learning and cooperation (see Martins and Martins, Chapter 7 in this volume). The led organization promotes individualism and hierarchy. The leaderless organization relies on the collective.

The concept of "situated learning" (Lave and Wenger 1991) takes on a particular significance in relation to leaderlessness (see Jørgensen and Ingman, Chapter 8 in this volume). A central tenet of situated learning is that learning is a social activity. People learn by, with and from others. It is the basis of human survival. The workplace is often a brutal and competitive place where people are judged, ranked and divided. These are hardly the conditions for productive and collaborative learning. Often, people at work in a led environment are not, as Knowles et al. (1998) expresses, in control of what and how they learn. Situated learning (Lave and Wenger 1991) theory perceives learning as a form of participation and is therefore complementary to and supportive of the concept of some form of self-organization.

Learning viewed as situated activity has as its central defining characteristic a process that we call legitimate peripheral participation. By this, we mean to draw attention to the point that learners inevitably participate in communities of practitioners and that the mastery of knowledge and skill requires newcomers to move toward full participation in the sociocultural processes of a community. [.....]. A person's intentions to learn are engaged and the meaning of learning is configured through the process of becoming a full participant in a sociocultural practice. This social process includes, indeed it subsumes, the learning of knowledgeable skills. (Lave and Wenger 1991, p. 29)

The key notion is "legitimate peripheral participation". Peripheral contrasts with full; it is a positive term and its conceptual antonyms are unrelatedness and irrelevance. It is a dynamic concept, suggesting an opening, a moving forward to greater participation in a sociocultural practice. This aspect of the theory of "situated learning" provides a basis for critically challenging the role of formal training in organizations, which places control for what is learnt in the hands of the organization and not the learner, and at the same time, it gives impetus to the value of informal, "situated learning".

The concept of situated learning provides a good basis for considering how such social learning may contribute to a leaderless organization. However, the concept has its problems. For example, rather than developing diversity, situated learning can lead to groupthink. In a leaderless organization, we argue that groupthink is inappropriate. The qualities of a self-led organization include creativity, innovation, self-motivation, flexibility and collaboration and these are not found in groupthinking. In groupthink, members of a social group agree and support one another without critical thought. People become socialized into the group and find it difficult to step out of the group. This is the case with professional groups, such as lawyers and doctors. They develop their own language and set of codes to communicate with each other and, as in neofeudalism, compliance to the rules is expected. This is clearly the case in the self-styled coaching professional bodies. An alternative to this is the concept of a community of discovery.

Based on humanism and the alternative coaching principles outlined above, a community of discovery asserts that to be creative, innovative and able to change requires new thinking, new ideas and new ways of working. It requires a complete understanding of the ecosystem to which an individual belongs and it relates well to Western's (2012) "network" discourse in coaching. The challenge, therefore, is to find ways forward for people to discover these ideas. It is not possible to learn about things that have not yet been discovered but we can learn about how to make discoveries. A community of discovery is a philosophical position with practical implications. It is, perhaps, a central philosophy to develop people within a leaderless organization.

The philosophy starts from the position that people exist in a meaningless world but continually strive to attribute meaning to their experiences. The human drive to do this explains the tendency to seek reductionism and simplification, or cause and effect thinking, which is allied to the performative goal orientation found in the managerialist discourse as discussed above. Additionally, religion, culture, science and the arts also provide vehicles for people to create meaning.

It is also apparent that no single human has the knowledge to understand all there is to know about creation, evolution and the structure of both the material and social worlds, despite the promotion of neofeudalist leaders as a societal mantra. Therefore, all human discoveries are collective and social achievements. For example, the emergence of the new vaccines for COVID-19 were not produced by anyone super person, despite the nationalistic claims of right-wing British neofeudalistic politicians. Rather, they were an international and global achievement.

Extending this view, the vaccine was not there waiting to be discovered any more than what there is to know or what is potentially knowable is not there already waiting to be discovered. It is, however, through a *sense* of discovery that people will create and transform everything that is currently claimed as knowledge. What is known is not just given, rather, it is constantly being discovered.

In practice, this means that discovery differs from one person to another and these differences move and extend across cultures. A led organization tends to view diversity through the lens of the managerialist discourse, which emphasizes compliance, and a lack of singularism; we argue that a leaderless organization, which focuses on collaboration and cooperation, needs to not only understand but also embrace diversity throughout the whole ecosystem of the organization. It is important therefore that in a leaderless context, diversity needs to be understood at many different levels, for example:

- whole culture level;
- local cultures;
- organizations and other groupings within their level;
- individual level.

Diversity is one of the biggest challenges facing humankind and it is daily under pressure by those who seek to polarize, separate and discriminate. Neofeudalist leaders fuel this separation because it is in their interest to do so in order to maintain their power base. In a leaderless organization, diversity is a central and active concept for it is through diversity that innovation and creativity come, rather than through hierarchies and group think. These qualities are necessary for leaderlessness to flourish.

Diversity thinking is about understanding how we come to know how to think within the frameworks of different cultures, social settings and the complexities of work. It is this understanding, when brought together that offers the biggest opportunity of innovation and change in a leaderless environment. Groupthink simply creates groupthink. It is diverse groups that, when brought together in open dialogue, make new discoveries. This generates two challenging questions:

- "How do people learn the fundamental categories of thought that bring coherence to the worldview of their society?
- How are people able to use these categories as a grammar of understanding and interpretation that enables them to live in and adapt to their world in ways that allow them to bring order and coherence to change and uncertainty?" (Garvey et al. 2018, p. 177)

As we are seeing in relation to the US 2020 election aftermath and the erosion of democratic values in other parts of the world, including the UK, developing such a grammar of understanding has never been more important, for without it, we condemn ourselves to increasing neofeudalist leadership.

The above arguments are central to the domain of sociological thinking. We accept that these arguments may seem rather abstract, in fact they are very practical. If we seek to understand the learning and development needs of a group of people in any organization, we have to find credible answers to the type of questions raised above.

To illustrate, imagine a leaderless business that wanted to develop multi-developmental networks. Using the themes cited above, the following questions may help them to do so:

- how do people in a leaderless organization perceive and understand coaching and mentoring?
- how does coaching and mentoring fit into their way of knowing about the world?
- what explains the differences in knowledge of coaching and mentoring competency among them?

- how far are such differences a product of their previous experience of coaching and mentoring?
- how does the prevailing work culture shape attitudes to coaching and mentoring?
- how can members of the leaderless organization best be helped to think about engaging in coaching and mentoring in their organization?

Answers to these questions cannot be found on Google or in a consultant's tool kit! These questions can only be addressed and the answers discovered through analysis, reflection, dialogue and experimentation. The coach's function here is to enable members of the organization to share their views openly and respectfully. In this way, they will learn from one another and through dialogue they will continue to discover new ways of engaging in coaching conversations. This approach becomes more possible in a leaderless organization because the hierarchy is not there to interfere or dictate what should happen with their imposed goals. Leaderless organizations, almost by definition, make it possible for a community of discovery to emerge.

The conditions necessary to create a community of discovery as an organization include:

- a different perspective on investment;
- expertise;
- diversity of knowledge and experience, culture and background;
- self-organization.

Investment of time, talent and funds is a core condition of a community of discovery. The revenues generated from the organizational innovations are not for the shareholders or for exorbitant pay for a few, rather, they are the funds that everyone has a stake in and everyone makes decisions about how they should be spent. This is leaderlessness in action.

There are other conditions necessary for the community of discovery philosophy to do its work in the context of a leaderless organization. These are:

- extensive social and developmental networking;
- product and service development;
- marketing.
  More subtle conditions are:
- a commitment to learn on the part of members of a group;
- extensive communication and dialogue;
- a diverse culture of excitement about change and ideas;
- curiosity and a commitment to and delight in discovery;
- determination to live in the world of ideas;
- toleration of complexity, a celebration of success;
- recognition that not all is controllable;
- a sense of mutuality in the learning process.

It is when there is this sense of excitement among members in an organization celebrate new ideas that these conditions will be met. When this happens, this is a community of discovery.

Conclusion

This chapter has argued in support of the realization of leaderless organization, which requires alternative practices of leadership development, and we proposed two different forms of coaching to facilitate people's learning and development within a leaderless organization. Table 3.2 offers a summary of the key components of the two approaches discussed in this chapter and their connections to leaderless organizations. The core principles of coaching, as outlined in our two examples, emphasizes humanism and the celebration of people's ability to learn, create and innovate collectively. It emphasizes diversity and equality. This, we believe, is the challenge of the twenty-first century for us to construct a new way of working and we argue that these two approaches, among others perhaps, offer a way of enabling people to take up the mantle of self-organization in a leaderless environment.

Table 3.2 Two eco-friendly coaching practices for leaderless organizations

Type of eco-friendly coaching practices	Learning-theory informed	Community of discovery	Connection to leaderless organizations
Type of learning	Individual Self-directed	Collective Situated learning	In leaderless organizations, learning should be customized for and by the actor involved in the learning processes
Assumptions about learning	Adults learn from experience Adults have distinctive learning styles Self-direction	Learning is a social activity	Leaderless organizations require situated bottom-up learning processes
Learning objectives	Reflexivity (see Jørgensen and Ingman, Chapter 8 in this volume)	Discovery; invention	Leaderless organizations require challenging the status-quo
Approach to coaching	A dialectical process and reflective space	Team or systemic coaching	Leaderless organizations require eco-friendly coaching practices

References

Alred, G., & Garvey, B. (2000). Learning to produce knowledge: The contribution of mentoring. *Mentoring and Tutoring, 8*(3), 261–272.

Amado, G. (2004). Le coaching ou le retour de Narcisse (in English, it would be something like "Coaching or when Narcissus is back"). *Connexions, 81*(1), 43–52.

Buechler, S. M. (1990). *Women's movements in the United States: Woman suffrage, equal rights, and beyond.* New Brunswick, NJ: Rutgers University Press.

Clutterbuck, D. (2007). *Coaching the team at work.* London: Nicholas Brealey.

Connor, M., & Pokora, J. (2012). *Coaching and mentoring at work: Developing effective practice*. Maidenhead, UK: McGraw-Hill.

Cornell, A. (2011). *Oppose and propose: Lessons from movement for a new society*. Edinburgh: AK Press Distribution.

Cox, E., Bachkirova, T., & Clutterbuck, D. (Eds.). (2014). *The complete handbook of coaching* (2nd ed.). London: Sage.

Downey, M. (2014). *Effective modern coaching: The principles and art of successful business coaching*. London: LID Publishing.

du Toit, A. (2014). *Making sense of coaching*. London: Sage.

Garvey, B., Stokes, P., & Megginson, D. (2018). *Coaching and mentoring theory and practice* (3rd ed.). London: Sage.

Garvey, B., & Williamson, B. (2002). *Beyond knowledge management: Dialogue, creativity and the corporate curriculum*. Harlow, UK: Pearson Education.

Gray, D. E., Garvey, B., & Lane, D. A. (2016). *A critical introduction to coaching and mentoring*. London: Sage.

Grint, K. (2020). Leadership, management and command in the time of coronavirus. *Leadership, 16*(3), 314–319.

Knowles, M., Holton, E., III, & Swanson, R. (1998). *The adult learner: The definitive classic in adult education and human resource development*. San Diego, CA: Elsevier.

Kolb, D. A. (1984). *Experiential learning*. Englewood Cliffs, NJ: Prentice Hall.

Lave, J., & Wenger, E. (1991). *Situated learning: Legitimate peripheral participation*. Cambridge, UK: Cambridge University Press.

Maslow, A. H., Fadiman, J., & Frager, R. (1987). *Motivation and personality* (3rd ed.). New York: Addison-Wesley.

Nadeem, I., & Garvey, B. (2020). Learning experiences for academic deans: Implications for leadership coaching. *International Journal of Evidence Based Coaching and Mentoring, 18*(2), 133–151.

Parsloe, E., & Leedham, M. (2009). *Coaching and mentoring: Practical conversations to improve learning*. London: Kogan Page.

Peltier, B. (2001). *The psychology of executive coaching: Theory and application*. New York: Brunner Routledge.

Rajasinghe, D. R. (2018). *Leadership development through executive coaching: An interpretative phenomenological analysis*. Unpublished PhD thesis. University of Leeds, UK.

Rogers, C. R. (1989). *The Carl Rogers reader* (H. Howard Kirschenbaum & and V. L. Henderson, Eds.). Boston: Houghton Mifflin.

Rogers, J. (2012). *Coaching skills: A handbook* (2nd ed.). Milton Keynes, UK: Open University Press.

Rosinski, P. (2004). *Coaching across cultures*. London: Nicholas Brealey.

Schön, D. (1983). *The reflective practitioner*. New York: Basic Books.

Self, T. T., Gordon, S., & Jolly, P. M. (2019). Talent management: A Delphi study of assessing and developing GenZ hospitality leaders. *International Journal of Contemporary Hospitality Management, 31*(10), 4126–4149. doi:10.1108/IJCHM-11-2018-0915.

Shearing, C. (2001). Punishment and the changing face of the governance. *Punishment & Society, 3*(2), 203–220.

Starr, J. (2008). *The coaching manual: The definitive guide to the process, principles and skills of personal coaching*. London: Pearson.

Stelter, R. (2019). *The art of coaching dialogue: Towards transformative exchange*. Abingdon, Oxon, UK: Routledge.

Stokes, P., Fatien Diochon, P., & Otter, K. (2021). Two sides of the same coin? Coaching and mentoring and the agentic role of context. *Annals of the New York Academy of Sciences, 1483*(1), 142–152. https://www.ncbi.nlm.nih.gov/pubmed/32083348. Accessed 25 Jan 2021.

Western, S. (2012). *Coaching and mentoring: A critical text*. London: Sage.

Whitmore, J. (2009). *Coaching for performance: Growing human potential and purpose* (4th ed.). London: Nicholas Brealey.

Zeus, P., & Skiffington, S. (2000). *The complete guide to coaching at work*. Sydney: McGraw-Hill.

4

When Matters Are Too Important to be Left to Leaders and Better Left to Democratic Control

Thomas Borchmann and Bendt Torpegaard Pedersen

Introduction

We live in a time when both management and leadership are often promoted as answers to the many challenges we are faced with. The call for more and better management and leadership is seen both in regard to the challenges associated with the growing environmental crisis (e.g., Woo and Kang 2020) and the widespread disengagement in the workplaces (e.g., Gallup 2013). However, when such calls are made, some questions also seem important to ask. One such question is, can the hopes we are supposed to have in leaders be labeled as realistic and well-founded? Another question is, what are the possible negative consequences of an increased investment of trust and resources in

T. Borchmann (✉) · B. T. Pedersen
Department of Psychology and Communication, University of Aalborg, Aalborg, Denmark
e-mail: borchman@ikp.aau.dk

© The Author(s), under exclusive license to Springer Nature Switzerland AG 2022
F. Hertel et al. (eds.), *Debating Leaderless Management*, Palgrave Debates in Business and Management, https://doi.org/10.1007/978-3-031-04593-6_4

management or leadership arrangements, which grant selected individuals a formal leadership position and privilege? Whereas the first question seems reasonable to ask for anyone who prefers to be guided by realistic views rather than fantasies, the second question is important because it directs our attention away from the promised gains and toward the risks and potential losses associated with the investment of trust and resources in management and leadership arrangements in general, which are rarely mentioned by management protagonists. As an example of such losses, one might fear that an increased investment of trust and resources in formal management or leadership arrangements can serve to weaken or even replace a variety of leaderless management arrangements. Examples of such practices are self-management, peer-regulated practices, democratic decision-making and democratic governance/control. Likewise, one might also fear that an increased investment of trust in formal management or leadership arrangements can produce a political apathy among the people being led (Marcuse 1964; Mills 1951). Thus, in this chapter, we will present different reasons to question some of the hopes that are put in management and leaders and also point at the possible negative consequences of investing too much hope in leaders. In relation to the overall theme of the present book, the articulated skepticism toward an investment of trust and resources in management or leadership arrangements naturally places us as being *against* management arrangements that grant selected individuals a formal leadership position and privilege, which is outside democratic control. The skepticism also puts us in favor of leaderless management practices in the form of democratic practices.

In the next section, we examine some of the different meanings being possible to associate with the term leaderless management. We point to the necessity of distinguishing between uses of the term leaderless management that has to do with the management of the organization as such and uses which only implies that certain aspects of organizational functioning are maintained—or that certain organizational domains are indeed managed—without the use of formal leadership arrangements. We also consider three different ways of questioning the importance of leaders and present the strategy of questioning pursued in this chapter. The specific organizational domain that we have chosen to focus on in our attempt to question the importance of leaders regards the management and maintenance of the psycho-social work environment. The reasons for our choice of focus on this domain are twofold. First, the psycho-social work environment is an interesting domain to choose, because it is a domain in which a leader in order to satisfy the inherent criteria of success would have to satisfy the needs and interests of the workforce, although a satisfaction of these needs and interests might easily conflict with the satisfaction of other organizational needs. Examples of such needs could be the need for numerical flexibility and the need for a continuous intensification of the work process. Secondly, one can see a heightened tendency to emphasize the importance of active leadership in this domain. Thus, in the third section, we show how this tendency manifests itself in a Danish context and also take a closer look at some of the different roles that are envisioned for leaders. We then point to a triad of constraints that makes the potential positive roles and contributions of leaders in this domain seem highly questionable. The first group of constraints we label *political* constraints. This group covers constraints stemming from the political interest in the pursuit of profit normally associated with the fulfillment of the managerial role. The second group of constraints we label *psychological* constraints. These constraints stem from the tendency of power to corrupt (Kipnis 1976), the stereotypical perceptions of subordinates that powerholders often have (Fiske 1993) and the decreased ability to understand the situation and perspectives of subordinates found among powerholders (Galinsky et al. 2012). Finally, the third group of constraints we label *practical* constraints. This group covers constraints stemming from the general characteristics of major organizations as such, and the deregulation of work in particular (Allvin and Aronsson 2003).

Finally, we take a closer look at some of the possible negative consequences of crediting leaders a more active and central role in the management and maintenance of the psycho-social work environment and also discuss possible alternatives. As an alternative to voicing hopes for an active and central role of leaders in the management and maintenance of the psycho-social work environment, we point to a strengthening of the worker collective, a strengthening of the workers' voice in the health and safety committees, and the formal organization of workers in unions. We also cast a short glance at the factors threatening the worker collective, the strength of workers' voice in the health and safety committees, and the organization of workers in unions, and argue that the tendency to naïvely credit leaders with a will and capacity they do not possess, is in fact one of these threats.

On Leaderless Management and Different Ways of Questioning the Importance of Leaders

The concept of "leaderless management" immediately leads us to think of activities being done and managed by one or more individuals without the presence and inputs by a leader or a formal distinction between people who are named and acknowledged as leaders and those who are not. These activities can take place within an organization or outside organizations or across the boundaries of two or more organizations. If we narrow our attention and focus exclusively on activities which take place within an organization, the notion leaderless management can make us envisage organizations which function and are managed without the use of a formal and institutionalized leadership arrangement, where some are leaders and others are not. However, this imply that the notion leaderless management has to do with the functioning of the organization as such. In contrast, the term leaderless management can also just make us think of specific aspects of organizational functioning or specific domains within the organization that either are or can be managed by self-management, peer control or democratic decision-making. These distinctions and the different scopes implied by the term leaderless management are important to keep in mind, when we go on to consider different ways of questioning the importance of leaders.

If one wants to argue against the importance of leaders in the functioning of organizations as such or just in relation to particular aspects of organizational performance, one can choose one of *three* strategies. A first strategy is to point to empirical studies which show how organizations are indeed getting by without leaders thus suggesting that leaders might not be necessary for the "survival" or general welfare of an organization, or whatever we perceive to be a reasonable end-goal or measure in this context. Research which focuses on the functioning of leader-free organizations include research on successful employee-owned companies, which are run collectively (e.g., Pierce and Rodgers 2004) and democratically governed institutions. Research which only focuses on the self-managing of particular aspects of organizational functioning includes, among other things, the delegation of planning and control of production to employees under the heading "organizational participation" (Heller et al. 1998) or "self-governing teams" (e.g., Hackman 1990).

A second strategy is to point at the lack of convincing evidence that documents the general importance of leaders. This strategy departs from a questioning of the clarity of the concept of leadership and its empirical foundation. Due to its focus on the concept as such, such critiques normally focus on the general functioning of organizations or overall organizational efficiency, rather than specific aspects of organizational functioning (e.g., Lakomski 2005; Pfeffer 1977).

Finally, a third strategy is to point at constraints which make it questionable to credit leaders with the will, abilities and possibilities to administer the many tasks and fulfill the many roles they are normally attributed, by the huge number of management consultants who make their living from cherishing and deifying management. This strategy, which questions the importance of leaders by questioning the adequacy of leaders in the management of organizational activities, is in our view best pursued by focusing on specific tasks or specific aspects of organizational functioning. As we will demonstrate later, this strategy is a strategy which can both draw on empirical evidence in the form of studies of neglect conducted by people in management positions (e.g., Rosskam 2007) and experimental research which can explain the possible causes for this neglect (e.g., Fiske 1993; Kipnis 1976).

Since the third strategy is rarely pursued, we have chosen to take up this strategy in this chapter. We will argue that there are weighty reasons to question the will, abilities and possibilities of leaders to manage and maintain the psycho-social work environment. We will also argue that the inadequacies displayed by leaders should not fuel hopes of more or better leadership, but rather make us realize that such hopes are not only naïve but also potentially harmful.

The Role of Leaders in the Management of the Psycho-Social Work Environment

The specific organizational domain that we have chosen to focus on in our attempt to question the importance of leaders is the management and maintenance of the psycho-social work environment. We start out by showing how a heightened tendency to emphasize the importance of leaders in the management and maintenance of the psycho-social environment manifests itself in a Danish context. We then go on to take a closer look at the potential but also questionable roles of leaders that are suggested in guidelines from the five national trade safety committees.

Today, it is possible to detect an increased tendency to emphasize the importance of leaders in the maintenance of the psycho-social work environment, at least in a Danish context. This tendency, which seems to be driven by occupational health researchers and practitioners, leaders and sometimes also unions, displays itself in many ways. Examples include a growing body of research addressing the role of leaders in the management of work environment issues (e.g., Limborg et al. 2020), the demand for voluntary courses in work environment issues for leaders in the government sector put forward as a union demand in the collective agreement of 2018 (SL 2021), and the guidelines for improvements of the psycho-social work environment suggested by the five national trade safety committees (APV-Portalen 2021).

To some, the aspiration to grant leaders a central and more proactive role in the management and maintenance of the psycho-social work environment might look unproblematic and a natural and progressive supplement to the work already being done by the mandatory safety and health committees. To others, this aspiration may also seem somewhat naïve. To be sure, a demand for the active engagement of management in work environment issues has often been put forward throughout the past 150 years, and it is also a demand that we support. However, we do not share the belief in a sudden transition of the role of leaders from political actors who reluctantly complied with the demands made by law or by trade unions to enlightened "agents of care" who proactively and progressively attend to the work environment. As we will explain later, we also consider a belief in such a transformation to be a potentially harmful belief.

The different sub-roles imagined for leaders in the management of the psycho-social work environment is clearly visible in the managerial tasks described in the so-called Iglo model. This model is widely promoted by national trade safety committees and also used as part of the curriculum in the voluntary leader courses in work environment issues (APV-Portalen 2021). The first role that leaders are believed to be able to play according to this model, is the role as "agents who take initiative and responsibility and make sure that activities aimed at improving the work environment take place and are granted the necessary time, resources and employee participation" (APV-Portalen 2021). This we can call the *proactive, organizing and policy enforcing role*. The second role is as caretakers and supervisors of each employee. In the description of this role, it is emphasized that "all employees are different, have different needs and limits, and that the leader should get to know how each employee experiences and expresses signs of lack of wellbeing, so that he/she can register any behavioral changes" (APV-Portalen 2021). This we can call the *attentive and caretaking role*. The third role is, finally, as role models. In the description of this role, it is emphasized that leaders are role models and have to be "good examples of work-life balance" (APV-Portalen 2021). Likewise, they have to "communicate politely even if under strain" and "show a positive way forward" (APV-Portalen 2021). This we can call the *exemplary and culture-bearing role*.

In what follows, we will argue that the belief that leaders are able to fulfill these roles is a belief which is both naïve and potentially harmful. The reason that this belief is naïve, is that there is a series of constraints that makes the potential positive roles and contributions of leaders seem highly questionable. The reason that this belief is harmful, is that a belief in leaders is a poor substitute for the management and maintenance of the psycho-social work environment offered by the active participation in the informal worker collective, the qualified backup (and control) of health and safety committee representatives and union membership.

A Leader-Maintained Psycho-Social Work Environment—Possible Constraints

In this section, we point at a triad of constraints that makes the potential positive roles and contributions of leaders in the maintenance of the psycho-social work environment seem questionable. The constraints can be divided into *political constraints*, *psychological constraints* and *practical constraints*.

Political Constraints

A first group of constraints which make it questionable to credit leaders with *the will* to fulfill their envisioned roles in the management and maintenance of the psycho-social work environment we label political constraints. This group covers constraints stemming from the political interest in the pursuit of profit normally associated with the fulfillment of the managerial role. This interest often leads to a neglect of important matters relating to occupational health and the psycho-social work environment, especially, if these matters threaten profit (Jakobsen 2011; Schnall et al. 2017).

Throughout history, one can see the tendency to ignore important matters relating to occupational health and the psycho-social work environment if these matters threaten profit. In his book *Velfærdens pris* (translated from Danish to English, it would be something like *The Cost of Welfare*), Jakobsen documents the origin and history of worker protection and regulation of work environment issues in a Danish context (Jakobsen 2011). Jakobsen points out how different interest groups; workers, health professionals, politicians and employers always have eagerly disputed—and confronted each other over—issues relating to workplace health and workers' rights. These disputes and confrontations have entailed questions concerning whether to regulate, what and how much to regulate, who must do the regulating and who must control whether regulations are followed. Examples include everything from unhygienic waste disposal and child labor over exposure to toxic chemicals and dangerous working conditions to unhealthy work organization and other psycho-social risk-factors, etc. Ignoring the odd references to the potential societal problems associated with idle children put forward in the defense of child labor (Jakobsen 2011, p. 59), the main arguments put forward by interest groups opposing regulations have always been the sovereign rights granted by ownership and the forces of competition which do not allow for costly employee-considerations. The main arguments put forward by interest groups in favor of regulations have been the need to secure workers' rights and the interests of the public as such as well as preserving an international reputation as a nation-state. As early as 1872, the argument that occupational health initiatives could have a positive effect on productivity and profit was also presented on a national industrial convention (Jakobsen 2011, p. 54). However, this argument always seemed more convincing in talk than in regular practice and never created a stable consensus on what and how much to regulate. What can be witnessed during history is rather a series of moments in which interests have often collided. Historically, workers have mostly been in favor of more and stricter regulations and thus opposed employers, who often were against regulations, but Jakobsen also gives examples of joint ventures between unions and employers. Some of these ventures led to an improvement of work environment issues and some led to serious neglects. An example of the latter is the joint pursuit of higher wages through time-motion studies in the 1950s and 1960s which left many occupational health issues ignored. Jakobsen also points out that although progress has taken place, it has been slow and sometimes even suffered drawbacks. One factor contributing to the lack of progress is the intentional neglect of laws displayed by companies and leaders (Jakobsen 2011).

The tendency among leaders to ignore important matters relating to the work environment, if these matters threaten profit or the ability to compete, is also visible in present times. In a report from 2007, an expert group of researchers identified the most important psycho-social risks of today. Among these, two important risks were precarious work arrangements and work intensification (EU-OSHA 2007). Both of these can be seen as risks which are widely ignored by leaders because precarious work arrangements and work intensification are seen as favorable because they allow for a cutting of costs (Kalleberg 2009). Likewise, one can also notice that the growth in precarious work arrangements and the increase in work intensification coincide with a decline of union strength (Case and Deaton 2020; Landsbergis et al. 2018). As Landsbergis et al. point out:

> with less union density and workers' power to protect working and employment conditions, what was formerly seen as a problem faced by poorer workers is increasingly recognized as an important structural factor for many. (Landsbergis et al. 2018, p. 296)

Finally, the interest in profit—and the associated tendency to ignore important matters relating to occupational health and the psycho-social work environment—can also manifest itself in a managerial preference for modeling matters of occupational health and the psycho-social work environment in terms of individual problems (Gordon et al. 2017; Willis 2018; Yuill 2009). Someone might object that the managerial tendency to model matters of occupational health and the psycho-social work environment in terms of individual problems are limited to specific cultural settings and not to be found in a Scandinavian context where occupational health issues traditionally have been looked upon through a structural prism. However, in a recent survey made by The Union for General Upper Secondary School Teachers in Denmark, 70% of the teachers strongly agree or somewhat agree that stress is conceived as an individual problem at their workplace (GL 2015). Confronted with the political constraints, which make it questionable to credit leaders with the will to fulfill their envisioned roles in the management and maintenance of the psycho-social work environment, there is reason to be skeptical of the potential value of the attempts to strengthen leadership in this organizational domain. Rather, the constraints serve to emphasize the need for leaderless management arrangements in the form of democratic control in order to secure that the consideration of profit does not overrule the considerations of workers health.

Psychological Constraints

A second group of constraints which make it questionable to credit leaders with *the abilities* to fulfill their envisioned roles in the management and maintenance of the psycho-social work environment, we label *psychological* constraints. These constraints originate from a tendency of power to corrupt (Kipnis 1976, 2006), from the stereotypical perceptions of subordinates that powerholders often have (Fiske 1993), and from the decreased ability to understand the situation and perspectives of the subordinates found among powerholders (Galinsky et al. 2012). From his studies of the effects of having power, Kipnis draws several lessons which illustrate the difficulties that leaders might face in their attempts to fulfill an attentive and caretaking role. In his early work, Kipnis finds that a powerful position is associated with a tendency to

> (a) increase attempts to influence the behavior of the less powerful, (b) devalue the worth of the performance of the less powerful, (c) attribute the cause of the less powerful's efforts to power controlled by themselves, rather than to the less powerful's motivations to do well, (d) view the less powerful as objects of manipulation, and (e) express a preference for the maintenance of psychological distance from the less powerful. (Kipnis 2006, p. 177)

In his later work, Kipnis shows that a powerful position is often associated with a tendency to ignore the perspectives of others as well as an instrumental view of subordinates as a means to realize one's own goal (Kipnis 1976). Kipnis's findings are supplemented by the work of Fiske (1993) who finds that people in power positions are characterized by having stereotypical views of their subordinates. This is partly due to the fact that people in power positions do not need to be attentive to the feelings, attitudes and motives of their subordinates, partly due to the fact that they don't have an easy access to these (Fiske 1993). In their work, Galinsky et al. point out that people in power positions do not need to be attentive to the feelings and motives of their subordinates because their positions do not depend on their subordinates (Galinsky et al. 2012, p. 19). Their research also documents a decreased ability to understand the situation and perspectives of subordinates among power-holders. The reason a powerful position seems to entail a decreased ability to understand the situation and perspectives of the subordinates is that this ability conflicts with the need for creating a psychological distance.

The lack of understanding, the devaluating and stereotypical view of subordinates, as well as the need to psychologically distance oneself from subordinates make the hope for an attentive and caretaking leader seem somewhat unrealistic. After all, how can you be trusted to be attentive to the needs of others and take care of their needs, if your position fosters an instrumental view of your subordinates and a decreased ability to understand their situation and perspectives? Confronted with the psychological constraints, which make it questionable to credit leaders with the abilities to fulfill their envisioned roles in the management and maintenance of the psycho-social work environment, there is reason to be skeptical of the potential value of the attempts to strengthen leadership in this organizational domain. Instead, the constraints give good reason to argue for the necessity of leaderless management arrangements in the form of strong democratic practices. These practices should include procedures, which secure that the perspectives of workers are brought forward by workers themselves, shared between them and transformed into—and treated as—collective demands, rather than being interpreted by leaders on an everyday basis and met on an individual basis.

Practical Constraints

A third group of constraints which make it questionable to credit leaders with *the possibility* to fulfill their envisioned roles in the management and maintenance of the psycho-social work environment we label *practical* constraints. This group covers constraints stemming from the characteristics of major organizations in general and the deregulation of work arrangements in particular (Allvin and Aronsson 2003).

The belief that leaders should be capable of watching the situation and well-being of each individual employee, and able to intervene proactively in order to avoid problems seems somewhat unrealistic at least in large organizations. One reason for this, is that information about the situation and well-being of individual workers requires a closeness—not to mention an amount of time—which does not exist for leaders in most organizations. The many attempts of developing tools which gather information on the well-being of individual workers in the form of digital apps document how this lack of information is indeed experienced by leaders. Although such tools are still in their infancy, one can easily envisage a number of problems associated with this approach, of which one is that the quality of information provided by such tools is potentially limited.

The hope that leaders can organize processes which lead to the formulation of policies which, once enforced, provide organizational settings in which workers' well-being is supported, can also be questioned. Allvin and Aronsson (2003) argue that a meaningful appeal to the concept of workplace environment can only take place if a job is clearly and centrally regulated in the dimensions time (when) space (where) and horizontal (how) and vertical organization (responsibility). This, they claim, is not the case for modern deregulated jobs, and hence such jobs do not have an objective environment which can be made the object of collective negotiation or management responsibility (Allvin and Aronsson 2003). While these claims perhaps seem a bit far-fetched since jobs still come with conditions, constraints, incentives and output expectations which create a shared environment that influence organizational behavior, the difficulties outlined do point to a series of practical constraints for crediting leaders with an ability to maintain and manage the psycho-social work environment through hands-on procedures.

Finally, one could also argue that a fulfillment of an exemplary and culture-bearing role is hindered by several "practical" issues too. One might wonder how the work-life balance of one person should in fact be visible to another person. One could also claim that the idea that leaders serve as role models and culture bearers who influence the thoughts and behaviors of so-called followers through their sporadic interactions is nothing more than a romanticized simplification of much more complex social processes (Ford and Harding 2018; Meindl et al. 1985). These practical constraints are the final constraints, which make it questionable to credit leaders with the possibilities to fulfill their envisioned roles in the management and maintenance of the psycho-social work environment. They are also constraints that should inspire us to look outside formal leadership arrangements and toward other types of arrangements if we want to strengthen the management and maintenance of the psycho-social work environment.

Concluding Remarks

In the beginning of the chapter, we stated a need for examining critically whether the hopes we invest in managers and leaders are realistic and well-founded. Focusing on the hopes, that are presently invested in leaders in the management and maintenance of the psycho-social work environment in a Danish context, we outlined a series of constraints which make it questionable to credit leaders with the will, abilities and possibility to fulfill their envisioned roles. The existence of these constraints positions us as being *against* an investment of trust and resources in management arrangements, which grant selected individuals a formal leadership position and privilege, which is outside democratic control. The constraints also position us as being *for* a strengthening of management through a variety of *leaderless* management arrangements. In order to overcome the political constraints that leaders are subjected to—and to secure that the pursuit of profits do not overrule the considerations of workers health—we have pointed to the necessity of *democratic control*. In order to overcome the psychological constraints associated with holding a power position, we have pointed at the necessity of leaderless management arrangements in the form of strong democratic practices. Such practices should include procedures, which secure that the perspectives of workers are brought forward by the workers themselves, shared between workers and transformed into—and treated as—collective demands, rather than being interpreted by leaders on an everyday basis and met on an individual basis. Finally, we have also argued that the lack of possibilities associated with a series of practical constraints should inspire us to look outside formal leadership arrangements and toward other arrangements, which are perhaps better suited for the task of managing and maintaining the psycho-social work environment.

Against the argument outlined here, one could claim that a strengthening of the role of leaders in the management and maintenance of the psycho-social work environment could take place without affecting existing practices or even include a parallel strengthening of democratic practices. However, another central issue, that fostered our initial worries—and also supports our position—was the fear of the potential negative consequences of placing more trust in formal leadership arrangements. Thus, we will finally turn our attention to the possible dangers of upkeeping a belief in leaders as proactive, attentive and quality-assuring actors in the context of the psycho-social work environment and explain what these are.

The main reason why we consider a belief in leadership to be a potentially harmful belief in the context of the management and maintenance of the psycho-social work environment, is that such a belief will be a poor substitute for the management and maintenance of the psycho-social work environment offered by a series of other and far more important channels. These channels are (a) the active participation of workers in the workers' collective which serves as an informal buffer against the demands put upon workers (Axelsson et al. 2019; Lysgaard 1971), (b) the qualified backup (and control) of representatives in the safety and health committees, which presently are the official channels for the discussion and negotiation of work environment issues within the organization and (c) union membership which historically has been a leading force in securing improvements in working conditions (McCluskey 2020).

Not only is an exaggerated belief in management a poor substitute for the before-mentioned channels, but it is also something which potentially threatens these channels. Personally, we have witnessed a growing number of colleagues who didn't see a need for union membership believing modern leaders to be a sufficient guarantee for a healthy and secure working environment. Due to the same belief, we have also seen safety and health committee representatives left to work without any backup or support by co-workers. We have also seen representatives who silenced their voice or ended up promoting managerial views to co-workers rather than promoting workers' views to management without being opposed or corrected by the workers they represent. Finally, we have also experienced weakened worker collectives in which fellow workers orient themselves toward leaders and their capacity to provide satisfying conditions for them as individuals rather than orienting themselves towards their peers and the shared conditions. And we also have experienced the many negative impacts on the work environment this orientation created. To be sure, there are many other threats to the organization of labor, the quality of the representation—and the political work conducted—in health and safety committees as well as threats to the workers' collective which we cannot hope to treat in any length here. However, compared to factors like actions directly aimed at weakening union membership; uncertainty; work intensification; and disciplinary regimes which weaken solidarity, a factor like an unjustified belief in leaders should be much easier to overcome or get rid of. All it takes is knowing what reasonably to expect from whom. Taken together, the lack of realism in the belief we can put in leaders and the dangers mentioned above are reasons to argue against the investment of trust in management arrangements, which grant selected individuals a formal leadership position and privilege. It also gives us reason to argue for a strengthening of leaderless management arrangements in the form of a strengthening of democratic procedures and democratic control.

References

Allvin, M., & Aronsson, G. (2003). The future of work environment reforms: Does the concept of work environment apply within the new economy? *International Journal of Health Service, 33*(1), 99–111.

APV-Portalen. (2021). Iglo-modellen: Hvem gør hvad? http://www.apvportal en.dk. Accessed 1 Mar 2021.

Axelsson, J., Karlsson, J. C., & Skorstad, E. J. (2019). *Collective mobilization in changing conditions: Worker collectivity in a turbulent time.* London: Palgrave Macmillan.

Case, A., & Deaton, A. (2020). *Deaths of despair and the future of capitalism.* Princeton, NJ: Princeton University Press.

EU-OSHA. (2007). *Annual report 2007*. Luxembourg: Office for Official Publications of the European Communities.

Fiske, S. T. (1993). Controlling other people: The impact of power on stereotyping. *American Psychologist, 48*(6), 621–628.

Ford, J., & Harding, N. (2018). Followers in leadership theory: Fiction, fantasy and illusion. *Leadership, 14*(1), 3–24.

Galinsky, A., Rus, D., & Lammers, J. (2012). Power: A central force governing psychological, social, and organizational life. In D. De Cremer, R. van Dick, & J. K. Murnighan (Eds.), *Social psychology and organization* (pp. 17–35). New York: Routledge.

Gallup. (2013). *State of the global workplace: Employee engagement insights for business leaders worldwide*. Omaha, NE: Gallup.

GL. (2015). *Gymnasielærernes stressundersøgelse 2015*. Copenhagen: Gymnasieskolernes Lærerforening.

Gordon, D. R., Jauregui, M., & Schnall, P. L. (2017). Stakeholder perspectives on work and stress. In P. T. Schnall, M. Dobson, & E. Rosskam (Eds.), *Unhealthy work: Causes, consequences, cures* (pp. 173–192). New York: Routledge.

Hackman, R. (1990). *Groups that work (and those that don't): Creating conditions for effective teamwork*. San Francisco: Jossey-Bass.

Heller, F., Pusic, E., Strauss, G., & Wilpert, B. (1998). *Organizational participation: Myth or reality*. Oxford: Oxford University Press.

Jakobsen, K. (2011). *Velfærdens pris: Arbejderbeskyttelse og arbejdsmiljø gennem 150 år*. Copenhagen: Gads Forlag.

Kalleberg, A. L. (2009). Precarious work, insecure workers: Employment relations in transition. *American Sociological Review, 74*, 1–22.

Kipnis, D. (1976). *The powerholders*. Chicago: University of Chicago Press.

Kipnis, D. (2006). Does power corrupt? In J. M. Levine, & R. L. Moreland (Eds.), *Small groups: Key readings* (pp. 177–186). New York: Psychology Press.

Lakomski, G. (2005). *Managing without leadership: Towards a theory of organizational functioning*. Bingley, UK: Emerald Group Publishing.

Landsbergis, P. A., Choi, B., Dobson, M., Sembajwe, G., Slatin, C., Delp, L., Siqueira, C., Schnall, P., & Baron, S. (2018). The key role of work in population health inequities. *American Journal of Public Health, 108*(3), 296–297.

Limborg, H. J., Pedersen, F., Nielsen, H. A., Jensen H. A., Just, I., & Jespersen, A. H. (2020). *Ledelse af det psykiske arbejdsmiljø: Håndtering og forebyggelse af psykisk arbejdsmiljø—udvikling af et praksisorienteret arbejdsmiljøsystem*.

Afslutningsrapport til Arbejdsmiljøforskningsfonden, Projekt nr.: 17-567/67-2017-03.

Lysgaard, S. (1971). *Arbeiderkollektivet: En studie i de underordnedes sociologi.* Oslo: Universitetsforlaget A/S.

Marcuse, H. (1964). *One-dimensional man.* Boston: Beacon Press.

McCluskey, L. (2020). *Why you should be a trade unionist.* London: Verso.

Meindl, J. R., Sanford B. E., & Dukerich, J. M. (1985). The romance of leadership. *Administrative Science Quarterly, 30*(1), 78–102.

Mills, C. W. (1951). *White collar: The American middle classes.* Oxford: Oxford University Press.

Pfeffer, J. (1977). The ambiguity of leadership. *Academy of Management Review, 12*(1), 104–112.

Pierce, J. L., & Rodgers, L. (2004). The psychology of ownership and worker-owner productivity. *Group & Organization Management, 29*(5), 588–613.

Rosskam, E. (2007). *Excess baggage: Levelling the load and changing the workplace.* New York: Baywood Publishing Company.

Schnall, P. T., Dobson, M., & Rosskam, E. (2017). *Unhealthy work: Causes, consequences, cures.* New York: Routledge.

SL. (2021). OK 2018. https://sl.dk/media/8890/ok-2018-staten-samlet-oversigt.pdf. Accessed 1 Mar 2021.

Willis, E. (2018). Foreword. In C. Peterson (Ed.), *Work stress: Studies of the context, content and outcomes of stress* (p. vii). New York: Routledge.

Woo, E.-J., & Kang, E. (2020). Environmental issues as an indispensable aspect of sustainable leadership. *Sustainability, 12*(17), 1–22.

Yuill, C. (2009). Health and the workplace: Thinking about sickness, hierarchy and workplace conditions. *International Journal of Management Concepts and Philosophy, 3*(3), 239–256.

5

Leaderless Management as the Solution to Struggles Over the Moral Center of Healthcare? Ward Nurses' Critique of Management as "Real Utopias" in the Public Sector

Rebecca Selberg and Paula Mulinari

Introduction

In 2017, Swedish poet and union activist Emil Boss published *Acceleration*, a poem written on a receipt roll from his employer Systembolaget (the state-owned chain of liquor stores). The poem mixed descriptions of repetitive, physically, and emotionally draining work under constant supervision with excerpts from management brochures on lean production and reflections on what work under such circumstances does to the human body and mind. He asked the critical question: *"Why do we accept leaving democracy behind as we enter our workplaces"*?[1] (Boss

R. Selberg (✉)
Department of Gender Studies, Lund University, Lund, Sweden
e-mail: rebecca.selberg@genus.lu.se

P. Mulinari
Department of Social Work, Malmö University, Malmö, Sweden

F. Hertel et al. (eds.), *Debating Leaderless Management*,
Palgrave Debates in Business and Management,
https://doi.org/10.1007/978-3-031-04593-6_5

2017). The poem was profound in its critique of work intensification and managerialism in the government's service.

This chapter heeds Boss' implicit claim that the voices from the shopfloor are not just relevant and legitimate, but powerful in their ability to elucidate power relations and articulations of alternative visions of organization of production and reproduction. Inspired by Boss' poem, we start there: in the radical notion that workers' critique and anger offer, to those who listen, a new way of thinking about organizations—a new way to imagine work. This new way of imagining work and organization is a contribution for leaderless management. Like Boss, we focus on the public sector, but the chapter deals with criticism expressed by ward nurses at hospital management. We approach the concept of leaderless management from a feminist-Marxist approach inspired by the work of Nancy Fraser (2014) and Erik Olin Wright (2011). We use this approach to analyze what nurses identify as central areas of conflict shaping their work, and what forms of structural and organizational change they view as necessary to create a more socially sustainable work situation.

Thus, we engage with leaderless management through exploring nurses' profound critique against the power of managers and what we conceptualize as a struggle over the moral center of the healthcare organization. We hope to show that workers within the public sector are key knowledge bearers and as such, central actors needed to confront what Fraser (2016a) has called the global care crisis, defined as the "growing strain" under neoliberalism on "the human capacities to create and maintain social bonds," including care work (Fraser 2014, p. 542). What this chapter proposes is that workers and not managers should be at the center of organizing care; we perceive leaderless management as a way of locating power and the moral center with workers, rather than managers. We argue that care workers do not need to be managed— they may need managerial tasks performed by managers, but they do not need managers to "lead." In this connection, the chapter returns to abandoned notions of the public sector as a real utopia and explores how nurses' knowledge about the workings of their workplaces can be used to improve healthcare. Thus, we argue for leaderless management and put forward powerful visions of what the public sector can offer in terms of new forms of organization. Leaderless management in care work is defined as a situation wherein leaders' roles are insignificant (Kerr and Jermier 1978) because it is the treatment of patients that takes center stage.

We begin by discussing the changing view on the public sector in Sweden, in order to historize its role and critical interventions regarding its functionality. After that we present, in the form of vignettes, results from an interview study with nurses working in Swedish hospitals and analyze their criticism of management. The interviews capture the problems with an organization in which management and managerial goals take center stage. Through nurses' critique we identify alternatives that essentially constitute an imagined real utopia of care work in which social reproduction takes center stage. These alternatives focus on the very processes through which care is performed—the interaction between carer and patient. Management should emanate from knowledge of these processes and thus resituates control of the work situation with nurses.

The Public Sector as Real Utopia

It is important to place public care work in a historical context, to understand the significance of our vision of leaderless management. Otherwise, it may come through as yet another recipe for "fixing" the public sector with a specific management program; from bureaucracy to New Public Management to trust-based management, for example (Olsen 2017). Our purpose is to move beyond promoting yet another "sophisticated system" wherein rules, policies and procedures are clearly set to produce predictable and measurable output (Kerr and Jermier 1978, p. 378). To argue for leaderless management based on care-centered and worker-led care, we need to contextualize the organizational (political, economic) landscape in the Swedish public sector.

Management in the public sector in the 1960s must be seen in the context of the expansion of the public sector. It came to as a *real utopia*, a concept defined by Erik Olin Wright (2011, p. 37) as capturing the spirit of a utopia while remaining attentive to what it takes to bring those aspirations to life. As historian Lars Ekdahl (2010, p. 15) notes, the "common sector" has constituted a vital feature in a political vision of a fairer, safer, and more equal society. Specifically, this has been a Social democratic vision of democratic socialism through public ownership of central resources and capabilities. However, two decades into the new millennia, both these contradictory visions appear to have lost their utopian power. For contemporary Swedish Social democrats, the public sector seems to have been reduced to a concrete feature of the "third way"—characterized by a meek defense of some core social democratic principles (the existence of public services) partnered with major concessions to neoliberal doctrines (market logics implemented throughout the public sector). For the capitalist class, the public sector is no longer a primary target for ideological critique as much as it is a central area for profit-making; it is in the opaque consultancy-run transformations of major hospitals (Röstlund and Gustafsson 2020) and the unique system of publicly funded private schools that astounding profits for venture capitalists are generating (Meagher and Szebehely 2019).

The hard turn to neoliberal economics in the late 1980s and early 1990s delivered a massive shift of resources from social reproduction commons to sectors of accumulation, as well as the ascendance of logics of private capital within the public sector (Therborn 2020). According to Patrik Hall (2013, pp. 408–409), the neoliberal turn also lead to a change in management, from input control to output control, from controlling the financial- and personal-related practice of the organization, to a control of the performance generated by the organization The leadership role changed from being marginal and administrative in relation to the work of professionals, toward being central and strategic in new public management and recent hybrid forms of the public sector.

One effect of this change in management regime is that the public sector seems to be a long way from the utopian visions it once captured, especially in terms of the extent to which employees can influence their work and the organizational logics, practices, and visions. However, even after many years of marketization, many professionals remain carriers of a utopian vision of the public sector, its role in social reproduction, and its potential of creating social and economic justice. Employees feel that management has become a menace due to it situatedness within a market logic. The utopian vision instead places the center of the formal organization of care at the point of interaction between medical and care professionals and patients. It is this point of interaction which renders managers if not obsolete than at least marginal in the healthcare system. It is this vision that we believe can be conceptualized as leaderless organization. It is not a new vision, however. In the transitional period of the early 1980s, when the discourse of "there is no alternative" was gaining strength, alternatives to bureaucracy were actually presented by public sector trade unionists, who suggested that a "more democratic work organization" built on intensified "democratic processes" and increased "employee influence" (Ekdahl 2010, p. 112) could renew the public sector and strengthen its declining legitimacy (cf. Pierre 1993).

But these calls went unanswered and instead the public sector, including the very idea of the public sector as a political project, dwindled. What came instead was more management and increasingly top-heavy organizations wherein quality measures are easily gamed to produce the quantitative outputs sought after in audits (Siltala 2013). Our vision of the public sector is antithetical to such managerialism. Leaderless management in the public sector is a notion that centers the responsibility of hospitals and clinics to deliver critical services to the public. Thus, expertise and responsiveness rather than management should take center stage. The life-sustaining services of the public sector can and should, we argue, be delivered by professionals through leaderless management.

Managers Changing the Moral Center of the Public sector—From Care to Efficiency

In the article *First, Let's Fire All managers*, Gary Hamel (2011) argued that "management is the least efficient activity in your organization." While we do not agree with Hamel's organizational vision, he posed an important question: what do managers contribute to? Do they in fact become an obstacle for the organization and its core purpose, for instance, to give people care. Our vision for leaderless management emanates from stories of public sector workers, as well as the vast research on the adverse development of working conditions since the restructuring of the Swedish public sector in the 1990s. Such research has illustrated that austerity politics and market reforms have resulted in a "renegotiation of working conditions" (Elomäki and Koskinen Sandberg 2020, p. 81) negatively impacting female-dominated public sector- and welfare state workers.

The implementation of Toyota-style managerialism in this sector, often referred to as New Public Management (NPM), has been identified as one of the central causes behind increasing workloads and growing dissatisfaction among welfare workers in the Nordic region (Mustosmäki et al. 2020; Newman and Lawler 2009; Selberg 2012). In the healthcare sector, NPM has created a shift in focus from patients to administration and budget restraints, and from workers to managers (Liff and Andersson 2013; Owens et al. 2019). It has further placed an increased emphasis on organizational professionalism at the expense of occupational professionalism, meaning objectives, tasks, norms, values, and quality are defined and controlled by the work organization, rather than the professions (Burton and van den Broeck 2009; Marklund et al. 2019; Welander et al. 2017).

The central question this research poses, is what do managers lead, who's interests influence leadership, and what forms of gender inequalities do NPM create? In this new organizational climate, nurses as one particular group of care workers are forced to maneuver increasingly complex and contradictory demands in slimmed-down organizations (Smeds Alenius et al. 2020). Our data show that nurses are deeply critical of management per se and managers' power, which many of the nurses interviewed by us tend to describe as an aspect of the devaluation of care work and human relations. Our interviews suggest that nurses experience the power of managers as a conflict over the moral center of the care work organization.

It is reasonable to interpret these conditions as local expressions of what feminist philosopher Nancy Fraser (2016a) calls a global care crisis. At the root of this is a social-reproductive crisis tendency inherent to capitalism: on the one hand, no society can endure without reproductive work, and on the other hand capitalism's strive for endless accumulation erodes the very foundation of this work. In capitalist societies, Fraser (2016b, p. 31) argues, the capacities for social reproduction are "taken for granted, treated as free and infinitely available as 'gifts,' which require no attention or replenishment." But like nature, social reproduction is a resource that can be "stretched to the breaking point" (2016b, p. 31). Across the world today, we are approaching such a breaking point, as society "withdraws public support for social reproduction and conscripts the chief providers of it into long and grueling hours of paid work," depleting the very social capacities on which it depends (2016b, p. 31).

Through a thematic analysis of in-depth interviews with 50 nurses working or having worked in hospitals in Sweden, we have identified three key leitmotifs of critique leveled against the healthcare organization and its management (Selberg et al. 2021). We introduce these themes through vignettes—short illustrative excerpts or renditions and compilations of multiple interviews which we find indicative of the broader material. Thus, these vignettes are based on the interview material, compiled of exact or slightly abridged quotes from one or several nurses. These themes help us illustrate a central problem of care delivery in the Swedish public sector today: the fact that managerial logics, and not responsiveness to patients, characterize the healthcare system. In support for our argument "for leaderless management," we argue that these themes point to a need for doing away with managerial logics altogether and instead radically centering control on the interactions between patients and carers.

Conflicts Around the Temporal Web of Care, or the Underestimated Value of Time

In support of leaderless management, we introduce a few themes illustrating the problem with leaderful management. The first theme is focused on time. Conflicts around what we call *the temporal web of care* are a central feature of nurses' profound critique of how the public sector healthcare organization functions. Nurses are left to solve the organization's lean greediness by working part-time, planning for early exit, and by accepting repetitive demands on their free time. They are also forced to balance increasingly complex demands on their labor while at work. Thus, one of the crucial tensions that arise in care work emanate from the different temporal logics at play in the organization of care—on the one hand, the temporal logic of caring for others and their recalcitrant bodies, on the other hand the temporal logic of providing efficient services within the realm of lean organizations (cf. Baines et al. 2014). Thus we introduce now the first vignette, capturing many nurses' experiences of the ever-present time-crunch in care work:

> I am not going to be able to stay on as a nurse until retirement, I know that already. I work part-time simply because of the huge workload at the ward. It is hard to work full-time; you cannot cope, you are tired all the time if you work full-time. Still, I never have enough time while at work. I don't have time for my patients, or family and kin of patients, I feel like I run in and out of the patients' rooms and even when I want to sit down and talk to them about their situation or just check if they want a cup of coffee, I never have time to do that. When a patient was leaving recently, I followed her down to the main entrance of the hospital where she was going to wait for a taxi. She was a bit unsteady; she really wasn't well. I had to just leave her there, even though I felt I should have stayed with her. It wasn't ethical to just leave her there and run back; I wasn't sure she'd figure it out with the taxi, or even if she'd be able to keep standing. But I knew I had to run back to the ward, I had other patients waiting, the pace is crazy. When I'm home, I'm not really free from work, because we're constantly called in, they call us and ask if we can take an extra shift, or they text us over and over again. As soon as I walk through the door at work, a manager will ask me: will you take an extra shift?
> Nurse employed at a ward treating stroke patients.

This critique is amplified by the fact that many nurses also expressed that the time-crunch was avoidable, if only managers had listened to their suggestions. One nurse told us that one solution would be to simply let nurses control the scheduling, since they know about each other's preferences and who's feeling tired or ready to work. Several nurses said that it would be possible to avoid constantly pressuring nurses to take on extra shifts, if they re-organized the ward to better fit with nurses' preferred structure of work. Many nurses argued that if they had a few more colleagues and were able to properly influence how the work was structured, the pressure would be reduced.

In the nurses' accounts of the temporal web of care, three alternative visions of leaderless management of time in care work can be envisaged. First and foremost, care takes time and should take time. However, this is not recognized or accepted by the healthcare organization or by managers. The fact that care takes time and should take time ought to be recognized as an essential value in care. Nurses want to have the possibility, should have the possibility, and the organization should have the resources for, spending *caring time*. Caring time, then, should be prioritized and valued as an asset for the organization. Nurses and other care workers would prioritize differently if they were left to manage and not just be managed in care.

Second, nurses have knowledge about themselves and their colleagues with whom they perform care work, and they see their caring capacities as interlinked with self-care and solidarity in the group. Thus, nurses should be granted power to organize or properly influence scheduling practices and periods according to notions of *time as self-care*. We argue that if nurses were made to lead, they would also be able to organize work time in more sustainable ways, which would strengthen the quality and the continuity of care delivery.

Third, the healthcare organization should prioritize care workers' time not just at but outside of work, and view nurses' efforts as performed in a web of relations and activities, in and outside of work. Nurses experience a growing neglect from managers of how they can combine paid work with all the responsibilities outside of work, such as for instance family. A leaderless organization that takes as its point of departure the time of workers, in and outside of work, could contribute to decrease the (often gendered) temporal conflict between paid and unpaid work. We make bold interpretations of nurses' critique of the temporal web of care that go beyond disagreeing with the current management regime or contemporary public sector administration. Instead, we take seriously nurses' disapproval and look for what visionary openings their criticism point to. We find a competing view on time, but also, and importantly, a competing narrative of knowledge, wherein nurses' experiences of time pressure challenge not only priorities in a slimmed-down organization, but also the power of management in time-management. We find, in nurses' accounts of the time-crunch, a different valorization of time in care work consistent with a vision of leaderless management.

Conflicts Around the Organization of Care, or the Underestimated Value of Caring

The next theme focuses on the conflicts around how the organization of care entails an underestimation of the value of caring. Immanent in the critique of management we saw in the interviews was direct suggestions of leaderless management. This second theme is introduced by our next vignette, which illustrates the conflicts around the value of caring:

> If I got to decide, I would get rid of all managers and have them replaced by people who have been inside and worked, who knew what the reality looks like. The only thing managers do, is to appoint even more managers. They get their salaries, while we the workers don't get anything, we who work on the floor, we don't get any appreciation, they don't see us or what we do. And that is sad, because it is down here that we should work, why do they have a hundred managers that all do the same job, I don't understand that. For me it is rather easy to see what changes are needed in order to make things better, but it doesn't happen. I don't know how many years nurses have shouted and screamed for help, that the healthcare system is falling apart, but nothing happens. There are no changes. Why do we employ people to handle all the financial stuff, and spend money on that, instead of on nurses or nursing assistants who do the real work?
>
> Nurse employed at a surgical ward.

When nurses stress the significant meaning that time has for them, and when they demand that managers respect their time, we see a language of resistance which is not often explicated in public sector research. While there is a lot of research on public sector governance that is deeply critical of the current management regime (Bornemark 2018; Bringselius 2019), our data show a more radical stance in which management per se is the problem. Often, radical ideas are expressed a bit jokingly, but very often they are delivered quite seriously, without comic relief. In an interview with a nurse working in a surgical ward at a university hospital, the issue of management's incompetence came up, as the nurse was telling a story of how she had fought back against scheduling changes. She suggested that the hospital should initiate workers' boards: "What if workers took control of the place?", she asked during the interview; "what if we planned the working hours and decided how to prioritize?". While not all nurses interviewed had such concrete suggestions as to how managers could be replaced, the notion of letting the employees run the organization was a common theme.

Often the critique against managers were not so much directed at ward managers (first line management) or even clinic leadership (second line management) as it was directed against higher management, where budgets are set and broader negotiations between workers and employers are played out. Central to nurses' argument was that managerial logics are not logical or even financially effective from the point of view of providing care. On the contrary, many nurses stressed that managers were the real cost of the organization, as they did not contribute to the production of care. The injustice they identify is that while they have the knowledge of how this work needs to be organized in order to be effective as care work, managers primarily are interested in controlling the organization based on principles that seem contradictory to care.

We suggest that, in the nurses' accounts of organizational conflicts, two alternative visions of leaderless organization of care work can be envisioned. First, care, in the broader sense of social reproduction, is the primary mission of the healthcare organization. Thus, those tasks that make up this undertaking should also be the center of the organization—these responsibilities, the people they are directed at and the people performing them, should thus be considered the *moral center* of the organization. In social psychology, it is understood that there is a "moral constitution to an intersubjective society, and focus on individuals' moral stances are constitutive (not simply incidental) to who we are" (Hitlin 2007, p. 249). Our moral sense, according to Hitlin, "comprises a series of horizons that shape our understandings of self and others" (Hitlin 2007, p. 249). The moral sense of the healthcare organization should emanate from the responsibility to care, meaning the power in the organization, and its key knowledge producers, should be considered to be those affected by and those performing tasks aiming at sustaining life in a social-reproductive sense. This supports an argument of leaderless management.

This leads to the second vision: a completely new set of priorities and structures need to evolve in the healthcare organization, in which attempts must be made to decouple organizational hierarchies, resource allocation and influence from social power structures and logics of accumulation under capitalism, and instead place the *center of operational logics* in the human interactions between patients, care providers and medical science. This would, in effect, reduce managers' power and strengthen medical professions and care workers', as well as patients and the public's role as key knowledge bearers and priorities in the organization. Such a move renders managers and managerialism almost obsolete. It is clearly a bold vision, and one that centers human connection and service of human bonds rather than bureaucratic structures, industrial management regimes and logics of capital. It is, put simply, a re-evaluation and valorization of the concept of care.

Conflicts Over Resources, or the Underestimated Value of Care

The third theme emanates from stories of conflicts over resources and leads to our third argument for leaderless management. The introduction of NPM within the public sector has led to a change of focus, from care to economic efficiently, and a lack of workers influence over the moral center of the organization. A central conflict experienced by the nurses we interviewed revolved around lack of resources. Austerity politics in Sweden are today permanent rather than temporary measures. Seymour (2014) distinguishes between conjectural austerity and permanent austerity. While conjectural austerity refers to "temporary measures in response to short-term problems," permanent austerity is "promoted in response to a 'chronic' crisis, real or manufactured" (Jessop 2019, p. 97) and intends to bring about a more lasting reorganization of the balance of forces in favor of capital. Permanent austerity thus "becomes a major vector of the colonization, commodification, and, eventually, financialization of everyday life" (2019, p. 97). Permanent austerity means that concepts such as cost and cost effectiveness, efficiency, production, and output shape the care process and penetrate the values and understandings of what care is. In the everyday of nursing, this means that much of the work nurses do becomes invisible, even if it is still essential, as it cannot be measured. We introduce this theme through the following vignette:

> The biggest problem is resources. For instance, at our ward, we only get to spend ten percent of our time meeting with patients who've been discharged, which means that we can't do proper follow-ups with patients, and it becomes difficult to measure the importance of it, and therefore it is difficult to say that it is important, even though we know it is. Because we cannot measure it, it's work that isn't given any room – we can't do the work that is really important for the patients. We are supposed to live up to something that is not there, there are no means to make it possible for us to live up to the goals that management demands of us to reach. I think you think differently when you are higher up, perhaps they think of money, money is what is important, that is what controls everything. It is all about the budget, we have new managers, and new demands, and new demands on cuts, and new budgets, and they refer to them all the time, they say 'we really appreciate what you have done, but we don't have the resources for it'. It's all about the money. And I am so fed up about that, that it's all about the money. Care is about care, not about saving money, care should be about giving care and instead they cut down on care and on care workers' salaries, the whole idea is wrong. They talk about production, but when you do care work, you can't see it as production, we don't produce. That is the first mistake they make when talking about this.
> Nurse employed at an intensive care unit.

Thus, what nurses and nursing science identifies as important is not important to the organization, which forces employees to either do it anyway (which increases their exploitation) or not do it (which negatively affects their sense of pride and commitment to the job and increases feelings of ethical stress). As one nurse alluded to, the healthcare system seems to create different forms of consciousness, and it is rarely the nurses' perspectives that count. In the nurses' accounts of conflicts over resources, two alternative visions of leaderless organization of care work can be envisaged. First, social reproduction comes at a cost. It is not a natural resource, simply there for the taking. It demands social efforts: complex, technical skills and instruments; time; human physical and intellectual exertion; and major societal inputs in different forms, from the construction of state-of-the-art hospitals to education of medical professionals to strategies around public health. All of this cost money, but there will never be a fully quantifiable output. Social reproduction is not a natural resource, but very much like a natural resource, it is finite.

Second, in order to sustain social reproduction, a new notion of value must evolve in society, one that places primacy on care instead of on accumulation. In the nurses' accounts, we see radical suggestions of a new system of value—one in which *care is the prime resource* and a prime profit. Such a vision moves beyond demands for new managerial models, such as trust-based management, and instead suggests a re-interpretation of how to measure output, and what to conceptualize as productivity. Such contention would demand leaderless management wherein the process and the result, from the standpoint of the interaction between patient and carer, is evaluated and learned from.

Conclusion

This chapter has argued for leaderless management. It has done so by illuminating what nurses' experience to be central conflicts shaping their everyday work, and what forms of injustice are born from those circumstances. We have thus engaged with leaderless management through nurses' critique against the power of managers and the struggle over the moral center of the healthcare organization. The argument for leaderless management is that workers and not managers should be at the center of organizing care. Care workers do not need to be managed—they may need managerial tasks performed by someone other than themselves, but they do not need managers to "lead." In this connection, the chapter returns to abandoned notions of the public sector as a real utopia and explores how nurses' knowledge about the workings of their workplaces can be used to improve healthcare. This sustains empirically Nancy Fraser's contention that we are amid a care crisis in which social reproduction is underinvested and underemphasized; energies, resources and capacities shifted toward for-profit sectors, and logics of accumulation dominate work aimed at sustaining humans and their relationships, despite the very sustenance of such relationships (Curty 2020). We have illustrated what this process is like from the standpoint of nurses.

In a Nordic context, there has been a growing critique around the implementation of NPM within the public sector. While we do not question this focus, we argue that there is a need for a radical organizational critique of managerial power and logics within the sphere of social reproduction that moves beyond a focus on management regimes and instead explores powerful collective ideas of alternate visions. Leaderless management is one of the visions that connect back to the ideas of real utopias framed in the early days of the Swedish public sector. Exploring real utopias, Erik Olin Wright (2011, p. 37) argued, implies "developing a sociology of the *possible*, not just the *actual*." We do not profess to develop a theory or even a suggestion of what is possible. What we do, however, is to attempt to broaden the horizon of what we may envision if we take seriously the critique of care workers as they speak of management and the functioning of the public sector healthcare organization. This requires engaging with Olin Wright's (2011, p. 37) definition of utopia—as something reflecting the "human longing for escape from the oppressions, disappointments and harsh realities of the real social world." We think of the concept of leaderless management as a form of real utopia, but in order for this concept to take meaning in the context of public sector care work, we must first understand the deeper meaning behind the problem with management as it is. And here, we argue, we find the changed visions of the public sector as real utopia, and managed leaderlessly, re-imagined.

Note

1. Swedish original: *Varför finner vi oss i att lämna demokratin när vi går till jobbet?*

References

Baines, D., Charlesworth, S., Turner, D., & O'neill, L. (2014). Lean social care and worker identity: The role of outcomes, supervision and mission. *Critical Social Policy*, *34*(4), 433–453.

Bornemark, J. (2018). *Det omätbaras renässans: en uppgörelse med pedanternas världsherravälde*. Stockholm: Volante.

Boss, E. (2017). *Acceleration*. Stockholm: Leid förlag.

Bringselius, L. (2019). *Uppföljning ur ett tillitsperspektiv* (rapport nr. 7). Stockholm: Tillitsdelegationen.

Burton, J., & van den Broek, D. (2009). Accountable and countable: Information management systems and the bureaucratization of social work. *The British Journal of Social Work*, *39*(7), 1326–1342. doi:10.1093/bjsw/bcn027.

Curty, G. (2020). Rethinking capitalism, crisis, and critique: An interview with Nancy Fraser. *Critical Sociology*, *46*(7-8), 1327–1337.

Ekdahl, L. (2010). *Välfärdssamhällets spegel: Kommunal 1960–2010*. Stockholm: Premiss förlag.

Elomäki, A., & Koskinen Sandberg, P. (2020). Feminist perspectives on the economy within transforming nordic welfare states, *NORA—Nordic Journal of Feminist and Gender Research*, *28*(2), 81–85. doi:10.1080/08038740.2020.1747248.

Fraser, N. (2014). Can society be commodities all the way down? Post-Polanyian reflections on capitalist crisis. *Economy and Society*, *43*(4), 541–558.

Fraser, N. (2016a). Contradictions of capital and care. *New Left Review*, *100*(Jul-Aug), 99–117.

Fraser, N. (2016b). Capitalism's crisis of care. *Dissent*, *63*(4), 30–37.

Hall, P. (2013). NPM in Sweden: The risky balance between bureaucracy and politics. In Å. Sandberg (Ed.), *Nordic lights: Work, management and welfare in Scandinavia* (pp. 406–419). Stockholm: Studieförbundet Näringsliv och samhälle.

Hamel, G. (2011). The world's most creatively managed company. *Harvard Business Review.*

Hitlin, S. (2007). Doing good, feeling good: Values and the self's moral center. *The Journal of Positive Psychology, 2*(4), 249–259. doi:10.1080/174397607 01552352.

Jessop, B. (2019). Authoritarian neoliberalism: Periodization and critique. *South Atlantic Quarterly, 118*(2), 343–361. doi:10.1215/00382876-738 1182.

Kerr, S., & Jermier, J. M. (1978). Substitutes for leadership: Their meaning and measurement. *Organizational Behavior and Human Performance, 22*(3), 375–403.

Liff, R., & Andersson, T. (2013). The multi-professional team as a post NPM control regime. Can it integrate competing control regimes in healthcare? *Scandinavian Journal of Public Administration, 16*(2), 45–67. doi:10.1080/ 14719037.2011.650053.

Marklund, S., Gustafsson, K., Aronsson, G., Leineweber, C., & Helgesson, M. (2019). Working conditions and compensated sickness absence among nurses and care assistants in Sweden during two decades: A cross-sectional biennial survey study. *BMJ Open, 9*(11), Article e030096. doi:10.1136/bmj open-2019-030096.

Meagher, G., & Szebehely, M. (2019). The politics of profit in Swedish welfare services: Four decades of social democratic ambivalence. *Critical Social Policy, 39*(3), 455–476. doi:10.1177/0261018318801721.

Mustosmäki, A., Oinas, T., & Anttila, T. (2020). The rise of lean organizations in Nordic countries: How recent changes in public sector management are shaping working life. In N. Foules Savinetti & A.-J. Riekhoff (Eds.), *Shaping and re-shaping the boundaries of working life* (pp. 123–138). Tampere, Finland: Tampere University Press.

Newman, S., & Lawler, J. (2009). Managing health care under new public management: A sisyphean challenge for nursing. *Journal of Sociology, 45*(4), 419–432. doi:10.1177/1440783309346477.

Olsen, J. P. (2017). An institutional perspective. In S. Van de Walle & S. Groeneveld (Eds.), *Theory and practice of public sector reform* (pp. 9–27). New York: Routledge.

Owens, J., Singh, G., & Cribb, A. (2019). Austerity and professionalism: Being a good healthcare professional in bad conditions. *Health Care Analysis, 27*(3), 157–170. doi:10.1007/s10728-019-00372-y.

Pierre, J. (1993). Legitimacy, institutional change, and the politics of public administration in Sweden. *International Political Science Review, 14*(4), 387–401. doi:10.1177/019251219301400406.

Röstlund, L., & Gustafsson, A. (2020). *Konsulterna: Kampen om Karolinska.* Stockholm: Mondial.

Selberg, R. (2012). *Femininity at work: Gender, labour, and changing relations of power in a Swedish hospital.* Lund, Sweden: Arkiv.

Selberg, R., Sandberg, M., & Mulinari, P. (2021). Contradictions in care: Ward nurses' experiences of work and management in the Swedish public sector. *NORA: Nordic Journal of Feminist and Gender Studies, 30*(2), 81–93. doi:10.1080/0803740.2021.1900910.

Seymour, R. (2014). *Against austerity: How we can fix the crisis they made.* London: Pluto.

Siltala, J. (2013). New public management: The evidence-based worst practice? *Administration & Society, 45*(4), 468–493. doi:10.1177/009539971 3483385.

Smeds Alenius, L., Lindquist, R., Ball, J. E., Sharp, L., Lindqvist, O., & Tishelman, C. (2020). Between a rock and a hard place: Registered nurses' accounts of their work situation in cancer care in Swedish acute care hospitals. *European Journal of Oncology Nursing, 47*, Article 101778. doi:10.1016/j.ejon.2020.101778.

Therborn, G. (2020). Sweden's turn to economic inequality, 1982–2019. *Structural Change and Economic Dynamics, 52*(Mar), 159–166. doi:10.1016/j.strueco.2019.10.005.

Welander, J., Astvik, W., & Hellgren, J. (2017). Stressrelaterad ohälsa och arbetstrivsel hos medarbetare och chefer i socialtjänsten. *Arbetsmarknad & Arbetsliv, 23*(2), 8–26.

Wright, E. O. (2011). Real utopias. *Contexts, 10*(2), 36–42. doi:10.1177/1536504211408884.

6

Dissolving the Leader–Follower Schism: Autonomist Leadership and the Case of Word of Warcraft

Shih-wei Hsu and Yafei Sun

Introduction

We start from the position of "for leaderless management." This is because we maintain the view that the very idea of one great leader is a negative thing. This idea of one great leader is represented in that dominant accounts of leadership start from the premise that "we need leaders." This premise is, in our view, an ideological appeal rooted in the romantic leader–follower dualism, which assumes that some people, with their personality or superior leadership skills, should lead, and others should follow. The leader–follower schism delegates to certain individuals the

S. Hsu (✉)
National Yang Ming Chiao Tung University, Taipei, Taiwan
e-mail: hsu_12_30@hotmail.com

Y. Sun
The Anyang Preschool Education College, Anyang, China

© The Author(s), under exclusive license to Springer Nature Switzerland AG 2022
F. Hertel et al. (eds.), *Debating Leaderless Management*,
Palgrave Debates in Business and Management,
https://doi.org/10.1007/978-3-031-04593-6_6

authority to lead and formulate the binary logic on which leadership rests: leaders lead and followers follow. However, from a postmodern sensibility, this binary logic is rooted in a self-other split, which tends to petrify a specific power distribution that authorizes and privileges certain individuals to lead others. Such a power structure also reproduces inequality and marginalizes certain voices.

We suggest that leaderless management should be an ideal state of management because it de-centers the very idea that leadership evolves around single individuals. We also suggest that, without leadership, an organization can still be "managed." We argue that the concept of Autonomist Leadership can be viewed as an example of leaderless management. The working definition of leaderless management is "management without fixed leadership in the center." In our account, Autonomist Leadership dissolves the leader–follower split whereas organizations can still be managed effectively.

Autonomist Leadership is different from, for example, the shared leadership theories (e.g., Hoch 2013) and the distributed leadership theories (e.g., Spillane 2006) which assume that leaders should let subordinates be involved in the decision-making process, or that followers should take part in the leadership activity to some extent. Autonomist Leadership is also different from "laissez-faire" leadership. Lewin et al. (1939) observed that such leadership exists when "All policies [are] a matter of group discussion and decision, encouraged and assisted by the leader"; "The leader was 'objective' or 'fact-minded' in his [sic] praise and criticism, and tried to be a regular group member in spirit without doing too much of the work" (p. 273). The "laissez-faire" leadership means "Complete freedom for group or individual decision without any leader participation"; "Various materials supplied by the leader, who made it clear that he [sic] would supply information when asked" (p. 273).

Superficially, the laissez-faire leadership seems to imply that leaders may limit their leadership to "information providers" and authorize followers to make decisions. However, upon closer examination, the leader–follower dualism remains intact: followers' decision-making power is bestowed by leaders and, as such, the binary logic that "leaders lead and followers follow" remains at work. This is supported by an

observation that power is often most effective without being physically exercised by leaders (Schmitt [1928]2008). Schmitt suggests that
power is not what a powerful person does to another person but what
the powerful person can do. Power's effectiveness thus resides in the
potentiality of its exercise. Such potentiality is also always present in
laissez-faire leadership. It follows that we must try to formulate perceptions of leadership that does not revolve around single individuals no
matter how soft, humanistic, or laissez-faire these leadership perceptions
may appear. Leaderless management is an opportunity to re-think how
to organize.

Insofar as a residual leader–follower split exists, there will be an asymmetry of power relations under which leaders are privileged to exercise
power over followers. We suggest that Autonomist Leadership may serve
as a vehicle for the development of leaderless management because
Autonomist Leadership has the potential to resist the binary logic of
leadership, i.e., leaders lead and followers follow. With the help of an
empirical case, the online computer game, World of Warcraft (WOW),
we will discuss how leaderless management may operate. The chapter is
structured as follows: first, we discuss the theory of Autonomist Leadership; second, we present the case of WOW and illustrate how the
leader–follower split may be dissolved practically; third, we identify
the implications for leaderless management and argue that leaderless
management is a desirable state of management.

The Autonomist Possibility

Autonomist Leadership represents an approach of leaderless management
because it shows how an organization can be managed without a fixed
leader–follower binary. In Western's (2014) account, Autonomist Leadership is a kind of "non-hierarchical, informal and distributed forms of
leadership founded in emancipatory social movements" (p. 673). The
philosophical ground of this idea comes from Anarchists such as Bakunin
([1882]2012) who offered an idea version of society: "Hierarchical order
and promotion do not exist, so the commander of yesterday can become
a subordinate tomorrow. No one raises above others, or if he does rise,

it is only to fall back a moment later" (Bakunin, cited in Joll 1979, p. 92). It is interesting to note that, with the advancement of the internet and social media, Bakunin's utopian ideal seems to gain a concrete sense because many of today's networked social movements are organized in such a manner (e.g., Wang 2015). Although much Anarchism has a strong implication for the concept of leaderless management, we should also point out that there also exist criticisms against leaderless activities because leaderless movements may include various activities ranging from the non-violent protest, civil disobedience and terrorism that seek to employ violence to achieve authoritarian goals (cf. Best and Nocella 2004; Joosse 2012). Here, it is important to briefly discuss the dark side of the leaderless movement because it helps to explain the merit of Autonomist Leadership.

Through a Lacanian lens, Western (2014) contends that the whole concept of leadership can be disavowed by many contemporary networked social movements, because "the term leaderless operates as an 'objet petit a,' an object that temporarily fills a gap" (p. 675), which rests on the conviction that "the disavowal of leadership represents a desire for a world that is freed from authoritarianism and power-relations" (p. 690; cf. Lacan 2007). In this process, being leaderless becomes "jouissance," a kind of enjoyment in Lacan's (2007) sense. Ironically, being leaderless can generate what is referred to as a "lack" because being leaderless is a "utopian fantasy" that "temporarily offers relief by filling the gap, and at the same time symptomatically points to the lack of, and the repressed desire for, leadership" (Western 2014, p. 690). Research has shown that social movements like the Occupy Movement were deeply inspired by the idea of being leaderless but many activists were in fact inspired by the carnival atmosphere wherein they fell in love with themselves (Strauss 2011; Žižek 2013), as described by Western (2014):

When protesters fall in love with themselves, they take "pleasure in their displeasure" enjoying being protesters too much, enjoying their oppression and in doing so maintaining the binary status quo of the oppressed and the oppressor, rather than working on creating a better society. (p. 690)

Western's (2014) argument reveals an important but disquieting reality of the leaderless context: stealth leadership may occur (cf. Freeman 1972). Stealth leadership refers to a leadership style wherein some individuals, de facto, lead the organization with their influence in a subtle way. In Underdahl's (2016) view, stealth leadership is well exemplified by Clive Woodward, a well-known rugby coach: "he does not charge in like a bustling sergeant major" but "encourages his group to buy into his way of thinking" (Kervin 2006, p. 347). In the context of leaderless social movement, what happened was that some elite in-groups or powerful individuals tool leadership without it being named and without consent (Western 2014, p. 690). If stealth leadership can be an inseparable dimension of a leaderless movement, it seems that the commitment to leaderless is merely a utopian fantasy that can hardly remove the leader–follower split. However, in this regard, Western (2014) argues that there exists an under-researched leadership concept, Autonomist Leadership, which reveals strong (emancipatory) potential for the development of leaderless management. There are five guiding principles associated with Autonomist Leadership (Western 2014, pp. 680–682).

- Spontaneity: Leadership emerges spontaneously; it is temporary without fixed roles.
- Autonomy: Anyone can take up leadership and there is no ranking or hierarchy; there are a heightened awareness and commitment to the autonomy of all, guarding against coercion and the manipulation of power.
- Mutualism: Leadership is enacted with mutual consent, mutual responsibility, and mutual benefits.
- Networks: The digital age has created new virtual platforms and/or social media that enable an active leadership dynamic that is fluid, ever-changing, and dispersed through the network.
- Affect: This is particularly associated with the context of social movements where activists show an emancipatory interest in resisting the predominant social norms and practices.

These principles imply a leadership style where the relationship between leaders and followers is dynamic and interchangeable, because leadership does not come from the hierarchical structure, but from the networks (of followers) which are fluid and changing. From the perspective of Autonomist Leadership, leadership is always in a state of shifting and waiting to be replaced. Autonomist Leadership does not privilege any individuals to act as leaders because leadership is considered as a temporary task based on organizational members' mutual consent and mutual benefits. Plainly, Autonomist Leadership differs from stealth leadership because Autonomist Leadership allows everyone to express his/her voice and function as a leader but stealth leadership seeks to encourage followers to "buy into" (to borrow Kervin 2006, p. 34) the leader's way of thinking other than followers' own.

However, although many contemporary social movements sought to operate in a leaderless way and enjoyed the idea of being leaderless, literature shows the ironic fact that the leaderless ideal often acted as an "objet petit a" (i.e., the unattainable object of desire) that, in turn, created space for stealth leadership to fill in. Such a paradox was owing to the reality that these social movements' wholesale rejection of leadership represented a utopian fantasy for a world free from power relations but power relations, as well as leadership, cannot disappear (cf. Western 2014, p. 679). Instead, as Freeman (1972) observed, leaderless movements may become "a way of masking power" and allowed "insidious elitists" to utilize "friendship and informal power networks" to dominant the movements and exclude out-groups (pp. 156–157).

In Western's (2014) account, Autonomist Leadership bypasses this "objet petit a" because Autonomist Leadership does not maintain the assumption that the world can be free from power relations. Autonomist Leadership recognizes the ontology of leadership but assumes that "no individual or group holds position, power or authority over others" (Western 2014, p. 685). Therefore, Autonomist Leadership is not "anti-leadership" or "leadership without leaders," as implicated in some CLS (Critical Leadership Studies) literature (e.g., Rachman et al. 2019; Sutherland et al. 2013). Autonomist Leadership implies "a form of individualized collective leadership" embedded in "networks and enacted by autonomous individual groups" (Western 2014, p. 693). In other words, Autonomist Leadership does not seek to discard the leader–follower schism but seeks to inspire a radically different form of leadership.

Instead of eliminating power itself, it gets rid of the eternal power brought to individuals by the leader's identity and status and makes equal power relations possible through power dynamics.

In this sense, Autonomist Leadership provides an effective framework for leaderless management and helps dissolve the leader–follower split. However, there arises a question. As we have noted above, if the leader–follower schism denotes an asymmetry of power relations, how can we ensure that this residual leader–follower split does not authorize some individuals or groups to exercise their power to influence and control others? In our view, if we can effectively resist this residual leader–follower schism, leaderless management may come true. In the next section, we will discuss an empirical case that shows that, in some specific social contexts, Autonomist Leadership entails followers to effectively resist the leader–follower split and makes leaderless management possible.

The Case of World of Warcraft (WOW)

The development of the internet and social media has triggered many new forms of organizations and leadership (e.g., Fuchs 2006) and, in our observation, some online games also offer a good opportunity to explore new leadership styles. In this chapter, we will use the online game, WOW (World of Warcraft), as an example to show the possibility of Autonomist Leadership and how Autonomist Leaders reveals potential for leaderless management. One of the authors is a WOW player and has three years of experience in this videogame. We share Cremin's (2015) vision that video games are a kind of canvas on which players generate sensations (p. 167). Although we understand that videogames are subject to company's commercial interests and the rules of the game are created by the program designers within relations of power, we suggest that, in a specific context, the players and their sensations may generate a fertile source for a radical understanding of social reality.

WOW is a massively multiplayer online role-playing game released in 2004 by Blizzard Entertainment. It was the world's most popular online games with ten million players in 2009. The game had 112,249,468

Table 6.1 A list of related important terms in WOW

	Definition	Leader–follower split
(Leisure) Guilds	A guild can be viewed as self-organization, established and organized by players. In this chapter, we will focus on what can be called "leisure guilds"	Leaders have some power to manage the organization (the guild) but leadership can be unstainable as followers can freely quit a guild
Temporary (tasked-based) teams	Players within a guild can freely team up and complete a task based on their will	Leadership is highly dynamic and temporary. The leader–follower split is unclear or can even be dissolved

subscribers and 4,265,480 active players by January 2021 (MMO Populations 2021). Within this virtual world, players can adventure, complete the task, explore the unknown world, kill monsters, and interact with NPCs (i.e., Non-Player Characters), as well as other players. In Table 6.1, we list a few important terms and concepts related to this chapter.

Guilds as Self-Organizations

In this chapter, our analysis will mainly be based on the leader–follower relations within a guild. In WOW, a guild can be viewed as self-organization and all players should work within their selected guild. WOW players can freely establish a guild and other players can join it. Once a player establishes a guild, the player will act as the leader of this guild. The leader of the guild has the power to accept and remove guild members, set certain rules, appoint officials, resolve conflicts, and allocate resources. However, followers can simply quit a guild if the leader cannot meet their requirement. In our observation, there are two general kinds of guilds: "performative" guilds and "leisure" guilds.

At the early stage of WOW, most guilds are the so-called performative guilds formulated by what can be called "hardcore players" who tend to "invest large amounts of time and resources toward playing video games and enjoy different games" (Juul 2010, p. 8). Some hardcore players may also act as "gold farmers" who seek to earn virtual currencies and items and sell them to other WOW players (e.g., Liboriussen 2016). Performative guilds are usually aggressive in terms of the performance in the game, and the leader–follower split is usually strong because guild leaders have the power to select guild members and allocate resources. Nevertheless, as time goes on, there have appeared many "leisure guilds" where one of the authors has been involved in a leisure guild for one year. Leisure guilds are often formulated by what can be termed "causal players" who tend to "commit small amounts of time and resources toward play video games" (Juul 2010, p. 29). In WOW, the function of leisure guilds is often to maintain friendship and, in leisure guilds, members are often not concerned with their performance and credits in the game. As such, this kind of (leisure) guilds formulate a particular social context for the understanding of Autonomist Leadership and we contend that leisure guilds, to a certain degree, also shed new light on leaderless leadership.

Although guilds are organized in a hierarchical way which offers guild leaders certain power (or authority) to "manage" the followers, the hierarchical rules may not always be effective, because guild members can freely quit a guild. That is, in an extreme case, if all guild members decide to quit, the guild will no longer exist and hence leadership will no longer exist either. In leisure guilds, the hierarchical rules have even less influence on followers because the members in the leisure guilds often enjoy the feeling of being with other anonymous players and not very concerned with their performance in the game. Therefore, when they are dissatisfied with the rules of this organization or other members, they can leave directly and join another guild. In WOW, players can also form temporary task-based teams and their goals are usually determined by all team members. Within a leisure guild, members often formulate temporary teams for specific tasks. When the task is completed, the team will disband. In these temporary task-based teams, the leadership structure can be highly dynamic, and leaders usually function as coordinators.

Overall, (leisure) guilds and temporary task-based teams can be viewed as self-organizations and they are borderless to a large extent. As we shall see, while WOW offers the guild and task-based leaders some power to manage their members, the leader–follower split often dissolves in the process of the game, which also paves the way for a condition under which followers have the power to force leaders to be "democratic."

Autonomist Leadership in WOW

The leisure guilds in WOW, when viewed through Western's (2014) lens, capture the spirit of Autonomist Leadership to a certain extent. How WOW does that can be discussed in relation to the five principles that is associated with Autonomist Leadership:

- Spontaneity: In both leisure guilds and temporary task-based teams, leadership is always spontaneous because online players do not have fixed time to play the game, and hence it is unlikely for the guilds or tasked-based teams to have fixed leadership. For instance, in WOW leaders frequently transfer their leadership roles to other players when they do not have time to manage a task. Players usually decide whether to join a guild based on the leader's ability or even based on their random choice. This spontaneity also implies that leaders and followers are highly interchangeable and dynamic.
- Autonomy: Leisure guilds and temporary tasked-based teams still have some (weak) hierarchies. Yet, members usually have much freedom to choose their roles. This is particularly evident in temporary task-based teams because the member's roles are usually based on mutual agreement and mutual selection between leaders and followers. Particularly, in temporary task-based teams, leaders can hardly make decisions without consultation with their followers because they have to discuss their strategy together. As such, followers usually have a strong power to make decisions in the game.
- Mutualism: In leisure guilds and temporary tasked-based teams, it is difficult for any leaders (either individuals or groups) to exercise their arbitrary power over other players. According to WOW's game setting, guild leaders may enact some rules but, in leisure guilds, it is unlikely for leaders to apply any rules without mutual consent between leaders and followers. Guild members have the power to negotiate with the leader in terms of how and when to complete a given task,

and followers may withdraw from any tasks if the leader fails to satisfy the follower's requirement.

- Networks: In WOW, leadership may pop up, disappear or reappear and is usually beyond single individuals. For instance, in temporary task-based teams, leaders only usually emerged in response to the task requirements. Network here does not mean that an individual can utilize his/her network to gain support from others. Instead, in leisure guilds and temporary tasked-based teams, participants remain anonymous and the network functions as a virtual platform that facilitates participants to achieve a goal collectively.
- Affect: In leisure guilds and temporary task-based teams, participants enjoy being with each other. Feelings like friendship and interaction with others play an important role. According to our observation, online players hardly meet each other in real life but, as time goes, they may develop strong friendships without know each other's real names. Especially, in leisure guilds, players often formulate or participate in a temporary task-based team only because they enjoy the feeling of being together.

The above shows general features of Autonomist Leadership. Under Autonomist Leadership, leadership becomes a "de-centered" concept because leadership and followership are interchangeable and shifting. This also means that the leader–follower schism can be dissolved. That is, when a leader fails to meet followers' expectations, the followers can simply remove or replace the leader. We consider this as leaderless management: an organization can be managed without leaders in the center. In the next section, we will discuss how Autonomist Leadership helps to realize leaderless management.

Leaderless Management

Conditions for Leaderless Management

In our observation, the context of WOW offers fertile soil for the development of Autonomist Leadership. Thus, it demonstrates how leaderless management is possible. We can identify three contextual factors in WOW that help to generate a condition for followers to "resist" the leader–follower split:

1. Borderless: A defining characteristics of WOW is that all guilds are borderless. In WOW, since members can quit guilds and temporary tasked-based teams at any time, leaders must meet follower's requirements. According to the author's experience, there was one occasion when the guild leader appointed her boyfriend as an official and, as a result, several guild members quit the guild. The remaining guild members asked the leader to abdicate and, consequently, the leader quit.
2. Smooth space: To some degree, WOW's cyberspace captures the spirit of what Deleuze and Guattari (2004) termed "smooth space." In Deleuze and Guattari's view, smooth space refers to a conceptual territory where individuals and concepts are "nomads" that can freely voyage and connect to each other without a given direction. At some levels, WOW creates a smooth space because each individual player can freely connect to others and generate their own guilds or temporary task-based teams.
3. Anonymity: The Internet provides online users with the freedom of expression and anonymity plays an important role (Joyce 2015). WOW can be viewed as an online platform where anonymous players interact with each other and have a certain freedom to express their opinions. This unprecedented anonymity also challenges the social ties in the conventional social structure and, in leisure guilds, members can freely question the authority and decisions of the leader.

The above three factors formulate the conditions under which followers have the power to confront the leadership. In such a context, followers can effectively force leaders to be "democratic" and, ultimately, dissolve the very notion, leadership. From the lens of CLS, many contemporary social movements failed to be "leaderless" as claimed, because the participants/activists cannot resist the "objet petit a." This is because social movements still required certain individuals or groups to lead their actions (Sutherland et al. 2013). Such a fact, in turn, produces a "lack" which ironically triggers a space for the development of stealth leadership (Western 2014). Yet, this is not the case with leisure guilds. As we have pointed out, most leisure guild members enjoy the feeling of "being with others" and there are no emotional attachments to "being leaderless" (i.e., a wholesale rejection of leadership). Although WOW does not reject power relations and leadership, the context of WOW restricts the power of leadership. It provides followers with the power to resist leadership. The phenomenon is particularly evident in leisure guilds, as leadership within leisure guilds is highly limited and leaders can only act as, or confined to, coordinators who should meet follower's requirements as much as possible.

As we have suggested, the leader–follower split is of importance to the very idea of leadership, because it is where the leader's "authority to lead" comes from. However, if followers have the power to remove this split, then the concept of leadership will be dissolved and the context may become "leaderless," at least temporarily. Hence, through the lens of Autonomist Leadership, the function of leadership is twofold: leadership means both "to lead" and "to resist" leadership itself. In this regard, we share Western's (2014) view that Autonomist Leadership represents a radically different version of leadership but we expand his argument that Autonomist Leadership requires some factors to support, including a borderless context, smooth space and anonymity.

Autonomist Leadership in WOW shows an example of leaderless management: leisure guilds can be well managed without clear leadership. Autonomist Leadership does not imply that an organization must be free from leaders. It implies that when the leader–follower split dissolves, followers will have effective power to decide, remove, or become leaders. However, some may argue, from the perspectives of mainstream leadership, that the concept of leadership in WOW seems to (superficially) share some features with humble leadership because humble leadership rests on the claim that it is a bottom-up approach to leadership that leaders should always satisfy follower's (physical or emotional) requirements (Owens and Hekman 2012; Walters and Diab 2016; Zhou and Wu 2018).

However, at the core of humble leadership theories is still a clear-cut split between leaders and followers. In leisure guilds, although there may appear a temporary leader–follower split, followers can easily dissolve this split by quitting a guild or forcing the leaders to abdicate. The leadership in leisure guilds also bears little resemblance with shared leadership and "laissez-faire" leadership, because they maintain the split between leaders and followers. Autonomist Leadership represents a radical version of democratic leadership. Autonomist leaders effectively manage the organization but there is no fixed leadership role in the center.

Conclusion

In this chapter, we have suggested that leaderless management can be an ideal state of management and Autonomist Leadership shows how leaderless management may function practically. Autonomist Leadership also serves as a vehicle for the understanding of leaderless management because it represents a dynamic, shifting, and interchangeable state of leadership and followership, and both leaders and followers have the power to "manage." Both leaders and followers have the power to make decisions in an organization. This implies that Autonomist Leadership also dissolves leaders' authority to "lead." Yet, Autonomist Leadership is not what Fairhurst (2008) proposed as "leadership without leaders" because, under Autonomist Leadership, leaders and followers still exist and they have clear roles to play.

Autonomist Leadership denotes a radical version of democratic leadership because, under Autonomist Leadership, followers have the effective power to resist, remove, or replace the existing leaders. This also means that Autonomist Leadership generates a context of forced democracy under which Autonomist Leaders have to meet followers' expectations and can hardly marginalize followers' interests. This chapter has set out to argue "for leaderless management." We aimed to show that, under certain conditions, the leader–follower split can be dissolved, which will also offer followers the power to de-center the very idea, leadership. When this happens, leaderless management may come true.

References

Bakunin, M. ([1882]2012). *God and the state.* New York: Courier Dover Publications.

Best, S., & Nocella, A. J. (2004). *Terrorists or freedom fighters?* New York: Lantern Books.

Cremin, C. (2015). *Exploring videogames with Deleuze and Guattari, towards an affective theory of form.* London: Routledge.

Deleuze, G., & Guattari, F. (2004). *A thousand plateaus: Capitalism and schizophrenia.* London: Continuum.

Fairhurst, G. (2008). Discursive leadership: A communication alternative to leadership psychology. *Management Communication Quarterly, 21*(4), 510–521.

Freeman, J. (1972). The tyranny of structurelessness. *Berkeley Journal of Sociology, 17*(1972–1973), 151–164.

Fuchs, C. (2006). The self-organization of social movements. *Systemic Practice and Action Research, 19*(1), 101–113.

Hoch, J. E. (2013). Shared leadership and innovation: The role of vertical leadership and employee integrity. *Journal of Business and Psychology, 28*(2), 159–174.

Joll, J. (1979). *The anarchists.* London: Methuen.

Joosse, P. (2012). Elves, environmentalism, and eco-terror. *Crime Media Culture, 8*(1), 75–93.

Joyce, D. (2015). Internet freedom and human rights. *European Journal of International Law, 26*(2), 493–514.

Juul, J. (2010). *A casual revolution: Reinventing video games and their players.* London: MIT Press.

Kervin, A. (2006). *Clive Woodward: The biography.* London: Orion.

Lacan, J. (2007). *The other side of psychoanalysis: The seminar of Jacques Lacan, book XVII.* London: W.W. Norton and Company.

Lewin, K., Lippitt, R., & White R. K. (1939). Patters of aggressive behavior in experimentally created social climates. *Journal of Social Psychology, 10*(2), 271–299.

Liboriussen, B. (2016). Amateur gold farming in China: "Chinese ingenuity", independence and critique. *Games and Culture, 11*(3), 316–331.

MMO Populations. (2021). World of warcraft stats historical (5-years) breakdown of the player and subscriber populations. https://mmo-population.com/r/wow/stats. Accessed 1 Jan 2021.

Owens, B. P., & Hekman, D. R. (2012). Modeling how to grow: An inductive examination of humble leader behaviors, contingencies, and outcomes. *Academy of Management Journal*, *55*(4), 787–818.

Rachman, G., Mander, B., Dombey, D., Wong, S., & Saleh, H. (2019). Leaderless rebellion: How social media enables global protests. https://www.ft.com/content/19dc5dfe-f67b-11e9-a79c-bc9acae3b654. Accessed 14 Jan 2021.

Schmitt, C. ([1928]2008). *Constitutional theory*. Durham, NC: Duke University Press.

Spillane, J. P. (2006). *Distributed leadership* (1st ed.). San Francisco: Jossey-Bass.

Strauss, J. (2011). Understanding Wall Street's "occupation". http://www.thenewsignificance.com/2011/10/07/jesse-strauss-understanding-wallstreets-occupation/. Accessed 29 Dec 2020.

Sutherland, N., Land, C., & Böhm, S. (2013). Anti-leaders(hip) in social movement organizations: The case of autonomous grassroots groups. *Organization*, *21*(6), 759–781.

Underdahl, L. (2016). Stealth leadership influences the culture of innovation. *Journal of Leadership Studies*, *10*(1), 70–72.

Walters, K. N., & Diab, D. L. (2016). Humble leadership: Implications for psychological safety and follower engagement. *Journal of Leadership Studies*, *10*(2), 7–18.

Wang, J. (2015). Mobilizing resources in networked social movements: Cases in Hong Kong and Taiwan. https://repository.hkbu.edu.hk/etd_oa/175/. Accessed 29 Dec 2020.

Western, S. (2014). Autonomist leadership in leaderless movements: Anarchists leading the way. *Ephemera*, *14*(4), 673–698.

Zhou, F., & Wu, Y. J. (2018). How humble leadership fosters employee innovation behavior: A two-way perspective on the leader-employee interaction. *Leadership & Organization Development Journal*, *39*(3), 375–387.

Žižek, S. (2013). Slavoj Žižek, speaks at occupy Wall St: Transcript of q&a. http://www.imposemagazine.com/bytes/slavoj-zizek-at-occupy-wall-street-transcript. Accessed 29 Dec 2020.

7

In Favor of Leader*less* Management: Follettian Perspective of Co-leadership

Ana Martins and Isabel Martins

Introduction

In this chapter, we argue for the leader*less* management position which we consider to be in harmony with the Follettian perspective of co-leadership leader*less* management. According to this perspective, leadership is inherent in and shared by the group and not in one specific single individual all the time. This chapter further demonstrates the importance of re-humanizing leadership and identity which is embodied in

A. Martins (✉)
Graduate School of Business and Leadership, University of KwaZulu-Natal, Durban, South Africa
e-mail: martinsa@ukzn.ac.za

I. Martins
School of Management, IT and Governance, University of KwaZulu-Natal, Durban, South Africa

© The Author(s), under exclusive license to Springer Nature Switzerland AG 2022
F. Hertel et al. (eds.), *Debating Leaderless Management*, Palgrave Debates in Business and Management, https://doi.org/10.1007/978-3-031-04593-6_7

111

relationships, context and made possible through groups and organizational culture. This chapter is organized in the following sections. First, we argue why we do not agree with the leader*ful* management position, neither the favorable nor less favorable lenses. Then, we argue why we agree with the co-leadership leader*less* management position, and herein we introduce our vision of an organization wherein a Follettian perspective of co-leadership leader*less* management prevails.

Why We Do Not Support Leader*ful* Management

In this first part, we argue the lens of the undesirable and inauspicious leader*ful* management perspective. This leader*ful* management is based on the dominant and militant principle combined with a relentless pursuit for surplus value. The great majority of inauspicious leader*ful* management is anchored on surplus-based management, which is considered autocratic, domineering, bellicose, and forceful (Follett [1949]1987). Moreover, unfavorable leader*ful* management tends to focus on hierarchical and autocratic structures and processes prevalent in the command-and-control environment, as Nielsen (see Chapter 2 in this volume) has previously explained.

During the 1980s and 1990s, the focus moved from managing to leading wherein leadership became an obsession (Alvesson and Spicer 2011) as leadership tended to concentrate on the individualistic paradigm and emphasized the leader and personality, based on the Scientific Management perspective. Studies on leadership further evidenced power instead of the essence of leadership itself. The roles of both managers and leaders have always portrayed a specific and important part in organizations and in society at large (Mintzberg 1973). These roles have also been the theme of research over many decades. However, this points to the undesirable leader*ful* management which encapsulates a single leader and which we are not in favor of. Moreover, a mindset based on rank that highlights the command-and-control thinking stifles the humane aspects of individuals as well as their intelligence. This mindset has arisen from the Scientific Management perspective wherein the leader takes on the autocratic and a military rank-based mindset. Furthermore, this mindset, evident in the undesirable leader*ful* management, is disheartening and intimidating because it restrains individuals from naturally wanting to participate.

Rank-based mental models, prevalent in undesirable leader*ful* management and advocated by the self-interest of leaders, uphold wicked, and malevolent contexts. As a consequence of the critique of rank, order, hierarchy, and power, as postulated by the anarchists, even in those situations where undesirable leader*ful* management is considered democratic and the leader appears to adopt a transformational leadership style, the leader possesses a command-and-control attitude because the leader considers individual employees as being a cog in the wheel of the organization. This type of organization alludes to the context of a machine, as Morgan (1986) substantiates. This context gives rise to the undesirable and inauspicious leader*ful* management perspective which can be as detrimental as the unfavorable leader*less* management perspective. Moreover, this machine metaphor has relegated the individual to the lowest possible state of being in the organization wherein all communication has broken down and the individual no longer has a sense of belonging to the organization. We are not in favor of the "hierarchization" of power, which is exercised by autocratic and dictatorial leaders, prevalent in undesirable leader*ful* management. In this context, creativity and innovation are stifled and this could impede the process of organizational learning, which can eventually result in the decline and possible stagnation of the particular organization.

Many contemporary organizations have become rife with undesirable leader*ful* management wherein leaders are characterized as being immoral greedy and lack humility because they are ruthless; their quest for profit and power is strengthened by their demeaning nature and by exploiting employees in their organization. This undesirable leader*ful* management perspective is directly associated with the production of surplus.

In summary, in this section we have essentially argued why we are against the leader*ful* management perspective, which is destructive, ruthless, exploitative, and usurps power of rank due to being focused on a single leadership figure. Therefore, the entire leader*ful* management perspective needs to be rethought in order for any positive and effective outcomes to be achieved and to harness the sustainability of an organization.

Why We Are in Favor of Leader*less* Management

This section entails two parts; first we put forward the Follettian co-leadership leader*less* management perspective which we consider as the favorable lens and which we espouse. Then, we argue the less inauspicious aspects of leader*less* management.

Favorable Co-leader*less* Management

In this part, we argue in favor of the desirable co-leader*less* management position which we embrace. We regard this perspective to be designated as the Follettian co-leader*less* management wherein the concept of being is the essential component.

Leader*less* management (Kotow 2019) may have benefits in so far as it focuses on peer instead of being based on rank, as Nielsen (Chapter 2 in this volume) has previously explained. This favorable leader*less* management position is regarded as the absence of single persons who take on the role of a leader. Thus, "effective management is a participatory, inclusive and non-hierarchical process—not a command and control, direction giving process" (Nelson 2017, p. 183). Indeed, organizations that are peer-based encourage the humane aspect of individuals by calling upon their heart and their intelligence. In these organizations which depict the less inauspicious leader*less* management approach, the shift in mindset may be endorsed because the common good is harnessed as opposed to the individual self-interest. Moreover, flat structures (Nielsen 2004) tend to be focused on instead of hierarchical structures because the latter are traditional and pyramid in nature with power and control being top down (Green 2007), as opposed to the flat structures which have participatory decision-making processes.

Furthermore, we draw inspiration from the pancake metaphor that Brafman and Beckstrom (2006) and Coop (2013) propose, to describe those organizations that have flatter structures. This flat structure seemingly alludes to a horizontal metaphor which highlights the disintegration of the traditional and pyramid-shaped organization by giving rise to a fundamentally different kind of structure, which, at first glance appears to be leader*less* and takes on an organizational structure that is considered flat in nature. Additionally, the fewer levels of management the organization has, the more conducive the environment is toward creating more flexible, creative and innovative individuals (Burns and Stalker 1961). This scenario may be favorable to the less inauspicious leader*less* management.

In line with the Follettian co-leader*less* management perspective, it is important to contextualize the notion and essence of being and its meaning. Our current globalized world, as we know it, seems to have fallen apart because the values of humanity, justice, and temperance have been overlooked in the quest for surplus value. The onset of the coronavirus disease which became known as the coronavirus (COVID-19) pandemic led to a compulsory change of how organizations operate, and this triggered the need for introspection. This urgency prompts a fresh opportunity for individuals and organizations to go back to the essence of being, the *raison d'être*. We draw upon Phenomenology in order to elucidate what is the meaning of being, and that meaning is circumstantial, endless, perceived as all-embracing and comprehensive (Merleau-Ponty [1945]1995). Being aware that we are alive is our first perception of what is the meaning of being human and, specifically contextualizing this meaning, and specifically in this context, what it means to be a co-leader. In perceiving our path in life, and our quest in attempting to understand why we are alive, we do so through introspection and language (Heidegger 2003). This inquiry, which Heidegger refers to as Dasein, where "Da" means "there" and "Sein" means "to be" or "being there." In this journey to comprehend the true meaning of being—the essence of co-leadership, it is necessary to substantiate and embody Dasein which is enabled through "...being ahead of oneself..." (Ricoeur 2006, p. 347). Additionally, in the exploration to understand being, we need to be aware of time in order to contextualize situations, as Follett posits. Moreover, we can draw a connection with the Follettian principles inherent in the "meaning of a situation" (Monin and Bathurst 2008, p. 450) which is understood as being linked to the elusive nature of both time and the situation itself. We can further draw a nexus with co-leader*less* management which concentrates on social interchange by espousing the co-leadership characteristics.

The notion of temporality further provides the context for "being" which is thus linked to time (Heidegger 2003). In an attempt to apply the metaphor of the clock to describe the Follettian principle of co-leader*less* management and linking this principle to the notion of time, it "is unusual in that it keeps time both for the individual's and the collective's authentic use of self and their engagement in and modelling of intention and purpose, creativity, experiential, and adaptive learning in relationship to their internal other and with others outside themselves" (Nelson 2017, p. 182). The notion of authentic human beings, considered the subject, arise from these social bonds. In this regard, the Follettian pragmatism provides a path to understand organizations and considers this activity as being reasonable.

The essence of Dasein resides in authentic and inauthentic existence (Heidegger 2003) which further corroborates the need for introspection. However, over the decades, this social context, based on the humanistic and holistic schools of thought, has unfortunately been neglected and even relegated to the wayside. What is more, the COVID-19 pandemic seems to have further eradicated the humane side of organizations and work. Additionally, the co-leader*less* management perspective, which is based on the Follettian principles of leadership, focuses on individualism and "plurivocality" (Monin and Bathurst 2008, p. 448). The group is composed of individuals who have attained self-actualization following a common purpose where there is no leadership arising from one single individual. Every situation is always in a process of becoming, just as we, humans, are also in a process of becoming. Heidegger (2003) termed this as "Being-in-the-world" which is considered as authentic existence. While inauthentic existence is portrayed when an individual is fulfilling a lifestyle which is pre-defined by the forces of society. This inauthentic existence supports the common existence which precludes and blurs the oneness.

Care and concern, therefore, are the ontological constructs associated with being and Dasein and embody the authentic existence. Indeed, the Follettian perspective of co-leader*less* management and the notion of re-humanizing leadership, address the aspect of bringing "concern and care" (Follett 1924) back into "being-in-the-world" into organizations as well, by bringing authenticity of existence into the meaning of temporality. Therefore, the authentic existence gains meaning when individuals are aware of their distinctive human beingness. This is fully envisaged in the Follettian co-leadership leader*less* management perspective. In accordance with this Follettian perspective, in an organization where everyone is actively involved, then the notion of a single individual as a leader becomes superfluous. This is very much in tune with the notion of group-based or shared leadership. This is possible when the organization develops four key elements, namely "collectiveness, concurrency, collaboration, compassion" (Raelin 2011, p. 16). These four elements are also considered as being anchors that facilitate the re-humanizing of the organization. In this context, the collective consciousness can be directed toward achieving the greater good of organizations and humanity at large. This a break away from the "hunt" for surplus value and is in line with the Follettian principle of leadership.

The Follettian perspective of co-leadership leader*less* management focuses on that authority which is based on knowledge and not on power of position. In the same vein, Foucault was "against scientific hierarchicalization of knowledge and its intrinsic power-effects" (Foucault 2003, p. 10), in spite of regarding knowledge as power. Foucault was also against authority based on position. This is further corroborated by Crossan et al. (2017) who created a leader-character framework which denotes a shift from the initial Scientific Management paradigm and now includes eleven virtues. These virtues entail the prudence dimension at the core of personality which can be regarded as diametrically opposed to the Scientific Management personality framework. This virtues framework is based on core and essential qualities that were first theorized by Plato (2021), then further developed by Aristotle (Barnes 1984), as well as the Chinese Confucian philosophy (Provis 2017), including the values of courage, justice, humanity, temperance, and transcendence.

These are the values that fortify the Follettian perspective of co-leader*less* management, which we argue in favor of.

The Follettian principle of co-leadership leader*less* management is described as group-based and as the rebel against the pursuit for surplus value. Furthermore, this Follettian perspective focuses on reciprocal relationships in groups enhancing "circular response" (Follett 1924, p. 53) giving rise to the notion of "power-with" (Follett 1941, p. 101) as opposed to power over. It is "power-with" that builds on integration because Follett attributed enormous importance on collaboration, shared purpose, commitment, and intent. Additionally, Follett was of the opinion that long-term sustainability engages individuals toward reaching the common good and taking into account the community. This type of Follettian co-leadership leader*less* management ensures that the integration of the wishes and needs of individuals, the community as well as organizations, takes place. For this reason, the main focus of the Follettian perspective is therefore, to ensure businesses are part of the broader community.

This Follettian perspective enables a balance to be achieved in the exploration—exploitation of co-leadership leader*less* behaviors, namely open (explorative and creative) and closed (exploitative and routine) behaviors (March 1991). In this regard, Burns and Stalker (1961) theorize a blend of mechanistic and organic structures. These evoke the Follettian perspective of collaborative leadership that entails human capital with expertise, social capital that is collaborative in nature, and organizational capital that is natural, green, and innovative. Furthermore, in open (exploration) and closed (exploitation) co-leadership leader*less* behaviors, harmonization, and co-ordination may occur because innovation is fostered through the exploitation and exploration of learning that individuals and groups engage in; this can lead to improved organizational performance. This Follettian co-leadership leader*less* management perspective promotes an auspicious learning culture which is nurtured through transformational co-leadership leader*less* behavior— as predicated by Nemanich and Vera (2009). Therefore, innovation arises because it is highly dependent on co-leadership behaviors, as O'Reilly and Tushman (2013) further substantiate. We are in favor of leader*less* management based on the Follettian co-leadership principles of collaboration and integration.

Additionally, in those organizations that enhance the Follettian co-leadership leader*less* management, these organizations do not demonstrate bureaucratic, hierarchical, and controlling processes. Furthermore, the abilities and qualities of co-leader*less* management are very much akin to those evident in distributed leadership, namely, to foster dialogue, adaptability, openness, and a culture that is in favor of innovation. These characteristics evoke the Follettian principles of co-leadership leader*less* management, that we advocate. In horizontal structures wherein power is driven by the community and learning is collaborative, no single individual is leader, but shared leadership is more relational and not individualistic (Endres and Weibler 2020). Moreover, this is analogous to what Proudhon termed "mutualism" (Edwards 1969). This is what we argue for in this chapter.

The Follettian view of integration also encapsulates cohesive yet divergent opinions which contemporary organizations have unfortunately, moved away from (Follett 1924). However, organizations with co-leadership characterized by the Follettian co-leader*less* management perspective display this humane aspect. This Follettian view of co-leadership leader*less* management emphasizes motivation, well-being, tasks, goals, and the performance of both the organization and its members (Bass 1990; DeRue et al. 2011; Skogstad et al. 2014; Yukl 2002).

We argue that a leadership management perspective in an organization should not simply achieve the needs of a particular individual but instead but should aim for the betterment of the organization. In essence, this transformation means re-focusing on the Follettian perspective of co-leadership leader*less* management and not on leaders as individuals. According to the Follettian perspective, leadership is inherent in the group and not in one specific single individual, as we have stated above. Reinforcing this perspective urges individuals in contemporary organizations to participate in collaborative activities with other individuals.

Inauspicious Leader*less* Management

In this part, we argue the inauspicious and less favorable leader*less* management lens by indicating that it can be based on the anarchists' dissociation of the western growth philosophy and its direct link with the hunt for surplus value (see also Hertel and Sparre, Chapter 9 in this volume). In organizations wherein leader*less* management prevails (Hansen 2016), the perception of this leader*less* management is analogous to the viewpoint espoused by the anarchists. Bakunin (Dolgoff 1972; Purkis and Bowen 2004) is a critic of organizational hierarchy because he concurs that the capitalistic production and its exploitative nature have dehumanizing corollaries. The production of surplus value is further critiqued by Kropotkin (Shatz 1995). There is insufficient empirical proof thus far about the effectiveness of leader*less* management perspective in organizations. Here, we draw inspiration from the double metaphor referring to the starfish and the spider, as Brafman and Beckstrom (2006) and Coop (2013) put forward, in order to distinguish between the progressive leader*less* peer-to-peer management model and the traditional top-down model. Brafman and Beckstrom (2006) further posit that the spider metaphor alludes to an organization where the head is centralized. This type of organization is hierarchical and top down in nature, where knowledge and power are concentrated at the top and the organization relies on a specific space in which to be located. If a unit is separated, this may affect the basic functioning of the organization. In contrast, the starfish metaphor alludes to a network organization without a head or some form of control; it is decentralized and fluid wherein power is diffused throughout and does not rely on a fixed space in which to function. If one arm of the starfish is removed, another arm is grown. Additionally, in so-called starfish leader*less* management, individuals unlearn the cultural information which enables the creation of new ideas which enthuse the group.

Moran (2015, p. 505) posits that in an organization which entails a leader*less* management approach, this leadership can be considered inefficient because it tends not to base decisions on facts or data ("data-less leadership"); naïve leadership behavior reveals an individual who is easily confused and is afraid of employees ("simply distracted leadership") and relies on others to make decisions; leader*less* management can also be evident in the so-called ostrich leadership approach which arises when problems are avoided in the hope that the issue gets resolved alone; and in the approach termed as "What would you do leadership?"—this leader*less* management approach demonstrates that the leader*less* management avoids making decisions because this type of individual neither knows how to manage nor wants to make the incorrect decision. The abovementioned type of leader*less* management approaches, as Moran (2015) further posits, reveal that there is an inquiry with other fellow employees to ascertain what they would do if they were in the leading position. The effect of the abovementioned leader*less* management styles on the organization has also been considered as a shortcoming because this type may give rise to feelings of perplexity, disorientation, as well as mistrust, skepticism, over-reliance on analysis and eventual organizational inertia. This scenario of leader*less* management can also be considered as detrimental to the well-being of the organization. In the leader*less* management scenario as Moran (2015) further describes, a blame culture surfaces, one in which the lack of morale predominates among individuals and the overall organizational climate is characterized by stagnation because individuals become averse to learning.

In summary, we are in favor of that specific co-leader*less* management which is based on constructive, transformational co-leadership behaviors inherent in the Follettian co-leadership management perspective.

Concluding Thoughts

In this chapter, we argued against the leader*ful* management perspective that is based on dominant and militant principles and their relentless pursuit for surplus value in undesirable leader*ful* management. We argued in favor of that leader*less* management perspective that is based on the Follettian co-leadership leader*less* management approach—wherein lies our definition of co-leader*less* management. We have put forth our definition of leader*less* management which is based on the anarchists' dissociation of the western growth philosophy and its hunt for surplus value. In this regard, co-leader*less* management should consider what is the essence of being. It is apparent that organizations require to re-humanize their principles and foster an environment imbued with humanity, virtuous, and values-based principles inherent in the Follettian co-leader*less* management perspective. The latter perspective entails principles which fortify a culture wherein all individuals are valued and respected. Creativity and innovation are fostered leading to the longevity of organizations. Furthermore, humanity is placed at the core and is considered the very essence for re-humanizing co-leadership in order to set organizations in this Follettian co-leadership leader*less* management direction, which we endorse.

References

Alvesson, M., & Spicer, A. (Eds.). (2011). *Metaphors we lead by: Understanding leadership in the real world*. London: Routledge.

Barnes, J. (Ed.). (1984). *The collected works of Aristotle*. Princeton, NJ: Princeton University Press.

Bass, B. M. (1990). *Bass and Stodgill's handbook of leadership: Theory, research and managerial applications*. New York: The Free Press.

Brafman, O., & Beckstrom, R. A. (2006). *The starfish and the spider: The unstoppable power of leaderless organizations*. New York: Penguin.

Burns, T., & Stalker, G. M. (1961). *The management of innovation*. London: Tavistock Publications.

Coop, T. (2013). Towards leaderless organizations? The impact of new technology on leadership and learning. In E. Avril & C. Zumello (Eds.), *New technology, organizational change and governance* (pp. 200–217). London: Palgrave Macmillan.

Crossan, M. M., Byrne, A., Seijts, G. H., Reno, M., Monzani, L., & Gandz, J. (2017). Toward a framework of leader character in organizations. *Journal of Management Studies, 54*(7), 986–1018.

DeRue, D. S., Nahrgang, J. D., Wellman, N. E. D., & Humphrey, S. E. (2011). Trait and behavioral theories of leadership: An integration and meta-analytic test of their relative validity. *Personnel Psychology, 64*(1), 7–52.

Dolgoff, A. (Ed.). (1972). *Bakunin on anarchy*. New York: Vintage Books.

Edwards, S. (Ed.). (1969). *Selected writings of P. J. Proudhon*. Garden City, NY: Doubleday & Company.

Endres, S., & Weibler, J. (2020). Understanding (non)leadership phenomena in collaborative interorganizational networks and advancing shared leadership theory: An interpretive grounded theory study. *Business Research, 13*(1), 275–309.

Follett, M. P. (1924). *The creative experience*. New York: Longmans.

Follett, M. P. (1941). Power. In H. C. Metcalf & L. Urwick (Eds.), *Dynamic administration: The collected papers of Mary Parker Follett*. New York: Harper & Brothers.

Follett, M. P. ([1949]1987). The essentials of leadership. In L. Urwick (Ed.), *Freedom and co-ordination: Lectures in business organization* (pp. 47–60). New York: Garland.

Foucault, M. (2003). *Society must be defended. Lectures at the Collège de France, 1975–1976* (trans: Macey, D.). New York: Picador.

Green, J. (2007). *Democratizing the future: Towards a new era of creativity and growth*. Amsterdam: Koninklijke Philips Electronics N.V.

Hansen, D. (2016, December 2). Is leaderless management a fad or the future of business? *Forbes*, pp. 1–9. https://www.forbes.com/sites/drewhansen/2016/03/08/leaderless-management/?sh=35a00d9b207f. Accessed 27 June 2021.

Heidegger, M. (2003). *Being and time*. Oxford: Blackwell Science.

Kotow, E. (2019). How realistic is a leaderless organisation? *Hedgetrade.com*. https://hedgetrade.com/how-realistic-is-a-leaderless-organization/. Accessed 30 May 2020.

March, J. (1991). Exploration and exploitation in organizational learning. *Organization Science, 2*(1), 13–31.

Merleau-Ponty, M. ([1945]1995). *Phenomenology of perception* (trans: Smith, C.). London: Routledge.

Mintzberg, H. (1973). *The nature of managerial work*. Englewood Cliffs, NJ: Prentice-Hall.

Monin, N., & Bathurst, R. (2008). Mary Follett on the leadership of "everyman". *Ephemera—Theory and Politics in Organization, 8*(4), 447–461.

Moran, J. (2015). Leaderless leaders: Leaders in title only. *Journal of Public Health Management Practice, 21*(5), 504–506.

Morgan, G. (1986). *Images of organization*. Thousand Oaks, CA: Sage.

Nelson, G. M. (2017). Mary Parker Follett—Creativity and democracy. *Human Service Organizations: Management, Leadership & Governance, 41*(2), 178–185.

Nemanich, L. A., & Vera, D. (2009). Transformational leadership and ambidexterity in the context of an acquisition. *Leadership Quarterly, 20*(1), 9–33.

Nielsen, J. S. (2004). *Myths of leadership: Creating leaderless organizations.* London: Nicholas Brealey Publishing.

O'Reilly, C. A., & Tushman, M. L. (2013). Organizational ambidexterity: Past, present, and future. *Academy of Management Perspectives, 27*(4), 324–338.

Plato. (2021). *The republic* (trans: Jowett, B.). https://www.gutenberg.org/files/1497/1497-h/1497-h.htm. Accessed 28 June 2021.

Provis, C. (2017). Confucianism, virtue, and wisdom. In A. J. G. Sison, G. R. Beabout, & I. Ferrero (Eds.), *Handbook of virtue ethics in business and management* (pp. 425–434). Dordrecht: Springer.

Purkis, J., & Bowen, J. (Eds.). (2004). *Changing anarchism: Anarchist theory and practice in a global age.* Manchester: Manchester University Press. https://library.oapen.org/handle/20.500.12657/35064. Accessed 1 May 2021.

Raelin, J. A. (2011). From leadership-as-practice to leaderful practice. *Leadership, 7*(2), 195–211.

Ricoeur, P. (2006). *Memory, history and forgetting* (trans: McLoughlin, K., & Pellaur, D.). London: The University of Chicago Press.

Shatz, M. S. (Ed.). (1995). *The conquest of bread and other writings.* Cambridge, UK: Cambridge University Press.

Skogstad, A., Aasland, M. S., Nielsen, M. B., Hetland, J., Matthiesen, S. B., & Einarsen, S. (2014). The relative effects of constructive, laissez-faire, and tyrannical leadership on subordinate job satisfaction. *Zeitschrift für Psychologie, 222*(4), 221–232.

Yukl, G. (2002). *Leadership in organizations.* Upper Saddle River, NJ: Prentice Hall.

8

Leaderless Leadership: Implications of the "Agora" and the "Public Library"

Kenneth Mølbjerg Jørgensen and Sissi Ingman

Introduction

Leadership education has become a billion-dollar business and is a popular field among researchers and students in universities. Multiple debates about what leadership is and how to perform it flourish. In a recent debate book, Anders Örtenblad (2018) has collected contributions that debate whether leadership should be a profession. Jørgensen and Svane (2018) argue that the answer is no to this question from the premises that leadership education would then be defined by the powerful and because it would entail an instrumentalization and standardization of leadership. Hertel and Fast (2018) suggest that leadership is connected to a certain way of being in a context. Therefore, they argue, that it is impossible to define universal principles of leadership.

K. M. Jørgensen (✉) · S. Ingman
Department of Urban Studies, Malmö Universitet, Malmö, Sweden
e-mail: kenneth.molbjerg-jorgensen@mau.se

© The Author(s), under exclusive license to Springer Nature
Switzerland AG 2022
F. Hertel et al. (eds.), *Debating Leaderless Management*,
Palgrave Debates in Business and Management,
https://doi.org/10.1007/978-3-031-04593-6_8

These arguments against turning leadership into a profession are grounded in the idea that leadership is a situated, relational and collective practice rather than a personal and a technical practice. Turning leadership into a profession implies the assumption that leadership emerges from the actions of superior individuals. These debates connect to our position regarding the central theme of the book, which is that we are *for* leaderless *management*. Using Hannah Arendt's (1998) distinction between *action* and *work*, we develop a position within leaderless management, which we call *leaderless leadership*. This position is founded upon action and involves specifying the critical dimension of democratic participation in decisions that concern the whole organization. Arendt argues that *action* is where people become political among other people. It presumes the perception of a common space among them. Action is thus where people assume responsibility for a world they have in common with others (Arendt 1998, pp. 50–55). Action is etymologically associated with leading and is not only a natural part of the human condition, but also an obligation because it implies taking responsibility for the complex matters of the world.

We define "leaderless leadership" as when people come together, meet as equals, and initiate collective action. These incidents take place in spaces in which everyday heroes can step forward and partake in action. Such spaces are neither organized around, nor governed by single persons. We argue that Arendt's use of the notion "agora" supplemented with a metaphor of the "public library," can inspire the design of such spaces. Leaderless leadership specifies that leaderless management goes beyond a decentralization of the control of one's personal work tasks. For Arendt (1998), *work* comprises the activity of fabrication and the production of cultural artifacts. Thus, work has a closer affinity to the performance of knowledge, skills, and judgment that craftsmen, professionals, and artisans do as an integrated part of managing their specific work task.

When leaderless management is only viewed from the perspective of work, the central question is more narrowly confined to if this work is controlled by practitioners themselves or if it is controlled by an external authority (see, e.g., Selberg and Mulinari, Chapter 5 in this volume). Leaderless leadership is naturally conditioned on, that practitioners control their work situation, but it also goes beyond this condition in suggesting that leaderless management also implies participation and control regarding strategic and political decisions concerning how the organization should position themselves in relation to its stakeholders.

It follows that leader*ful* leadership is a type of leader*ful* management that refers to when strategic and political decisions are determined and structured around what single leaders think and do. This may involve dialogue and communication with the subordinates. The decisive point in leaderful leadership is that action is determined either directly by the single leader or through the sheer presence of this leader. The image of the great man is often embedded in ideas of leaderful leadership (Spector 2016). When leaderful management is only seen from the perspective of work, this involves external control of work tasks. Such control can be performed by single persons, as in direct supervision, but in this case, it also refers to systemic modes of control that are inscribed into and exerted through technologies of power (Foucault 1977). The central point is here that performing individual work tasks is not controlled by employees but by managers, supervisors, or systems.

This chapter takes the position of being *for* leaderless *leadership*. It implies both that employees have reasonable control of their individual work situations and have possibilities of participating in strategic decision-making. We present the agora as an idea of workplace democracy in which leaderless leadership is possible. We furthermore suggest the metaphor of the public library for understanding how organizations can organize a collective memory through which experiences are passed on between members and to newcomers, and through which a common space among participants therefore can be developed and maintained. The next section discusses the distinction between action and work in relation to leaderless management. This section ends with an argument for how leaderless management can relate to Arendt's concept of work. We then proceed to discuss leaderless management from Arendt's concept of action. We then argue for the use of the metaphors of agora and the public library for enhancing the political quality of organizations. We argue that putting action into the center of leaderless management implies *first*, that creative solutions are more probable if plural people are invited into the debate concerning the organization's strategic decision-making. *Second*, because participation according to Arendt is a human condition, leaderless leadership is a condition for the creation of a shared identity where individuals can confirm a sense of belonging. *Third*, great and visionary ideas require that they mature through a process of dialogue, debate, and conversation among equals.

Leaderless Management and Work

Our argument for leaderless leadership is based on Arendt's distinction between work and action. This distinction has implications for the conceptualization of leaderless and leaderful management in this book. Most contributions that are for leaderless management situate it in opposition to leaderful organizations. In opposition to leaderful management, Hsu and Sun (Chapter 6 in this volume) proposes Autonomist leadership as a more situated, emergent and collective leadership process based on voluntary participation. Garvey and Fatien Diochon (Chapter 3 in this volume) propose a form of leaderless organization that are based on coaching and communities of discoveries. They define a leaderless organization as one that works based on collaboration in communities.

Likewise, the contributions, which are against leaderless management, do it with a reference to the need for single person, who take the initiative and act. Gobind (Chapter 15 in this volume) defines leaderless management as the absence of a leader. For her this absence entails the absence of leadership. Gerwel Proches (Chapter 18 in this volume) argues that centrally positioned leaders have enabling roles in times of crisis. These contributions center the debate for or against leaderless management upon the figure of the "the great leader." The central question here is if sound leadership is performed by single persons, who have extra-ordinary knowledge and skills (Spector 2016) or if leadership is a more collective endeavor? The imagination of a single great leader featured prominently in the writings on corporate culture in the 1980s (Deal and Kennedy 1982) in which the values of the founding fathers of corporations were being hailed. The learning organization (Senge 1990) followed as a new "big fix" approach to organizations in the 1990s but without changing the basic perception that at the heart of great organizations stands a great leader. Reflexive and relational leadership (Cunliffe and Eriksen 2011) also presume the presence of a leader. Generally, however, there is also a need to address another central question concerning leaderless or leaderful management. Does leaderless or leaderful relate the control of work or the control of action? Hsu and Sun as well as Garvey and Fatien Diochon seem to relate leaderless management to action. Selberg and Mulinari (Chapter 5 in this volume) and Flanigan (Chapter 10 in this volume) relate their arguments for leaderless management to the control of work.

Arendt distinguished work from labor, which corresponds to the biological process of the human body (Arendt 1998, p. 7). *Work* corresponds to "the unnaturalness of human existence" (Arendt 1998, p. 7). It provides an artificial world of things. Unlike labor, a work process has a definite beginning and a definite end. Human experience of mastery comes from working skills in causing ends and controlled use of violence in fabrication. Work is associated with "tékhnē", i.e., craft and art, and thus the material practices by which we produce cultural artifacts and produce a distinct human world. In organizations, labor is typically used to denote repetitive, unskilled activities. We labor in order to earn a pay, while there is no intrinsic motivation. True work, on the other hand, involves professional pride, dedication, and control of the activity.

In early prescriptions of organizations, scientific management and the bureaucracy, work was transformed into labor, and this labor in the form of routines was then separated from what was considered the mind of organizations (engineers, bureaucrats, managers). Thus, we witnessed a separation of the production process and control of this production process. Today, work has seen a renaissance in organizations as organizational activities have become more knowledge intensive. In the Western world, labor-intensive activities are taken over by automation, robots and machines or are outsourced. Instead, the presence of highly skilled and educated people is frequent. However, the basic leadership models are still leaderful.

Many critics of leaderful management is based on, that professionals should have control of their complex work task. One example is the critique of new public management, which uses standardized measurement systems to control how professionals should manage and handle complex, contextual, and ambiguous problems. The reflective practitioner (Schön 1983) and situated learning (Lave and Wenger 1991) are on the other hand examples of leaderless management practices where work practices are controlled by practitioners. The relations between practitioners may however still be hierarchical in the sense that the experienced practitioners pass on their knowledge to apprentices or other legitimate peripheral participators in practical work situations.

The professional bureaucracy left it to practitioners to control and manage their complex work practices. The question is however if we should reserve the debate about leaderless management to a concern for who should control practitioners work situation. Even if leaderless management clearly involves control of work, we argue that we need to focus upon the political and participative dimensions that Arendt associates with the last of her three human activities, namely *action*, in order to grasp the full implications of leaderless management.

Leaderless Leadership and Action

Action is associated with politics and takes place in the spaces between people (Arendt 1998; Jørgensen 2022). As noted by Arendt (1998, p. 177) "to act" means taking an initiative and it is related to "to begin", "to lead," and to rule. For Arendt, "to act" or "to lead" corresponds to the human condition of having political agency in the world (Jackson 2013). Therefore, leaderless leadership connects with workplace democracy in a broader sense in which it connects with questions concerning participation in strategizing, policymaking and in the organization's collective responses to the challenges it faces. Leaderless Leadership moves beyond the control of the individual work situation and relate to broader common issues.

Arendt's notion of action implies that leaderful organizations are untenable because they take the political agency and the capacity of action away from people. In other words, leaderful management destroys the creative potential that lies in that plural people can take the initiative, experiment, and create from the passions of their heart and from their interests and intentions. The challenge is to create conditions where everybody can take an initiative and lead. Such conditions of mutual respect and reciprocity among a community of plural beings recognizes that despite their differences, they share a world and have a space of action through which they can intervene into this world. This impulse to act and create resides for Arendt in the simple fact of being born. She uses the notion *natality* to argue that to begin again in action is a human condition (Arendt 1998, pp. 176–178). Thus, leaderful management not only destroys the human potential of acting. It also destroys the possibilities of creating a shared identity and horizon among people. As a final point, action is not tied to a notion of liberalism, which emphasizes the pursuit of individual freedom. Action and freedom are the same but only from the viewpoint that freedom is never free from interdependence of others (Arendt 1961). Action takes place within and supported by a web of relations and interests.

Following Arendt, the problem with leaderful management is that it rejects the principle of plurality by inhibiting it and in trying to contain and control it. Human beings are managed as if they were laborers instead of agents. Skilled work is transformed into steps of repeatable labor. Work's dignity is threatened when the skilled process becomes the end, and any result is a potential bi-product or waste, turning the world into a heap of rubbish. Action's dignity is offended when used as a resource for wealth accumulation. Following Arendt, the logic of the leaderful management models is out of bounds. Instead of providing spaces where people come together, organizations become suppressive, exploitative, and destructive structures.

She argues (1998, p. 190) that as a process, action has a definite beginning, but no end, because every action is inserted into a web of human relations. Furthermore, action is boundless because every reaction is a new action with unforeseeable consequences. She argues that action is miracle-making because it may begin new processes that are completely unexpected and because it—by forgiving—has the power to stop a process that otherwise might go on forever (Arendt 1998, p. 247). This revolutionary quality is not limited to political action involving a multitude of people. Instead, she notes (1998, p. 190) that the smallest acts bear the seed of the same boundlessness. Sometimes one word suffices to change a whole constellation.

After we have produced arguments for leaderless leadership, we will now proceed to illustrate how it might look like in practice. We will use the metaphors of "agora" and "the public library". The agora is used to rethink the organizational space from a space of work as labor to a collective space of action. The library is a metaphor for *organized remembrance*.

The Agora as Places and Spaces for Leaderless Leadership

Leadership and organizational development studies and practice use metaphors of dialogue and reflexivity for establishing alternative humanistic and democratic practices that are different from bureaucratic and machine-like organizations (Hersted 2016). However, generally, they tend to favor or at least accept the necessity of a leader in the center of activities. Not even Critical Performativity, suggested as an interventionist stream of critical management studies (Spicer et al. 2009), breaks with the mainstream model.

In contrast, Arendt's notion of action implies the suspension of leaders (Jørgensen 2022) in the sense that leadership only can emerge in spaces where people can come together as equals. It takes place in what she calls *a space of appearance*—the space that come into being whenever people appear to each other as human beings and make themselves seen and heard before others (Arendt 1998, pp. 198–199). She describes it by the example of the agora, the ancient Greek public square. It is a space where plural people meet for collective action. This space is leaderless but invites leadership to emerge from everyday people who temporarily can become everyday heroes (Tassinari et al. 2017). These spaces invite plural participation where everyone can be a beginner, leader as well as a supporter. The space of appearance is connected to a physical place but is otherwise a space that can emerge whenever people are together. In such spaces, "… people are with others and neither for nor against them" (Arendt 1998, p. 180). Thus, they are together as "equals". She argues here that the term "equality" designates situations where people can appear and be recognized based upon *who* they are as opposed to *what* they are.

The agora is a metaphor for workplace democracy. Workplaces might have formally assigned or elected managers that govern and see to that the rules of the democratic decision-making process are followed and enacted into practice. The plurality of "equals" that characterize the agora is not restricted to decision-making spaces but is grounded in a way of being together. We use the agora as a metaphor of a space for organized and unorganized meetings. It is a space where people go to meet and to find out what is happening. The agora is a stage where action can take place and where people choose to make things—announcements, opinions, stories, and invitations for joint action, artifacts and inventions—public. It allows for *co-presence* in time and space. Such collective spaces are important in organizations even if their value is currently underrated in favor of time management and exploitation of time. The agora celebrates excess and redundancy of sharing stories and communicating across boundaries. It is based on the love of small conversations, coffee-breaks and all the multiple ways of coming together in both organized and unorganized meetings and work situations—all the things we have lost during the corona pandemic.

Using the agora as a metaphor for organizational space entails that everybody has the right to participate in outlining and designing work as well as policies and strategies. In organizations such collective spaces weave stories and people together into a shared community that contain within them the participants' unique identities. Our own space, Malmö University can be seen as designed to afford such coming together. The material spaces are designed for the possibilities of appearing before others and for coming together. Six floors are connected and are open. They contain generous spaces for students that are free for visitors with sofa groups and chairs allowing half-privacy. Anyone can use the small and everyday concrete things in-between us—the coffee, exotic tea bags, and private teacups—to start a convivial and non-obliging conversation. Often you can listen to and join as people talk as peers sharing pragmatic ups and downs—breakdowns during the morning meetings or work with the students or things that have worked out better than expected—and opinions on how the work situation could be improved. In this semi-public space, a momentary space of appearance is opened as people standing nearby listen to the peer presenting a problematic situation, they all can relate to from their own experience and join the short conversation.

This small-scale organizing, coordination, and informal leadership adds to the political quality of the organization when people share their world and make sense of it together. These spaces are then supplemented with other spaces, which are more concerned with essential work activities. The research seminar is, for example, an indispensable part of academic communities, which unfortunately also is fading in value. When such seminars work, they confirm the common space between people and allow for organizing and creating a world-sharing activity. They become arenas for leadership if the issues that are spoken about concern the practice shared by the peers. If this includes questions that go beyond the pragmatic "what works" and concern the role of their practice in the common world and how they could act on the responsibility that comes with this, the informal and collective leadership that rises in togetherness has a truly political quality (Vino 1996).

The agora requires both physical places and structural arrangements that may enable people coming together. On the other hand, the space of appearance is always potentially there when people get together. It is an act and obligation that rests with how people choose to engage and share experiences with each other. Leaderless leadership takes place in such spaces in which ordinary people can take an initiative are obliged to listen and respond to each other's different viewpoints and concerns. Such spaces are momentary supplements to the practices of work, but they correspond to a basic human experience that has existed on earth as long as there have been people getting together. According to Arendt, power is a potential that actualizes when people who speak together develop a common sense and horizon that allows them to form a group and act-in-concert (Arendt 1972, p. 143).

"The Public Library" as a Space of Collective Remembrance and as Generosity

If the agora is metaphor for the public place of the *present*, the public library is metaphor for the ways we keep, take care of, and relate to experiences and voices from the *past*. Chilean poet, Roberto Bolaño notes that,

> A library is a metaphor for human beings or what's best about human beings, the same way a concentration camp can be a metaphor for what is worst about them. A library is total generosity. (Bolaño 2009, p. 48)

In the library, our first books may lie next to notes written yesterday, waiting to be read, listened to, gathered around, interpreted, translated, and engaged with, by individuals in withdrawal as company in their thinking processes, and by people getting together to speak and make sense of them. Existentially, the library is a way of dealing with equality, and it also ensures equality in the sense of availability—experiences and knowledge from the past are available to everyone.

Libraries are spaces where people of all ages can learn. It is "total generosity." The library metaphor is meaningful for reflecting on how we as human beings can organize for leaderless leadership. In a strictly Arendtian sense, the library (as materiality) stands for an organized world that each generation lives in and passes on to the next. As process and activity, the library stands for "organizing remembrance" (Arendt 1998, p. 198), by creating and adding thought-things to the world, and as taking care, preserving and dwelling in a world that allows each and every one to choose what she calls "...his company among men, among things, among thoughts, in the present as well as in the past" (Arendt 2006, p. 226).

The concentration camp as an exact opposite of the library as what is best about us also rhymes with an Arendtian view on what organizing can achieve (Ingman 2016). The concentration camp is a counterpart to the agora and the library. It is an organizing that denies even the right to belong to a community (Arendt 1968, pp. 296–297). As a counterpart to "organized remembrance" which is captured by the agora and the library, Arendt spoke of totalitarian practice as "organized oblivion" (Arendt 1968, p. 452). A *public* library symbolizes generosity by dwelling among and inserting ourselves in a community and plural voices from the past and present. The library, freed from authority of tradition, saving originals as well as translations, is where we are free to "discover the past for ourselves" (Arendt 2006, p. 204).

Two examples can illuminate how the library can be used as a metaphor for organized generosity. One is inspired by Arendt's reflections on the old library in Baghdad, and the other is inspired by Deleuze. Both are suggestive for how we may enact generous, welcoming, and affirmative organizing that enhances plurality, crucial for leaderless leadership. In a library, we are free to take inspiration from a plurality of thinkers, from different times and places, if the principles of generosity and affirmation are respected. In the aversion toward coercion and in the respect for all forms of life, which together actualizes what Arendt spoke of as plurality as "the law of the earth" (Arendt 1978, p. 19), we find a common denominator between an Arendtian and a Deleuzian idea of organizing for spaces that allow, protect, and celebrate plurality.

The old library in Baghdad—the House of Wisdom—was a center of translation, gathering people from different generations and places in the world. Exploring how houses of Wisdom could be enacted in the twenty-first century Barbara Cassin (2018) proposes translation as "a know-how with differences," as a paradigm for contemporary citizenship (Cassin 2018, p. 132). Her initiative is inspired by Arendt's (2003, pp. 42–43) reflections on the plurality of languages, distinguished not only by vocabulary but by grammar, that is their manner of thinking. This points to the absurdity of a universal language and the wonder at the fact that languages are not owned but are all learnable. One way of exploring the metaphor of the library as organizing is to start from the fact that we have a plurality of languages, which we can share and that open the world and accompany our experiences in different ways.

Cassin (2018), for example, enacts practices of translation, the "de-essentializing" movement between at least two languages serving as hosts for each other, as a political "antidote" against the prevailing, universalizing, and essentializing trend associated with expertise, evaluation, ranking, and the "economy of knowledge". In organizational settings that take living experience and language seriously, translation could be part of organizing principles aiming at dismantling the kind of jargon that make up both management and (great man) leadership discourses, the one mixing and re-compartmentalizing labor and work logics, and the other mixing and perverting work and action logics.

Janning (2014) uses the library metaphor in another way. He interprets the generosity of the library as a metaphor for the generosity of life in a reflection on ethical leadership from a Deleuzian poetic perspective. He argues that "...the human being of today is living more in a moralistic concentration camp than in a library. ... surrounded by a moral rhetoric where leaders try to cultivate certain values and norms" (Janning 2014, p. 31). Janning (2014, pp. 25, 31) suggests an ethical form of leadership that is based on a continuous "poetic" dialogue between creation and affirmation and argues that we should create spaces in which lives can remain different. Thus, an organization that works as a library implies the idea that organizational living and working is one of mutual generosity and recognition among participants. Gaining experiences are free. Living each life, furthermore, passes on experiences to the next generation for free. For organizations, this entails that the participants can shape their own lives and create an enjoyable living in organizations according to who they are and what they want to achieve in life if they respect the principle of plurality and interdependence—basic principles in all Arendt's writings.

Thought of as living generously, the library directs attention to how organizations might be framed as living networks of affordances for shaping lives, identities, and political agencies; second, how organizations can be living reservoirs through which people can connect, reiterate, and revitalize the past in the present and the future. This does not only entail a space where people can be together but also that the intimate spaces of work are designed from a principle of generosity in which experiences can be passed on from masters to apprentices and from principles of exploration, artistry, artisan—as well as craftsmanship. The political agencies within the space of appearance are in the end intimately connected to such spaces of work just as the material practices of work give material substance to action. The material practice of work is fused with politics and requires consciousness of a common world and responsibility for this world.

Conclusion

We have proposed leaderless leadership as a contrast to leaderful management and as a concept that goes beyond when employees control their individual work tasks. Leaderless leadership is based upon Arendt's twofold definition of the Greek polis as organizing remembrance (the library) and as a place for distinction, debate, communication and collective sensemaking (the agora). Together they offer potential spaces of appearance for voices in the present as well as from the past. Neither define specific roles that limit responsibility but rather open spaces for responsiveness. As physical or virtual places they are not solely the result of action but need making and caring. As Spoelstra (2010, pp. 91–92) has noted, there is an analogy between Arendt's account of the Greek polis and contemporary business discourses on creating environments for innovation and creativity. This does not call for "Great man leaders" but rather everyday heroes who—knowing how to protect plurality—design, produce, organize, enact, and take care of the public spheres in the world.

A critique of modern management under capitalism needs to consider that it tends to feed on anything, including humanist or post-humanist methods used to resist it (Boltanski and Chiapello 2007). If capitalism has proven capable of sucking human communicative skill into its mills, why would a turn to collective action not only become one more of its victims? It would be naïve to ignore a structural antagonism inherent in capitalist logic, and the risks that creative spaces of appearance within organizational settings automatically also become spaces of surveillance and exploitation (Fleming 2009; Marquez 2012). Thinking with Arendt means turning attention away from subjects to things between us that we can share. The principles we have presented take their inspiration from her suggestions that people together need to deal with the *things* in our human world and that we need to understand the material conditioning of public spaces that allows for collective participation. This contrasts with the engineering of *people* manifested in management science and contemporary great man leadership.

References

Arendt, H. (1961). Freedom and politics. In A. Hunold (Ed.), *Freedom and serfdom: An anthology of western thought* (pp. 191–217). Heidelberg: Springer.

Arendt, H, (1968). *The origins of totalitarianism.* San Diego, CA: Harcourt Brace.

Arendt, H. (1972). *Crises in the republic.* San Diego, CA: Harcourt Brace.

Arendt, H. (1978). *The life of the mind: The groundbreaking investigation on how we think.* San Diego, CA: Harcourt Brace.

Arendt, H. (1998). *The human condition* (2nd ed.). Chicago: University of Chicago Press.

Arendt, H. (2003). *Denktagebuch, Vol. 1: 1950–1973.* München: Piper Verlag.

Arendt, H. (2006). *Between past and present.* San Diego, CA: Harcourt Brace.

Bolaño, R. (2009). Literature is not made from words alone. In M. Maristan (Ed.), *Roberto Bolaño: The last interview, & other conversations* (trans: Perez, S., pp. 42–50). Brooklyn, NY: Melville House Publishing.

Boltanski, L., & Chiapello, E. (2007). *The new spirit of capitalism.* London: Verso.

Cassin, B. (2018). Translation as politics. *Javnost—The Public, 25*(1–2), 127–134.

Cunliffe, A. L., & Eriksen, M. (2011). Relational leadership. *Human Relations, 64*(11), 1425–1449.

Deal, T. E., & Kennedy, A. A. (1982). *Corporate cultures: The rites and rituals of corporate life.* Boston: Addison-Wesley.

Fleming, P. (2009). *Authenticity and the cultural politics of work: New forms of informal control.* Oxford: Oxford University Press.

Foucault, M. (1977). *Discipline and punish: The birth of the prison.* New York: Vintage Books.

Gobind, J. (2022). Against leaderless management. In F. Hertel, A. R. Örten-blad, & K. M. Jørgensen (Eds.), *Debating leaderless management—Can leaders do without managers* (this volume). London: Palgrave Macmillan.

Hersted, L. (2016). *Relational leading and dialogic process.* PhD thesis, Aalborg University Press, Aalborg.

Hertel, F., & Fast, M. (2018). Can leadership become a profession? In A. Örtenblad (Ed.), *Professionalizing leadership: Debating education, certification and practice* (pp. 125–139). London: Palgrave Macmillan.

Ingman, S. (2016). Dignity in organizing from the perspective of Hannah Arendt's worldliness. In M. Kostera & M. Pirson (Eds.), *Dignity and the organization* (pp. 11–36). London: Palgrave Macmillan.

Jackson, M. (2013). *The politics of storytelling: Variations on a theme by Hannah Arendt.* Copenhagen: Museum Tusculanum Press.

Janning, F. (2014). Affirmation and creation—How to lead ethically. *Tamara Journal of Critical Organization Inquiry, 12*(3), 25–35.

Jørgensen, K. M. (2022). Storytelling, space and power: An Arendtian account of subjectivity in organizations. *Organization, 29*(1), 51–66. doi:10.1177/1350508420928522.

Jørgensen, K. M., & Svane, M. (2018). Against professionalizing leadership: The roles of self-formation and practical wisdom in leadership. In A. Örtenblad (Ed.), *Professionalizing leadership: Debating education, certification and practice* (pp. 141–160). London: Palgrave Macmillan.

Lave, J., & Wenger, E. (1991). *Situated learning: Legitimate peripheral participation.* Cambridge, UK: Cambridge University Press.

Marquez, X. (2012). Spaces of appearance and spaces of surveillance. *Polity, 44*(1), 6–31.

Örtenblad, A. (Ed.). (2018). *Professionalizing leadership—Debating education, certification and practice.* London: Palgrave Macmillan.

Schön, D. M. (1983). *The reflective practitioner: How professionals think in action.* London: Routledge.

Senge, P. M. (1990). *The fifth discipline: The art and practice of the learning organization.* New York: Doubleday/Currency.

Spector, B. (2016). *Discourse on leadership: A critical appraisal.* Cambridge, UK: Cambridge University Press.

Spicer, A., Alvesson, M., & Kärreman, D. (2009). Critical performativity: The unfinished business of critical management studies. *Human Relations, 62*(4), 537–560.

Spoelstra, S. (2010). Business miracles. *Culture and Organization, 16*(1), 87–101.

Tassinari, V., Piredda, F., & Bertolotti, E. (2017). Storytelling in design for social innovation and politics: A reading through the lenses of Hannah Arendt. *The Design Journal, 20*(Suppl. 1), S3486–S3495.

Vino, A. (1996). Telling stories, reflecting, learning: Hannah Arendt and organization. *Studies in Cultures, Organizations and Societies, 2*(2), 309–325.

9

Beyond Leaderlessness: Even Less Than Nothing Is Way Too Much

Frederik Hertel and Mogens Sparre

Introduction

In this chapter, we argue *for* the content of leaderless management—thus, for the absence of any leaders and non-leaders—and we take the argument even further and argue against leaderless management as a concept. The leader concept can, because of our dialectical approach, only be defined in terms of what it is not, its nonidentity. This means that the non-leader concept is essential for understanding the leader concept. Non-leaders can be defined in terms of what leaders are not and it,

F. Hertel (✉)
Aalborg University Business School, Aalborg University, Aalborg, Denmark
e-mail: fhl@business.aau.dk

M. Sparre
Department of Culture and Learning, Aalborg University, Aalborg, Denmark

© The Author(s), under exclusive license to Springer Nature
Switzerland AG 2022
F. Hertel et al. (eds.), *Debating Leaderless Management*,
Palgrave Debates in Business and Management,
https://doi.org/10.1007/978-3-031-04593-6_9

therefore, involves, e.g., workers, employees, and members of the organization. However, it also involves a leader, e.g., losing his/her footing as a leader and turning into a non-leader. The non-leader concept is (re)activated whenever the leader concept is applied and vice versa. This means that strategies to end authority, order, and hierarchy enforcing all to become non-leaders will just re-activate the leader concept on a higher and more abstract level. We will further elaborate and argue for our approach in the current chapter.

We perceive the leaderless management concept as intended to reflect Kropotkin's (2005) classic Anarchists' ideal where organizations, as well as society, are organized without hierarchy, order, authority, and the production of surplus-value. The surplus-value must here be understood in Marx's terms (1993) and it is simply explained a matter of the employee adding more value to the product or service than he/she is being paid. This is a vision based on the principle of federalism, free communes, free associations, and free agreements created by free women and men. The vision, furthermore, involves self-governed, self-created, and non-surplus value organizations. Our chapter will uncover two interconnected challenges that relate to the significations (or connotations) of leaderless management. The immediate issue relates to the concept of leader*less* management since it presumes that there is "someone" (that is, leaders) being absent. To the contrary of this concept, we argue for another ideal based on the non-existence of leaders *and* non-leaders. To turn all into non-leaders (labor) receiving equal wages as suggested by Proudhon (2011) will just produce an abstract capitalist society (Marx 2019, p. 81) where capitalists are being replaced by a "social system" or "society," e.g., personified in the previous Soviet system by the apparatchiks.

The consequence of our position is that we reject Kinna's (2014) and Ward's (1966) Anarchist principle of fluctuating leadership as self-contradicting since replacing "fixed leadership" with "flexible leadership" will enforce others to become non-leaders and therefore continuously re-activate leadership. The second challenge connected with the connotations of leaderless management is the inability in present time to imagine a leaderless future without, consciously or not, reproducing the contemporary leadership and its uninhibited hunt for surplus-value which is devastating for the inner nature, for other people's inner nature, and the external nature. Contemporary leaders and managers are installed in organizations to ensure the production of surplus-value (Marx 2019) and the production of surplus-value will therefore frame leadership and management. To exclude leaders and managers without canceling the hunt for surplus-value will not end the essence of leadership but just transfer the managerial tools and leadership to others.

Against the Concept of Leaderless Management

We will in this section argue against leaderless management as a concept. Leaderless is a compound word composed of two parts: "leader" and "less". In connection, the expression connotes a social entity existing without a leader. The leader concept not only connotes a social entity with authority, hierarchy, and (social) order, but also it furthermore includes its contradiction: the non-leader. The non-leader is of essential importance since leaders and managers occupied getting aims through others (Mintzberg 2011, 2013), e.g., to ensure the production of surplus-value. The reason for the leader being absent is probably of secondary importance compared to the connotation of the image of a social entity being without and thereby, somehow lacking a leader.

We, therefore, argue that the expression "leaderless" presupposes the image of a social entity described in everyday language as an *organization.* The emerging image of the organization will, because of the absence of a leader, implicitly connote the meaning: an incomplete organization. The organization lacking a leader connotes the image of members of the organization somehow dealing with and probably also compensating from the present short (leader) supply situation. Following this series of connotations implies that the "natural" or "normal" configuration of an organization includes a leader and that the disadvantages of the leader's absence will force the employees to develop a strategy for compensating for the lacking leadership. Being "leaderless" connotes the image of an organization in an "unnatural situation." We argue against this assumption and claim that people neither need contemporary leaders nor that the production of goods and services should be governed by a hunt for surplus-value.

We furthermore argue that the expression "leaderless" cannot stand alone but implies and reintroduces the leadership concept, which means the image of the contemporary leadership ideal and practice. To fully dismiss contemporary leadership implies rejecting the concept of "leaderless" or "leaderlessness" and it furthermore implies a consciousness developed in a social reality organized without leaders and non-leaders. However, if we, instead of connoting the absence of leaders, divide the expression in two and focus on "less" as an isolated expression, then we would connote the meaning of a minor portion or amount of something. This means that we deal with an organization containing a varying portion of or amount of leader(ship). No matter how we approach the expression "leaderless" is it impossible to break away from the impression that the organizational situation includes a leader either being present or absent.

Leaderlessness must, as a concept, be understood as the negation of and therefore interconnected with the leader/leadership concept. The leader/leadership concept cannot only be defined in terms of non-leaders as we did above. It must also be defined in terms of being in opposition to management.

We have in this section showed that the leaderless management concept which intends to produce the image of a social entity or organization managing without leaders is, in our viewpoint, erroneous since it requires and re-activates its negation: leaders and leadership. Re-activating the leader and leadership content makes it impossible to use the leaderless management concept to produce the desired leaderless alternative. After summing up, we will now extend our argument to show how the second part of the expression (management) produces comparable challenges.

To manage means to handle something and the expression is, therefore, interrelated with activities or action(s). Based on the meaning of the expression "to manage" we could probably expect that the expression "management," like a limp twig, somehow would cling to those handling something in everyday organizational life. By the expression "those handling something," we refer to the employees being involved in the production of goods, products, and services. The expression "management" refers to those people (managers) overseeing the production and to those monitoring and controlling the work of the employees being actively involved in the everyday production. We have in the above argued against the concept of "leaderless management," but this does in no way—as we will see in the next section—imply that we are arguing *for* leader*ful* management.

Against Leaders and Leadership

In the following two sections, we will explain our humanistic and political approach to a critique of leadership/management. We should probably also note that our humanistic critique of leadership/management is based on arguments found in the Kantian phenomenology. Thus, we do not mean to say that Kant intended or would have agreed in our use or misuse of his concepts.

The Humanistic Approach

We find inspiration for the humanistic critique of leaders and leadership in Kant's (2017) ethics which is founded on a Christian belief. The Kantian idea is that humans must be an end in themselves and therefore should not be reduced to a means for something else. Leadership, as well as management, will as mentioned above be perceived as a common way of obtaining aims through others in the hunt surplus-value.

The most important issue is probably that human beings a priori must be considered ends "in themselves" and consequently that no one should in the name of surplus-value reduce others or themselves to pure means. Furthermore, such reduction of others to means will in our understanding violate the Kantian categorical imperative (Kant 2017) which requires that one must act in a way that enables one's act to be considered suitable as a general law of ethics. Since leadership and management are based on rationality where aims are obtained through others in the hunt for surplus-value it will inevitably result in reducing others and in some cases probably also "self" to means. The latter probably requires slightly more explanation than the former. Reducing oneself to a means can be the consequence of self-management. Nevertheless, self-management is a complex concept since it applies to both leaders/managers as well as to their employees. In both cases, we argue that it reflects what we perceive as the immanent rationality founding management/leadership and further explained the following lines. One of us has previously explained self-management (Hertel and Fast 2013) as a way of outdistancing one from oneself to obtain aims, e.g., in connection with the production and exchange of goods or services. Self-management can be a matter of "self-reduction" probably somehow comparable to Buber's (2004) description of the fireman who becomes one with the process of feeding coal to the flames. It is the type of instrumentality Marcuse (2010) once defined as technical rationality. Where the former (Buber) is closer to our second key inspiration (Levinas 2020) and belongs to the Jewish (religious) phenomenology the latter (Marcuse) belongs to a political phenomenology represented by the first generation of the Frankfurter school (critical theory). In other words, we here see a meeting point for the humanistic and political critique of leadership/management.

So, the key argument against leadership is that participating in what we could call or define as the "leader/management game" results in others, and to some extent also the leaders/managers' selves are being reduced to a mean. This reduction of others and self contradicts the Kantian categorical imperative. However, when others are reduced to means is it both the result of and the constitution of immanent rationality included in the "leader/manager game." To focus on immanent rationality is not a way of downgrading the importance of the everyday physical and emotional interactions between actors. On the contrary, we find such interactions and the relation between actors determining the accessibility or immanence of everyday rationality. Our experiences are that the more one-eyed, commanding, and thereby authoritarian leaders/managers act during everyday interactions the more manifest will the rationality appear for the involved actors.

The humanistic critique of the leader/manager game assumes that immanent rationality influences and transforms the involved actors' lifeworlds from otherness to sameness (Levinas 2020). It is a process reducing the complexity and the content of the lifeworld which enables the actors to fit the crippled simplicity of everyday rationality. Actors are not reducible to weak-willed creatures but humans accepting and, consciously or not, actively involved in fitting the frame of the "leader/manager game" and thereby the immanent rationality. We here use the Levinasian concept of otherness (Levinas 2020, p. 29) to refer to the lifeworld perceived as a stranger in the sense of being an absolute other and thereby free. The lifeworld's character of being another (otherness) is fading during the "leader/manager game" and language somehow seems to lose its capacity to mediate between lifeworlds. The domesticated residues of the actor's lifeworlds become controllable and simple (lifeless) technical tools in the hand of management and leaders. Technical is here intentionally applied since it is identical or at least comparable with Marcuse's (2010) concept of technical rationality. It is this rationality that reduces the human being to means and it is this reducible process transforming the human being to sameness.

Political Approach

The political ground for arguing against leaders and leadership is shared by Socialists, Marxists and Libertarian Socialists. "[T]o fight for a new society in which there will be neither masters by birth, titles, or money, nor servants by origin, caste, or salary" (Reclus 2018, p. 72). With the quote of Reclus, we here pay a tribute to the Communards in the sesquicentennial of the Parish Commune of 1871. We will use the sesquicentennial as our opportunity to underline that the Communards argued *for organizing and managing without leaders*. Nevertheless, is it not our claim that the Communards were organized without leaders, but we do claim that the vision about managing without leaders was common among the Communards and especially among the fractions of Socialists and Libertarian Socialists, the latter also known as Anarchists.

One important aspect of the Socialists' and Libertarian Socialists' efforts was to encourage workers to take control of workshops and establish self-organized and self-managed cooperatives responsible to produce goods and services (Schulkind 1960, p. 412). The difference between Marxist and Libertarian Socialists is that the Libertarian Socialists argue against leaders and leadership. Marxists critique mainly contemporary leaders and leadership for being a representation of the hegemony (Gramsci 1992) in society.

Contemporary leaders and leadership are both a sign of the exploitation of employees and a tool for increasing the surplus-value A consequence of the hunt for surplus-value is that the social relations between humans involved in the production become thing-like (dinglich) and that the relation between things (commodity) take the form of social relations (Marx 1982, p. 166). This is named reification and Marx uses the expression: *the fetish of the commodity* to describe how the reification is installed in modern society.

Critical theory and the Frankfurter School is of interest here since it illustrates an alternative strategy toward the critique of leaders and leadership. Adorno (2017) developed a method for an immanent critique of contemporary society and its cultural phenomena. The method uncovers inner contradictions in the phenomena studied and tends to show how the contradictions make the studied phenomenon fall from within. What we notice here is that the phenomenon studied (leaders and leadership) can be studied both from a position within and from without. The within position is bound to a critique of present conditions, and it does therefore not consider replacing leaders or leadership. Based on this, we conclude that Marxists and Neo-Marxists display a critique of the present leader and leadership. Neo-Marxists do not reflect on leaders or leadership in general while traditional Marxists turn to leaders and leadership as a means for transforming the production and distribution of goods and thereby the society in general. The Neo-Marxists and the Marxists contribute with insights but as positions, they are in this context probably not radical enough and we will in the following section turn to Libertarian socialism for a profound argument against leaders and leadership.

For Libertarian Socialists, the situation is slightly different since Anarchism means the government of the none, and consequently, we regard leaders and leadership as a problem in-it-self. However, using singularities and presenting Anarchism as a unified approach is a serious simplification and probably also a mistake. Even a fast look at the historical and contemporary "Anarchism" clearly exposes a whole universe of highly varying Anarchist approaches and understandings. It is probably more appropriate to apply the metaphor of a variety of loosely coupled systems (Weick 2001) or maybe is it even better to use the expression of family resemblance (Wittgenstein 2009, p. 36) to describe the relationship between the large varieties of Anarchist's ideas such as Anarcho-Primitivism, Anarcho-Communism, Mutualism, Individualist Anarchism, Anarcho-Syndicalism, etc. Nevertheless, we will in this section stick to inspiration from the classic Anarchist tradition of Libertarian Socialists which includes Kropotkin, Bakunin, Proudhon, etc. The Anarchists' tradition varies but Anarchists share the perception of themselves as the left-wing of the Socialist's camp. This also means that we object against private ownership and as a resulting protest the very existence of surplus-value (Kropotkin 1911, 1976, 2005, 2006). The classic Anarchists are against private ownership and the production of surplus-value since it conflicts with what they consider justice and the dictate of utility. Libertarian Socialists perceive leaders and leadership as the exercise of authority, order, and hierarchy. Therefore, we both reject contemporary leaders and even Socialist or Marxist leaders attracting followers to transform contemporary society. They strongly object to what we see as the state-socialism of Marxists and Socialists.

In this chapter, we pursue and outline our Anarchist's critique of leaders and leadership. We mainly follow inspiration from Kropotkin since he combines three essential elements. Firstly, a critique of the very existence of surplus-value, secondly a demand for radical democracy, and thirdly a demand for pursuing well-being for all with the lowest possible waste of human energy. Finally, we should probably note that Kropotkin's critique of the surplus-value is undoubtedly both different from and inspired by Marx's work.

Against So-Called Anarkist's Organizations

We will in the following argue that existing descriptions of Anarchist's organizations will express either a past or contemporary social consciousness which makes such characterizations unsuited as a means for our ideal on self-organizing organizations and communities. We generally regard contemporary sketches (Kinna 2014; Parker et al. 2020) of Anarchist inspired organizations as a bizarre synthesis of elements from existing leadership and its negation.

We argue against the above-mentioned sketches of a so-called anarchist-inspired organization intended to handle authority or more precisely the absence of authority, hierarchy, and order. We furthermore disagree with Ward's (1966) description of Anarchist's organizations, and against Kinna's (2014, p. 613) fluid organizational practice. The temporary existing organizations are according to Ward (1966) expected to produce a time-limited spontaneous order. We think that the best way of describing Ward's principle is to apply the model of a Hegelian-inspired (Hegel 2019) process continuously bringing organizations and, therefore, leadership into existence, which furthermore implies a dialectical interplay between organizational being and nothing. The principle of a fluid leadership practice refers to the constant change of leadership (De Geus 2014; Land and King 2014, p. 926; Reedy 2014). Land and King (2014) furthermore argue that the essential idea in this principle is that the authority or leadership changes to ensure correspondence between competencies and tasks. We should probably underline that this approach is comparable with the idea introduced by Bakunin (2017) and which starts with rejecting a state of fixed and constant authority. He replaces it with a continual exchange of mutual, temporary, and voluntary authority and subordination. To fully understand Bakunin's (2007, 2017) idea, we should probably add that his masterpiece rejects both state and religion, which he describes as an absolute authority and replaces it with a conviction of science. To glorify and express such a belief in science reflects Bakunin's contemporary enlightenment period.

Choosing authority, as Bakunin as well as the above-mentioned Anarchists suggests, is in the aftermath of populists such as President Bolsonaro, Trump, and Prime Minister Orban probably not the answer.

The idea about spontaneous order is neither a proper solution since the dialectics of organizational being and nothing is an infinite circle of re-established contemporary leadership, order, authority, power, and hierarchy. We need to bring Social Libertarianism to its extremes to obtain a new organizational practice where the past contradictions between leadership and non-leadership (authority and non-authority) have passed away. An organizational practice, where the principle of "well-being for all" (Kropotkin 2005) has replaced the contemporary marked logic. It would be a situation where both authority and the absence of authority are rejected because of a social consciousness enabling the creation of a production founded on the principle of "each in correspondence to his/her needs."

Epilogue

We have in this chapter rejected the connotations connected with the leaderless management expression. As a result, we have rejected the leaderless management concept. The essential idea about managing without leaders can in our opinion only be expressed as the negation of leaders *and* non-leaders. This aim is in our opinion, unattainable within the frame of the leaderless management expression. Exchanging leaderless management with self-management appears at first glance obvious but must be rejected since it simply means managing the manageable. The concept cannot transgress reality and is, therefore, unable to silhouette the Anarchist's utopia.

Rhetorically we phrase the question: how much leadership is included in Leaderless management? When it comes to leaders, we do believe that even leader*lessness* introduces far too much leadership. If we were to present a sign following our organizational ideals it would be a sign which connotes an organization without leaders and non-leaders. We regard self-organizing as a means to express our organizational ideal and as a situation where all organizations, as well as society, are organized without hierarchy, order, authority, and surplus-value. It is an ideal involving self-governance, autopoiesis (or self-creation), and it discontinues the production of surplus-value. However, it is also a vision that requires a social consciousness to come. This is the utopia of Libertarian Socialism and if we could exclude the possible misconceptions, we would upfront declare our support to the realization of Proudhon's (2011) watchword: "the government of the none."

References

Adorno, T. W. (2017). *Negativ dialektik*. Aarhus, Denmark: Klim.
Bakunin, M. (2007). *Statism and anarchy*. Cambridge, UK: Cambridge University Press.
Bakunin, M. (2017). *God and the state*. Dumfries & Galloway, UK: Andos Books.
Buber, M. (2004). *Jeg og du*. Gylling, Denmark: Hans Reitzels Forlag.
De Geus, M. (2014). Peter Kropotkin's anarchist vision of the organization. *Ephemera—Theory & Politics in Organization, 14*(4), 853–871.
Gramsci, A. (1992). *Selections from the prison notebooks*. New York: International Publishers.
Hegel, G. W. F. (2019). *Åndens fænomenologi*. Aarhus, Denmark: Gyldendal.
Hertel, F., & Fast, M. A. (2013). Et signalement af ledelsesdilemmaet. *Akademic Quarter, 6*, 68–80.
Kant, I. (2017). *Grundlæggelse af sædernes metafysik*. Gylling, Denmark: Hans Reitzels forlag.
Kinna, R. (2014). Anarchism and critical management studies. *Ephemera—Theory & Politics in Organization, 14*(4), 639–658.
Kropotkin, P. (1911). Anarchism. In H. Chisholm (Ed.), *The Encyclopedia Britannica* (11th ed., pp. 914–919). New York: Cambridge University Press.
Kropotkin, P. (1976). *The essential Kropotkin*. London: The Macmillian Press.
Kropotkin, P. (2005). *The conquest of bread*. New York: Cambridge University Press.
Kropotkin, P. (2006). *Mutual aid*. New York: Dover.
Land, C., & King, D. (2014). Organizing otherwise. *Ephemera—Theory & Politics in Organization, 14*(4), 923–950.
Levinas, E. (2020). *Totalitet og uendelighed*. Aarhus, Denmark: Hans Reitzels Forlag.

Marcuse, H. (2010). *One-dimensional man*. Suffolk, UK: Routledge.

Marx, K. (1982). *Capital* (Vol. 1). Bucks, UK: Penguin Books.

Marx, K. (1993). *Grundrisse*. Suffolk, UK: Penguin Classic.

Marx, K. (2019). *Economic and philosophic manuscripts of 1844*. New York: Dover.

Mintzberg, H. (2011). *Managing*. Gosport, UK: Financial Times Prentice Hall.

Mintzberg, H. (2013). *Simply managing*. San Francisco: Berrett-Koehler.

Parker, M., Stoborod, K., & Swann, T. (2020). *Anarchism, organization, and management*. New York: Routledge.

Proudhon, P.-J. (2011). *Property is theft!* Oakland, CA: AK Press & Distribution.

Reclus, E. (2018). Inquiry on the commune. In M. Abidor (Ed.), *Communards* (pp. 70–76). Ashland, OH: Bookmasters Inc.

Reedy, P. (2014). Impossible organisations: Anarchism and organisational praxis. *Ephemera—Theory & Politics in Organization, 14*(4), 639–658.

Schulkind, E. W. (1960). The activity of popular organizations during the Paris Commune of 1871. *French Historical Studies, 1*(4), 394–415.

Ward, C. (1966). The organization of anarchy. In L. I. Krimerman & L. Perry (Eds.), *Patterns of anarchy* (pp. 386–396). New York: Anchor Books.

Weick, K. E. (2001). *Making sense of the organization*. Singapore: Blackwell.

Wittgenstein, L. (2009). *Philosophical investigations*. Singapore: Wiley-Blackwell.

Part II

In Between For and Against Leaderless Management

10

Leaderless Work and Workplace Participation

Jessica Flanigan

Introduction

Leaderless management is an organizational approach that deemphasizes hierarchical relationships in the workplace by distributing power and authority among employees, rather than concentrating power and authority in the hands of a few leaders or supervisors. One of the more compelling moral reasons for leaderless management is that it promotes more egalitarian relations between workers, often through workplace democracy or more worker participation. But, as I argue in this chapter, proponents of leaderless management needn't support reforms that promote workplace participation in order to achieve their egalitarian aspirations.

J. Flanigan (✉)
Jepson School of Leadership Studies, University of Richmond, Richmond, VA, USA
e-mail: flanigan@richmond.edu

© The Author(s), under exclusive license to Springer Nature Switzerland AG 2022
F. Hertel et al. (eds.), *Debating Leaderless Management*, Palgrave Debates in Business and Management, https://doi.org/10.1007/978-3-031-04593-6_10

In its most general form, leaderless management involves a "flat" organizational structure where employees collaborate to make strategic decisions (Kastelle 2013). Many organizational commentators tout the benefits of a leaderless management approach (Coop 2013; Kastelle 2013; Kotow 2019; Peterson 2018; Ross 2011). Proponents of leaderless workplaces tend to equate this approach with reforms that give workers more opportunities for workplace participation and collaboration. For example, this was CEO Tony Hsieh's argument for eliminating management roles at the online retailer Zappos (Guzman 2016). In practice, leaderless management structures can resemble small-scale participatory democracies (Ross 2011). One commentator writes, "[leaderless management] structures demand a more inclusive, democratic leadership style" (Hansen 2016). Philosophers who are proponents of workplace democracy also defend a more participatory organizational structure on the grounds that hierarchy is morally objectionable.

Yet, there are also downsides to democratic workplaces. In this chapter, I make the case that proponents of leaderless management should not necessarily favor more participatory workplaces as a way of making work more egalitarian. My position in the leaderless management debate is not that leaderless management is good or bad regardless of the context. Though there are egalitarian reasons to favor a leaderless approach, workers may have good reasons to prefer a more hierarchical workplace because it benefits them in other ways. Rather, my position is that in contexts where a leaderless management approach is justified, proponents of leadership management should not interpret the reasons in favor of a leaderless approach as reasons in favor of more workplace participation. For example, organizations can promote the egalitarian aspirations of leaderless management by encouraging workers' *independence* rather than workers' *participation.*

So while proponents of leaderless management are right to point out the value of creating workplaces that respect workers' autonomy and promote more egalitarian relations between workers, they shouldn't necessarily interpret this value as requiring a more participatory workplace. To establish this claim, I first describe the philosophical case for a moral presumption in favor of workplace democracy and codetermination. I then argue that this case is mistaken. And this argument also applies more generally to moral defenses of other workplaces that include similarly participatory institutional arrangements. Next, I argue that participatory workplaces aren't necessarily more efficient either. Despite this case against leaderless management, understood as workplace participation, I agree with workplace egalitarians that hierarchical leadership is often morally fraught. For this reason, I then outline some more promising egalitarian alternatives to participatory workplaces. I conclude that rather than addressing the moral costs of a hierarchical leadership structure by sharing responsibility and decisional authority, people should consider structuring organizations in ways that promote independent work and minimize the degree that people have authority over each other at all.

The Case for Participation

The moral case for a participatory workplace often appeals to egalitarian principles. For my purposes in this essay, I am focusing on the relational egalitarian tradition, which includes several prominent criticisms of workplace hierarchy. Relational egalitarians argue that everyone should have a broadly democratic relationship with their partners, compatriots, and coworkers, characterized by equal respect and shared decision-making (Lippert-Rasmussen 2018). The relational egalitarian case against hierarchical workplaces is grounded in the idea that treating people as equals is inconsistent with hierarchy. The argument goes like this:

> Premise 1: People have very strong moral reasons to relate to each other as equals.
> Premise 2: Workplace hierarchy prevents people from relating to each other as equals.
> Conclusion 1: Therefore, people have very strong moral reasons to avoid forming hierarchical relations in the workplace.

This argument is valid, so if its two premises are true, the argument establishes a moral presumption against forming hierarchical workplace relations. There are also good reasons to accept the premises, as I show in this section, so there are good reasons to accept a moral presumption against hierarchical relations in the workplace. Proponents of the argument then sometimes take the argument further, arguing:

Premise 3: Policies such as workplace democracy and codetermination can prevent people from forming hierarchical relations in the workplace.
Conclusion 2: Therefore, people have very strong moral reasons to support workplace democracy and codetermination.

This further argument suggests that limiting the influence of management or leaders in the workplace can promote relational egalitarianism at work. In the next few sections, I dispute this additional argument as well as the claim that people's strong moral reasons to avoid workplace hierarchy are decisive in light of other morally relevant considerations.

The first premise is that all people have very strong moral reasons to relate to each other as equals. This relational egalitarian premise refers to a conception of equality that is grounded in the liberal tradition. Relational egalitarians emphasize the value of equal autonomy and freedom. These liberal egalitarians also emphasize the moral importance of ensuring that everyone has equal freedom or equal rights. This approach to equality stands in contrast to egalitarians who advance more "distributive" interpretations of egalitarianism. Whereas distributive egalitarians focus on the moral reasons in favor of creating an equal distribution of resources, relational egalitarians focus on the moral imperative to foster relationships of non-domination.

The second premise is that relations of hierarchy that assign formal power to a boss or a leader cause people to relate to each other in a subordinating way. Hierarchy prevents people from sharing in decision-making authority. Since people have strong moral reasons to relate to each other as equals, they, therefore, have strong moral reasons to avoid forming undemocratic, hierarchical relationships (Kolodny 2014). For the sake of argument, let us grant this first premise, that people have strong moral reasons to try to relate as equals. The second premise, that workplace hierarchy prevents people from relating as equals, is partly an empirical claim. It states that, in practice, hierarchical workplaces are counterproductive to the goal of fostering egalitarian relationships. Proponents of this argument, most notably the philosopher Elizabeth Anderson, are, therefore, very critical of the modern workplace. Anderson argues that the same reasons against a dictatorial government are reasons against a dictatorial workplace. She writes,

> We talk as if workers *aren't* ruled by their bosses. We are told that unregulated markets make us free and that the only threat to our liberties is the state. We are told that in the market, all transactions are voluntary. We are told that since workers freely enter and exit the labor contract, they are perfectly free under it. We prize our skepticism about "government" without extending our critique to workplace dictatorship. (Anderson 2017, p. xx, emphasis in original)

Anderson then provides evidence that many workplaces, especially in America, are relevantly similar to tyrannical political communities. Workers have little say in the nature or terms of their labor. They are constantly surveilled, prevented from taking bathroom breaks, they must undergo drug testing, they are policed by their supervisors, and bosses suppress unions when workers attempt to improve their conditions. According to Anderson, the modern workplace is undemocratic and disrespectful—exactly the sort of institution that all people who are committed to relating with others as an equal ought to reject. Following this argument, Anderson and other relational egalitarians conclude that there are strong moral reasons to avoid a hierarchical workplace.

In light of this argument against workplace hierarchy, relational egalitarians generally favor regulations, incentives, legal protections, or economic policies that give more power to democratic institutions. For example, Anderson advocates for policies that promote workers' autonomy by enabling them to leave, such as a ban on noncompete clauses in labor contracts (Anderson 2017, p. 66). She also proposes policies that prevent people from alienating their basic rights as part of the terms of their labor, including rights to speech, association, and privacy. And Anderson also favors policies that would strengthen the rights of labor unions and give workers a voice at the table through codetermination, a system where workers are guaranteed representation in decisions that affect them and seats on corporate boards (Anderson 2017, p. 70).

Other relational egalitarians favor different policies to ensure workers' rights on similar grounds. Alex Gourevitch defends the right to strike "as a way of resisting intertwined forms of structural and personal domination associated with the modern labor market" (Gourevitch 2016, p. 307). Sam Arnold (2012) argues in favor of workplace regulations that would compel employers to promote employees' capacities for deliberation and foster greater self-realization at work. Arnold makes a case for these policies on the grounds that otherwise, people will be less capable of participating as free and equal citizens in a fair society. Philosophers have also called for minimum wage legislation and maximum hour laws on the grounds that these policies would reduce workplace domination (Kates 2015, 2019).

In addition to workplace regulations, relational egalitarian political philosophers also defend proposals to restructure firms (O'Shea 2020). These proposals include workplace democracy and collective ownership of firms. The idea of workplace democracy developed in the theoretical work of thinkers as varied as Karl Marx, John Dewey, and John Stuart Mill (Frega et al. 2019). More recently, neo-republican theorists have argued in favor of workplace democracy on the grounds that it would minimize relations of subordination (Breen 2017; Dagger 2006; González-Ricoy 2014). Anderson's work can be characterized in this way, too (Anderson 2015). Some argue that, in general, workplaces should be as democratic as possible (Collins 1997; Gerlsbeck and Herzog 2020; Landemore and Ferreras 2016). Others hold merely that all workers should have the choice as to whether they work in a democratic firm (Jacob and Neuhäuser 2018). A different argument for workplace democracy is that it is a part of cultivating civic virtue or maintaining the politically important practice of democratic participation during times when there is not an election (Graham 2000; Kohler 1994).

Collective ownership and codetermination are also justified by an appeal to relational egalitarian ideals. For example, workers in Germany have legal rights to participate in management decisions if they work for large companies, including rights to substantial worker representation on corporate boards. Codetermination is justified primarily on the grounds that giving workers a greater say in the terms and conditions of their labor will improve workers' well-being and ensure greater protections for workers' rights, but it is also justified on relational egalitarian grounds. For example, Elizabeth Anderson argues that codetermination is a promising strategy for giving workers a greater voice in hierarchical labor relations (Anderson 2017). In response, Tom O'Shea argues that codetermination is likely insufficient to ensure meaningful voice because it is limited to employment issues rather than broader strategic decisions for a company (O'Shea 2020).

These arguments show that philosophers have defended leaderless approaches such as workplace democracy and codetermination on the grounds that these policies better approximate or promote the ideal of social equality. People who defend these policies argue that hierarchical relationships at work, or workplaces with leaders and subordinates, are in some way unjust to workers even if they are not unjust on balance. They also argue that workplace hierarchy will, empirically, reduce workers' autonomy or frustrate equal relations between people. In the next two sections, I will argue that neither of these two assumptions clearly weighs in favor of workplace democracy. Policies that aspire to leaderless management by way of greater worker participation may just trade one form of hierarchy and subordination for another. I then suggest that there are alternatives that are potentially more promising means for pursuing a non-hierarchical workplace and confronting the moral risks of hierarchy at work.

Problems with Participation

In the previous section, I described the relational egalitarian case against workplace hierarchy and for workers' participation. Hierarchy is antithetical to workplace equality, the argument goes, and therefore, it seems plausible to think that distributing some of a leaders' power to workers would reduce hierarchy. In this section, I argue that limits on leaders' workplace authority wouldn't necessarily promote equality at work for two reasons. First, workers may experience participatory remedies to workplace inequality as a mere shift of subordination and domination from one's leaders to one's coworkers. Trading a single boss for dozens of bosses won't make workers more equal or free—it may just make them need to go to more meetings. And second, non-hierarchical workplaces can amplify underlying inequalities in the workplace rather than mitigating them.

The first reason to be skeptical that a participatory or leaderless workplace structure will secure equality is that workers may not appreciate "flat" workplaces. Treating people as an equal typically involves deferring to their judgment about what is best, so if workers do not judge that a democratic or participatory workplace is best, then it could be wrong to impose it on them. For example, when Tony Hsieh reorganized Zappos in an effort to create a more democratic, leaderless structure, 21% of the workforce chose to leave the company in response to the reorganization (Hodge 2015).

So while it may look like worker empowerment is best achieved by encouraging workers to participate in managing themselves and their workplaces, some workers may not value self-management and more opportunities for participation. For workers who judge that they are better suited for a more hierarchical workplace, subordinating them to an organizational change that forces them to participate in decision-making at work is unlikely to foster equal relations between workers in practice. In general, the best way for a group to foster egalitarian relations is to organically adopt a broad principle of deference to those who are actually in the relationship, even if they don't value formal structures that would appear to promote equal power between them.

As a further illustration of this point, consider how worker participation often looks in practice. Meetings and votes do not necessarily ensure that workers relate as equals or that they are treated with respect and dignity at work, and the process of including workers in decisions can be frustratingly inefficient. As John Tomasi writes,

> I invite readers, whatever their profession, to ask whether they would forego greater wealth for greater political control of their workplaces....Personally, I would not accept such sacrifices for the opportunity

to have longer and more frequent department meetings...My point is more general: professors are not the only people who value their work, who find rhythms and comforts in their workdays, and would hear the clang of a bell calling them to a workplace committee meeting as an infringement on their independence rather than as an enlargement of it. (Tomasi 2013, p. 191)

Tomasi's argument attempts to place an economic value participation. If there are any tradeoffs between economic prosperity or occupational freedom and participatory rights, Tomasi suggests that most people would value economic prosperity and occupational freedom more. But even if one denies the value Tomasi places on wealth and occupational freedom, Tomasi's objection to meetings is also a persuasive case against workplace democracy even if frequent meetings don't force these trade-offs. To the extent that participatory workplaces involve more meetings, they can make everyone worse off just by wasting people's time with decisions and tasks that could have been handled by a manager.

The second reason to be skeptical that a participatory or leaderless workplace structure will secure equality is that shared decision-making can backfire when workplaces include a minority of workers who may feel oppressed, harassed, marginalized, or excluded by a socially empowered majority of workers. For example, American labor unions historically opposed efforts to address and reduce workplace harassment. And some prominent unions have struggled to address sexual harassment within their own worker-led organizations (Avendaño 2018). And even if labor unions historically promoted egalitarian relations between workers in a narrow sense, they were exclusive and hostile to outsiders. For example, labor unions have historically been anti-immigration, which may not have undermined social equality within workplaces but plausibly undermined social equality within their broader political communities (Gonyea 2013). So taking a wider lens, reducing hierarchy at work could, therefore, exacerbate hierarchies in society, including hierarchies of race, gender, and national origin.

These examples do not establish that unionization and efforts at workplace empowerment exacerbate discrimination on balance—there is some evidence that unions do effectively promote wage equality among workers (Rosenfeld and Kleykamp 2012). Rather, they show that sharing decisional authority among workers doesn't guarantee relational equality, and in some cases, workers' participation can further entrench preexisting social inequalities. When this happens, their influence potentially undermines relational equality at work.

These two arguments challenge the egalitarian case for a presumption in favor of promoting worker participation. Though I have focused on the philosophical arguments in favor of and against more democratic workplaces, these arguments extend more broadly to discussions of leaderless management because other participatory organizational structures raise similar concerns. In the next section, I consider whether reasons related to efficiency and productivity are reasons to make workplaces more democratic.

A Practical Case for Participation?

Proponents of leaderless management may respond to the foregoing arguments against a more participatory workplace structure, by arguing that even if participatory policies are not required by a commitment to equality in principle, they are better than hierarchical alternatives. One may argue, for example, that workplace participation promotes egalitarian relations between workers and advances the material conditions of workers more than the status quo. Or, one may make the practical case that participatory workplaces are more efficient than those with more hierarchical organizational structures.

There is some evidence in support of these pragmatic arguments for participation when it comes to policies like codetermination and worker ownership of firms. For example, some scholars argue that democratic workplaces, understood as those with democratic ownership, are healthier and more productive (Foley and Polanyi 2006; Levin 2006). Other research finds that worker-owned firms are more likely to survive, plausibly due to less employee turnover and more stability (Park et al. 2004). Similarly, codetermination agreements do not seem to reduce productivity or innovation, though they also do not clearly promote profitability (Boneberg 2011; Kraft et al. 2011; Renaud 2007). On the other hand, empirical studies of these worker-owned businesses are generally limited to sectors or markets where worker ownership is common, so the external validity of these claims is unclear.

Turning to workplace democracy, there is less evidence in support of the claim that a participatory or democratic workplace is comparatively more efficient. Some leadership scholars argue that whether a more democratic, inclusive leadership style is more efficient depends on the context, including the tasks involved in managing people and the organizations' culture (Maner 2016). For example, one recent analysis of leadership styles finds that democratic leadership styles are more effective when employees are highly skilled and experienced (Khan et al. 2015). To the extent that hierarchical workplaces are more efficient for less experienced workplaces, workers also benefit from their firms' gains in productivity in the form of more job security or potentially better wages.

More participatory workplaces can also struggle to scale. For example, the online publishing company Medium experimented with participatory workplace structure but decided to back away from the model on the grounds that "it was difficult to coordinate efforts at scale… for larger initiatives, which require coordination across functions, it can be time-consuming and divisive to gain alignment" (Doyle 2016). Zappos also moved away from its earlier participatory organizational structure as the company grew (Albert-Deitch 2020; Groth 2020). More generally, meaningful participation becomes more challenging as organizations grow (Bernstein et al. 2016; Swanner 2018).

For these reasons, the participatory organizational structures that proponents of leaderless management support can not only fail to deliver the moral benefits of fostering more egalitarian workplaces, but they can also fail to deliver the productivity benefits that some supporters cite in their favor.

Alternatives to Participatory Approaches

Participatory approaches to leaderless management involve sharing power in the workplace. Sharing power in the workplace can involve unionization, codetermination, flat organizational structures, or workplace democracy. I have argued that these participatory institutional reforms do not necessarily promote egalitarian values, either in principle or in practice. Nevertheless, egalitarian critics of hierarchy at work are on to something, and the most promising moral justification for leaderless management is an egalitarian one. Egalitarian critics of hierarchical workplaces are right to denounce organizational cultures of domination or subordination, even if they should also be skeptical of promoting more workers' participation. They should aim to reduce the extent that workers or citizens are required to subserviate themselves to a leader even if they should be reluctant to implement workplace democracy.

In this section, I make a case for an alternative ideal for organizations—an independent ethos instead of a participatory ethos. Rather than sharing power, I argue that workplaces should be structured in ways that minimize leaders' influence on people's daily work lives without requiring that they actively participate in their workplaces. Whereas the aforementioned institutional attempts at leaderless management involved empowering workers to shape their workplaces, I propose that organizations also promote equality by empowering workers to work independently from their workplaces.

In other words, I am arguing that the practice of encouraging workers' independence rather than workers' participation can also achieve the egalitarian aspirations of leaderless management. In principle, this means that people should *aspire to equal freedom from bosses rather than equal power with their bosses*. In practice, this ideal involves policies that encourage independent work as much as possible. To these ends, I favor workplace policies such as incentive pay, salary transparency, and telework.

Consider a political analogy that illustrates this point. One way to reduce the moral risks of bosses is to make everyone a boss. The problem with this strategy, I've argued, is that even if an individual worker shares the power to lead with their fellow employees, they have, in a sense, traded one boss for hundreds of thousands of bosses. Another way to reduce the moral risks of bosses is to reduce bosses' scope of authority. Many countries have constitutional provisions that protect citizens' rights from executive or democratic encroachment. Courts uphold these rights and order public officials to enforce them even in cases where the rights are unpopular among citizens and elected officials.

Similarly, workplaces often guarantee rights to workers within labor agreements. These rights include provisions that ban harassment, specify rates of overtime pay, or describe fair procedures for the allocation of office space, for example. These workplace protections are not good for workers because workers secure them through a democratic process; rather, a workplace democratic process is often justified on the grounds that it secures these protections.

Participatory rights in politics are only justified to the extent that voters promote just outcomes more reliably than unelected leaders would (Brennan 2016). So too, workplace democracy is justified to the extent that worker participation secures better conditions for workers, and the organization workplace democracy does not reliably improve workers' conditions relative to alternatives; it risks exposing workers to even more points of workplace domination than more hierarchical alternatives.

One reason to think that workplace democracy is not necessary for creating better conditions for workers is that other interventions in labor agreements may similarly reduce leaders' discretionary control over workers. I will now discuss three organizational reforms that can empower workers without expanding their participation in the workplace. First, incentive pay can potentially liberate employees from leaders' subjective judgments of their performance. Second, salary transparency can empower workers to hold their leaders publicly accountable, and it can reveal patterns of discrimination and inefficiencies. Third, technology can give workers more control over their workplaces without sacrificing productivity or workers' autonomy.

Consider first practices like commission and incentive pay. Workers are subordinated when they are vulnerable to arbitrary, non-transparent systems of punishment and reward and when they lack control over the terms and conditions of their labor (Lovett 2001; Pettit 2005). Policies that transparently pay workers for what they produce, such as commission agreements that pay workers a percentage of all sales or incentive programs that pay workers for producing more, can potentially reduce the potential for arbitrary interference in a workplace. Some egalitarians may object to these kinds of payment schemes on the grounds that they can create very unequal wages, but there are also egalitarian reasons to object to a more egalitarian pay system where more productive workers may feel exploited by their less productive colleagues who are paid the same.

The second intervention which could potentially prove liberatory for workers is salary transparency. Among its many virtues, pay transparency also holds leaders accountable and enables employees to monitor the distribution of benefits and rewards, prompting leaders to uphold fairer standards. And as Jeffery Moriarty argues, it is also potentially more efficient, and pay transparency can also prevent unjust discrimination (Moriarty 2018).

Technology can also free workers from excessive oversight and domineering leadership at work. For example, many workers are increasingly shifting part or all of their workweek to telework. Telework can free workers from the oppressive gazes of bosses or fellow workers. It is easier for remote workers to avoid office politics and surveillance, for example, and telework also has less potential for physical intimidation and harassment (though workers can still be harassed or intimidated online). Telework also may protect workers from discrimination to the extent that it gives workers more anonymity. And teleworkers have more autonomy to shape their working environment and more flexibility in scheduling their days. Remote work is not feasible for all workers, but giving workers the option to work remotely when it is feasible can be an effective strategy for empowering workers without sacrificing productivity (Bloom et al. 2015).

One may object to these proposals on three grounds. First, one may object that they are infeasible. Second, one may reply that the aforementioned reforms are likely to be unprofitable or inefficient. And third, one may object that independent work is potentially worse by relational egalitarian standards to the extent that gig work deprives workers of the ability to collectively organize and subjects them to unpredictable demands and constant surveillance.

To the first objection, I reply that independent work is no less feasible than other egalitarian proposals, which require cultivating a sufficient democratic ethos to enable shared decision-making. If anything, the proposals I advance are more feasible because they do not require large-scale collective action or political change. The reforms I propose can be implemented in a piecemeal way. And these reforms are also potentially more feasible because, paradoxically, leaders can act unilaterally to limit their role going forward, rather than proposals such as workplace democracy, which may require a broader base of support among employees.

To the second objection, I grant that implementing workplace protections, telework, salary transparency, and incentive pay could be more costly or less efficient than a hierarchical workplace in some cases. Whether these policies would be costly and inefficient relative to existing practices is an open empirical question and is surely industry-specific. I mentioned evidence that salary transparency and incentive pay would not be costly, whereas the evidence for telework is more mixed, depending on the industry.

The third objection is that the aforementioned proposals for independent work, especially telework and incentive pay, could make workers more vulnerable to workplace domination by depriving them of the ability to organize and subjecting workers to heightened surveillance and precarity. This is a compelling objection to proposals for independent work. On my view, workers are entitled to organize, but public officials should neither promote nor discourage collective organization. Elsewhere, I argued that to the extent that there is a tradeoff between respecting workers' economic freedom and promoting collective action, officials should respect individual workers' voluntary choices even if those choices undermine workers' efforts at collective bargaining (Flanigan 2016). This argument assumes that individual rights constrain groups' interests, an assumption which is consistent with relational egalitarians' emphasis on the moral importance of individual autonomy and freedom.

In any case, the relevant question is not whether the policies I propose would be more costly and less efficient than the status quo. The relevant question for proponents of leaderless management, who are concerned about workplace hierarchy, is whether these reforms would be better than more participatory proposals. I have argued that contractual protections, pay transparency and incentive pay, and telework would not undermine social equality. And a more participatory institutional structure, such as workplace democracy, risks backfiring and being counterproductive by relational egalitarian standards of workplace justice. For this reason, organizational leaders have presumptive reasons to prefer independent approaches to participatory approaches to leaderless management.

Conclusion

Leaderless management is a compelling idea for people who are committed to relational equality and are opposed to hierarchy. And participatory policies that aim to reduce leaders' influence, such as workplace democracy and codetermination, may improve workers' conditions in some contexts. But these policies are only instrumentally justified. If they do not improve workers' material conditions and reduce subordination, then there is no non-instrumental reason to prefer a more participatory approach. For these reasons, proponents of leaderless management should not necessarily favor reforms that promote more workplace participation. Participatory policies may fail to promote workplace equality, and they can be inefficient. People who are committed to achieving greater workplace egalitarianism through a leaderless approach to management should therefore consider other promising workplace reforms, such as expanding opportunities for independent work, as alternatives to collective leadership.

References

Albert-Deitch, C. (2020). Zappos CEO Tony Hsieh's biggest management experiment is evolving again (in a very intriguing way). *Inc.com* https://www.inc.com/cameron-albert-deitch/zappos-tony-hsieh-holacracy-market-system.html. Accessed 23 July 2021.
Anderson, E. (2015). Equality and freedom in the workplace: Recovering republican insights. *Social Philosophy & Policy, 31*(2), 48–69.

Anderson, E. (2017). *Private government: How employers rule our lives.* Princeton, NJ: Princeton University Press.

Arnold, S. (2012). The difference principle at work. *Journal of Political Philosophy, 20*(1), 94–118.

Avendaño, A. (2018). Sexual harassment in the workplace: Where were the unions? *Labor Studies Journal, 43*(4), 245–262. doi:10.1177/0160449X1 8809432.

Bernstein, E., Bunch, J., Canner, N., & Lee, M. (2016). Beyond the holacracy hype. *Harvard Business Review.* https://hbr.org/2016/07/beyond-the-holacr acy-hype. Accessed 23 July 2021.

Bloom, N., Liang, J., Roberts, J., & Zhichun, J. Y. (2015). Does working from home work? Evidence from a Chinese experiment. *The Quarterly Journal of Economics, 130*(1), 165–218.

Boneberg, F. (2011). The economic consequences of one-third co-determination in German supervisory boards. *Jahrbucher fur Nationalokonomie & Statistik, 231*(3), 440–457.

Breen, K. (2017). Non-domination, workplace republicanism, and the justification of worker voice and control. *International Journal of Comparative Labour Law and Industrial Relations, 33*(3), 419–439.

Brennan, J. (2016). *Against democracy.* Princeton, NJ: Princeton University Press.

Collins, D. (1997). The ethical superiority and inevitability of participatory management as an organizational system. *Organization Science, 8*(5), 489–507. doi:10.1287/orsc.8.5.489.

Coop, T. (2013). Towards leaderless organizations? The impact of new technology on leadership and learning. In E. Avril & C. Zumello (Eds.), *New technology, organizational change and governance* (pp. 200–217). London: Palgrave Macmillan. doi:10.1057/9781137264237_13.

Dagger, R. (2006). Neo-republicanism and the civic economy. *Politics, Philosophy & Economics, 5*(2), 151–173.

Doyle, A. (2016). Management and organization at medium. *Medium.* https://blog.medium.com/management-and-organization-at-medium-222 8cc9d93e9. Accessed 23 July 2021.

Flanigan, J. (2016). Sweatshop regulation and workers' choices. *Journal of Business Ethics, 153*(1), 79–94. doi:10.1007/s10551-016-3395-0.

Foley, J. R., & Polanyi, M. (2006). Workplace democracy: Why bother? *Economic and Industrial Democracy, 27*(1), 173–191. doi:10.1177/014383 1X06060595.

Frega, R., Herzog, L., & Neuhäuser, C. (2019). Workplace democracy—The recent debate. *Philosophy Compass, 14*(4), Article e12574.

Gerlsbeck, F., & Herzog, L. (2020). The epistemic potentials of workplace democracy. *Review of Social Economy, 78*(3), 307–330. doi:10.1080/003 46764.2019.1596299.

Gonyea, D. (2013). How the labor movement did a 180 on immigration. *NPR.org.* https://www.npr.org/2013/02/05/171175054/how-the-labor-mov ement-did-a-180-on-immigration. Accessed 4 Jan 2021.

González-Ricoy, I. (2014). The republican case for workplace democracy. *Social Theory and Practice, 40*(2), 232–254.

Gourevitch, A. (2016). Quitting work but not the job: Liberty and the right to strike. *Perspectives on Politics, 14*(2), 307–323.

Graham, J. W. (2000). Promoting civic virtue organizational citizenship behavior: Contemporary questions rooted in classical quandaries from political philosophy. *Human Resource Management Review, 10*(1), 61–77.

Groth, A. (2020). Zappos has quietly backed away from holacracy. *Quartz.* https://qz.com/work/1776841/zappos-has-quietly-backed-away-from-holacr acy/. Accessed 23 July 2021.

Guzman, Z. (2016). Zappos CEO Tony Hsieh on getting rid of managers: What I wish I'd done differently. *CNBC.* https://www.cnbc.com/2016/09/ 13/zappos-ceo-tony-hsieh-the-thing-i-regret-about-getting-rid-of-managers. html. Accessed 23 July 2021.

Hansen, D. (2016). Is leaderless management a fad or the future of business? *Forbes.* https://www.forbes.com/sites/drewhansen/2016/03/08/leader less-management/. Accessed 23 July 2021.

Hodge, R. D. (2015, October 4). First, let's get rid of all the bosses. *The New Republic.* https://newrepublic.com/article/122965/can-billion-dollar-corpor ation-zappos-be-self-organized. Accessed 23 July 2021.

Jacob, D., & Neuhäuser, C. (2018). Workplace democracy, market competition and republican self-respect. *Ethical Theory and Moral Practice, 21*(4), 927–944.

Kastelle, T. (2013). Hierarchy is overrated. *Harvard Business Review.* https:// hbr.org/2013/11/hierarchy-is-overrated. Accessed 23 July 2021.

Kates, M. (2015). The ethics of sweatshops and the limits of choice. *Business Ethics Quarterly, 25*(2), 191–212.

Kates, M. (2019). Sweatshops, exploitation, and the case for a fair wage. *Journal of Political Philosophy, 27*(1), 26–47.

Khan, M. S., Khan, I., Qureshi, Q. A., Ismail, H. M., Rauf, H., Latif, A., & Tahir, M. (2015). The styles of leadership: A critical review. *Public Policy and Administration Research*, *5*(3), 87–92.

Kohler, T. C. (1994). Civic virtue at work: Unions as seedbeds of the civic virtues. *Boston College Law Review*, *36*, 279–304.

Kolodny, N. (2014). Rule over none II: Social equality and the justification of democracy. *Philosophy & Public Affairs*, *42*(4), 287–336. doi:10.1111/papa. 12037.

Kotow, E. (2019, October 21). How realistic is a leaderless organization? *Hedgetrade.com*. https://hedgetrade.com/how-realistic-is-a-leaderless-organization/. Accessed 23 July 2021.

Kraft, K., Stank, J., & Dewenter, R. (2011). Codetermination and innovation. *Cambridge Journal of Economics*, *35*(1), 145–172.

Landemore, H., & Ferreras, I. (2016). In defense of workplace democracy: Towards a justification of the firm-state analogy. *Political Theory*, *44*(1), 53–81. doi:10.1177/0090591715600035.

Levin, H. (2006). Worker democracy and worker productivity. *Social Justice Research*, *19*(1), 109–121.

Lippert-Rasmussen, K. (2018). *Relational egalitarianism: Living as equals*. Cambridge, UK: Cambridge University Press.

Lovett, F. N. (2001). Domination: A preliminary analysis. *The Monist*, *84*(1), 98–112.

Maner, J. (2016). Good Bosses switch between two leadership styles. *Harvard Business Review*. https://hbr.org/2016/12/good-bosses-switch-between-two-leadership-styles. Accessed 6 Jan 2021.

Moriarty, J. (2018). Against pay secrecy. *Journal of Applied Philosophy*, *35*(4), 689–704.

O'Shea, T. (2020). Socialist republicanism. *Political Theory*, *48*(5), 548–572. doi:10.1177/0090591719876889.

Park, R., Kruse, D., & Sesil, J. (2004). Does employee ownership enhance firm survival. *Advances in the Economic Analysis of Participatory and Labor-Managed Firms*, *8*(1), 3–33.

Peterson, J. (2018). Want to get the most from your millennial employees? Start using 'leaderless teams'. *Inc.com* https://www.inc.com/joel-peterson/millennials-are-independent-flexible-heres-how-you-can-turn-that-into-an-advantage.html. Accessed 23 July 2021.

Pettit, P. (2005). The domination complaint. *Nomos*, *46*, 87–117.

Renaud, S. (2007). Dynamic efficiency of supervisory board codetermination in Germany. *Labour*, *21*(4–5), 689–712.

Rosenfeld, J., & Kleykamp, M. (2012). Organized labor and racial wage inequality in the United States. *AJS: American Journal of Sociology, 117*(5), 1460–1502. doi:10.1086/663673.

Ross, C. (2011). *The leaderless revolution: How ordinary people will take power and change politics in the 21st century.* New York: Simon & Schuster.

Swanner, N. (2018). Why holacracy is such a poor management structure. *Dice Insights.* https://insights.dice.com/2018/08/03/holacracy-tech-compan ies-poor-choice/. Accessed 23 July 2021.

Tomasi, J. (2013). *Free market fairness.* Princeton, NJ: Princeton University Press.

11

Who Sustains Whose Passion?

Marjo Siltaoja and Suvi Heikkinen

Introduction

This chapter invites the reader to ponder the thoughts on position in between leader-centered management (LCM) and leaderless management (LLM). In particular, we are concerned how portraying passionate individuals as necessary for organizational success contribute to this debate. We situate our provocation as a part of trending discussion, according to which all organizations need passionate employees and how this allegedly results in leaderless management, something we perceive

M. Siltaoja (✉) · S. Heikkinen
Jyväskylä University School of Business and Economics (JSBE), University of Jyväskylä, Jyväskylä, Finland
e-mail: marjo.siltaoja@jyu.fi

S. Heikkinen
e-mail: suvi.s.heikkinen@jyu.fi

© The Author(s), under exclusive license to Springer Nature Switzerland AG 2022
F. Hertel et al. (eds.), *Debating Leaderless Management*,
Palgrave Debates in Business and Management,
https://doi.org/10.1007/978-3-031-04593-6_11

as a phenomenon that places emphasis on individual's self-management and leaderless organizing, making leader-figures unnecessary. However, we argue that such discussion silences from situations when the purpose of passionate individuals is actually to enforce the passions of a leader-figure, resulting in more leader-centered management. We do not take a stance here on whether LLM is better than LCM. We are more concerned whether passion discourse is a wolf in sheep's clothing-used to obscure the relation between LLM and LCM.

We build our provocation on what such discussions on passion in organizations entail and on the other remain silent on. The hunt for passion as a leader attribute was first mainstreamed in the influential consultancy book by Peters and Austin (1985). In the contemporary consultancy industry, the argument has been extended from leaders to all members through arguments that future knowledge-oriented "organizations need workers with passion to realize extreme sustained performance improvement" (Bersin 2013, p. 5). Management books continue to promote organizations, such as Patagonia, as exemplary firms in combining individual passion, tenets of leaderless organization, and of course, sustainability (Sisodia et al. 2003). Scholars have further shown how some modern-day organizations discursively emphasize passion, play, and fun at work (Fleming and Sturdy 2009). The central idea is that people who are deeply connected to a cause do not need directives, rewards, or leaders to tell them what to do because inflamed and passionate people are inspiring and productive. Thus, leaderless organizations are borne because of such self-driven organizing, making leader-figures unnecessary.

However, we argue that harnessing passion does not generate merely positive results. Passion-driven people can engage in extreme means to support their causes and perform in their work (Wheatley 2007). Accordingly, there are more ethical complexities than the current discourse suggests. Our argument builds on two elements that tend to remain silent in the promotion of passion. First, the idea of passionate individuals has been legitimized with the underlying claim pertaining to how passion would strive people to do the "right things." However, that is a dangerous simplification. For example, studies on terrorist organizations have brought forward the unifying element of members' passion and individualism for collective behavior (Freeman 2014; Kruglanski et al. 2013; Wheatley 2007). Thus, passion does not guarantee that pursued aims would be right, nor that those aims would be pursued in an appropriate manner. Second, passion seems to be the twenty-first-century label used to replace charisma. More specifically, charisma has been perceived hard to acquire but passion is marketed as approachable and reachable for every individual, as people just need to find their passion! However, whether it is just an old idea rephrased to maintain organizational power hierarchies needs more attention.

We elaborate our argumentations through scholarly literature by discussing how emphasis on passion does not automatically translate into ethical behavior or leaderless organizations. Our empirical illustration comes from the field of high-performance sports, which is generally promoted as a field where passion is considered a necessity for success. In our empirical section, we examine how people define attributes of passionate leader and leadership style, in which we focus on a central leader-figure in the upper echelons of Finnish sport management. In our discussion section, we elaborate on why passionate leader behaviors might be misaligned with collectively shared and negotiated ethical practice. We end by discussing whether and how shared leadership could help solve some of the ethical tensions.

What Is Passion About in Organizations?

Even though contemporary societal discourse emphasizes and promotes passion and the need for engagement in order for us to thrive as good leaders or as ideal workers in the workplace, this has definitely not always been the case. The English word "passion" has its roots in the Latin "passio," which means "suffering" (Höpfl and Linstead 1993). Traditionally, the passions widely referred to emotions. Aristotle perceived passion as a part of desire; thymos—meaning passion—carries the sense of "heart," "courage," or "spirit" in relation to life and strong feeling (Linstead and Brewis 2007). Later, philosophers were particularly concerned about the relationship between reason and emotion. For example, for Immanuel Kant (2013, 2016), passions were desires, yet they were somehow evil, and illnesses of the mind prohibited people from engaging with reason and moral behavior. The understanding and conceptualization of passion then began to have an important role in controlling human behavior. This discussion, however, took a turn, as philosophers argued that passions (emotions, desires) stand for liberation and act as a source of self-knowledge, self-control, and power over others, moving away from the treatment of passions as something one must restrain if being virtuous (Gherardi et al. 2007; Thanem 2013). Thus, philosophers have, in a sense, debated whether emotions, such as passion, are problematic or whether they motivate or drive us toward pursuing unethical outcomes. As Linstead and Brewis (2007, p. 352) point out that passion is not a wholly pleasant concept. It may involve pain and, in its more obsessive forms, can consume, displace, even destroy the self or others the pursuit of something external or transcendent. In addition, passion is also always related to other(ness) meaning that the more we know about the material or phenomenological worlds of other people, the more we can locate them in relation to our own so that, at the very least, we are able to act in relation to them without personal risk (Linstead and Brewis 2007).

Social psychologists have treated passion as something that helps direct one's attention and actions (e.g., Vallerand 2012). Passion is thus a motivational construct that contains affective, cognitive, and behavioral components. For example, Vallerand et al. (2003) defined passion as "a strong inclination toward an activity that people like, that they find important, and in which they invest time and energy" (Vallerand et al. 2003, p. 756). Recent scholarly work has promoted the idea that there exist two different forms of passion: harmonious and obsessive. For example, harmonious passion in working life and for work refers to willed, controllable job integration, in which work is seen as important but not all-consuming (Bélanger et al. 2013; Vallerand et al. 2003). In contrast, an obsessive passion for work refers to a strong and uncontrollable urge to partake in work despite experiencing dysfunctional consequences. In the organizational setting, this dualistic assumption of passion focuses on how work is internalized in an individual's identity (in a controlled or a pressured way) and whether the person has control over their engagement at work. Thus, it is different from the idea of whether the action or target of passion is ethically valid or a preferable thing to do.

Passion and (Mis)alignment with Ethics and Leaderless Organizations

Perhaps the most influential leadership theory that promotes passion as a feature of leadership is charismatic leadership (see Burns 1978). Charismatic leaders summon their subjects through "an emotional form of communal relationship" (Weber 1947, p. 360) by expressing passionate emotions to attract passionate followers toward social and organizational change. The central idea of charismatic leadership emphasizes a leader's ability to engage in symbolic behavior and visionary and inspirational messages, and appeal to their subordinates' values and stimulate them intellectually. Thus, such behavior is perceived as providing meaningfulness to the workplace beyond traditional incentives. However, charismatic leadership literature is far from promoting leaderless management but on the contrary, emphasizes leaders passion and personal influence as focal methods.

Studies on passionate leadership have not received similar attention as a single construct as charismatic leadership has (see for a review Banks et al. 2017). However, Linstead and Brewis (2007) argued that the prevalent interpretation of passion in the literature of organizations is teleological (i.e., that of a powerful, purposive motivation to achieve an end result). For example, passion is perceived as a success factor of educational leadership (e.g., Blackmore 2004; Davies and Brighouse 2008; Day 2004) and is further associated with an enthusiasm for achievement, collaboration, trust, care, and inclusivity. The literature further tends to build on the assumption that leaders will be more successful at inspiring and motivating followers by being in touch with and leading through their own passions. However, studies have also found that passionate leaders typically ignore the fact that followers may not share the leader's passion (Munro and Thanem 2018; Thanem 2013) or that they exploit their own passions to engender ecstatic dedication and excessive performance in their followers (Sosik 2005). Additionally, studies have also shown how a passionate manager can cast the employees in passive roles in terms of developing new ideas and acting innovatively, as leaders want innovation to be developed according to their passionate view (Aromaa et al. 2020). However, when the collectively shared passion is missing, followers may instead be irritated, frustrated, and demotivated (Thanem 2013), and this can lead to ethical tensions. As Munro and Thanem (2018) argue, the existing research on ethical leadership does not currently fully acknowledge the problems inherent in passionate leaders or leading passions ethically.

Therefore, we must ask ourselves, does passionate leadership equal charismatic leadership? Both approaches do rely on people's affective tendencies. A crucial difference we suggest here is that charisma is generally perceived as an individual attribute promoting the leader's influence and is not generally attached to leaderless organizations whereas passion is perceived both as an individual and a collective attribute and promoted as a mean to generate both leader-focused and leaderless organizations. However, aforementioned studies show that rather than enabling self-management and leaderless management, passionate managers enforce leader-centric management. The assumption of leaderless activity comes particularly from studies that have examined passion as a shared attribute among activist (see, e.g., Scully and Segal 2002). However, activist organizations are often romanticized and the ways of interaction in these organizations may or may not correspond to those of business organizations (see Chowdhury et al. 2021). Both charismatic and passionate leadership approaches further tend to underplay the ethical capacities of followers by presuming that they are in need of direction or care by some great leader who guides them to be passionate or visionary for the right causes. Accordingly, attributing too much faith in the ethical behaviors of passionate, charismatic leaders omits the fact that passion and charisma also feature irrationality (Beyer 1999), crisis (Tourish and Vatcha 2005), and resistance to change (Levay 2010). Thus, what end result passionate behavior seeks and how the focal target is achieved is at the core of our discussion pertaining to passionate behavior and ethicality in organizations; yet, this discussion tends to gain less space in the quest for passion. In the next section, we move on to our empirical illustration of a passionate leader in the field of sports.

Empirical Illustration of a Passionate Leader in Sport Management

We used the data of 40 sport leader interviews collected in a research project where decision-making in publicly funded top sport organizations in a Nordic country between the years 2016–2019 was examined. We applied stimulus-based interviews, in which participants are shown visual or textual materials and are asked to make sense of that stimulus. The example used here focuses on a specific photograph of a leader commonly labeled as "a passionate leader," a longstanding figure in the field of ice hockey. He, Kale as people call him, has had an extensive management career in national and international sport organizations for several decades (e.g., currently acting as a Vice President of the International Ice Hockey Federation). He has also been involved in politics as a former member of the Parliament of Finland from 1999 to 2003. In the national media and public discussion, he is one of the central figures one uses as an example of a passionate leader, but not when talking about ethical manner in leadership.

We asked respondents what they saw in the photo (in the photo, he was a recognizable person, having badges of honor attached to his suit) or what comes to mind when seeing the photo of the person in question. The respondents then described the character of this person, his leadership styles, and his efforts for the sporting community. While some had a close personal relationship with him, for others he was more of an icon, a person they had met but had not worked with in close proximity. In our analysis, we wanted to understand how ethicality was aligned with conceptions of a passionate leadership style. We analyzed the attributes used to describe Kale as a leadership figure and his leadership style, as well as what were not attached to either of these dimensions.

Findings

Our data shows that the passionate leader in question was portrayed as a strong-minded person, a leader with a clear mind-set regarding leadership, and a person who stands for his determination and does his work efficiently. He is described as an internationally acknowledged leadership figure and is referred to as impressive and powerful; above all, he is seen as passionate for sports. He was also perceived as reliable, as he does not shy away from difficult situations. In the data, interviewee 1 (*E1*) reflected on this by saying, "In difficult situations, this man does not hide. And I appreciate that. [...] Of course, Kale has his own reputation, the reputation of the iron chancellor, his decision-making is probably quite straightforward, such as a strong-willed person is likely to have." Interestingly, he was often described with strong images, such as the iron chancellor (a common nickname for him in the national media), patron, dictator, big shot, or master of the house.

Indeed, the passionate leader was valued and admired through his performance and achievements, and in particular, the economic wealth and success he created for the country's ice hockey federation. His leadership style is described as someone who clears the way, authoritarian, arrogant, and strategic, but simultaneously as impulsive and preferring ad hoc thinking. Thus, the attributes placed him as the top and front figure in the field. Part of his "charm" was that he was seen as "traditional" and "strong," giving off an impression of a steady and successful, yet authoritarian leader. The adjectives used to describe his style were firm, unethical, resolved, straight, frightening, and determined, all of which grounded his leader-centered position in the sport organization. Thus, he has achieved what he had pursued in the field. In the valuation of his style, outcome mattered more than the process—successful outcomes legitimized his acts. His leadership style was referred to as an "old" model, yet it was not contested.

Interestingly, the respondents tended to justify his leadership style in terms of how they knew him by person, which was in contradiction and distanced from his leadership style. The following quotations from two separate interviewees (*E2* and *E4*) illustrate these contradictions: "When I worked as a board member, I came to know him in person, as a person, he is an amazing sport leader; he is so passionate about it. Thus, if the image is of this old, cartridge-like, dictatorial leader that this is being sought, then I don't agree with such opinion... because he has a lot of warm heart in him" (*E2*) and "He is a really a nice person...like in person, he has a sense of humor, he is tolerant and kind. Then, when he opens his mouth in this [leader] role, there is no limit, no limit. He has done a lot of good work for sports, especially for hockey" (*E3*). Although the achievements were admired, the majority of the respondents raised ethical and moral concerns in relation to achieving these goals and how such a leadership style was outdated.

The leader's passion for sport was perceived as the foreground of his leadership. He was described as a sportsman with big "S," a man who took every breath for sports. His leadership style was described as straightforward—excluding women and those who are not a part of the inner circle. It was even said that he is not willing to talk to every woman, and that some people are or "should be" actually frightened of him. An illustration from an interviewee (*E5*) points this out: "Like first of all, female leaders are afraid of Kale. Not all even dare to talk to him. And he does not talk to all the women." In the data, he was described as a leader who is an impulsive bulldozer, or as a gambler who favors his "guys" and his "inner" circle. His strong masculine image was never questioned in the data, yet it was more commonly boosted. As a result, he was perceived as an efficient, yet despotic leader who favors top-down management— him in the lead—without asking any other opinions. Yet, the empirical illustration points out that this type of leadership ability, to make "bad" or unfavorable decisions, is admired if it generates positive results for the predetermined target.

In particular, when ethics was discussed, the passionate leader-figure seemed to be lacking central attributes. In the data, this meant that the passionate leader was described as missing the participatory, open, and transparent processes of decision-making. The respondents, despite their praise, claimed that the leaders of today should have an interactional approach with constant interaction and discussion with followers. Integral to the type of leadership were mentoring and coaching. Adjectives such as equal, inclusive, open, transparent, dynamic, trustworthy, honest, talkative, professional, ethical, moral, sustainable, and change-seeking were not related to the passionate patron leader, but to future leadership- something that respondents expected to take place after the passionate leader leaves his position. The "new" leaders were expected to have an emphasis on group achievement and equality, and that leaders would be easily approachable. These types of leaders no one mentioned by name but seemed to await. However, for a small minority in high positions, this "iron grip leader method" represented the only path to success, perceiving that the future would still "rest on the shoulders of passionate leaders such as Kale who give all their effort and time for developing sport."

To sum up, as passion is related to something or someone, passionate leaders in our data were valued as being passionate about sport and achieving the (predetermined) end results for the sake of the sport, and not for how responsibly they acted as a leader. The attributes attached to passionate leaders in scholarly literature, such as an enthusiasm for achievement, collaboration, commitment, trust, and inclusivity, were not the central attributes attached to the leadership style illustrated in our case example, whereas attributes such as inner circle, determination, unethical behavior, sole decision-maker, and maintenance of organizational inequality gained much more emphasis. Of course, the presented data here was based on the figure and leadership style of one individual in one specific ice hockey context, and the limitations should be acknowledged accordingly. Next, we move on to discuss what can be learned from this empirical illustration.

Passion and Ethical Organizations: Toward Shared Leadership

Howell and Avolio's (1992) article of nearly 30 years ago states as follows: "Wanted: Corporate Leaders. Must have vision and ability to build corporate culture. Mere managers need not apply" (p. 43). Accordingly, this suggests that little has changed in the search for excellent leaders. The quest has only moved from charismatic leaders to passionate leaders, yet the underlying message is still the same.

We have sought to argue here that emphasis on passion does not equal with leaderless organizations but can actually enforce leader-figure-centric management. The reliance on one's passionate drive can bypass many ethical issues prevalent in organizations (Brown et al. 2005). The questions that remain are as follows: Why does passion actually translate into leader-centered activity? Why is it hard to connect passion with shared, democratic leadership even though it might be a possible path? One reason is that we might force the phenomenon to be a part of collectives that it actually does not fit well for. More specifically, the literature suggests how one needs to develop one's passion, but in the organizational reality, the targets and purposes of organizations are already set. This means that individuals should then make their passion "fit" within the organizational targets, which can be complex. In addition, the management literature still relies on the ability of passionate leaders to make others alike. More specifically, we found that because individuals' passions have been known to generate self-striven motivation, the management literature is interested in how to harness such passion for the sake of the organizational bottom line. This means that the literature tends to cherry pick romanticized ideals from grassroots communities and how these communities are borne around a shared common goal and how they pursue this goal passionately despite scarce resources. However, grassroots organizations feature a number of struggles over power, leadership, and shared goals (Chowdhury et al. 2021), yet these features are less emphasized in romantic translations to business organizations.

Another reason for the complexity of creating passionate leaderless organizations is in the individualization of passion. Particularly, in the media, passionate individuals are narrated as people who kept going against the mainstream, persisted in following their own path, and in the end, were somehow victorious. Indeed, being passionate does not automatically translate into more favorable treatment, even in the world of business (Chen et al. 2009). Furthermore, the stories behind visionaries, such as Elon Musk, Steve Jobs, and Mark Zuckerberg, are portrayed as passionate leaders and individuals who tend to be more about the pursuit of individual visions than emphasis on ethics in organizational relations.

We suggest that in future organizations, we do not need a complete transition to leaderless management where people are self-managed by their "passions," nor do we need strong leader-focused management where managers tell people how and for what should they be passionate about. We need discussions and debates on shared leadership centered on what kind of targets can be collectively generated, what collective behaviors are ethical ones, and how one can ensure that these targets and behaviors, particularly if passionately pursued, can be pursued in an ethical manner. This then means a more in-depth focus on the cultural, social, and moral norms what is perceived as passion and what ethical harnessing of passion means (see Turner 2009). No organizational member can be forced to share a passion for something that is predetermined. Passion is also temporal. Being constantly passionate over something can be energizing, but also consuming. Organizational members may well reject the passionate claims exhorted by management and choose to distance themselves from this (Holmer-Nadesan 1996). Therefore, we need accountable leaders more than we need passionate leaders. As an extension to passionate organizations, we need ethically aware organizations who are concerned and willing to foster ethics as central, not peripheral, modes of collective work.

References

Aromaa, E., Hytti, U., & Aaltonen, S. (2020). The dark side of entrepreneurial passion. In A. Örtenblad (Ed.), *Against entrepreneurship* (pp. 185–201). London: Palgrave Macmillan.

Banks, G. C., Engemann, K. N., Williams, C. E., Gooty, J., McCauley, K. D., & Medaugh, M. R. (2017). A meta-analytic review and future research agenda of charismatic leadership. *The Leadership Quarterly, 28*(4), 508–529. doi:10.1016/j.leaqua.2016.12.003.

Bélanger, J. J., Lafrenière, M. A. K., Vallerand, R. J., & Kruglanski, A. W. (2013). When passion makes the heart grow colder: The role of passion in alternative goal suppression. *Journal of Personality and Social Psychology, 104*(1), 126–147. doi:10.1037/a0029679.

Bersin, J. (2013). *Predictions for 2014*. Bersin by Deloitte Consulting LLP.

Beyer, J. M. (1999). Taming and promoting charisma to change organizations. *The Leadership Quarterly, 10*(2), 307–330. doi:10.1016/S1048-984 3(99)00019-3.

Blackmore, J. (2004). Restructuring educational leadership in changing contexts: A local/global account of restructuring in Australia. *Journal of Educational Change, 5*(3), 267–288. doi:10.1023/B:JEDU.0000041044. 62626.99.

Brown, M. E., Treviño, L. K., & Harrison, D. A. (2005). Ethical leadership: A social learning perspective for construct development and testing. *Organizational Behavior and Human Decision Processes, 97*(2), 117–134. doi:10.1016/j.obhdp.2005.03.002.

Burns, J. M. (1978). *Leadership*. New York: Harper & Row.

Chen, X. P., Yao, X., & Kotha, S. (2009). Entrepreneur passion and preparedness in business plan presentations: A persuasion analysis of venture capitalists' funding decisions. *Academy of Management Journal, 52*(1), 199–214. doi:10.5465/amj.2009.36462018.

Chowdhury, R., Kourula, A., & Siltaoja, M. (2021). Power of paradox: Grassroots organizations' legitimacy strategies over time. *Business & Society, 60*(2), 420–453. doi:10.1177/0007650318816954.

Day, C. (2004). *A passion for teaching*. London: Routledge.

Davies, B., & Brighouse, T. (Eds.). (2008). *Passionate leadership in education*. London: Sage.

Freeman, M. (2014). A theory of terrorist leadership (and its consequences for leadership targeting). *Terrorism and Political Violence, 26*(4), 666–687.

Fleming, P., & Sturdy, A. (2009). "Just be yourself!": Towards neo-normative control in organisations. *Employee Relations, 31*(6), 569–583. doi:10.1108/01425450910991730.

Gherardi, S., Nicolini, D., & Strati, A. (2007). The passion for knowing. *Organization, 14*(3), 315–329. doi:10.1177/1350508407076146.

Holmer-Nadesan, N. (1996). Organizational identity and space of action. *Organization Studies, 17*(1), 49–81. doi:10.1177/017084069601700103.

Höpfl, H., & Linstead, S. (1993). *Emotion in organizations*. London: Sage.

Howell, J. M., & Avolio, B. J. (1992). The ethics of charismatic leadership: Submission or liberation? *Academy of Management Perspectives, 6*(2), 43–54.

Linstead, S., & Brewis, J. (2007). Passion, knowledge and motivation: Ontologies of desire. *Organization, 14*(3), 351–371. doi:10.1177/1350508407076149.

Kant, I. ([1788]2013). *Puhtaan järjen kritiikki. Suom. Markus Nikkarla*. Helsinki: Gaudeamus.

Kant, I. ([1781/1787]2016). *Käytännöllisen järjen kritiikki. Suom. Markus Nikkarla*. Helsinki: Gaudeamus.

Kruglanski, A. W., Bélanger, J. J., Gelfand, M., Gunaratna, R., Hettiarachchi, M., Reinares, F., Orehek, E., Sasota, J., & Sharvit, K. (2013). Terrorism—A (self) love story: Redirecting the significance quest can end violence. *American Psychologist, 68*(7), 559–575. doi:10.1037/a0032615.

Levay, C. (2010). Charismatic leadership in resistance to change. *The Leadership Quarterly*, *21*(1), 127–143. doi:10.1016/j.leaqua.2009.10.010.

Munro, I., & Thanem, T. (2018). The ethics of affective leadership: Organizing good encounters without leaders. *Business Ethics Quarterly*, *28*(1), 51–69. doi:10.1017/beq.2017.34.

Peters, T. J., & Austin, N. (1985). *A passion for excellence: The leadership difference*. New York: Random House.

Scully, M., & Segal, A. (2002). Passion with an umbrella: Grassroots activists in the workplace. In M. Lounsbury & M. Ventresca (Eds.), *Social structure and organizations revisited*. Bingley, UK: Emerald Group Publishing.

Sisodia, R., Wolfe, D., & Sheth, J. N. (2003). *Firms of endearment: How world-class companies profit from passion and purpose*. Hoboken, NY: Pearson Prentice Hall.

Sosik, J. J. (2005). The role of personal values in the charismatic leadership of corporate managers: A model and preliminary field study. *The Leadership Quarterly*, *16*(2), 221–244. doi:10.1016/j.leaqua.2005.01.002.

Thanem, T. (2013). More passion than the job requires? Monstrously transgressive leadership in the promotion of health at work. *Leadership*, *9*(3), 396–415. doi:10.1177/1742715013486037.

Tourish, D., & Vatcha, N. (2005). Charismatic leadership and corporate cultism at Enron: The elimination of dissent, the promotion of conformity and organizational collapse. *Leadership*, *1*(4), 455–480. doi:10.1177/1742715005057671.

Turner, J. H. (2009). The sociology of emotions: Basic theoretical arguments. *Emotion Review*, *1*(4), 340–354. doi:10.1177/1754073909338305.

Vallerand, R. J. (2012). The role of passion in sustainable psychological well-being. *Psychology of Well-Being: Theory, Research and Practice*, *2*(1), 1–21. doi:10.1186/2211-1522-2-1.

Vallerand, R. J., Blanchard, C., Mageau, G. A., Koestner, R., Ratelle, C., Léonard, M., ... & Marsolais, J. (2003). Les passions de l'ame: on obsessive and harmonious passion. *Journal of Personality and Social Psychology*, *85*(4), 756–767.

Weber, M. (1947). *The theory of social and economic organization*. New York: Oxford University Press.

Wheatley, M. J. (2007). Leadership of self-organized networks lessons from the war on terror. *Performance Improvement Quarterly*, *20*(2), 59–66. doi:10.1111/j.1937-8327.2007.tb00440.x.

12

Leaderless Organization Versus Leading for Creativity: The Case for Creative Leadership

Camille A. McKayle

Introduction

We are living in what is often described as a VUCA world, filled with *v*olatility, *u*ncertainty, *c*omplexity, and *a*mbiguity. This acronym has made its way into business writings, though it started in the Army War College in the mid-1980s. Few would argue that the description does not fit our current circumstances. Though the use of the acronym might lead us to thinking about VUCA as one state, each of the four states is different from the others and requires a different approach. Thus, to be successful today, we need to adopt a leadership approach that will be able to address volatility, uncertainty, complexity, and ambiguity in a natural way. To be effective, I argue that one must be deliberate in the approach to leadership.

C. A. McKayle (✉)
University of the Virgin Islands, St. Thomas, VI, USA
e-mail: cmckayl@uvi.edu

© The Author(s), under exclusive license to Springer Nature
Switzerland AG 2022
F. Hertel et al. (eds.), *Debating Leaderless Management*,
Palgrave Debates in Business and Management,
https://doi.org/10.1007/978-3-031-04593-6_12

Creativity in organizations and innovation in output are often the goal of leadership. Leaderless management, or leaderless leadership, seeks to flatten the hierarchy in organizations and decentralize decision making (see, e.g., Kotow 2019). It leans on self-management and participatory democracy. Often, this leads to creativity and innovation, and sets up a situation where organizations are flexible and better able to address volatility, uncertainty, complexity, and ambiguity. A creative leadership approach is one in which there is a deliberate guidance of the team toward working together to realize novel and innovative outcomes (Puccio et al. 2011). The creative leadership stance from which I approach this debate is one in which the leader is creative and leads for creativity. When provided the choice between a leaderless approach and a creative leadership approach that is intentional in its application, my position is that the creative leadership approach will be more effective and predictable in realizing innovative outcomes than a leaderless management approach.

In this chapter, we will first look at various views of leadership and leaders with the intent to give context to leadership. The needs of the twenty-first-century workplace will be explored, as this is what has primarily given rise to the need for a new type of leadership. We will review leaderless leadership and creative leadership as two approaches that could address the needs of the twenty-first-century workplace, especially with an eye toward creativity and innovation. The resulting conclusion is that a more direct and effective way to achieve creativity from groups and innovation from organizations is through creative leadership.

Leadership Defined

The concept of leadership is one that has long been studied. Many see leadership as a way to have influence over others. Thus, a deep understanding of leadership can lead one to amass power or create change, for better or for worse. Northouse (2016) explores the evolution of leadership definitions, starting with the early 1900s through to the twenty-first century. Early on, leadership was seen as domination over others, leading to obedience and loyalty. The emphasis was on control. The focus on qualities that individuals (primarily male) possess, and especially from the point of view that leaders were born with these traits or qualities, is sometimes referred to as the Great Man theory of leadership (Puccio et al. 2011, p. 6). The definition has gone through periods where the emphasis was on the traits of the individual and how those traits interacted with the group, as well as an emphasis on the behavior of the person. Common to those definitions of leadership was the ability to influence or persuade others (rather than dominating them). By the 1960s, there was agreement on the definition as "behavior that influences people toward shared goals" (Northouse 2016, p. 3). By the 1970s, leadership was viewed from the organizational standpoint. The goals of the organization were seen to be held by both leaders and followers, and leadership involved mobilizing groups and organizations to achieve organizational goals (Northouse 2016, p. 3). From the 1980s to present, the subject of leadership has become more nuanced and more diverse. Though influence and individual traits are still seen as important, there are discussions about the difference between leadership and management, as well as analysis of various leadership approaches.

Northouse (2016) adopts the following definition of leadership to discuss various approaches and theories of leadership: "Leadership is a process whereby an individual influences a group of individuals to achieve a common goal" (p. 6). Puccio et al. (2011, pp. 6–11) look at various contemporary leadership theories, as well as various leadership myths. They focus on leadership as a collection of skills and traits, and note that leadership is not about position, but about what people do. The practices of leadership posited by Kouzes and Posner (2017; Kouzes et al. 2010) are also held up as exemplary: Model the Way; Inspire a Shared Vision; Challenge the Process; Enable Others to Act; and Encourage the Heart.

With the abundance of writing about leadership, Winston and Patterson (2006) sought to understand leadership as a whole by looking at 160 books and articles with a definition or construct of leadership. They hoped to synthesize this information to arrive at an integrative definition of leadership. Their definition starts with the following:

A leader is one or more people who selects, equips, trains, and influences one or more follower(s) who have diverse gifts, abilities, and skills and focuses the follower(s) to the organization's mission and objectives causing the follower(s) to willingly and enthusiastically expend spiritual, emotional, and physical energy in a concerted, coordinated effort to achieve the organizational mission and objectives (Winston and Patterson 2006).

The definition goes on to describe the process of leadership, including how leaders exert influence, how they interact with others, and how they grow as leaders. Throughout this integrative definition, however, is still the assumption that there are leaders and there are followers, reflecting the historical approach to defining leadership through the focus on leaders.

Why Rethink Leadership: Twenty-First-Century Organizations

It is difficult to discuss leadership without noting that twenty-first-century organizations and factors are vastly different from those of the 1900s. Uhl-Bien et al. (2007) remind us that we have shifted from the industrial era to the knowledge era and thus need a different approach to leadership. They posit that leadership should be seen as an "emergent, interactive dynamic" and base their framework in the field of complexity adaptive systems. Thus, leadership is distinguished from leaders and is seen more as a process. In recognition of the new organizational structures and units of the knowledge era, Uhl-Bien et al. (2007) develop *Complexity Leadership Theory* which incorporates bottom-up behavior and systems needed to respond to the "dynamics of interdependent learning, creativity, and adaptability." In this complexity leadership theory, there are three leadership functions: "adaptive, administrative, and enabling." The adaptive function refers to the dynamics that occur between "agents." The administrative leadership function refers to the more managerial tasks, including budgets, structuring tasks, etc., but also encompasses some areas that are often seen as leadership roles, such as building vision. The enabling function focuses on the environment that will ensure that the other two leadership functions (adaptive and administrative) are able to flourish. The administrative functions are in line with a top-down view of leadership, while the adaptive function may be less formal. The interplay between these functions will depend on the nature of the conditions that the organization faces. When viewed this way, context is important for leadership. "Adaptive leadership is not an act of an individual, but rather a dynamic of interdependent agents" (Uhl-Bien et al., p. 307). These complex networks produce creativity and adaptability. One recognizes adaptive leadership through its impact.

There seems to be uniform agreement that future organizations will not look like past organizations. Many point to the rapidly changing environment that will require organizations to adjust quickly and be continuously adaptable. Kotter (2012, p. 169) addresses this head on when describing organizations of the future, noting that given the predicted increase in environmental volatility, what we now know as standard organizations will be a thing of the past. There will be what Kotter refers to as a persistent sense of urgency. Given this, organizations will have to embrace greater distribution of data, thus creating more honesty and transparency. There must be greater candor within the organization, and greater reliance on teamwork. He also refers to promoting a team, with persons with big egos less likely to rise. There must be greater empowerment of all members of the organization, as everyone's knowledge will be needed to address quickly changing environments. Organizations will become flatter and leaner. Kotter (2012, p. 23) describes an eight-stage process for managing change: establishing a sense of urgency; creating the guiding coalition; developing a vision and strategy; communicating the change vision; empowering broad-based action; generating short-term wins; consolidating gains and producing more change; and anchoring new approaches in the culture. The organizations of the twenty-first century will find themselves in constant change, thus continuously managing change.

Organizational Creativity and Innovation

In addition to being in a state of constant change, twenty-first-century organizations are also focused on innovation. Focus on change and innovation are, in fact, connected (Puccio and Cabra 2010). The authors go on to note that, because we are living in a world that is undergoing change at a "breakneck pace," if organizations do not change, they will be left behind. However, the ways in which an organization changes are through its people. If employees are not able to adapt, then the organization cannot. It is for this reason that there is increased emphasis on creativity and creative problem-solving skills in the workplace. Anderson et al. (2014) propose the following integrative definition of creativity and innovation:

> Creativity and innovation at work are the process, outcomes, and products of attempts to develop and introduce new and improved ways of doing things. The creativity stage of this process refers to idea generation, and innovation to the subsequent stage of implementing ideas toward better procedures, practices, or products. Creativity and innovation can occur at the level of the individual, work team, organization, or at more than one of these levels combined, but will invariably result in identifiable benefits at one or more of these levels of analysis.

This definition shows the inextricable link between creativity and innovation. Creativity is one of the more highly sought-after skills in the twenty-first-century workplace (Puccio et al. 2018, p. xiv; Reiter-Palmon et al. 2019). Thus, crucial for leading in today's world is doing so in such a way as to maximize creativity both at the individual and the organizational levels.

Toward a Creative Outcome: Leaderless Leadership and Creative Leadership

After years of study of leaders and leadership, attention now turns to describing and studying leaderless organization. We note that the Winston and Patterson's (2006) exhaustive and integrative definition of leadership was based on a review of 160 articles and books, which led to more than 1000 constructs categorized into over 90 dimensions of leadership. When contemplating a "leaderless" organization, there needs to be an understanding of what is being discussed. With so many constructs for leadership, might there be an amalgamation or combination of existing ones that would lead to the outcomes desired in a leaderless organization?

Many leaderless leadership models are proposed as a way of moving away from a top-down approach and toward a peer-based approach. Nielsen (2004) equates leaderless companies with peer-based organizations (loc. 77). In a peer-based organization, everyone is on equal standing with regard to decision making and information sharing (loc. 1705). Nielsen posits that the three "hallmarks" of peer-based strategy are shared decision making; employee wisdom privileged over outsider wisdom; and information sharing throughout the organization (loc. 1711).

Brafman and Beckstrom (2006) describe the difference between a centralized (coercive) system and a decentralized one by using the analogy of the spider and the starfish. The two organisms appear to have a great deal in common, with appendages, etc. However, they are vastly different. The analogy of the spider describes an organization where the decision making is centralized. If the head of the spider goes, then so does its ability to move forward. In contrast, the starfish moves forward by convincing all parts that this is the way to go. Each appendage mimics the whole and is at the same level as any of the others. If one piece of the starfish is damaged, the organism can regenerate. In particular, if an appendage is cut off, two new starfish will result, with each piece regenerating to become the whole.

Brafman and Beckstrom (2006) describe the five legs that are integral to a successfully decentralized, open system: circles, which have no hierarchy or structure and members are inspired to contribute to the best of their abilities; catalysts, who may start a circle, but who then step back and the circle operates on its own, with ownership transferred to the circle; ideology, which offers a sense of community, hence leading members to join a circle; a pre-existing network, which may serve as a launchpad for the decentralized organization; and a champion, who is "relentless in promoting a new idea" (loc. 1021). Whereas the catalyst champions and inspires, the effort is less overt compared to the effort of the champion.

Other approaches, such that of Carne Ross in *The Leaderless Revolution*, make the case for "participatory democracy" (Ovans 2012) where decisions are made through "civilized debate." The experiment at Zappos under CEO Tony Hsieh (Hodge 2015) focused on Holacracy, a system of self-management, which led to Hsieh making a bold move of doing away with all the people managers. Interestingly, the word Holacracy comes from the concept of a holon, which is like a fractal (Hodge 2015). Fractals are self-replicating forms, where each piece is a replica of the whole. This is the same concept used in describing the starfish organizations, as starfish are able to self-replicate even from a limb. Leaderless organizations are described as organizations where workers do not need to be "babysat" (Kotow 2019).

Creative Leadership

A review of research in creativity and leadership led to the conclusion that leadership is an important factor for enhancing or hindering creativity in the workplace (Hughes et al. 2018; Mumford et al. 2019). Though that review did not arrive at specific answers regarding leadership behaviors that foster workplace creativity (Hughes et al. 2018), there are other constructs that define creative leadership and that delineate the skills needed to lead for creativity.

The most established leadership theory that is most closely aligned with creative outcomes of followers is that of transformational leadership. Transformational leadership incorporates four factors: idealized influence; inspirational motivation; intellectual stimulation; and individualized consideration (Northouse 2016, p. 167). Puccio et al. (2011) note that there is a strong positive relationship between transformational leadership and team innovation. There are research studies that showed that leaders exhibiting transformational leadership behaviors contributed to individual and team creativity (Mumford et al. 2019). Creativity can be enhanced through the transformational leadership approach by, among other things, focusing intellectual stimulation on creativity. Creativity, or the ability to creatively solve problems, is seen as an essential workplace skill, and there are myriad studies that point to the fact that creativity is a teachable skill (Scott et al. 2004). Puccio et al. (2011) define Creative Leadership as:

> the ability to deliberately engage one's imagination to define and guide a group toward a novel goal—a direction that is new for the group. As a consequence of bringing about this creative change, creative leaders have a profoundly positive influence on their context ... and the individuals in that situation. (Puccio et al. 2011, p. 13)

The definition addresses the methods used, and the desired outcomes. Thus, the leader is called upon to utilize creativity in order to realize a creative outcome. Mumford et al. (2019) recognize that leading creative efforts can be quite complex and involves three key functions: leading the work; leading the group; and leading the firm. Taken together, these functions can yield a deeper understanding of what it takes to lead for creativity.

Creativity results from the interplay of person, process, product, and environment (press), known as the 4Ps of creativity (Rhodes 1961). Many articles point to the importance of the leader in creating the environment that results in a creative approach (Amabile and Khaire 2008; Hughes et al. 2018; Li and Yue 2019; Puccio et al. 2011; Zhou and George 2003). Anderson and West (1998) point out the importance of vision, participative safety, task orientation, and support for innovation. These four factors work together to create a climate for innovation. There are various leadership behaviors that can increase the likelihood of this climate arising. Leader creativity is essential (Li and Yue 2019), as it works to set an example for the team. There are known inhibitors of creativity in an environment, including bureaucracy, lack of resources, and time pressures, while Amabile and Kramer (2011, pp. 104–108) found seven major catalysts in the work environment: setting clear goals; allowing autonomy; providing resources; giving enough time; help with the work; learning from problems and successes; and allowing ideas to flow. Many of the advantages of "leaderless organizations" focus on creative and innovation output. If the goal is creativity, then leading specifically for creativity may be a simpler solution. In moving to the concept of a leaderless organization, it appears that what is defined as leadership is primarily a top-down, hierarchical approach to leadership. Starting from this point of view leads to various observations that might not be true in a creative leadership approach.

Brafman and Beckstrom (2006) posit that the starfish organization leads to creativity, whereas the hierarchical organization limits creativity. When describing the catalyst, one of the "hidden powers" mentioned was "tolerance for ambiguity." Puccio et al. (2011) delineate various cognitive and affective skills for creative leadership, many of which are grounded in approaches to creative problem-solving; tolerance for ambiguity (p. 64) is among the affective skills.

Brafman and Beckstrom (2006) also describe leaders in a top-down organization as wanting to control what is happening, thus limiting creativity. Closely watching employees limits the likelihood that they will take risks and innovate (loc. 1344). When leading for creativity, the leader should be fully aware of the need to create an environment in which persons can be innovative. The leader is important for setting the tone for creativity and innovation. One might argue that when Zappos CEO wrote "As of 4/30/15, in order to eliminate the legacy management hierarchy, there will be effectively no more people managers" (Hodge 2015), he was working to set the tone for creativity, building on previous actions taken by the company to ensure a culture that was "positive and caring and fun as possible." Leadership is important for setting the climate, and there are research-based aspects of work climate that are shown to encourage, or hinder, creativity. Puccio et al. (2011) argue that there are behaviors of transformational leaders that can foster a climate for innovation and creativity. In creating this environment, the leader is "open to change; involves followers in problem-solving efforts; responds positively to new ideas; is supportive of new ideas; encourages debate and entertains different perspectives; allows freedom and autonomy, is not controlling; and encourages risk taking and accepts failure." Thus, leading for creativity is an act of leadership, rather than accepting that the opposite of leadership is a leaderless approach.

The creative leadership approach is in keeping with the peer-based practices outlined in *The Myth of Leadership* (Nielsen 2004). Nielson compares the rank-based practices vs. peer-based practices in the following way: controlling vs. sharing; mindless vs. mindful; top-down vs. freeing; fearful vs. creative; and bureaucratic vs. flexible. This comparison will not apply to the creative leader, where necessary affective skills include (among others) sensitivity to environment; mindfulness; sensing gaps; avoiding premature closure; and tolerance for risks (Puccio et al. 2011, p. 73). In *Creative Leadership: Skills that Drive Change*, Puccio et al. (2011) conclude the following: creativity is an essential skill for leadership. They put forward the following five tenets:

1. Creativity is a process that leads to change; you don't get deliberate change without it.
2. Leaders help the individuals and organizations they influence grow by deliberately facilitating productive change.
3. Because leaders bring about change, creativity is a core leadership competence.
4. An individual's ability to think creatively and to facilitate creative thinking in others can be enhanced.
5. As individuals develop their creative thinking and master those factors that promote creativity, they enhance their leadership effectiveness (p. 289).

The creative leader's approach will ensure a deliberate shaping of an environment through the following behaviors (Puccio et al. 2011):

Engaging in deliberate creative problem-solving efforts;
Empowering others to solve problems;
Monitoring creative progress in a timely manner (vs. checking on the status of assigned work too often);
Set goals, expectations, and job requirements that explicitly challenge team members to be creative;
Structure work environment to match the creative role expectations of jobs;
Socializing, developing healthy relationships with team members;
Disclosing personal information and feelings;
Acting on team members' ideas or wishes;
Asking for team members' ideas and opinions (Puccio et al. 2011, pp. 284–285, abbreviated).

The creative approach, by definition, creates an environment where all ideas are equal and more ideas are better than fewer. The leader ensures processes are consistent with getting a diversity of input and provides training for everyone in order to create processes that will lead to creativity. We recognize that if the goal is innovation, as displayed in the products, then focus needs to be on the persons and processes involved, and the environment created (press), as delineated in the 4Ps of creativity in Rhodes' Analysis of Creativity (Rhodes 1961).

Conclusion

There is great overlap between the case for leaderless leadership and creative leadership. The goal of creativity and innovation is often seen as a by-product of leaderless organizations, whether they are seen as peer-based (Nielsen 2004), holacracy (Hodge 2015), decentralized (Brafman and Beckstrom 2006), or self-management (Hansen 2016; Kotow 2019). Hansen (2016) concludes that maybe we are not looking for leaderless organizations, but leader-full organizations. This is in keeping with providing an environment for personal growth and recognizing that everyone's input is valid. What we need is not leaderless organizations with the hope of igniting a creative approach, but a deliberate approach to leadership that sets the stage for creativity; this is creative leadership.

References

Amabile, T., & Kramer, S. (2011). *The progress principle*. Boston: Harvard Business Review Press.

Amabile, T. M., & Khaire, M. (2008). Creativity and the role of the leader. *Harvard Business Review, 86*(10), 100–109.

Anderson, N., Potočnik, K., & Zhou, J. (2014). Innovation and creativity in organizations: A state-of-the-science review, prospective commentary, and guiding framework. *Journal of Management, 40*(5), 1297–1333. doi:10.1177/0149206314527128.

Anderson, N. R., & West, M. A. (1998). Measuring climate for work group innovation: Development and validation of the team climate inventory. *Journal of Organizational Behavior, 19*(3), 235–258. doi:10.1002/(SICI)1099-1379(199805)19:3<235::AID-JOB837>3.0.CO;2-C.

Brafman, O., & Beckstrom, R. A. (2006). *The starfish and the spider: The unstoppable power of leaderless organizations*. New York: Penguin Group [Kindle Edition].

Hansen, D. (2016). Is leaderless management a fad or the future of business? *Forbes*. https://www.forbes.com/sites/drewhansen/2016/03/08/leaderless-management/. Accessed 2 Nov 2022.

Hodge, R. D. (2015). First, let's get rid of all the bosses. *The New Republic*. https://newrepublic.com/article/122965/can-billion-dollar-corporation-zappos-be-self-organized. Accessed 2 Nov 2022.

Hughes, D. J., Lee, A., Tian, A. W., Newman, A., & Legood, A. (2018). Leadership, creativity, and innovation: A critical review and practical recommendations. *Leadership Quarterly, 29*(5), 549–569. doi:10.1016/j.leaqua.2018.03.001.

Kotow, E. (2019). How realistic is a leaderless organization? *Hedgetrade.com*. https://hedgetrade.com/how-realistic-is-a-leaderless-organization/. Accessed Feb 2022.

Kotter, J. P. (2012). *Leading change*. Boston: Harvard Business Review Press.

Kouzes, J. M., & Posner, B. Z. (2017). *The leadership challenge: How to make extraordinary things happen in organizations* (6th ed.). Hoboken, NJ: Wiley.

Kouzes, J. M., Posner, B. Z., & Biech, E. (2010). *A coach's guide to developing exemplary leaders* (pp. 11–300). San Francisco: Pfeiffer.

Li, T., & Yue, C. (2019). Working with creative leaders: An examination of the relationship between leader and team creativity. *Social Behavior and Personality: An International Journal, 47*(6), 1–12. doi:10.2224/sbp.8084.

Mumford, M. D., et al. (2019). Leading for creativity. In J. C. Kaufman & R. Sternberg (Eds.), *The Cambridge handbook of creativity* (2nd ed., pp. 546–566). Cambridge, UK: Cambridge University Press.

Nielsen, J. S. (2004). *The myth of leadership: Creating leaderless organizations* (1st ed.). Boston: Davies-Black, Nicholas Brealey Publishing [Kindle Edition].

Northouse, P. (2016). *Leadership: Theory and practice* (7th ed.). Thousand Oaks, CA: Sage.

Ovans, A. (2012). When no one is in charge. *Harvard Business Review, 90*(5), 146–147.

Puccio, G. J., & Cabra, J. F. (2010). Organizational creativity. In J. C. Kaufman & R. J. Sternberg (Eds.), *The Cambridge handbook of creativity* (pp. 145–173). Cambridge, UK: Cambridge University Press. doi:10.1017/CBO9780511763205.011.

Puccio, G. J., Cabra, J. F., & Schwagler, N. (2018). *Organizational creativity: A practical guide for innovators & entrepreneurs* (1st ed.). Thousand Oaks, CA: Sage.

Puccio, G. J., Mance, M., & Murdock, M. C. (2011). *Creative leadership: Skills that drive change* (2nd ed.). Thousand Oaks, CA: Sage.

Reiter-Palmon, R., Mitchell, K. S., & Royston, R. (2019). Improving creativity in organizational settings. In J. C. Kaufman & R. Sternberg (Eds.), *The Cambridge handbook of creativity* (2nd ed., pp. 515–545). New York: Cambridge University Press. doi:10.1017/9781316979839.

Rhodes, M. (1961). An analysis of creativity. *The Phi Delta Kappan, 42*(7), 305–310.

Scott, G., Leritz, L. E., & Mumford, M. D. (2004). The effectiveness of creativity training: A quantitative review. *Creativity Research Journal, 16*(4), 361–388. doi:10.1080/10400410409534549.

Uhl-Bien, M., Marion, R., & McKelvey, B. (2007). Complexity leadership theory: Shifting leadership from the industrial age to the knowledge era. *The Leadership Quarterly, 18*(4), 298–318. https://reader.elsevier.com/reader/sd/pii/S1048984307000689?token=C8DBE631E5B802D088F5EB9484235C02E265A1AE2094CAC3FC318079C894065487F902AB3B79CDE3ED75E2B26FF7D716.

Winston, B., & Patterson, K. (2006). An integrative definition of leadership. *International Journal of Leadership Studies, 1*(2), 6–66.

Zhou, J., & George, J. M. (2003). Awakening employee creativity: The role of leader emotional intelligence. *Leadership Quarterly, 14*(4–5), 545–568. doi:10.1016/S1048-9843(03)00051-1.

Part III

Against Leaderless Management

13

Why Leaders Are Necessary

Yusuf M. Sidani and Yasmeen Kaissi

Introduction

Leaders provide direction in institutional settings; they create vision, empower strategy development, provide alignment among various organizational elements, organize tasks, mold organizational cultures, instill shared values, foster relationships, inspire, empower, intellectually stimulate the intellect of followers, act as agents of change, and provide direction and comfort during times of uncertainty and crisis (Cashman 2010; Earl 2007; Kotter 1990; Mintzberg 2009; Siltaoja and Heikkinen, Chapter 11 in this volume). Organizational scholarship and practice have long celebrated the key roles played by leaders often giving them a larger-than-life image. Leaders, rightfully or wrongfully, are often credited for

Y. M. Sidani (✉) · Y. Kaissi
American University of Beirut, Beirut, Lebanon
e-mail: ys01@aub.edu.lb

© The Author(s), under exclusive license to Springer Nature
Switzerland AG 2022
F. Hertel et al. (eds.), *Debating Leaderless Management*,
Palgrave Debates in Business and Management,
https://doi.org/10.1007/978-3-031-04593-6_13

organizational successes and blamed for organizational failures (Svensson and Wood 2005).

Despite all of those various roles that leaders occupy, some argue that there is indeed room for organizations that do not need leaders. Some organizational settings do not require leaders, they argue, because organizational members might have reached a level of maturity where leaders are not really needed (Dissanayake and Takahashi 2012; Gerwel Proches, Chapter 18 in this volume). Or it could be the case that, for example, self-managing groups operate on their own; so the need to a leader would not be warranted (Côté et al. 2010). Moreover, there could be very clear and advanced organizational processes that are well documented and communicated that make the presence of a leader an act of redundancy. Against such arguments, we argue that leaders are invariably needed for proper organizational functioning. While there are situations that reduce our dependency on leaders, there are no circumstances—excluding very short intervals of organizational functioning—where organizational members are able to operate effectively on their own.

This chapter is structured as follows. First, we present our conceptualization of what is meant by a leaderless organization. Then we present our rationale for the necessity of leaders. We explain why the leader's emotional and inspirational roles cannot be replaced. We also explore how leadership cannot be substituted. Finally, we explain the role of leaders as irreplaceable shapers of organizational values.

Leaderless Organizations

Before explaining our arguments for the necessity of leaders, we present how we understand what is meant by a "leaderless organization." One of the primary ways that we might think of a "leaderless organization," where leaders are not needed, less needed, or redundant, is embodied in a body of scholarship termed "substitutes for leadership." Kerr and Jermier (1978), in a seminal article about substitutes for leadership, explored the conceptualization and operationalization of such an approach. They asserted that a wide array of individual, task, and organizational factors would temper the relationship between leader's behavior and organizational outcomes to the extent that at a certain point, a leader's role becomes insignificant or *relatively* inconsequential. For example, organizations would not need leaders, or—at least—not to the same extent, in the presence of able, experienced, trained, and mature followers who have a need for autonomy, and who do not rely on organizational rewards (Nielsen, Chapter 2 in this volume; Hsu and Sun, Chapter 6 in this volume). Moreover, organizations do not need leaders when tasks are clear, well structured, and intrinsically motivating. Finally, organizations do not need leaders when there are sophisticated systems (Selberg and Mulinari, Chapter 5 in this volume), where rules, policies, and procedures are clearly set, and there are "highly specified and active advisory and staff functions [and] closely knit, cohesive work groups" (Kerr and Jermier 1978, p. 378). If this rationale is carried to the extreme, one can indeed talk of situations where a leaderless organization becomes a matter of fact.

Why Leaders Are Necessary

We do not agree with the notion that leadership is substitutable to the extent where leaders become redundant or unnecessary. We argue that leaders are indispensable for organizational functioning for three main reasons. First, a leader's emotional and inspirational roles cannot be replaced. Second, alternative arrangements such as self-leadership or self-managing teams do not nullify the need for leaders, but these only moderate dependency on them. Third, leaders are markers of organizational values, in a sustained manner; without them an organization would quickly drift from its core values and lose its identity. In what comes, we will address each point explaining our reasoning.

A Leader's Emotional and Inspirational Support Cannot Be Replaced

Leaders need to be present because their role is not only to establish routines and norms whose very existence nullifies our need for them over time. People need continuous emotional support, they need sustained inspiration, and they need to be reminded of what things are important and why these are important. Organizational members often forget and things get lost over time. Organizations need leaders not because of what they do at a certain point in time. Organizations need leaders to continuously keep the organizations and organizational members in the right direction.

The psychological and emotional role of leaders is widely accepted in leadership research (Siltaoja and Heikkinen, Chapter 11 in this volume). Whether one is addressing transformational leadership (Bass 1999; Bass and Riggio 2006; Nielsen, Chapter 2 in this volume), authentic leadership (Avolio and Gardner 2005; Gerwel Proches, Chapter 18 in this volume; Kenny-Blanchard, Chapter 17 in this volume; Luthans and Avolio 2003), servant leadership (Greenleaf 2002; Van Dierendonck 2011), or charismatic leadership (Conger and Kanungo 1998; House and Howell 1992; Siltaoja and Heikkinen, Chapter 11 in this volume) among the myriad of leadership approaches, the persona of the leader is considered to be extremely critical to the leadership phenomenon, and the ensuing outcomes. Leadership is a quality that is often understood in terms of one's charisma or psychological standing and ability to influence resulting in follower and organizational outcomes including follower commitment, satisfaction, and motivation in addition to organizational performance. In that, leadership is not a replaceable resource, among others, that are collectively responsible for organizational performance and follower outcomes. In explaining performance, access to knowhow might compensate for the absence of financial resources; a research capability might compensate for the absence of proprietary technology; but a robot cannot compensate (at least not till now!) for the presence of a leader. Many resources are substitutable; leadership is not one of them.

If one accepts this notion of a leader, then one might be inclined to embrace the heroic perspective of a leader (Garvey and Fatien Diochon,

Chapter 3 in this volume), the superman (or superwoman), whose presence is ever needed.[1] Yet, within this notion of leadership is an underlying assumption that perhaps we need leaders not because they are needed for organizational performance per se; we need leaders because they are good for us, organizational members. We yearn for leaders, we celebrate their successes, and we attribute (and perhaps sometimes over-attribute) organizational performance to their own doings. This romance for leadership (Meindl 1995; Meindl et al. 1985) stems from an instinctive attachment to a larger power that helps us understand the world in which we live, very similar to the yearning of a child to her mother. In that sense, leadership is needed, not as a necessary cause of organizational performance, but more as an inspirational phenomenon reflecting the needs of organizational members for a reference point and a source of comfort. Yet, even if leaders are only needed for the need to attribute success or failure to a certain party, this means that leaders are indeed needed irrespective whether they are genuinely responsible for organizational outcomes or not.

Leadership Cannot Be Totally Substituted

Early conceptual papers that addressed the concept of substitutes for leadership aspired to a world where leadership is not necessary; later developments found that this would be an untenable objective or situation:

> Although early conceptual papers on leadership substitutes by Kerr (1977), Kerr and Jermier (1978), Howell, Dorfman and Kerr (1986), and Howell, Bowen, Dorfman, Podsakoff, and Kerr (1990) indicated that all leadership might become "unnecessary and impossible," a clearer understanding of the substitutes construct has shown that this expectation was not necessary and probably not reasonable. (Dionne et al. 2005, p. 176)

The substitutes for leadership model and the empirical studies related to it led some scholars to conclude that often "substitutes" do not really substitute for leadership. Some empirical studies have found disappointing empirical support for this theory (Podsakoff et al. 1993) despite its conceptual attractiveness. In a subsequent meta-analysis, Podsakoff et al. (1996) found that:

> the combination of leader behaviors and substitutes for leadership accounted for the majority of the variance in employee attitudes (75%) and role perceptions (60%) and a substantial proportion of the variance in performance (21%). This suggests the addition of the substitutes variables substantially improves our ability to explain the variance in a wide range of employee criterion variables. (Podsakoff et al. 1996, p. 395)

The above indicates that the addition of substitutes greatly augments the power of the leader. Simply stated, a leader would be able to do better in the presence of facilitators to his/her leadership, such as capable followers or facilitative organizational structures. Podsakoff et al. (1996) continue to assert that "on average, substitutes for leadership uniquely account for more variance in criterion variables than do the leader behaviors" (p. 395). While this suggests an even greater role to some variables other than leaders or their behaviors, this does not reach the level by which one concludes that leaders are dispensable or not needed if some other factors are present.

There is growing evidence supporting the notion that when placed in a leaderless environment, individuals tend to exhibit self-leadership. Self-leadership can be understood as a process by which one tends to motivate and influence one's self in order to achieve the needed direction to perform the necessary tasks (Dissanayake and Takahashi 2012; Houghton and Yoho 2005). Yet the emergence of self-leadership does not necessitate that a leader is not needed. It is actually the case that effective leaders are those who are able to develop their followers into self-leadership (Gardner et al. 2005). Self-leadership becomes rather an outcome of excellent leadership rather than a by-product of an absence of leadership or failed leadership.

Yet, it could be convincing to note that sometimes the absence of leaders would lead to organizational members taking ownership of their own functioning and leading themselves. In the absence of good leadership, some people might emerge as organizational intrapreneurs who would take the initiative into guiding their own behaviors within their own settings. Yet, this is not evidence of the power and success of a leaderless entity. It is rather evidence of the emergence of another type of leaders, those who are able to recognize the failings of their own leaders, and thus become proactive in filling the void that exists. A leaderless organization is argued by some to be the one that doesn't engage in "exerting influence" over human behavior in order to achieve the set-out tasks (Dissanayake and Takahashi 2012). Yet, this perspective might fail to note that the absence of top-down hierarchical influence does not mean the absence of any influence at all. Those organizational intrapreneurs are those who initiate influence because of the absence of the otherwise expected influence from the designated leaders.

The label "leaderless" would seem awkward to proponents of the above-mentioned leadership schools; after all, leadership is defined by people who are behind this phenomenon, "leaders." Without discounting follower-centered approaches to those perspectives (Bligh 2011; Kohles et al. 2012; Sidani and Rowe 2018; UhlBien et al. 2009), the position of a "leader" is considered to be an integral part of this phenomenon. The drive toward follower-centered approaches did not aim at reaching organizations that are leaderless, but rather at broadening our understanding of the role of followers in the leadership relationship. This aimed to complement the role of leaders rather than to replace their positioning within organizational functioning.

Sometimes the absences of effective top-down leadership lead to leadership that is diffused and distributed across the organization or within the organizational units. In such instances, teams become able to lead their work collectively and independently of a domineering powerful figure that monitors other members (Choi and Schnurr 2014). In such instances, team members show engagement in common distributed leadership as they work collaboratively by actively listening and exploring each other's ideas and suggestions toward developing solutions to organizational problems. As opposed to the top-down and hierarchical leadership model that exists in the traditional context, "distributed leadership" is much less authoritative and much more liberal but doesn't demolish the significance of leadership and leaders. Moreover, the existence of diffused leadership, particularly when intended, could be an act of leadership in itself. If not-intended, then leadership would be ascribed to those leaders distributed across the organization (Martins and Martins, Chapter 7 in this volume), who are collectively responsible for its functioning. People assume more of their own functioning not waiting for external guidance, collaborating more with each other, sharing duties and responsibilities among themselves, and engaging in collective visioning (Dissanayake and Takahashi 2012; Pasini et al. 2015). This would not be evidence of a leaderless organization, as a truly leaderless team often fails (Moran and Beitsch 2015). On the contrary, this would rather be evidence of a different form of leadership embedded within the organizational structure.

Leaders as Irreplaceable Shapers of Organizational Values

Leaders play an instrumental role in the process of transmitting values and creating values-based organizational cultures. Advocates of the "leaderless organization" focus on the flexibility, freedom, and creativity that such a model offers (Brafman and Beckstrom 2006; Garvey and Fatien Diochon, Chapter 3 in this volume). We argue that this runs the risk of organizations drifting from the values on which they were founded. With a core value system, organizations cease to exist as social units (Buchko 2006). Organizations are entities in which people get together to serve a common purpose with an underlying common set of values or shared principles. Leaders provide the initial spark that shapes organizational values, and their continued presence to preserve the value structure. Moreover, leaders are necessary in reinforcing behaviors that align with organizational values (Blanchard and O'Connor 2003). Leaders have a critical role in shaping organizational cultures. Moreover, leaders have a role in managing and sustaining an organizational culture after it is established (Fairholm 1994) through reinforcement of the value system. Even when there are events or contingencies that necessitate some departure from this core value system, a leader is necessary to guide the organization through this transformation.

To be able to function, organizational members agree on a set of values that guide their behaviors. This, of course, does not mean that each and every member embraces those values to the same level of depth. There are instances when there are degrees of misalignment between individual values and organizational values. Indeed, sometimes people function in organizations without any commitment to its underlying values. This does, however, create a risk of creating organizations that have weak organizational cultures with varying, sometimes competing values. This ultimately negatively impacts the ability of the organization to deliver on its desired objectives. The world of management celebrates organizations which are able to perform under a set of commonly held value systems that individuals embrace and act upon.

Values are mental ideals that motivate behavior through positive guidance done with empathy shaping individual action (Grojean et al. 2004). Values are essential as they shape behavior and ultimately affect performance (Frost 2014; Lumpkin and Doty 2014). They are needed to shape attitudes, direct behavior, guide decision-making, and dictate what is moral or immoral. While values alone are essential, a leader implementing these values and leading by example seems to really bring out the best of any organization with a values-based culture. Values-based leaders are imperative to the well-functioning and sustainability of an organization (Taylor 2007) as they are the main way that values are transmitted and sustained. According to several articles in the literature, it is a leader's show of integrity, display of honesty, fairness, and the values by which he or she wishes to lead that motivate members to apply themselves in living up to these standards and achieving better results (Dolan 2015; Frost 2014; Lumpkin and Doty 2014; Taylor 2007; Whetten 2001).

To begin with, there is ample evidence showing that hierarchical systems and bureaucracy have had a negative effect on employees who end up being stripped of creativity and losing motivation (Dolan 2015). However, according to Dolan (2015), the best leaders must find the balance between maintaining control and allowing their employees the necessary freedom to allow their creativity to flow. To achieve this, it would require the leader to establish core values to start with and understand that these values need to be given room to evolve and change through the consideration of inputs from employees, customers, suppliers, or shareholders (Whetten 2001). It is, therefore, imperative for a leader to be self-aware, aware of others around him/her, and aware of the values of the organization (Frost 2014) in order to be able to lead with humility and achieve alignment between the values of the organization and those of the employees (Taylor 2007).

Furthermore, the relationship linking shaping values and a leader's behaviors is rather direct. In order for any organization to succeed, a leader must adhere to the values of the organization; he/she must reflect those values in their actions and lead by example (Buchko 2006). In that, for a healthy leadership relationship, they need to transcend their own needs and desires keeping the collective goals of the organization in mind (Dolan 2015; Lumpkin and Doty 2014; Taylor 2007).

A leaderless organization will find it harder to maintain its values and will become more prone to go down a slippery slope and thus risks compromising those core values. Leaders do not only show followers what needs to be done, but also have to show how things are done, and within which value system. Indeed there are organizations led by selfish "leaders" who only care about goal accomplishment irrespective of any dearly held value or principle guiding organizational behavior. While such organizations might reach certain goals, the long-term sustainability of such organizations is doubtful not only from a goal-oriented perspective but also from an ethical perspective. Without leaders who have certain qualities and who consistently refer to a set of core and shared values, it is difficult to have a healthy work environment established on trust, competence, excellence, and integrity (Dominick et al. 2020). Values-based cultures require the presence of leaders in a *sustained* manner. Ethical leaders act as role models, helping organizational members to focus on what is right, not only in terms of doing things efficiently and effectively, but also in terms of doing things ethically. When leaders disappear, cultures are more prone to fall into ethical blindness (Palazzo et al. 2012), and they might gradually go down on a slippery slope. The presence of ethical leaders is not only necessary to develop such cultures, but also to keep them going. As such, we argue that leaderless management is not possible in creating or sustaining those types of cultures (Gobind, Chapter 15 in this volume; Siltaoja and Heikkinen, Chapter 11 in this volume).

In sum, the continuous presence of leaders is crucial not only for the transmission of values, but also for the sustained presence and reinforcement of such values. In theory, one can advance the notion that organizations can set along "negative" core values or no core values at all. Yet, such an organizational presence is not likely to reach desired objectives in a consistent manner. Even criminal organizations operate along a set of values. The presence of a leader to reinforce such values would be needed to divert people who experience a reawakening of conscience and keeping them attached to the negative course of that organization. Likewise, and perhaps more importantly, in a healthy organization revolving around a positive value system, the presence of a leader is needed to help prevent organizational members from drifting into adopting value systems and behaviors that are inconsistent with the firm identity and core value system (Gerwel Proches, Chapter 18 in this volume). A leader is the person who (1) has the courage to embrace a value system, (2) convinces followers of the validity and vitality of such a system, and (3) incessantly works to plant it deep in the organizational memory.

Final Words

We argue that leaders are invariably needed for proper organizational functioning. While there are situations that reduce our dependency on leaders, there are no circumstances—excluding very short intervals of organizational functioning—where organizational members are able to operate effectively on their own. We have argued that leaders are indispensable for organizational functioning for three main reasons. First, a leader's presence, as a source of emotional and inspirational support, cannot be replaced. Leaders are needed because, among other things, they provide a sense of security and comfort to organizational members. Second, alternative arrangements such as self-leadership or self-managing teams do not nullify the need for leaders, but these only moderate dependency on them. Those arrangements are often an outcome of good leadership rather than an outcome of absent or failed leadership. Third, leaders are markers of organizational values, in a sustained manner; without them an organization would quickly drift from its core values and lose its identity. Ethical leaders act as role models, helping organizational members to focus on what is right, not only in terms of doing things efficiently and effectively, but also in terms of doing things ethically.

Even if one is to embrace the notion that at a certain point in time, organizations can operate on their own with no leader interference, this lack of leadership is not sustainable over a long period of time. Like humans, organizations are learning entities, and much like humans, things get lost with time. Value systems that leaders implement and work on building into organizational structures need continuous nourishment and protection. Values that have been embedded into organizational cultures and routines need unwavering reinforcement by leaders. No substitute may exist whereby an organizational value is able to renew itself autonomously through independent feedback mechanisms. As time passes, priorities change, and organizational members might focus on things that are not necessary aligned with the deeply held organizational values planted by the leader. Organizational history is replete with examples where organizations lose focus and lose their way in the absence of capable and visionary leadership. Even in those cases where leaders are able to implement mechanisms and create structures that reduce their own importance, and even making them redundant, this is indeed an act of leadership in and of itself. In other words, "if the creation of substitutes is an act of leadership, then how can substitutes, per se, exist?" (Dionne et al. 2005, p. 182). One can argue that many leadership functions can be replaced by novel organizational structures, norms, or routines, yet nothing makes up for the process of developing, protecting, and sustaining organizational values. In that, leaders are not substitutable.

Note

1. Moving beyond the heroic perspective of leadership, there is much to support the notion of leadership as a phenomenon, or a relationship, that includes many other needed ingredients including followers and elements of various organizational structures and contingencies (Hernandez et al. 2011).

References

Avolio, B. J., & Gardner, W. L. (2005). Authentic leadership development: Getting to the root of positive forms of leadership. *The Leadership Quarterly, 16*(3), 315–338.

Bass, B. M. (1999). Two decades of research and development in transformational leadership. *European Journal of Work and Organizational Psychology, 8*(1), 9–32.

Bass, B. M., & Riggio, R. E. (2006). *Transformational leadership.* New York: Psychology Press.

Blanchard, K., & O'Connor, M. (2003). *Managing by values: How to put your values into action for extraordinary results* (2nd ed.). San Francisco: Berrett-Koehler Publishers.

Bligh, M. C. (2011). Followership and follower-centered approaches. In A. Bryman, D. Collinson, K. Grint, B. Jackson, & M. Uhl-Bien (Eds.), *The Sage handbook of leadership* (pp. 425–436). Thousand Oaks, CA: Sage.

Brafman, O., & Beckstrom, R. A. (2006). *The starfish and the spider: The unstoppable power of leaderless organizations.* New York: Portfolio.

Buchko, A. (2006). The effect of leadership on values-based management. *Leadership & Organization Development Journal, 28*(1), 36–50.

Cashman, K. (2010). Lead with energy. *Leadership Excellence, 27*(12), 7.

Choi, S., & Schnurr, S. (2014). Exploring distributed leadership: Solving disagreements and negotiating consensus in a "leaderless" team. *Discourse Studies, 16*(1), 3–24.

Conger, J. A., & Kanungo, R. N. (1998). *Charismatic leadership in organizations.* Thousand Oaks, CA: Sage.

Côté, S., Lopes, P. N., Salovey, P., & Miners, C. T. (2010). Emotional intelligence and leadership emergence in small groups. *The Leadership Quarterly*, *21*(3), 496–508.

Dionne, S. D., Yammarino, F. J., Howell, J. P., & Villa, J. (2005). Substitutes for leadership, or not. *The Leadership Quarterly*, *16*(1), 169–193.

Dissanayake, K., & Takahashi, M. (2012). Emerging organizational structures: Implications for leaderless organizations. *Colombo Business Journal*, *3*(2), 17–26.

Dolan, S. (2015). Values, spirituality and organizational culture. *Developing Leaders Quarterly*, *23*(21), 22–27.

Dominick, P., Iordanoglou, D., Prastacos, G., & Reilly, R. (2020). Espoused values of the "Fortune 100 best companies to work for": Essential themes and implementation practices. *Journal of Business Ethics*, *173*(1), 69–88. doi:10.1007/s10551-020-04564-8

Earl, J. (2007). Leading tasks in a leaderless movement: The case of strategic voting. *American Behavioral Scientist*, *50*(10), 1327–1349.

Fairholm, G. W. (1994). *Leadership and the culture of trust*. Westport, CT: Praeger Publishers.

Frost, J. (2014). Values based leadership. *Industrial and Commercial Training*, *46*(3), 124–129.

Gardner, W. L., Avolio, B. J., Luthans, F., May, D. R., & Walumbwa, F. (2005). Can you see the real me? A self-based model of authentic leader and follower development. *The Leadership Quarterly*, *16*(3), 343–372.

Greenleaf, R. K. (2002). *Servant leadership: A journey into the nature of legitimate power and greatness*. Mahwah, NJ: Paulist Press.

Grojean, M., Resick, C., Dickson, M., & Smith, D. (2004). Leaders, values, and organizational climate: Examining leadership strategies for establishing an organizational climate regarding ethics. *Journal of Business Ethics*, *55*(3), 223–241.

Hernandez, M., Eberly, M. B., Avolio, B. J., & Johnson, M. D. (2011). The loci and mechanisms of leadership: Exploring a more comprehensive view of leadership theory. *The Leadership Quarterly*, *22*(6), 1165–1185.

Houghton, J. D., & Yoho, S. K. (2005). Toward a contingency model of leadership and psychological empowerment: When should self-leadership be encouraged? *Journal of Leadership & Organizational Studies*, *11*(4), 65–83. doi:10.1177/107179190501100406

House, R. J., & Howell, J. M. (1992). Personality and charismatic leadership. *The Leadership Quarterly*, *3*(2), 81–108.

Kerr, S., & Jermier, J. M. (1978). Substitutes for leadership: Their meaning and measurement. *Organizational Behavior and Human Performance, 22*(3), 375–403.

Kohles, J. C., Bligh, M. C., & Carsten, M. K. (2012). A follower-centric approach to the vision integration process. *The Leadership Quarterly, 23*(3), 476–487.

Kotter, J. P. (1990). *A force for change: How leadership differs from management.* New York: The Free Press.

Lumpkin, A., & Doty, J. (2014). Ethical leadership in intercollegiate athletics. *The Journal of Values-Based Leadership, 7*(2), 1–11.

Luthans, F., & Avolio, B. J. (2003). Authentic leadership development. In K. S. Cameron, J. E. Dutton, & R. E. Quinn (Eds.), *Positive organizational scholarship* (pp. 241–258). San Francisco: Berrett-Koehler Publishers.

Meindl, J. R. (1995). The romance of leadership as a follower-centric theory: A social constructionist approach. *The Leadership Quarterly, 6*(3), 329–341.

Meindl, J. R., Ehrlich, S. B., & Dukerich, J. M. (1985). The romance of leadership. *Administrative Science Quarterly, 30*(1), 78–102.

Mintzberg, H. (2009). *Managing.* San Francisco: Berrett-Koehler Publishers.

Moran, J., & Beitsch, L. (2015). Leaderless leaders: Leaders in title only. *Journal of Public Health Management and Practice, 21*(5), 504–506.

Palazzo, G., Krings, F., & Hoffrage, U. (2012). Ethical blindness. *Journal of Business Ethics, 109*(3), 323–338.

Pasini, E., Magatti, P., & Bruttini, P. (2015). The three paradoxes of the "leaderless organization". *Organizational & Social Dynamics, 15*(1), 79–100.

Podsakoff, P. M., MacKenzie, S. B., & Bommer, W. H. (1996). Meta-analysis of the relationships between Kerr and Jermier's substitutes for leadership and employee job attitudes, role perceptions, and performance. *Journal of Applied Psychology, 81*(4), 380–399.

Podsakoff, P. M., MacKenzie, S. B., & Fetter, R. (1993). Substitutes for leadership and the management of professionals. *The Leadership Quarterly, 4*(1), 1–44.

Sidani, Y. M., & Rowe, W. G. (2018). A Reconceptualization of authentic leadership: Leader legitimation via follower-centered assessment of the moral dimension. *The Leadership Quarterly, 29*(6), 623–636.

Svensson, G., & Wood, G. (2005). The serendipity of leadership effectiveness in management and business practices. *Management Decision, 43*(7-8), 1001–1009.

Taylor, D. (2007). *The imperfect leader.* Bloomington, IN: AuthorHouse.

UhlBien, M., Pillai, R., & Bligh, M. C. (Eds.). (2009). *Follower-centered perspectives on leadership: A tribute to the memory of James R. Meindl.* Greenwich, CT: Information Age Publishing.

Van Dierendonck, D. (2011). Servant leadership: A review and synthesis. *Journal of Management, 37*(4), 1228–1261.

Whetten, D. A. (2001). What matters most. *The Academy of Management Review, 26*(2), 175–178.

14

Ghostbusters! On the Narrative Creation of (Absent) Leader Characters

Tommi Auvinen, Pasi Sajasalo, Teppo Sintonen, and Tuomo Takala

Introduction

While arguments for self-governance and increased local autonomy as a viable option for organizations, akin to the notion of leaderless management, have emerged in management literature over the years (Balkema and Molleman 1999; see also Sidani and Kaissi, Chapter 13 in this volume), self-organization of workgroups (e.g., Cummings 1978), or entire organizations, has turned out to be more of an inspiring and empowering idea with little substance to it, rather than a standing practice (Manz and Sims 1987).

Organizations characterized as being leaderless—or self-governed—are purported by some (see, e.g., Nielsen 2004) as the way forward to

T. Auvinen (✉) · P. Sajasalo · T. Sintonen · T. Takala
School of Business and Economics (JSBE), Jyväskylä University, Jyväskylä, Finland
e-mail: tommi.p.auvinen@jyu.fi

© The Author(s), under exclusive license to Springer Nature Switzerland AG 2022
F. Hertel et al. (eds.), *Debating Leaderless Management*,
Palgrave Debates in Business and Management,
https://doi.org/10.1007/978-3-031-04593-6_14

rectify the failings of the "rank-based leadership" marked by command-and-control management and the assumed superiority of those in charge of organizations based on their hierarchical position.

However, our point of departure is that leaders as organizational actors play such an important role for the organizational members, not as organizational hierarchy "placeholders" but as organizational "functionaries," that in the event of even a temporary absence in the corporeal realm, a leader is constructed in the narrative, non-corporeal realm by the organizational members. Therefore, our core argument in this chapter building on empirical data from a Finnish high-tech organization is that leaderless management, or any variant of effective goal-oriented organized leaderless activity, can be said to be a myth (see also Manz 1992).

In this chapter, by studying the physical or non-physical (i.e., the corporeal or non-corporeal) existence of leaders and their leadership influence, we seek to "bust out"—in the sense of making discernible— "ghost leaders" appearing in discursive organizational reality by scrutinizing narrated characters manifesting leadership influence to discuss the inherent challenges related to leaderless management. We utilize a simple working definition for leaderless management as literally representing orientation to management without leaders (as corporeal organizational actors).

In the following sections, we demonstrate how organizational members narrate leader characters into existence in the non-corporeal realm during an organizational change to fill the void of a corporeal leader. By taking the all-important non-corporeal aspect of leadership and leadership influence into account, we further challenge the notion of leaderless management.

We will show that also in situations of organizations emphasizing the autonomy of the staff or self-organized workgroups (i.e., allegedly "leaderlessly" managed organizations), leadership influence manifesting in the discursive and narrative realm still exists and affects organizational members in various ways. Thus, we will demonstrate how narrated leader characters and their leadership influence challenge the notion of leaderless management; even if corporeal leaders are temporarily absent, the narrated leader characters, the ghost leaders, and their leadership influence on the organizational members are not.

Theoretical Underpinnings

This chapter builds on discursive orientation to leadership study, dissecting the interactional, relational, socially, and symbolically constructed discursive processes that constitute leadership (Bryman et al. 2011; Fairhurst 2009) to bring out a powerful, typically neglected aspect of leadership studies: the influence of non-corporeal phenomena (Hartt 2013) beyond simple human interaction (Bass 1998). Auvinen (2012) frames this as "ghost leadership"—a leadership power construct where external and internal leader-related meanings are intertwined in organizational narration. Incorporating the immaterial aspects of leadership provides further insight into organizational power construction, particularly the influence of a leader, corporeal or non-corporeal.

We take the criticism of traditional leadership studies being overly focused on the leader as a person and approaches to the leadership process tied to the ongoing activities of an embodied actor seriously (see Boje 1991; Boje et al. 2011; Cunliffe and Coupland 2012). Therefore, we approach the idea of leaderless management from the point of view of the discursive, and especially narrative, organizational realm.

We illustrate the influence of corporeal leaders and non-corporeal leader characters on organizational members by focusing on the narration process among a leader and four of his colleagues/followers. Thus, our consideration includes designated hierarchical positions but also covers leadership influence detached from such formal structures. This allows us to identify informal leader characters and their leadership influence as well as sense indirect resistance (e.g., Bryman et al. 2011; Collinson 2000), constructed, conveyed, and challenged by the organizational members through narration (e.g., Auvinen et al. 2019; Boje and Rhodes 2006; Denning 2005).

To sum up: We argue that leaderless management is a myth. Leaders may appear not only as actual corporeal entities, as typically perceived in leadership theorizing, but—more importantly—as virtual, symbolic, narrated non-corporeal leader characters (Auvinen 2012; Boje et al. 2011; MacAulay et al. 2010) exercising leadership influence. From this discursive vantage point in particular, "leaderlessness" of any kind may be considered more of an optical illusion rather than an actual state of an organization as will be demonstrated below. Thus, when it comes to corporeal leaders or non-corporeal leader characters and their leadership influence—what is captured by the mind, rather than what meets the eye—is what matters to organizational members.

Now You See Me, Now You Don't—The Case of Tech Ltd

The case organization serving as a vehicle of discussion on the challenges of the leaderless management notion is a large high-tech research company operating primarily in the field of printed intelligence. It is a globally networked research organization ranking among the largest multi-technological applied research organizations in Europe, employing some 3,500 people. For confidentiality reasons, the organization's identity is hidden, and further details will not be disclosed. It is hereby referred to as "Tech Ltd."

At the time of data collection, Tech Ltd was aiming for a major strategic and cultural change, marked with the entry of a new leader hereby known as "Luis." His task was to both implement a strategic change and inspire personnel to embrace it. Over a period of four years, we interviewed Luis five times, and his colleagues (referred to as Col 1 ... Col 4) twice, to compile a dataset of 13 thematic interviews (approximately seven hours total, 120 pages of single-spaced transcribed text).

The informants were invited to casually consider the organizational culture before and after the strategic change. Leadership, commitment, and attitude toward the ongoing change were also discussed. Moreover, the interviewees were encouraged to raise topical issues they had encountered during the strategic and leadership changes.

The Emergence of a Ghost Leader and Leadership Influence

Next, we demonstrate the ways a non-corporeal leader character is constructed in organizational storytelling prior to, during, and after their corporeal presence in the organization. By doing so, we demonstrate how the absence of a corporeal leader does not amount to leaderless management. This is because both the narrated leader character—the ghost leader—and the leadership influence of this non-corporeal leader character had tangible effects on the organizational members and their behavior.

As noted above, Luis was primarily employed to lead a major strategic change program initiated around 2005–2006. Tech Ltd hired him to develop the commercialization of technological innovations. In terms of leadership and influence, his major task was to transform the mindset of Tech Ltd researchers from research and security-oriented to marketing-oriented and more entrepreneurial instead.

It is interesting to consider Luis' relationship with Tech Ltd against the backdrop of the notion of leaderless management, both during his introduction to the organization and his pre-existence as a non-corporeal leader character for the members of Tech Ltd. Despite Luis being officially a new actor in the organization, he was already familiar with Tech Ltd, and therefore, something was "known" about him by the members of Tech Ltd before he joined in 2007, due to having previously been employed by a large client of Tech Ltd.

Prior to joining, Luis had concerns that his background would be unfavorable for his upcoming role as a leader in a major strategic and cultural change, as he had worked as a sales expert and manager with no subordinates in his earlier career. However, the pre-existing organizational stories of Luis as an expert in the field seemed to support the new formal leadership position. Similarly, stories regarding Luis' leadership skills were favorable and preceded his entry to Tech Ltd as described by a colleague:

> I had heard loads of stories about Luis. He was familiar with us as we had cooperated with his former employer in the past. In that sense, we knew

Luis. He really has experienced a lot in the business world. He knows it well and has, you know, rubbed elbows with the really big boys. (Col 3)

Thus, positivity dominated the organizational narrative regarding the upcoming leader. It is, nevertheless, impossible to point out explicitly when, how, or where these purported leadership acts had taken place, or whether they were fictional. However, the above instance follows the leadership influence process outlined by Denning (2005, 2010): the influential leader character is an outcome of narration among the followers. In our case, the non-corporeal leader character appearing in the positive narration already granted Luis leadership influence among his colleagues/followers prior to his entry as a corporeal actor, and later, support as a formal leader corporeally present for the organizational members. Therefore, even when Luis was not corporeally present, he already pre-existed and had leadership influence among his followers.

The classic chicken-and-egg dilemma of which comes first, the corporeal leader or the story, was a non-issue as the latter appeared first: narration about Luis preceded him in the organization and made Luis an influential leader character among organizational members before his corporeal entry to the organization. The mechanism at play is narrative rationality (Fisher 1985, 1987, 1994)—the coherence and fidelity of the narrative coupled with the characterological behavior of the narrated leader character. Hence, the above marks the advent of leadership influence of the discursive leader character instead of an embodied, corporeal person with physical existence.

This is the first instance allowing us to bust out the ghost leader, challenging the idea of leaderless management. While Luis was not corporeally present, his leadership influence had already entered the organization and thus, the new leader pre-existed in the form of a narrated leader character for the organizational members—a ghost leader—before appearing to them corporeally. Therefore, we may argue, that even if Tech Ltd was without a formal flesh-and-blood leader, it was neither a leaderless nor leaderlessly managed organization prior to Luis' entry: The ghost leader narrated into pre-existence had already entered the organization and had an influence on its members.

After corporeally entering the organization, Luis' leadership influence was further reinforced in his followers' narrations, still boosted by the organizational stories regarding his previous experience and career at his former employer. His breadth of experience was generally appreciated and additionally, his leadership influence was amplified by stories of external authorities praising Luis:

> We had one Japanese firm here, and Luis was presenting the new technology. The Japanese CEO said that this is how things should be. He kind of admitted that Luis was right. This Japanese CEO was a true kingpin. (Col 4)

Apart from being impressed with Luis as a corporeal formal leader in addition to his pre-existing narrated leader character, the followers seemed to be supportive of the ongoing organizational change. They particularly appreciated Luis' experience in business development, commercializing technology, and his social and communication skills. The era from Luis' narrative pre-existence as a leader character for organizational members to the beginning of his work as a formal, corporeal leader seemed to be a harmonious honeymoon phase for everyone involved.

A Rupture in the Positive Leadership Influence Spiral—The Springboard Speech

The honeymoon ended abruptly with Luis' first public speech to the organizational members which outlined the idea of mindset change. He aimed to inspire the organizational members by offering them a springboard story (Denning 2005, 2010; Sintonen and Auvinen 2009). He recollects the "awakening narrative" as follows:

> There were about 33 people present, most of them meeting me in the flesh for the very first time. I introduced myself but hadn't prepared properly. I did not have a compelling story in mind. Instead, I started to narrate off-the-cuff. My first words were that we will have succeeded

in this organizational transformation if less than 50% of those present in this room work for Tech Ltd in five years. (Luis)

His—admittedly less than ideally communicated—idea was that half of the workforce would work for technology spin-offs that relied on technology developed by Tech Ltd within the specified timeframe. According to Luis, he faced quiet resistance at first, only to face strong resistance later, seemingly simmering all around the organization. While the organizational members never openly disagreed with Luis' idea, they consistently pointed out that an organizational faction, the "old researchers," was not going to play along with the efforts to instill the new mindset but would obstruct any attempts at it.

In terms of leadership influence, Luis represented the official, corporeal leader, but instead of inspiration, the springboard speech created an informal, non-corporeal leader character: the old researcher, whom, nevertheless, we never found as a corporeal entity in the organization. This incident illustrates the emergence of organizational resistance through a non-corporeal leader character without a formal position of power in the discursive and narrative realm of the organization. This non-corporeal leader character—another ghost leader—however, transformed into a highly influential autonomous entity for both Luis and organizational members alike.

In terms of leaderless management, the additional dimension offered by accounting for the non-corporeal aspect of leadership challenges the notion of leaderless management. This incident manifests a situation where a corporeal leader is present but accompanied by two non-corporeal leader characters—his own, and that of the informal ghost leader (old researcher)—both exerting leadership influence on the organizational members. Interestingly, it appears that both the corporeal and non-corporeal forms of leadership can exist simultaneously and be relatively independent of each other.

Ghosts Battling It Out—The Struggle Over the Change Efforts

The struggle over the targeted changes were eventually fought in the realm of meanings between two influential non-corporeal leader characters that emerged in organizational narration: the ghost of the—now previous—formal leader, and that of the informal ghost of the old researcher. The targeted mindset changes among the researchers eventually took place, albeit only after Luis had already left Tech Ltd. A former colleague mused the developments a year after Luis's departure:

> We have made substantial progress. While Luis demanded at least five spin-offs per year way back when we will have launched already eight this year. (Col 3)

It is interesting to note the reference to the already departed Luis as a leadership authority this way. At the time, the organization already had a new formal leader, but in the discourse related to the organizational change and its goals, Luis still existed as a highly influential non-corporeal leader character.

He thus had become a post-existent ghost leader for the organizational members by defeating another narrated ghost leader—the old researcher—who fiercely resisted any attempts at mindset change. Similar to Macaulay et al.'s (2010) findings, a non-corporeal leader character became a persevering actor in the organizational narration of Tech Ltd, and one could virtually hear the persistent ghostly footsteps of the now-absent CEO walking in the halls. In our case, Luis appeared as a victorious ghost leader character having defeated the opposing forces within the organization.

This situation resembles what Boje et al. (2011) term the orders of virtual leadership, entailing: (1) the imitation of a former flesh-and-blood leader, (2) a creative re-presentation of a former leader, and (3) a fabricated leader with no direct reference to an actual person. In our case, the re-presentation of a former leader is what especially takes place. The staff creates a non-corporeal leader although the corporeal leader has left the organization. Furthermore, the Tech Ltd case is also an example of how

leadership influence does not disappear with a corporeal leader, and nor does it mean an organization becomes leaderlessly managed upon their departure.

Figure 14.1 (temporally organized to reflect our case data) summarizes in which forms (formal/informal, corporeal/non-corporeal), and in which instances (prior, during, after), the various leader characters emerged in Tech Ltd. This extends the perception of leaders and their leadership influence to allow discussion of learnings concerning the notion of leaderless management from the case of Tech Ltd.

An interesting point that can be made concerning the notion of leaderless management based on Fig. 14.1 is that Luis, as a formal leader, had a non-corporeal existence that far exceeded his corporeal existence for the members of Tech Ltd. Thus, Luis, as a non-corporeal leader character, both pre-existed and post-existed, along with existing corporeally, for the Tech Ltd organizational members, backing up our initial claim of leaderlessness being a myth or optical illusion, as implied by the heading above.

		Pre-existence of the leader	Entrance of the new leader	Leader's springboard speech	The departure of the leader
FORMAL	Corporeal		x	x	
LEADER	Non-corporeal	x	x	x	x
INFORMAL	Corporeal				
LEADER	Non-corporeal	(x)	(x)	x	(x)

Fig. 14.1 Leader characters busted: x denotes the form and instance of leader emergence while (x) indicates latency

Learnings and Takeaways from the Tech Ltd Case

Traditional approaches to leadership predominantly emphasize real-world entities, such as leaders with their static attributes and traits, or seek to fix leadership with an ideal person or person-situation combination (e.g., Bryman et al. 2011; Grint 2011). Recently, however, interest in the study of leadership has shifted from hierarchical and managerialist perspectives toward self-leadership and autonomous, team-centered approaches (e.g., Auvinen et al. 2018). The interest in the notion of leaderless management follows suit. While the emphasis has been shifting away from a person—a leader—toward collectives of people and self-governance of workgroups, the emphasis on real-world entities has remained.

The case of Tech Ltd demonstrates that instead of focusing solely on real-life entities that would lead to the omission of the important non-corporeal aspect of organizations, adopting a narrative orientation allows light to be shed on the all-important aspects of the non-corporeal dimensions of leadership and leadership influence in the spirit of discursive leadership inquiry, stemming from social constructionism and interpretivism (Fairhurst 2011; Riessman 2008). This opens avenues in the narrative construction of reality (Boyce 1995; Bruner 1991; Fairhurst 2011), be it narration among organizational members, stories about great leaders, or future-oriented sensemaking (Boje 2008; Czarniawska 1998). Due to humans having an innate ability and tendency to make sense of their social experiences in narrative form, stories become the currency of human behavior in organizations (e.g., Boje 1991, 1995; Gabriel 1995). Furthermore, since stories as discursive entities also participate substantially in the construction of organizational reality and leadership (Boje 1995, 2011; Czarniawska 1998), they open a window into the non-corporeal realm of leadership.

Boje et al. (2011) propose a framework for studying non-corporeal leadership by introducing the concept of "virtual leadership" to refer to an entity performing leadership functions for an organization. This kind of narrative leadership influence construction involving both corporeal and non-corporeal elements is, however, still underdeveloped, and it is suggested by Boje and Rhodes (2006) and Flory and Inglesias (2010), among others, that more empirical explorations, such as this chapter based on empirical case data, are needed. The idea of virtual leadership strengthens our argument of the existence of non-corporeal leadership and as such, further questions the viability of the notion of leaderless management or leaderlessly managed organizations. The idea of a fabricated leader appears particularly promising for further elaboration.

As proposed by Denning (2005, 2010), narratively mediated virtual leadership may result from the following process: First, there is an action by a leader with eyewitnesses; second, the eyewitnesses create stories about the incident and distribute the first oral accounts of the qualities of the leader. Based on our exposition of the Tech Ltd case, we add to this that a leader may emerge in organizational storytelling before their physical presence in the organization. This may take place when the members of an organization are discussing and combining their existing pre-knowledge about their leader-to-be. As our case clearly demonstrates, the dynamics of human behavior are an outcome of the dynamic flux of organizational stories regardless of their corporeal reference existing or not (see, e.g., Boje 2008; Gabriel 2000). The pre-entry stories of Luis' character and competencies serve as fitting examples of the flux of organizational stories having performative effects on organizational members as they built the future leader's leadership influence well before his corporeal entry into the organization.

Like Collin et al. (2011) finding a leader character influencing follower behavior regardless of the physical presence of the leader, we observe the same phenomenon taking place in Tech Ltd. Collin et al. (2011) noted that organizational newcomers learned to adapt their organizational behavior according to the characteristics of leaders even before meeting them in person. Such behavior may seem peculiar to an outsider but makes sense to the organizational members and is thus only rational: The coherence and rationality of human order "require that characters behave characteristically" (Fisher 1985, p. 47). Therefore, entities of social construction in the discursive realm—such as leadership, leader characters, or their leadership influence—do not necessitate corporeal materiality but exist primarily in organizational discourse (Fisher 1985; Gabriel 2000), as also demonstrated by the Tech Ltd case in this chapter.

In summary, the Tech Ltd case allowed us to address the interplay between non-corporeality and corporeality in organizational narratives. We showed how a non-corporeal leader character may appear discursively in advance in organizational stories. The appearance of the upcoming leader took place in informal conversations based on the pre-existing knowledge and perceptions of organizational members. Additionally, we were able to show how, after the corporeal leader had already left the organization, the influential non-corporeal leader character still appeared in the organization in narrative form. Thus, the leader can be said to appear as a ghost leader both before and after corporeal presence in the organization, which is at odds with the working definition of leaderless management in this chapter, and further stresses our argument against the notion of leaderless management.

Discussion

This chapter set out to illustrate how organizational members narrate leader characters into existence to fill a perceived leadership void resultant of temporary corporeal non-existence of a leader in the organization undergoing an organizational change, and thus, where leadership influence is located. We focused particularly on the influence of corporeal leaders and non-corporeal leader characters—ghost leaders—on organizational members by drawing from case study data. We identified the forms (how and when) leadership is present in relation to intended organizational change and which forms it may assume. Based on our case, leadership may attach to a formal or informal, corporeal, or non-corporeal leader character.

During organizational change, an informal leader character emerged to resist the change. This informal leader character, however, never had a corporeal presence in the organization. Nevertheless, it appeared prominently in the narration of both the formal leader and the organizational members. Our observations contribute to narrative leadership discussions focusing on the leadership influence (Boje and Rhodes 2006; Snowden 2003) of non-corporeal leader characters (e.g., Auvinen 2012; Auvinen et al. 2019; Boje et al. 2011; MacAulay et al. 2010) by showing the dialectic relationship between the two forms of leadership in our case organization.

The resistance appearing within the organization was thus narrated into existence in the form of the old researchers—a hazy group of organizational members fiercely resisting the execution of the organizational change. The narrated group of old researchers received its influence, and thus non-corporeal leadership influence, within the organization from the implicit seniority and experience of its members. In this process, we can illustrate the non-corporeality of influential leader characters.

To conclude, we return to our initial argument related to the mythical qualities of leaderless management. In our context of organizational change, leaderless management appears to be an oxymoron. Despite that goal-oriented organizational activity might not always require a leader as a corporeal actor to be present, the exercise of leadership influence, however, requires a meaningful leader character to lead followers toward goals. In the event of the absence of a corporeal leader, as demonstrated in this chapter, organizational members create an appropriate form of leader for themselves in the creative process of organizational narration, mixing formal and informal, and corporeal and non-corporeal dimensions, which exposes the inherent fallacy of leaderlessness as a principle of organization.

Therefore, while an organization may declare itself to be leaderless, and it may—temporarily at least—cope without corporeal managers or leaders in the short term, we maintain that leaderless management is without substance, and organizations characterized as being leaderlessly managed are, in fact, not. Similarly to the natural tendency of vacuums being filled, leaderlessness creates such a vacuum for organizational members, that removing corporeal leaders, non-corporeal leader characters, or their leadership influence among organizational members is not sustainable in the long run. Leaders, or more specifically their leadership influence, are simply needed, though they need not always be formal leaders, nor corporeal leaders for that matter. This is especially true in situations characterized by change. As Ovans (2012, p. 147) points out, "to turn [organizational members'] myriad passions into productive change, leaders will have to emerge."

Conclusion

To conclude, we wish to offer suggestions for future research based on our findings on leaderless management to allow it more substance in a more focused domain within leadership and management literature. A field within management and leadership literature bordering leaderless management revolves around advanced digital technologies and their application to leadership. This appears an especially promising field of literature in terms of developing ideas related to leaderless management further within a focused domain. The advances in digital technologies provide interesting resources for management and leadership as a source of automating some aspects of leadership (Derrick and Elson 2019). As managerial supervision and routine tasks are already replaceable by artificial intelligence (Noponen 2019), artificial intelligence-based leadership is an interesting case of virtual leadership (Boje et al. 2011) as it is purely non-corporeal. This highlights the non-corporeal aspect of leadership brought up by our findings in this chapter and brings up the non-corporeal dimensions in organizations occurring through pre-reflective, non-representational, affective processes, and embodied practices (cf. Cunliffe and Coupland 2012) as an important aspect for future studies to explore more thoroughly, as we understand very little of the implications of artificial leadership thus far.

References

Auvinen, T. (2012). The ghost leader: An empirical study on narrative leadership. *EJBO Electronic Journal of Business Ethics and Organization Studies, 17*(1), 4–15.

Auvinen, T., Riivari, E., & Sajasalo, P. (2018). Lessons learned from traditional and "new-age" leadership. In A. Eskola (Ed.), *Navigating through changing times* (pp. 95–112). New York: Routledge.

Auvinen, T., Sajasalo, P., Sintonen, T., Pekkala, K., Takala, T., & Luoma-aho, V. (2019). Evolution of strategy narration and leadership work in the digital era. *Leadership, 15*(2), 205–225.

Balkema, A., & Molleman, E. (1999). Barriers to the development of self-organized teams. *Journal of Management Psychology, 14*(2), 134–149.

Bass, B. M. (1998). *Transformational leadership: Industrial, military, and educational impact*. Mahwah, NJ: Lawrence Erlbaum Associates.

Boje, D. (1991). The storytelling organisation: A study of story performance in an office-supply firm. *Administrative Science Quarterly, 36*(1), 106–126.

Boje, D. (1995). Stories of the storytelling organisation: A postmodern analysis of Disney as 'Tamara-Land'. *Academy of Management Journal, 38*(4), 997–1035.

Boje, D. (2008). *Storytelling organisations*. London: Sage.

Boje, D. (2011). Introduction to agential antenarratives that shape the future of organizations. In D. M. Boje (Ed.), *Storytelling and the future of organizations* (pp. 1–22). New York: Routledge.

Boje, D., Pullen, A., Rhodes, C., & Rosile, G. A. (2011). The virtual leader. In A. Bryman, D. Collinson, K. Grint, B. Jackson, & M. Uhl-Bien (Eds.), *The Sage handbook of leadership* (pp. 518–530). London: Sage.

Boje, D., & Rhodes, C. (2006). The leadership of Ronald McDonald: Double narration and stylistic lines of transformation. *The Leadership Quarterly, 17*(1), 94–103.

Boyce, M. (1995). Collective centring and collective sense-making in the stories and storytelling of one organisation. *Organisation Studies, 16*(1), 107–137.

Bruner, J. (1991). The narrative construction of reality. *Critical Inquiry, 18*(1), 1–21.

Bryman, A., Collinson, D., Grint, K., Jackson, B., & Uhl-Bien, M. (2011). *The Sage handbook of leadership*. London: Sage.

Collin, K., Sintonen, T., Paloniemi, S., & Auvinen, T. (2011). Work, power and learning in a risk filled occupation. *Management Learning, 42*(3), 301–318.

Collinson, D. (2000). Strategies of resistance: Power, knowledge and subjectivity in the workplace. In K. Grint (Ed.), *Work and society: A reader* (pp. 162–195). Cambridge, UK: Polity Press.

Cummings, T. (1978). Self-regulating work groups: A socio-technical synthesis. *Academy of Management Review, 3*(3), 625–634.

Cunliffe, A., & Coupland, C. (2012). From hero to villain to hero: Making experience sensible through embodied narrative sensemaking. *Human Relations, 65*(1), 63–88.

Czarniawska, B. (1998). *A narrative approach to organisational studies*. London: Sage.

Denning, S. (2005). *The leader's guide to storytelling*. San Francisco: Jossey-Bass.

Denning, S. (2010). *The leader's guide to radical management*. San Francisco: Jossey-Bass.

Derrick, D. C., & Elson, J. S. (2019). Exploring automated leadership and agent interaction modalities. In *Proceedings of the 52nd Hawaii International Conference on System Sciences*. http://hdl.handle.net/10125/59461. Accessed 14 Apr 2021.

Fairhurst, G. T. (2009). Considering context in discursive leadership research. *Human Relations, 62*(11), 1607–1633.

Fairhurst, G. T. (2011). Discursive approaches to leadership. In A. Bryman, D. Collinson, K. Grint, B. Jackson, & M. Uhl-Bien (Eds.), *The Sage handbook of leadership* (pp. 495–517). London: Sage.

Fisher, W. R. (1985). The narrative paradigm: In the beginning. *Journal of Communication, 35*(4), 74–89.

Fisher, W. R. (1987). *Human communication as a narration: Toward a philosophy of reason, value, and action*. Columbia, SC: University of South Carolina Press.

Fisher, W. R. (1994). Narrative rationality and the logic of scientific discourse. *Argumentation, 8*(1), 21–32.

Flory, M., & Inglesias, O. (2010). The role of rhetoric and narratives in management research and practice. *Journal of Organizational Change Management, 23*(2), 113–119.

Gabriel, Y. (1995). The unmanaged organisation: Stories, fantasies and subjectivity. *Organisation Studies, 16*(3), 477–501.

Gabriel, Y. (2000). *Storytelling in organisations: Facts, fiction and fantasies*. Oxford: Oxford University Press.

Grint, K. (2011). A history of leadership. In A. Bryman, D. Collinson, K. Grint, B. Jackson, & M. Uhl-Bien (Eds.), *The Sage handbook of leadership* (pp. 3–14). London: Sage.

Hartt, C. M. (2013). *The non-corporeal actant as a link between actor-network theory and critical sensemaking: A case study of Air Canada*. Halifax, NS: Saint Mary's University.

MacAulay, K. D., Yue, A. R., & Thurlow, A. B. (2010). Ghosts in the hallways: Unseen actors and organizational change. *Journal of Change Management, 10*(4), 335–346.

Manz, C., & Sims, H. (1987). Leading workers to lead themselves: The external leadership of self-managing work teams. *Administrative Science Quarterly, 32*(1), 106–129.

Manz, C. C. (1992). Self-leading work teams: Moving beyond self-management myths. *Human Relations, 45*(11), 1119–1140.

Nielsen, J. (2004). *The myth of leadership: Creating leaderless organizations.* Palo Alto, CA: Davies-Black Publishing.

Noponen, N. (2019). Impact of artificial intelligence on management. *Electronic Journal of Business Ethics and Organization Studies, 24*(2), 43–50.

Ovans, A. (2012). When no one's in charge. *Harvard Business Review, 90*(5), 146–147.

Riessman, C. K. (2008). *Narrative methods for the human sciences.* Los Angeles: Sage.

Sintonen, T., & Auvinen, T. (2009). Who is leading, leader or story? *Tamara Journal, 8*(1), 95–109.

Snowden, D. J. (2003). *Narrative patterns: The perils and possibilities of using story in organisations.* Oxford, UK: Oxford University Press.

15

Against Leaderless Management: What Leaderless Means in South Africa

Jenika Gobind

Introduction

This chapter argues against leaderless management. Speaking from South African experiences, I define leaderless management as the absence of leadership (see also Jørgensen and Ingman, Chapter 8 in this volume). This is different from perceptions of leaderless management embedded in an anarchist's vision for organizations and society as a whole. Here, leaderless management is perceived as the direct consequence of the Anarchist's rebel against hierarchy, order, and authority (Bakunin 2007; Kropotkin 1976; see also Hertel and Sparre, Chapter 9 in this volume). In this case, leaderless management is a matter of leaving organizing to cooperatives based on bottom-up democracy, self-management, and self-organization. Such leaderless management is based on trust, ethics, and

J. Gobind (✉)
Wits Business School, Wits University, Johannesburg, South Africa
e-mail: jenika.gobind@wits.ac.za

© The Author(s), under exclusive license to Springer Nature   **245**
Switzerland AG 2022
F. Hertel et al. (eds.), *Debating Leaderless Management*,
Palgrave Debates in Business and Management,
https://doi.org/10.1007/978-3-031-04593-6_15

collaboration. If these conditions are not present, leaderless management develops into an absence of leadership.

Therefore, I argue against leaderless management. I argue instead for the need for ethical leaders. The contemporary lack of ethical leadership results in substantial waste of resources in South African society. These resources could have helped solve urgent social, cultural, and health issues. I do not believe that South African society is ready for leaderless management based on the anarchist's vision. Instead, we need ethical leaders, who act in the world for the purpose of moral and ethical transformation. It is an empirical fact that some individuals are positioned in privileged decision-making positions. It is essential that those individuals recognize their moral and ethical responsibilities and lead.

An ethical leader is an individual that is committed and present. Such leadership is a contrast to uncommitted, unethical, and absent leadership, which unfortunately characterizes the situation in South Africa (Moran and Beitsch 2015, p. 504). This unfortunate surge in absence of leadership and selfishness disturbingly occurs in both the state and private organizations. The experience is that absence of leaders neither results in equitable ethical decision-making (Kotow 2019; Peter 2018), nor does it result in collaborative non-hierarchical context resulting in cooperative leadership (Endres and Weibler 2020, p. 306; see also Martins and Martins, Chapter 7 in this volume). The lack of leadership entails in this situation the absence of ethical leadership and is in reality a failure of management (Moran and Beitsch 2015, p. 504). We need strong ethical leadership that prevents the rise in corruption that has become apparent in both public and private organizations.

South Africa suffers from absence of leadership. The roots of unethical leadership in South Africa are historical. Unethical leadership permeates the mind of current leaders. This chapter discusses the role history has played in fostering absent and discouraging ethical leadership. Second, it explores the belief that to lead in South Africa, one must replicate a leadership style that mirrors unethical practices of apartheid predecessors. I argue that democratic processes of sharing power may help curtail unethical and absent leadership provided ethical leadership becomes a norm. So far, these circumstances reinforce the stance that leaderless management has no room in South Africa.

Against Leaderless Management

South African leaders are the architects of the present absence of leadership. Buried in their self-gain and lack of ethics these leaders continue to flourish while the rest of South Africa dissipates into economic decline. Former Minister of Finance Tito Mboweni recently spoke out against leaders who pursued personal wealth rather than fulfilling their leadership duties (Omarjee 2021). Adding that "all the systems we have in place to protect much-needed resources and prevent looting can only go so far when there are people who seek to manipulate processes to steal public funds" (Omarjee 2021). The present hardship of the South African people is a direct consequence of the historical development and conditions.

South African history is embedded in the hierarchical apartheid regime and unethical leadership practices that have indoctrinated leaders into embracing unethical practices. This has predictably resulted in the reluctance to move away from the apartheid regime to one of ethical leadership. To understand the attraction for the indoctrination is to explore the historical imprint that has crafted an absent leadership style that is unique to South Africa. This imprint is an effect of the accumulative suppression of a hierarchical apartheid regime based on an ideology that was cultivated by the Dutch, reinforced by the British and later perpetuated by an apartheid government (O'Malley 2008). The apartheid government's strict policy of racial segregation became the vehicle for the creation of a black separatist state (O'Malley 2008). The alienation of the black majority and the deliberate coalition of other minorities allowed for the entrenchment of a regime that inculcated subservience.

Years of subservience created the belief that one race was ranked higher than the other, creating a so-called hierarchy of races (Ruben and Bobat 2014). This hierarchy permeated the government, workplace, and the mindset of individuals and began to foster a perception that leadership rested with the race that remained at the apex. To attain a role similar to the apex race was an achievement and highly sought after. Unfortunately, post-democratic South Africa inherited the belief that to lead, one needs to adopt leadership style of the apartheid oppressor, thereby creating a new hierarchy under the guise of a democratic government. As a result, South Africa sees a rise in unethical and absent leaders who chose to gain power through unethical means often retreating into the shadows when true leadership is required.

I think that the present hardship and the obvious waste of the nation's limited resources preclude the Anarchist's vision on leaderless management (see also Hertel and Sparre, Chapter 9 in this volume). I simply ask: How can people in the township who are suffering from a devastating healthcare system, lack of nutrition and poor education find the resources to engage in endless discussions on leaderless management? At present the South African society simply needs trustworthy leaders who are able to re-distribute resources thereby improving living conditions, healthcare system and education for every South African, particularly those in our poorest communities. The syphering siphoning of much-needed resources by individuals in leadership positions has resulted in a government that is tethering on bankruptcy. Poor health care, dysfunctional service delivery, and escalating food prices have resulted in unprecedented economic inequality. People of South Africa need answers and are demanding restitution. South African society and its people simply lack time to await the possible (or impossible) materialization of beautiful visions of leaderless management.

Dismantling a Hierarchical Regime

Dismantling the hierarchical regime requires that the South African state and organizations scrutinize leadership practices. This process has the potential to expose existing leaders who currently engage in unethical practices. Consequently, there is resistance to dismantle the hierarchical regime for fear of being exposed. However, to continue with the norm will allow unethical leaders to continue with their unethical practice to the detriment of the country. Former president of South Africa, Jacob Zuma, is the perfect example of a leader who used his position within government hierarchy as a veil to pursue unethical practice (Cocks and Roelf 2021). Had the former president dismantled the hierarchy, this would have allowed for greater transparency and less room for unethical practice (see also Nielsen, Chapter 2 in this volume). However, the former president chose to use his position, as a vehicle to drive the country into recession. When ethical leadership was sought, the former president retreated into the shadows continuing to remain absent during his presidency.

The Challenge remains replacing unethical leaders with those, who are driven by ethics and integrity. The transference of leadership qualities of the past is a cause of concern, as, current leaders tend to succumb to values of the past thus allowing room for unethical practices. The need to break the dependency on the past is key to rehabilitation and moving South Africa toward virtuous leadership. The unethical leader has since changed demographic and in turn, has unknowingly undergone a process of transference. The impact of a history that has changed a nation continues to influence the ideology of leaders who view leadership in a historical oppressive sense, as the ideal. Apartheid ideology paved the belief, that to lead with power, wealth and influence are necessary to achieve success (Graybeal et al. 2019). These beliefs are ingrained in current leadership who unashamedly strive to attain wealth and status through unethical means.

This has led to what some call a *cycle of transference*. This cycle emanates from the indoctrinated hierarchical regime and apartheid ideology has manifested in the unethical practice of South African leaders. The nature of transference has been studied by many psychoanalysts over the years. The process has subsequently been used by many to advance political careers. South African leaders have displayed tendencies of transference, they have absorbed leadership qualities of past leaders. It is these traits of transference that one sees in South African leaders particularly, in the way they lead and conduct themselves. The idealization of leaders whom they have perceived, as influential and yielding power is seen as the ideal form of leader, "where leadership is conflated with being governed by another" (Western 2014, p. 677).

South African leaders have become followers of leaders that have led before them and they, in turn, are generating a form of leadership by transference that creates leaders that repeat actions of individuals that they perceive to have influenced them. To change South African leadership style is to break the cycle of transference that has allowed South African leaders to replicate leadership that are similar to their hierarchical apartheid counterparts and more recently unethical leaders that refuse to concede to allegations of unethical practice. Demonstrating transference is a facilitator of fellowship, which in turn destroys objectivity (Maccoby 2004). Follow the leader has disadvantaged leaders of a young democracy.

The fixation on nationalist paternal leadership has allowed for the replication of a leadership style that does not accommodate ethical leadership. For South African organization to realize the potential of leadership within their organizations, leaders of the said organization need to break the cycle of attempting to replicate leaders whose goals and ambitions were based on power, control, prejudice, and corruption. The stereotypical or traditional perception of idealized apartheid leadership remains a driver of organizations and are unable to liberate their employees or a nation. The reluctance to move away from a hierarchical regime to one of leadership is an impediment that anchors South Africa in apartheid fostering unethical and absent leadership.

Unethical and Absent Leadership

In recent years, ethical leadership in South Africa has been demanded by the masses and yet disregarded (Harding 2020). A country that is familiar with historical unethical leadership today remains oblivious when faced with a resurgence. This stance of indifference has resulted in unresponsiveness and reluctance to demand ethical leadership (Cowan et al. 2021a, 2021b). The unethical behavior of South African leaders is often identified but overlooked. Various commissions and investigations are undertaken in the hope that these investigations will yield findings that will incriminate those being investigated (Hosken and Skiti 2021; Malala 2021).

Unfortunately, the findings of these investigations are held captive in the clutches of corruption and are seldom published (Botha 2019). Individuals supposedly found guilty of these transgressions are never held accountable. Investigative findings are briefly mentioned and systematically removed from the face of media to conceal and appease interest (Botha 2019). Years of indoctrination on the merits of unethical leadership has tarnished individuals in leadership roles and has transformed these individuals from products of democracy to malversation. In an interview conducted by Omarjee (2021), former Minister of Finance Tito Mboweni outwardly stated that "there is virtue in living simply and rejecting the temptation to consistently chase ill-gotten wealth, which clearly leads people to corruption and other forms of malfeasance."

In a country like South Africa, the title of leader is highly sought after. To question these titles is unacceptable. Therefore, diminishing the status associated with titles may be the first step to restoring ethical leadership. This would be a situation where leaders lead with integrity and not power in pursuit of wealth. The move toward ethical leadership in South Africa would mean moving away from indoctrinated thinking to ethical practices. In so doing, individuals that are currently in leadership roles, are required to initiate a shift in leadership style to be directly involved if change is sought. Current leaders are concerned that these changes would alter their much sought-after position of power and control threatening their ability to acquire personal wealth (Chabalala 2021).

In a context where the ability to attain a position of authority is highly sought, the need to remain in control is a prized possession in the backdrop of post-apartheid South Africa. The title, role, and the impact the title lends to social standing is a valued badge of achievement however, the effort that is required in deserving the title is absent. With the leadership title, comes the opportunity to establish personal wealth (see also Borchmann and Pedersen, Chapter 4 in this volume). Rather than uplifting communities and actively addressing and resolving needs South African leaders seek to impoverish communities. Their absence one may argue is deliberate, being absent at the scene of a crime negates blame.

The former Minister of Home Affairs is an example of an unethical leader in pursuit of a title. In a recent testimony, the minister was found to have taken a series of bribes, abusing his position and purpose in government (Malala 2021). These proceedings are underway, the outcome of which may not be revealed and may surface once the memory of the incident fades. The minister will continue to live unethically remaining unaccountable while South Africa plays catch-up (Gumede 2020; Malala 2021). Work undertaken during his appointment is unaccounted for.

The state and private organizations are no different. The entities are not exempt from unethical leaders who in their role as leaders conceal their unscrupulous practices behind the veil of their titles periodically surfacing when being investigated for corruption. One such example in practice is the state-owned entity Elektrisiteitsvoorsieningskommissie (Eskom), a beacon of unethical leadership that has forced the country into darkness (Chabalala 2021; Cowan et al. 2021a, 2021b; Hosken and Skiti 2021; Seeletsa 2021). Unethical leadership practices have resulted in a snowball of underhanded practices and a barrage of leaders who are unable to lead the organization out of corruption. This state entity bleeds the country of resources and hope (Cowan et al. 2021a; Hosken and Skiti 2021).

The absence of ethical leadership has forced the state-owned entity to siphon resources leading the country to impoverishment. Following suit is the country's national carrier South African Airways (SAA), which is an example of holding on to a status that has run aground due to corruption like Eskom which siphons needed resources (Govender 2021; Smith 2020). The national carrier duped by foreign investors sold lucrative airline routes only to fund pockets of leaders that brokered the sale (Kapoor 2018). The airline now grounded is a metaphoric symbol of unethical leadership that has prevented a country from reaching greater heights. These are but two examples of unethical leadership that have surfaced and vaporized.

An example of unethical leadership where leaders remain unchallenged often orchestrated by politicians that remain behind the veil of their political positions (Goge and Letshwiti 2020). Unethical leaders thrive under investigator fatigue. This has hardened South Africans, who display a sense of indifference, as corruption becomes ingrained to a point of normality, a role played by history. The suggestive alternative to unethical leadership is the adoption of shared leadership.

Adopting Shared Leadership

Shared leadership may be described as the shared initiative to motivate and collectively achieve success. Shared leadership may be described as "a dynamic, interactive influence process among individuals in groups for which the objective is to lead one another to the achievement of group or organizational goals or both" (Pearce and Conger 2003, p. 1). This form of leadership has the potential to remove South African parastatals like Eskom and SAA out of corruption and into profit. Unfortunately, the current disjointed leadership does not allow for shared leadership, as leaders are not prepared to work toward a sustainable organization. Individual agendas have led to individual wealth. Shared leadership is where teams come together and demonstrate their collective leadership (Cox et al. 2003; see also Martins and Martins, Chapter 7 in this volume), one could argue that this is, in essence, the missing ingredient in the South African context. Shared leadership has the potential to remove the element of power and control from the hands of a singular leader. This in turn will inadvertently deter corruption and unethical practices that often breeds within leadership cartels and political circles while restoring the presence of leadership.

Independent studies have shown that shared leadership has demonstrated positive outcomes and higher team performance (Hoch et al. 2010; Nicolaides et al. 2014; Wu et al. 2020, p. 60). With shared leadership comes collaborative behavior that allows for individuals to share new knowledge and develop trust (Hill 2005), thereby removing the need for power and control (see also Martins and Martins, Chapter 7 in this volume; Siltaoja and Heikkinen, Chapter 11 in this volume), which sequentially will negate the opportunity for unethical practices. Research has established that shared leadership is advantageous for teams in developing competencies in self-management and self-leadership (Bell and Kozlowski 2002). These skills have the potential to strengthen existing leadership that foster higher levels of commitment that is currently lacking. Shared leadership in South Africa will allow for ethical leadership, as leadership will be shared by a set of leaders that are committed and present. Collective accountability will prevent unethical practices and the abuse of power and position. Thus, harnessing shared leadership has the potential to lead from within without the control of a designated leader. However, these expectations are limited within the South African context, because the mind shift that is required to embrace self and shared leadership remains bound to the need to lead traditionally in an idealized apartheid leadership style. Individuals in leadership roles are not prepared to share leadership, as this may result in the loss of power and control.

The uptake of ethical leadership in South Africa is unrealistic, as there is disinterest in the concept that is unfathomable. In a nation where leaders once fought tenaciously for democracy and ethical leadership have opted to follow a path that contradicts the values and ethical practices that have underpinned ethical leaders of the past. South Africa has eradicated apartheid and prides itself in the advances made toward democracy. A relatively young democracy that has tried to undo past injustices particularly in the workplace has made strides in enacting progressive labor legislation that has attempted to return authority to previously disadvantaged individuals' remains infatuated with power and wealth.

In an attempt to afford rights, a democratic government has counteracted their actions by enforcing an administration that has, in turn, re-enforced segregation within the country by creating a divide between wealthy and poor. Unethical leadership has resulted in wealth creation among a few while impoverishing the very country they have sworn to protect and serve. The absence of ethical leadership is experienced in daily interactions and functions in the life cycle of the South African from birth to death. At no point can one point to ethical leadership. This is a concern. Unethical practices continue to be the norm and leaders continue to remain detached and absent.

Conclusion

The focus on South Africa as a backdrop to this chapter is somewhat symbolic. One would anticipate that a country that once sustained heightened levels of prejudice and unethical leadership, in the wake of apartheid would lead with tenacity and resilience. A country emerging from the ashes into a new world of leadership, that is based on ethics and justice. A country dedicated to being at the forefront of establishing and upholding democratic and ethical leadership. A country that once fostered discrimination would now afford individuals of every race and creed an equal opportunity to lead indiscriminately. However, the expectation to uphold democracy and the opportunity, to lead ethically has never been achieved. South Africa has in turn succumbed to corruption and the unethical leadership forcing the nation into economic hardship.

Poor health care, dysfunctional service delivery, escalating food prices, and unprecedented economic inequality have become the new normal. Lessons learnt during apartheid have not altered how current South African leaders' lead. Years of subservience have resulted in the reversal of roles, which are now driven by corruption and unethical practices. Therefore, examining the absence of ethical leadership in a country that fought against unethical leadership is of interest. Looking to South Africa a country with a historical past unlike any other. Where the country remains in search of the ideal leader remains entrenched in a past forged in a dispensation that established a hierarchical culture based on racial segregation, mistrust, and suppression. Although, the evolutionary path of democracy has forced South African leaders to take charge and lead. The approach used in South Africa is unlike leadership that one associates with, ethics and virtue. Ethical leadership in South Africa is non-existent.

Absent leader has become the norm, and absent leaders continue to occupy themselves with unethical practices. Absent leaders need to be held accountable irrespective of their leadership role and political allegiances. If South Africa is expected to thrive and overcome present challenges uncommitted, unethical, and absent leadership should be eradicated in its, entirety. Then one day, one could probably start discussing leaderless management.

References

Bakunin, M. (2007). *Statism and anarchy*. Cambridge, UK: Cambridge University Press.

Bell, B. S., & Kozlowski, S. W. J. (2002). A typology of virtual teams: Implications for effective leadership. School of Industrial and Labor Relations, Cornell University. http://digitalcommons.ilr.cornell.edu/hrpubs/8/. Accessed 3 Jan 2021.

Botha, C. (2019). How corruption impacts on your media rand. *Daily Maverick*, April 12. https://www.dailymaverick.co.za/opinionista/2019-04-12-how-corruption-impacts-on-your-media-rand/. Accessed 8 May 2021.

Chabalala, J. (2021). Order granted to seize R1.4bn worth of assets belonging to former Eskom exec Hlakudi and other Kusile accused. *News24*, May 4. https://www.news24.com/fin24/economy/eskom/order-granted-to-seize-r14bn-worth-of-assets-belonging-to-former-eskom-exec-hlakudi-and-other-kusile-accused-20210504. Accessed 3 May 2021.

Cocks, T., & Roelf, W. (2021). S. Africa's ex-president Zuma pleads not guilty to corruption charges. *Reuters*, May 26. https://www.reuters.com/world/africa/safricas-ex-president-zuma-appears-court-corruption-plea-2021-05-26/. Accessed 28 May 2021.

Cowan, K., Masondo, S., & Karrim, A. (2021a). The Eskom files I Exclusive: Power utility's R178 000 000 000 dodgy tender tsunami. *News24*, May 3. https://www.news24.com/news24/southafrica/investigations/eskomfiles/the-eskom-files-exclusive-power-utilitys-r178-000-000-000-dodgy-tender-tsunami-2021a0503. Accessed 3 May 2021.

Cowan, K., Masondo, S., & Karrim, A. (2021b). The Eskom files I FBI, Hawks probe General Electric's R30m "donation" to DD Mabuza Foundation. *News24*, May 3. https://www.news24.com/news24/southafrica/investigations/eskomfiles/the-eskom-files-fbi-hawks-probe-general-electrics-r30m-donation-to-dd-mabuza-foundation-2021b0502. Accessed 3 May 2021.

Cox, J. F., Pearce, C. L., & Perry, M. L. (2003). Toward a model of shared leadership and distributed influence in the innovation process. In C. A. Pearce & J. A. Conger (Eds.), *Shared leadership: Reframing the hows and whys of leadership* (pp. 69–102). Thousand Oaks, CA: Sage.

Endres, S., & Weibler, J. (2020). Understanding (non)leadership phenomena in collaborative inter-organizational networks and advancing shared leadership theory: An interpretive grounded theory study. *Journal of Business Research, 13*(1), 275–309. doi:10.1007/s40685-019-0086-6.

Goge, S., & Letshwiti, P. (2020). Senior ANC officials allegedly "captured" by cartel. *eNCA*, November 26. https://www.enca.com/news/exclusive-senior-anc-officials-allegedly-captured-cartel. Accessed 8 May 2021.

Govender, P. (2021). "A travesty": Well-run parastatal has to slash staff by half to fund SAA bailout. *Times* LIVE, May 4. https://www.timeslive.co.za/sunday-times-daily/news/2021-05-04-a-travesty-well-run-parastatal-has-to-slash-staff-by-half-to-fund-saa-bailout/. Accessed 4 May 2021.

Graybeal, P., Franklin, M., & Cooper, D. (2019). Principles of accounting, volume 2: Managerial accounting. https://openstax.org/details/books/princi ples-managerial-accounting. Accessed 9 Dec 2020.

Gumede, W. (2020). Why corruption killed dreams of a better South Africa. *The Walrus*, January 10. https://thewalrus.ca/corruption-why-corruption-kil led-dreams-of-a-better-south-africa/. Accessed 8 May 2021.

Harding, A. (2020). Ferraris and frustration: Two faces of South Africa's corruption battle. *BBC News*, October 10. https://www.bbc.com/news/world-afr ica-54480257. Accessed 28 May 2021.

Hill, N. S. (2005). Leading together, working together: The role of team shared leadership in building collaborative capital in virtual teams. In M. M. Beyerlein, S. T. Beyerlein, & F. A. Kennedy (Eds.), *Collaborative capital: Creating intangible value. Advances in Interdisciplinary Studies of Work Teams* (Vol. 11, pp. 183–209). Bingley, UK: Emerald Group Publishing.

Hoch, J. E., Pearce, C. L., & Welzel, L. (2010). Is the most effective team leadership shared? *Journal of Personnel Psychology, 9*(3), 105–116.

Hosken, G., & Skiti, S. (2021). Senior Eskom manager's bank account frozen, with R11m in it. *Times* LIVE, May 7. https://www.timeslive.co.za/news/south-africa/2021-05-07-senior-eskom-managers-bank-account-fro zen-with-r11m-in-it/. Accessed 7 May 2021.

Kapoor, S. (2018). Questions over Gupta role in SAA halting its flights to India. *IOL*, March 11. https://www.iol.co.za/sundayindependent/ana lysis/questions-over-gupta-role-in-saa-halting-itsflights-to-india-13706694. Accessed 8 Aug 2022.

Kotow, E. (2019). How realistic is a leaderless organization? https://hedgetrade. com/how-realistic-is-a-leaderless-organization/. Accessed 20 Feb 2021.

Kropotkin, P. (1976). *The essential Kropotkin*. London: The Macmillan Press.

Maccoby, M. (2004). Why people follow the leader: The power of transference. *Harvard Business Review*. https://hbr.org/2004/09/why-people-follow-the-leader-the-power-of-transference. Accessed 31 Dec 2020.

Malala, J. (2021). As long as Cyril keeps cadres in key posts, state capture agents will walk free. *Times* LIVE, May 2. https://www.timeslive.co.za/sunday-times-daily/opinion-and-analysis/2021-05-02-justice-malala--as-long-as-cyril-keeps-cadres-in-key-posts-state-capture-agents-will-walk-free/. Accessed 2 May 2021.

Moran, J., & Beitsch, L. M. (2015). Leaderless leaders: Leaders in title only. *Journal of Public Health Management and Practice, 21*(5), 504–506. doi:10.1097/PHH.0000000000000282.

Nicolaides, V. C., LaPort, K. A., Chen, T. R., Tomassetti, A. J., Weis, E. J., Zaccaro, S. J., & Cortina, J. M. (2014). The shared leadership of teams: A meta-analysis of proximal, distal, and moderating relationships. *The Leadership Quarterly, 25*(5), 923–942.

O'Malley, P. (2008). *Shades of difference: Mac Maharaj and the struggle for South Africa.* London: Penguin Books.

Omarjee, L. (2021). Mboweni: "Rats and mice" acting as leaders have worsened the economic crisis. *News24*, October 5. https://www.news24.com/fin24/economy/mboweni-rats-and-mice-acting-as-leaders-have-worsened-the-economic-crisis-20211005. Accessed 5 Oct 2021.

Pearce, C. L., & Conger, J. A. (2003). All those years ago: The historical underpinnings of shared leadership. In C. L. Pearce & J. A. Conger (Eds.), *Shared leadership: Reframing the hows and whys of leadership* (pp. 1–18). Thousand Oaks, CA: Sage.

Peter, P. (2018). Leaderless management: What I discovered this week. LinkedIn, August 15. https://www.linkedin.com/pulse/leaderless-management-what-i-discovered-week-patrick-peter?trk=public_profile_article_view. Accessed 20 Feb 2021.

Ruben, S., & Bobat, S. (2014). Constructing racial hierarchies of skill—Experiencing affirmative action in a South African organisation: A qualitative review. *SA Journal of Industrial Psychology, 40*(1), Article a1158. doi:10.4102/sajip.v40i1.1158.

Seeletsa, M. (2021). R178 billion just the tip of Eskom corruption iceberg. *The Citizen*, May 4. https://citizen.co.za/business/2483443/r178-bn-just-the-tip-of-r800-bn-eskom-corruption-iceberg/. Accessed 4 May 2021.

Smith, C. (2020). Gordhan | SAA no garage sale for someone waiting in the wings. *News24*, May 15. https://www.news24.com/fin24/companies/industrial/gordhan-saa-no-garage-sale-for-someone-waiting-in-the-wings-20200515-2. Accessed 8 May 2021.

Western, S. (2014). Autonomist leadership in leaderless movements: Anarchists leading the way. *Ephemera: Theory and Politics in Organization, 14*(4),

673–698. http://www.ephemerajournal.org/sites/default/files/pdfs/contribut
ion/14-4western_0.pdf. Accessed 2 Jan 2021.

Wu, Q., Cormican, K., & Chen, G. (2020). A meta-analysis of shared leadership: Antecedents, consequences, and moderators. *Journal of Leadership &
Organizational Studies, 27*(1), 49–64. doi:10.1177/1548051818820862.

16

Leaderless Management: No! Leaders at All Levels: Yes!

Warren Blank

Introduction

What is "leaderless management?" Does it enable organizations to be successful? I offer responses to these two questions and propose that "leaderless" management does not really exist. "Leaderless" ignores the realities required for goal-oriented, organized action among interdependent people. It obscures recognizable, valid, and reliable differences between the leader and the manager roles. I suggest that organizations need "leadership-fullness" or "leadership at all levels." This chapter describes these concepts, offers examples, and suggests how they can provide a way forward in the disruptive, unprecedented changes experienced globally in 2020–2021.

W. Blank (✉)
The Leadership Group, Vero Beach, FL, USA
e-mail: leaderwb@gmail.com

© The Author(s), under exclusive license to Springer Nature Switzerland AG 2022
F. Hertel et al. (eds.), *Debating Leaderless Management*, Palgrave Debates in Business and Management, https://doi.org/10.1007/978-3-031-04593-6_16

The Leaderless Management Concept

I define leaderless management as an organization's efforts to minimize reliance on formal authority to guide and direct the work of subordinates. These efforts also include organizations reforming their management control and direction systems (e.g., strategies, goals, plans, rules, regulations, policies, and procedures) and structuring their hierarchy to minimize reliance upon formal position power to influence employees. The logic behind these efforts is to allow employees greater autonomy in their work roles. Research suggests doing so yields higher levels of employee production and satisfaction (Oldham and Hackman 1976). People are more motivated to perform well when they have more autonomy over their work and related decision-making (Pink 2009). From these perspectives, leaderless management is a positive way to design and implement a management system and to manage people. Employees can self-manage their time and behavior on the job, and they want more flexibility in their work life. Said more bluntly, employees do not need to be "babysat" to be productive (Kotow 2019).

Organizations apply leaderless management in various ways. Some decentralize their structure to allow for local-level decision-making versus reliance on a top-down approach. This means employees do not have to "run ideas up the chain of command" and wait until the boss approves their decision choices to implement them. Organizations also apply leaderless management by investments in managerial training. Such training focuses on providing knowledge and skills that managers can use to: engage staff to fulfill responsibilities without much oversight; involve and include staff in problem-solving; empower staff to take on responsibilities with increased decision-making latitude; and enable staff to operate as self-directed teams (Blank 2001).

The explosion of digital communication and use of telework or work-from-home allows for the use of more horizontal power structures and less direct managerial oversight (Kellerman 2012). Flextime and work-from-home practices give employees freedom from having to "punch in" and to be at their office desk/workplace to control their behavior and to be productive.

Organizational culture transformation efforts also attempt to implement leaderless management (Champy and Hammer 2003). Such transformations aim to establish systems, processes, norms, and values that cultivate peer collaboration and coordination, all-way communication, and employee engagement as "the way we do our business." The HR manager of WL Gore explains his organization's intent with leaderless management: "It's about making sure something is happening, but not taking control, you're not managing people, you're letting the team work out the how and then get on with it" (Kotow 2019).

Leaderless management approaches appear to yield valuable benefits. Overall, organizations that implement telework have experienced generally positive results (Hickman and Robison 2020). The 2020–2021 pandemic demanded large percentages (often 100%) of employees be required to work-from-home and rely on virtual interaction through digital communication. While this dramatic pandemic event certainly created disruption, discomfort, and dismay, overall many organizations adapted well enough and experienced how a significant change and reduction in hierarchical oversight could work. Companies such as Morning Star, retailer John Lewis, Beverly Cooperative Bank in Massachusetts, Denmark's Lynetten Wind Cooperative, Organic Valley, etc., report a fair degree of success based on how they use leaderless management (Kotow 2019).

Answers to the first two questions proposed above (What is "leaderless management?" Does it enable organizations to be successful?) can be provided. Leaderless management, as I defined it, the design and implementation of organizational control processes to allow employees greater autonomy, and less reliance on formal authority by managers, appears to enable organizations to fulfill dimensions of their overall objectives.

Yet, I suggest that truly "leaderless" management does not exist. It is actually a misnomer, a wrong or inaccurate use of a name or term. This is not mere semantics. The linkage of the labels "leaderless" and "management" does not account for how organized action among interdependent people actually occurs. It also obscures the distinctions between the leader and manager roles which are described below. Increased autonomy and empowerment do have a positive impact. People do respond better when their managers rely less on influence rooted in command, demand,

and require (i.e., "Obey, I am in charge") tactics. However, how people working in organizations actually get things done requires multiple people at all levels to demonstrate leadership or "leadership-full" behaviors (i.e., provide direction, as is outlined below). Such behaviors have always been significant driving factors for organizational action. They are even more important because of the complexity and uncertainty organizations face today.

The remainder of this chapter describes the leader-manager differences and offers examples of the varieties of leadership at all levels. I then offer a "way forward" by suggesting the need for a paradigm shift in the meaning of leadership and management to respond more successfully to the complexity of today's world.

The Differences Between the Leader and Manager Roles

My definition and description of the leader role and its clearly recognizable distinctions from the manager role (see Table 16.1) suggest that organizations need leadership-fullness or leadership at all levels not leaderless management because action within groups requires someone to provide direction and, if that person is not a formal manager, it is a person who "takes the lead." Managers and a management system are designed to get things done within organizations. Yet, it often takes leadership at all levels to achieve an organization's desired outcomes.

Think of your own experience to reveal the distinctions noted in Table 16.1. Recall a time when you were called by your manager (i.e., 1a, see Table 16.1) to attend an in-person or virtual meeting which had no agenda. The lack of an agenda signals a poorly executed element of a management system and an ineffective manager (i.e., 4a, see Table 16.1). An agenda offers a local-level plan and procedure to direct action. Effective managers establish agendas to prescribe a meeting's path toward established goals for which they are responsible (i.e., 3a, 5a, see Table 16.1). That limitation aside, imagine that you arrived at the meeting on time, and the members, all of whom you knew, were chatting amiably in pairs or trios about non-work-related matters. The participants' dialogue

Table 16.1 Recognizable differences between the manager and leader roles

1a. Managers are assigned subordinates	1b. Leaders gain willing followers
2a. Managers and employees are separated by a management system of rank, role, and responsibilities; terms like "superior," and "subordinate" reinforce this separation	2b. Leaders and followers are a unified "whole;" followers are a leader's allies whose voluntary support "creates" the leader; "true leadership" is the leader–follower interaction
3a. Managers have formal authority derived from their "position power" and can command, demand, and require staff to "carry out orders" and "obey" through the use of "force" based on sanctions if necessary	3b. Leader influence is beyond authority, "person power," based on commitment and desire that inspires voluntary support by followers; no one can be forced to willingly follow
4a. Managers direct employees to fulfill established, "prescribed paths" of action based on the management system (strategy, goals, plan, policies, procedures, rules, and regulations)	4b. Leaders offer direction as a response to a need to lead along "non-prescribed paths" when opportunities and obstacles arise that are not addressed by existing organizational plans and processes
5a. One manager oversees a unit of an organization (e.g., office, division, etc.)	5b. Multiple leaders can and do step up at all organizational levels

Source Blank (2008)

continued for several minutes past the expected meeting start time. The manager had still not arrived. Being responsible and accountable for simple requirements like on-time behavior is a key element of a well-honed management system and of an effective manager's behavior (i.e., 4a, see Table 16.1). All of the meeting participants were your peers and no one had any form of seniority. The informal dialogue continued for several more minutes.

At this point, did your awareness go to thoughts such as, "Are we waiting for the manager to come to get started?" or "Does anyone know our agenda?" Imagine then that a colleague asked, "How about using our time to discuss…. (a work related issue) to be productive until the manager arrives?" (i.e., 4b, see Table 16.1) Did you say, "Yes!" in response to this question because it matched your expectation about a need for direction? (i.e., 1b, 4b, see Table 16.1) Assume then that others gave verbal or non-verbal signals of agreement to take work-related action which resulted in the group being focused on getting something done (i.e., 1b, 2b, 3b, 4b, see Table 16.1).

I label what happened in this situation as leadership-full behavior or leaders at all levels. Your colleague "took the lead" by offering a course of action where none existed (i.e., 4b, see Table 16.1). There was no prescribed path set by the management system (i.e., 4a, see Table 16.1). Your colleague motivated you into action. You were a willing follower (i.e., 2b, see Table 16.1). Followership is an overlooked aspect of what people think about and discuss as an element of what I call, "true leadership." My experience indicates many people view followers as, "second class citizens." I often hear the comment, "You don't want to be a follower, be a leader!" I argue that no one can be a leader without willing followers (i.e., 1b). Willingness is the key word. Followership is voluntary (i.e., 3b, see Table 16.1). When we hear the comment, "Follow orders," in a highly centralized, command and control system, what is actually meant is, "obey," not, "commit" (i.e., 3a, see Table 16.1) (Blank 1995).

Followers, especially "first followers," matter because their initial support gives someone who tries to influence others that first important boost that enables them to lead. Without followers, there is no leadership, only ideas that fall on infertile ground. Furthermore, a leader's direction translates into impact when a "critical mass" of followers commit to it. The critical mass could be "enough" followers (e.g., a majority of others) or one or a few "key" followers (e.g., those who have significant credibility that attracts others to follow). Critical mass was established in the meeting when the other members also supported your colleague's initiative (Blank 2021).

This meeting did not illustrate leaderless management. Leadership-full behaviors occurred. A leader (the person who suggested, "How about using our time to discuss….") and followers (your comment, "Yes") took action (i.e., 2b, see Table 16.1). The meeting illustrated the value of "leadership-at-all levels." When there is a need for direction, someone must step up and others must follow for work to get done (i.e., 4b, see Table 16.1). Anyone can contribute as a leader to provide such direction and, often times multiple leaders do take such initiative (i.e., 5b, see Table 16.1) (Blank and Brown 2006). Anyone can step up to be a first follower.

Organizations that claim to institute "leaderless management" by decentralizing their structure, managerial training, culture transformation, etc., must reframe what they actually do as a leadership at all levels approach (Blank 1995). The need for multiple leaders stems from the reality no organization can create a perfect plan, implement fool-proof systems, or cover every contingency. Change happens. And, as the events of 2020–2021 revealed, change can be unprecedented, complex, turbulent, and volatile. As the military motto indicates, "No plan survives first contact with the enemy." Or, as Murphy's Law suggests, "If something can go wrong, it will." Furthermore, managers do not always hold employees accountable in ways that promote positive performance results. In fact, some use the term "leaderless management" in reference to managers who have difficulties exercising control and influence over their staff (Heah 2016). I argue this is not leaderless action since being a manager does not make someone a leader, and leaders may not be managers. Managers that fail to fulfill the requirement of accountability illustrate "worst boss" characteristics.

When there is no prescribed path, someone must step up, "take the lead," the "risk of initiative" and offer an idea to get something done (i.e., 4b, see Table 16.1). And, others need to take the risk of willing followership and support the initiative. True leadership then occurs. Leadership at all levels does not mean a *break down* in a management system or the use of formal authority. Instead, it creates a *build-up* of leadership-full behavior.

Consider some alternate scenarios for how the meeting could have played out. No one offered a direction and the meeting drifted aimlessly like a rudderless boat. Or, no one else but you willingly embraced your colleagues' comment. You and your colleague could not force others to follow since neither of you had formal authority. The necessary critical mass is not established. Nothing got done. Or image your colleagues' comment and your first follower response were met with someone else saying, "We should wait for the manager to arrive before we do anything." If that comment got multiple nods or comments of agreement and the participants just continued to sit and chat, the operative reference point of awareness was "subordinate compliance" to hierarchical command (i.e., 3a, 3b, see Table 16.1). It was a, "Take no risk outside what we are supposed to do," quality of thinking and doing. And, imagine one more possible scenario. You did not support your colleague's comment, and after a few more minutes, people got calls or texts and left the in-person meeting or signed off to the virtual meeting. As you left the in-person version of the meeting, you walked with your colleague and said, "I liked your idea," or, you sent a text or email after the virtual meeting with the same sentiment. Did your colleague respond, "Then why didn't you speak up?" This scenario illustrates the need and value of a first follower. True leadership requires a leader–follower connection (i.e., 2b, see Table 16.1).

Situations like the meeting outlined above happen every day at all organizational levels among interdependent people. Leaders and followers must respond to get things done in a non-prescribed situation (i.e., 2b, 4b, see Table 16.1). The reality is different when people do not need guidance because they can figure out how to take action that does not involve others, i.e., their work is essentially independent. People also do not need direction when an organization's established guidelines offer direction for clear courses of action. Such guidelines, in the form of strategies, plans, goals, rules, regulations, policies, procedures, etc., are necessary and useful for orderly interdependent action toward desired goals (i.e., 4a, see Table 16.1). Organizational action benefits from managers who, at a minimum, communicate guidelines, monitor action, and assess results.

Managers are typically looked to first by their staff to provide direction in non-prescribed situations. "Best bosses" respond to this need and use leader versus manager influence approaches. They seek commitment first. They resort to demanding compliance with their position power last. When managers seek commitment first to attract willing followers, they are viewed as boss-leaders. Best boss managers are also willing to be part of true leadership by being "first followers." Such managers are not overwhelmed with an exalted sense of self-importance. Their motivation is "mission-first" not "me-first." Managers who embrace, successfully implement, and support others who lead are still managers. They are also models of a leadership at all levels approach.

Varieties of Leadership at All Levels

Multiple leaders and followers can and do exist at all organizational levels (Blank and Brown 2006). They have impact at various levels and in varying degrees. Some leader–follower actions are broad and far-reaching. Consider an inspiring organizational vision or long-term strategy that a critical mass of an organization's members readily embrace as a meaningful direction and commit to its implementation over a long time frame. Think of the response to President Kennedy's, "Put a man on the moon in this decade." Publications typically tout such visions as "great leadership." I agree that this level and degree of leadership has substantial impact. Yet, in my experience, what makes a difference in the long run are many more brief instances of the leader–follower connection. The "core cadre of the committed" throughout an organization who step up to lead and willingly follow in more narrow scopes of action ultimately help organizations to be successful. It is the many soldiers in the trenches who trudge forward step-by-step and hill-by-hill that defeat an enemy and win a war. It is the multitude of leaders and followers who connect at every level that enable an organization to achieve its vision and implement its strategy. Books and films about the moon-mission illustrate how NASA's success resulting from examples of thousands of leaders at all levels action to figure out how to achieve the vision.

Managers and managerial systems can thwart leadership at all levels by being too "rule minded" and overly command and control. Efforts to empower and engage people at all levels counter these barriers to leadership-full behavior. And, a manager can implement and take initiative to create and support leaders at all levels. A personal example illustrates this. In the early 2000s, I had the privilege of providing several leadership development courses for a U.S. government organization. In the first few courses, participants explained to me that their direct supervisors were not usually receptive to their leadership initiatives. They indicated the management system was rooted in more command and control, "Do what you are told," methods. I recalled conversations with the senior manager who engaged me to conduct these courses and the motivation behind it. The manager, who had taken one of my courses, embraced the need for leadership at all levels as essential for the organization's success. I contacted the manager and described the feedback I received. The manager indicated action would be taken.

Several weeks later, while conducting another course with the organization, I mentioned the senior manager's name. A participant asked if I had heard what the manager had done a few weeks earlier. I indicated I did not. The participant then explained that the manager sent an email to everyone in the organization asking for their ideas about how to improve the organization. The manager committed to give consideration to those initiatives that enhanced the organization's ability to fulfill its mission. Two-thousand responses were provided within five days. The manager then closed the invitation, reviewed the responses, and made a commitment to see that two-hundred of them were implemented. Consider that. Leaders stepped up at all levels. The senior manager was the "key" first follower. The tone of that course and subsequent courses I conducted visibly changed. Participants were empowered, energized, and engaged to think and act like leaders: leadership-full behavior, leadership at all levels.

Examples of Leadership at All Levels

Since 1972, Orpheus, a New York city-based orchestra, had operated without a formal conductor. It has no "manager." Yet, it is not leaderless. A core group convenes to make decisions about the total orchestra's direction. This happens when someone in the core group suggests a direction, and gains a consensus, critical mass of followers within that group. The idea is then brought to the full orchestra. And, the process of gaining committed followers continues by someone clarifying the direction and working the process to gain consensus among all the musicians. Subsequent performances are guided by another, sometimes different make up of individuals (Satell 2012). In every case, members of a core group take the lead, offer initiatives, and/or engage the group to generate ideas. Decisions are made when a critical mass of the group follows.

Anonymous is a group of online chat rooms, forums, and software protocols. There is no hierarchical structure or even designated membership. Things happen when someone gets an idea for an operation (i.e., sees the need to lead) and/or recruits others (i.e., followers) through chat rooms. Action plans are created by ad hoc groups in special private chats. Leaders and followers emerge to guide this group's action (Satell 2012).

Jack Welch, former CEO of GE, is often touted as a great manager and highly successful leader. He demonstrated both the application of managerial formal influence and the recognition that leaders at all levels add value. Welch wielded his formal, position-based authority like a surgeon when he unceremoniously cut businesses in which GE could not dominate the market in first or second positions. He established a performance evaluation system that required firing the bottom 10% of employees and managers. Welch also introduced a "corporation without boundaries" vision. His "boundaryless" model sought to: break down walls that separate people within the organization from their core external stakeholders; remove barriers among traditional functions; and "recognize no distinctions" between domestic and foreign operations. He wanted to "ignore or erase group labels such as 'management,' 'salaried,' or 'hourly,'" which he argued get in the way of people working well together (Hirschhorn and Gilmore 1992, p. 104). Welch illustrated the use of a highly directive management system and strong use of the command and control action of a hard-nosed manager. On the other hand, he encouraged leadership at all levels by his focus on boundaryless behavior that aimed to eliminate stove-piped barriers among people and reinforce more fluid interactions among all.

Consider President Joe Biden's plan to inoculate 100 million people with the COVID-19 vaccines within his first 100 days in office. Think of the hundreds of thousands of people it took to achieve this goal. I recall my wife and I getting our shots. We arrived at a facility a short time before our scheduled appointment and noticed two lines of people formed along a walkway in front of the location. It was unclear which line we should join. A woman holding a clipboard was standing nearby. I asked, "Are you in charge?" She smiled and replied, "No, I'm just a volunteer," and asked me, "Are you here for the vaccine?" I told her we were, she looked at her clipboard and asked for our names. She indicated that we were on the list for this day at this location at the time we had been assigned. She then directed us to join one of the lines. I asked her to describe the steps in the overall process. The volunteer explained it. I then said, "Thanks for taking the lead." The woman gave me a somewhat curious look and said, "I'm not in-charge. I'm just helping out to keep things moving." I responded, "That's an important part about what being a leader is." The woman was clearly taken aback, yet she smiled, and said, "I guess you're right."

I was delighted this person recognized the important contribution she made to President Biden's incredibly complex and significant plan. When we entered each of what turned out to be the three stages to get the vaccine, I recognized a clearly outlined, pre-determined, prescribed process for each stage. Yet, I observed several citizens who had concerns and needed clarity of direction on what to do within each step of the process. Volunteers cheerfully and kindly answered. Throughout our time there, my wife and I heard many comments such as, "This is well-organized." "Everyone is doing a good job." And, "I was concerned about how this would work, but the people in-charge were really helpful." The irony to me is none of the volunteers felt like they were in-charge. They operated without formal authority and did not demand compliance. They were examples of action by leadership at all levels.

The author, Frederric Laloux, stated:

> The tasks of management, setting direction and objectives, planning, directing, controlling, and evaluating, haven't disappeared. They are simply no longer concentrated in dedicated management roles. Because they are spread widely, not narrowly, it can be argued that there is more management and leadership happening at any time in self-managing organizations despite, or rather precisely because of, the absence of full-time managers. (Kotow 2019).

A Way Forward

My position, leaderless-management, "No!" and leaders at all levels, "Yes!" could be summed up by a quote from the Hall of Fame baseball player Yogi Berra: "If you don't know where you're going, you may end up someplace else" (Goodreads 2021). Someone must provide direction when people do not know how to achieve organizational goals. Managers are expected to do so, and, as argued above, a manager is not a leader without willing followers. Organizations and managers can enable non-managers to do so and to become leaders when others willingly follow. The result is not leaderless-management, but leaders at all levels.

In my 35-plus years' experience training, consulting, speaking, and coaching with hundreds of organizations and thousands of people around the world, I often ask, "Do you view every boss you ever had as a leader?" Most people respond, "No." I also ask, "Have you been in situations where you perceived someone as a leader who was not a manager?" and almost always get a, "Yes," response. People obviously recognize there is a difference between the leader and manager roles. Yet, it is fairly common for people to refer to their manager or their organization's management as, "the leadership." Countless individuals in my training and consulting work have said to me, "I can't be a leader because I am not in charge." Something is amiss in the language and labels we use to describe these roles. This impacts people's recognition of the impact they can have. It limits them "stepping up" to meet the need to lead.

We need a paradigm shift in how we think about, discuss, and use the labels of leader, manager, management, and leadership to respond to the complexity of today's world. We need to clarify, promote, educate for, and reward what I call the "true leadership" mindset. This quality of perception and action means people embrace being leaders and followers with reference points of awareness such as "ownership" (i.e., "I am responsible, able to respond") and "adaptability" (i.e., "I can confront and change my thinking and behavior in response to my environment"). They demonstrate higher levels of "grit," defined as passion for an outcome and the perseverance to "stick with it" in the face of adversity (Duckworth 2016). They also exhibit "self-efficacy": a belief in their ability to succeed in specific situations or accomplish a task (Bandura 1977).

The true leadership mindset is essential as we attempt to forge forward through the many challenges we face today: a global, interconnected, and often fragile economy; multiple instances of racist, sexist, etc., discrimination; increased dependency on technology and concomitant vulnerability to cyberattacks; rampant expressions of misleading and false communication and slanted "news" coverage. And, we must now recognize the "butterfly" effect of how a tiny virus molecule can spread across the globe and create a devastating pandemic of unprecedented proportions. Leaders and followers at all levels, who recognize, address, and persevere to resolve these issues must step up. Leadership at all levels is everybody's business, a way to create better standards of living and higher standards of life that bring fulfillment.

References

Bandura, A. (1977). Self-efficacy: Toward a unifying theory of behavioral change. *Psychological Review, 84*(2), 191–215.

Blank, W. (1995). *The nine natural laws of leadership.* New York: AMACOM.

Blank, W. (2001). *The 108 skills of natural born leaders.* New York: AMACOM.

Blank, W. (2008). *Leadership for smart people book I: The five truths.* Vero Beach, FL: Leadership Group Press.

Blank, W. (2021). What explains the quality of today's leaders? In A. Örtenblad (Ed.), *Debating bad leadership: Reasons and remedies* (pp. 163–179). Cham, Switzerland: Palgrave Macmillan.

Blank, W., & Brown, A. (2006). *The leadership event: The moments of true leadership that move organizations.* Vero Beach, FL: Leadership Group Press.

Champy, J., & Hammer, M. (2003). *Reengineering the corporation.* New York: Harper Collins.

Duckworth, A. (2016). *Grit.* New York: Simon and Schuster.

Goodreads. (2021). Quotable quote, Yogi Berra. https://www.goodreads.com/quotes/23616-if-you-don-t-know-where-you-are-going-you-ll-end. Accessed 23 Apr 2021.

Heah, M. (2016). Are you a leaderless leader? *Leaderonomics.com.* https://www.leaderonomics.com/articles/personal/leaderless-leader. Accessed 23 Mar 2021.

Hickman, A., & Robison, J. (2020). Is working remotely effective? *Gallup Research.* https://www.getabstract.com/en/summary/is-working-remotely-effective-gallup-research-says-yes/38866. Accessed 23 Feb 2021.

Hirschhorn, L., & Gilmore, T. (1992). The new boundaries of the "boundary-less" company. *Harvard Business Review, 70*(3), 104–115.

Kellerman, B. (2012). *The end of leadership*. New York: Harper Collins.

Kotow, E. (2019). How realistic is a leaderless organization? *Hedgetrade.com*. https://hedgetrade.com/how-realistic-is-a-leaderless-organization/. Accessed 11 Mar 2021.

Oldham, G., & Hackman, R. (1976). Motivation through the design of work: Test of a theory. *Organizational Behavior and Human Performance, 16*(2), 250–279.

Pink, D. (2009). *Drive*. New York: Riverhead Books.

Satell, G. (2012). The leaderless organization. https://digitaltonto.com/2012/the-leaderless-organization/. Accessed 7 Feb 2021.

17

Principled Leadership: The Antidote to Leaderless Management

Sharon E. Kenny-Blanchard

Introduction

The effectiveness of a leader is directly related to their leadership approach and while achieving results is key, what they bring, give, and how they support their team is even more important (Avolio and Bass 2002; Becker 1998; Denison and Neale 1996; Kerr 2013; Kotter 1990, 2002; Kouzes and Posner 2017; Lawrence and Pirson 2015; Parameswar and Prasad 2017; Petrie 2014; Schein 2010). An effective leader can be described as one who is self-aware, works to win the souls and hearts of their people, understands the organizational culture, its strengths, and weaknesses, and clearly understands their role and the context of their actions in order to act as responsible stewards of organizations and society (Gill 2003; Lawrence and Pirson 2015; Parameswar and Prasad

S. E. Kenny-Blanchard (✉)
Principled Leadership Institute, Twizel, New Zealand
e-mail: sharonekennyblanchard@gmail.com

© The Author(s), under exclusive license to Springer Nature
Switzerland AG 2022
F. Hertel et al. (eds.), *Debating Leaderless Management*,
Palgrave Debates in Business and Management,
https://doi.org/10.1007/978-3-031-04593-6_17

2017). Denison and Neale (1996) further define effective leaders as those who build human capacity, empower, and build their team, develop organizational capability, and create change.

Understanding leadership is key to unpacking how an organization functions within the context of leaderless management. I have concluded that leaderless management can be understood as a group of individuals who work collectively in an attempt to meet organizational goals and objectives and is devoid of formal leadership (Choi and Schnurr 2014; Cook et al. 2020; Nielsen 2011; Rojek 2014). While the gap between leadership and management continues to be widely debated, it provides an opportunity to validate the need for leadership within organizations. The difference can be illuminated within the context of transformation leadership theory, where "leadership is essentially concerned with bringing about transformational change. Management is primarily concerned with achieving stability and predictability by ensuring that subordinates comply with the rules, regulations and working procedures" (Burnes and Todnem 2012, p. 241). If we believe that management requires a leader who is responsible for guiding, enabling, empowering, enacting change, and is accountable, then leaderless management organizations won't have the capacity to be responsive to change, in fact, they will be ineffectual. Given the expansive evidence supporting the need for leadership (Avolio and Bass 2002), one wonders why leaderless management is considered. In theory, it may be posited but in practice leaderless management has yet to be demonstrated to be effective, sustainable, or lacking in leadership (Choi and Schnurr 2014).

Whether a leader is effective or ineffective can also be debated given that an effective leader can be constructive and destructive at the same time; positively impacting the organization while damaging individuals along the way, resulting in a non-sustainable leadership approach (Einarson et al. 2007; Padilla et al. 2007; Schyns and Schilling 2013; Shaw et al. 2011). Given this, principled leadership theory offers the proposition that an organization lead by principled leaders will ensure that leaderless management does not emerge or will even need to be considered. Principled leadership is defined as a leader who is rooted in authentic behaviors, free from the influence of one's ego, firm in the knowledge of self through identity, has a balanced perspective based on strong morals and values, and works in service of others based on love and respect (Blanchard 2018). The principled leader provides a sustainable example of effective leadership and why organizations need leadership to function. Teams require leaders. Organizations need structure, accountability, and depend on leadership. There is no room for leaderless management and if an employee feels that there is no need for a leader, then the leader has most certainly done their job, and that may not necessarily be a bad thing.

The chapter presents arguments for why leaderless management is not practical or sustainable, they are: (1) People need to be led: they require boundaries, structures, and frameworks; (2) Leaderless management leads to the status quo; and (3) the principled leader advantage is offered as a sustainable antidote to the conceptualization of leaderless management. My leadership research and professional experience throughout my career provide a basis and framework for these arguments.

People Need to Be Led

Rojek shared that "leaderless events have been regarded as improbable as spontaneous combustion is in the natural sciences" (Rojeck 2014, p. 352). In theory, leaderless management appears to be democratic, socially inclusive, equitable, and non-hierarchical collectives, but in reality could be the "holy grail of cultural management" (Rojek 2014, p. 362). It is highly improbable that leaderless management in practice can exist without the emergence of leadership in some shape, leading to my next argument supporting why leaderless management isn't practical, people need to be led.

In arguing for leadership, that people need to be led, you could post the question of accountability and who is ultimately responsible for the organization. In answering this, the words of Tzu (2021) provide insight: A leader is best when people barely know the leader exists, when their work is done, their aim fulfilled, the people will say: we did it ourselves (Tzu 2021). Rather than question whether this is attainable, it is worth discussing if it can be sustainable and that by our human nature, people need to be led (Bolino et al. 2010; Neves 2009). To explain this further, I offer the following example: there have been many times throughout my professional career while in positions of leadership where I experienced my team to be ticking along quite seamlessly; everything was operating smoothly, folks were happy, we were reaching our strategic goals, and the team didn't need me to be with them every single minute. This didn't mean that they didn't need me, their leader, in fact it was most probable that in those moments they had simply achieved the ability to be the best version of themselves in their role thus enabling the overall team to efficiently operate. During these times, I believe they could say, they did it themselves, or did they? I have concluded this was when the members of my team felt the most empowered, capable, motivated, efficient, but most importantly, supported. I often wonder, did they begin to think that they could do it alone, didn't need the boss around? If a leader is subtle enough, this amazing ticking along could, and probably should, become a regular thing. As a leader there's no better feeling than this, the realization of achieving your leadership and organizational goals. However, there is one caveat. Having experienced the other side of leadership as a member of a team, I have observed there can be a very fine line between the awareness of perceived great leadership-in-action and the team thinking they are doing all of the work, on their own, without leadership. It was during the times when we didn't have strong leadership that we became stagnated, maintained systems and processes, but did not develop further, advance, or progress. In fact, we didn't have a mechanism for growth. We needed the empowerment, direction, and guidance, the reinforcement that a leader provides.

The leader is ultimately responsible for ensuring the team's growth and development in achieving successful outcomes for the organization. In peer-based organizations (Nielsen 2011), peers are considered to be equal but leadership isn't about inequality, it's about responsibility. You can be equal with your peer, but you may have a higher level of responsibility. Choi and Schnurr (2014) discussed that even in leaderless organizations, there was evidence of leadership emergence questioning whether or not leaderless management can work in practice. To further explain this, Wendover (2002) observed that nines hire tens, and sevens hire fives (Wendover 2002). What does this mean? A leader who is authentic, courageous, and confident will hire someone they believe is more competent than themselves, a ten. Whereas, a less confident leader, will hire someone that isn't as competent as they perceive themselves to be and who they can control; someone they can manage, who doesn't pose a threat to their current position. Great leaders hire tens. They surround themselves with an incredible team, exploding with skill, experience, and technical acumen to work in unity. These leaders work to build a team where each individual will become the best they can be in their role, they provide them the opportunity to grow, develop, and to be nurtured in return for a positive, engaging, and stable work environment. That's why things appear to be seamless when things are ticking along, it's not due to the lack of leadership, it's because the leader has done his job. An effective leadership culture creates the ability for this to happen where the leader is the visionary or catalyst for the organization and has direct responsibility and accountability for this.

People need to be led, guided, and supported in order to flourish as an individual member of the team, to ensure that they can contribute as part of a larger team, and ultimately work to ensure they meet the goals and outcomes as set by the leader who has the ultimate responsibility and accountability for this (Avolio and Bass 2002; Badura et al. 2020; Kouzes and Posner 1999, 2017). A lack of direction, support, and responsibility can lead to chaos, and raises the point that leadership is a necessary and integral component of formal organizational structures. Why? What does the leader really have to ensure? Reaching and exceeding organizational benchmarks and goals, understanding the centrality of key performance indicators, yes, fiscal acumen, absolutely. Being responsible, accountable, of course. Individual team members have various degrees of experience, knowledge, skills, and expertise, and their accountability and responsibility within the organization needs to be aligned with this. By their very human nature, people do need guidance, boundaries, and parameters, and even though when we establish these in an equal opportunity dynamic, it isn't bullet-proof (Bolino et al. 2010; Neves 2009). Which leads to my position supporting the need for leadership; that people need to be led, guided, and supported, and organizations are better when a stable environment is created through strong leadership. This further points to why leaderless management is not practical or sustainable and will lead to the status quo which will be reviewed next as part of the argument for why leaderless management is not effective or practical.

Leaderless Management Leads to the Status Quo

The previous section put forward that people need to be led, that supportive and enabling leadership empowers individuals to flourish and reach their potential as part of reaching organizational goals and objectives (Avolio and Bass 2002; Badura et al. 2020; Kouzes and Posner 1999, 2017). This next section provides further evidence for the impracticality of leaderless management, that without leadership enactment, individual and team efforts will lead to the status quo.

In examining effective leadership as part of understanding why leaderless management can lead to the status quo, it was important to ask whether leaders impact organizations and if so, to step back further to understand what are the perceived expectations of effective leadership. In discussing leadership effectiveness, Svensson and Wood (2005) ascertained that leadership effectiveness and organizational achievements may be dependent upon a serendipitous event or series of events rather than skillfulness, questioning contemporary leadership effectiveness. I agree with their argument that it is an evolutionary process of interconnected events, but argue that the impact of these events is dependent upon the leader and not interconnected, timely events (Svensson and Wood 2005). What does this have to do with the status quo? You need leaders to keep things moving, shifting, and responding. Even though leaderless management environments can be considered to be highly collaborative collectives, a coordination of problem solving with shared responsibility, there isn't evidence that they are dynamic and responsive to change (Choi and Schnurr 2014; Rojek 2014). The leader ensures the organization is dynamic, moving, changing, and responsive because this is the essence of leadership whether it be due to an inherent, conscious, or subconscious leadership approach (Badura et al. 2020; Yukl 2013). This motivation to lead and the ability to influence others as a means of accomplishing shared objectives are core components of leadership

(Badura et al. 2020; Yukl 2013). Leaders undertake positions requiring a high level of accountability and responsibility where they are called to empower, motivate, and enable others. A leader further connects personal meaning to a higher purpose to create belief and a sense of direction, and works to create a sense of connection, collaboration, and unity for the whole team and organization (Kerr 2013, p. 35).

Why is leadership needed? What's the difference? When everything is the status quo and things are running smoothly, no one is looking for the leader. However, when the going gets tough, in times of need, and in a crisis, you need a leader who is enabling, empowering, guiding, and most importantly, affirming. We need leaders who are continually aware, responsive, and operating at a level where they see everything, respond to everyone, and ensure the needs of the team are a priority where we don't have to be perfect but "engaged and committed to aligning values with action" (Brown 2012, p. 172). The responsibility of the leader is one of unity; they are responsible for everyone and ensuring cohesion among the organization or area in which they have responsibility. Brown (2012) describes this as a daring leadership strategy, crucial in understanding the spaces between where we currently are and where we desire to be in the future. Given the absence of a leader to guide and enact change, a leaderless management environment is not equipped to respond to anything but the status quo; there is no clear pathway for responsibility and accountability, enabling individual and team development, ensuring a micro and macro focus on employee development to achieve organizational goals and objectives (Kotter 1990, 2002; Kouzes and Pozner 2017; Neves 2009). It is void of a healthy balance; one that can be found through a principled leadership approach put forward as the antidote to leaderless management in the next section.

Principled Leadership: The Antidote

The leadership literature reveals substantial evidence of ineffective or bad leadership and whether ineffective leadership leads to a desire for a leaderless management environment will continue to be debatable (Badura et al. 2020; Einarson et al. 2007; Kelemen et al. 2020; Padilla et al.

2007; Schyns and Schilling 2013; Shaw et al. 2011). The key question to ask is if a leader's attributes and characteristics create an effective leadership approach where they positively impact their working cultures, and the attitudes and behaviors of those they lead for the long term? This section focusses on principled leadership as the antidote for leaderless management; a leadership approach that moves beyond traditional forms of leadership and toward an approach where the leader truly cares for and sees their people as the integral component of their leadership approach. Within the context of this chapter, antidote is defined as a way of preventing something bad and in this case, principled leadership offered as the way to avoid leaderless management environments (Cambridge English Dictionary 2021).

In their seminal work, Kouzes and Posner put forward that leadership is dichotomous, it is "about toughness and tenderness. Guts and grace. Firmness and fairness. Fortitude and gratitude. Passion and compassion" (Kouzes and Posner 1999, pp. xv–xvi). The definition of principled leadership is aligned with their approach as a principled leader is rooted in authentic behaviors, free from the influence of one's ego, firm in the knowledge of self through identity, has a balanced perspective based on strong morals and values, and works in service of others based on love and respect (Blanchard 2018). This passionate and compassionate approach enables the leader to be tough and kind. Principled leadership provides evidence that a sustainable, effective leadership approach comes from being authentic, honest, caring for others, acknowledging vulnerability, being capable of building trust, demonstrating integrity, humility, upholding the respect and dignity of others, and having courage (Avolio and Gardner 2005; Blanchard 2018; Sergiovanni 2005). Authenticity is at the core of principled leadership. People simply know when a leader is being honest and become accepting of tough love in the presence of authenticity (Avolio and Gardner 2005; Blanchard 2018). Equally important to honesty is integrity. I do believe that great leaders are bubbling with integrity but how can we build a sustainable leadership practice with trust, respect relationship and a cooperative, healthy team at the center? A principled leadership approach provides a sustainable leadership practice and is the antidote to contemporary leadership cultures driving the discussion of leaderless management.

Principled leaders provide the antidote to leaderless management because they work from a place of service and care, they put others first and work hard to make their individual team members thrive from a health and safety perspective, and, it seems, they do this from an almost altruistic stance. It is a leadership approach grounded in an honest endeavor to build individuals first, then the team, as step in achieving organizations' goals and strategies (Blanchard 2018). Accountability is key to this leadership approach.

A principled leadership approach is steeped in accountability and framed so as to ensure that the team has the opportunity to develop, to be the best that they can be, both individually and collectively, while ensuring the goals of the organization are achieved. The principled leader goes further, deeper, not only to successfully achieve and perform at a high level, but labors to get the most out of their people; to ensure they meet their own, the individual, and the team's goals. To do this, the leader's primary goal is creating a healthy environment in which everyone can thrive. The World Health Organization (WHO 2006) defines health and well-being as not simply the absence of disease but an overall balance of physical, mental, and social well-being. A principled leader ensures this balance is maintained in themselves and equally, in their people. I believe that the antidote to leaderless management is moving beyond traditional forms of leadership to principled leadership where the focus is on developing the individual as part of a wider team.

When you have honest, authentic, principled leaders, great organizations emerge. A principled leader operates from a deeper leadership approach that is based on a love that is truly beyond serving the needs of the self, and organization, and moves toward serving others for their better good (care), and service of a greater cause. Humility can be found at the core of their practice where it begins with a level of interpersonal communication, enabling an interrogative, facilitative learning environment in which no one has all the answers (Kerr 2013, p. 18). This environment requires trust, vulnerability, and courage.

Within this leadership approach, the motivation to lead may be innate, natural, or a directed behavior, and when it comes from an authentic, honest, principled intrinsic desire, the pathway, although not easy, will hopefully lead to fulfillment for the individual and those they work for. As a leader, I purposely, always use the term we as I do not believe that anything I do is of my own accord. I do not have an affinity or desire to be called the boss. When you have humility at the core of your practice, you don't need to receive the accolades, the title, the hierarchical reference of where you are in the organizational chart. You know what you have to do, you have a full awareness of your role and its associated responsibility and accountability; you are part of the greater team ensuring that everyone is capable of achieving individual and team goals. Using terminology such as we and team doesn't mean that you don't confidently step into your role as leader, it means you know who you are, what you do, and the critical importance of every member of the team, and how they uniquely contribute. This is principled leadership in action. This is what provides a sustainable leadership approach ensuring that a healthy organizational culture negates the development of leaderless management.

Concluding Thoughts

It was the intention of the author to put forward the notion that leadership is needed and when approached from a principled leadership approach provides a proactive response to the conceptualization of leaderless management. I believe leaderless management is steeped in the status quo, with a lack of focus and accountability resulting in eventual mismanagement, disharmony, and even chaos due to a lack of visionary, efficacious leadership that can foster innovation and entrepreneurial progress. Leaderless management in theory may be posited, but in practice is not sustainable. If you have an organization built upon the shoulders of principled leaders, you don't need leaderless management.

The concept of leaderless management provides the opportunity to review the leadership map with a mindful frame of the influence of power and privilege, and what it is that motivates an individual to desire to be working within the leadership realm. There is also the concept raised within this chapter that perhaps leaders inadvertently create leaderless teams; or is this simply the perception of the team? Is leaderless management a situation where you don't know where to put the cart or the horse? Leadership in twenty-first-century organizations need the cart, they require the horse, and without a driver, one continues to ponder, how they can be sustainable without the presence of a leader.

References

Avolio, B. J., & Bass, B. M. (2002). *Developing potential across a full range of leadership: Cases on transactional and transformational leadership.* Mahwah, NJ: Lawrence Erlbaum Associates.

Avolio, B. J., & Gardner, W. L. (2005). Authentic leadership development: Getting to the root of positive forms of leadership. *The Leadership Quarterly, 16*(3), 315–338. doi:10.1016/j.leaqua.2005.03.001.

Badura, K. L., Grijalva, E., Galvin, B. M., Joseph, D. L., & Owens, B. P. (2020). Motivation to lead: A meta-analysis and distal-proximal model of motivation and leadership. *Journal of Applied Psychology, 105*(4), 331–354. doi:10.1037/ap1000439.

Becker, T. (1998). Integrity in organizations: Beyond honesty and conscientiousness. *Academy of Management Review, 23*(1), 154–161.

Blanchard, S. (2018). *Exploring principled leadership in higher education: A study of president's, provosts', and deans' leadership approaches while managing a change agenda.* Ed.D. Dissertation, University of Calgary, Alberta.

Bolino, M., Valcea, S., & Harvey, J. (2010). Employee, manage thyself: The potentially negative implication of expecting employees to behave proactively. *Journal of Organizational Psychology, 83*(2), 325–345. doi:10.1348/096317910X493134.

Brown, B. (2012). *Daring greatly: How the courage to be vulnerable transforms the way we live, love, parent, and lead.* New York: Penguin Group.

Burnes, B., & Todnem, R. (2012). Leadership and change: The case for greater ethical clarity. *Journal of Business Ethics, 108*(2), 239–252.

Cambridge English Dictionary. (2021). https://dictionary.cambridge.org/dictionary/english/antidote. Accessed 8 Nov 2021.

Choi, S., & Schnurr, S. (2014). Exploring distributed leadership: Solving disagreements and negotiating consensus in a leaderless team. *Discourse Studies, 16*(1), 3–24. doi:10.1177/1461445613508891.

Cook, A., Zill, A., & Meyer, B. (2020). Observing leadership as behavior in teams and herds—An ethological approach to shared leadership research. *The Leadership Quarterly, 31*(2), 1–14. doi:10.1016/j.leaqua.2019.05.003.

Denison, D. R., & Neale, W. S. (1996). *The Denison leadership development survey.* Ann Arbor, MI: Aviat.

Einarson, S., Aasland, M. S., & Skogstad, A. (2007). Destructive leadership behaviour: A definition and conceptual model. *The Leadership Quarterly, 18*(3), 207–216. doi:10.1016/j.leaqua.2007.03.002.

Gill, R. (2003). Change management—Or change leadership? *Journal of Change Management, 3*(4), 307–318. doi:10.1080/714023845.

Greenleaf, R. K. (2002). *Servant leadership: A journey into the nature of legitimate power and greatness* (25th Anniversary ed.). Mahwah, NJ: Paulist Press.

Greenleaf, R. K. (2003). *The servant-leader within: A transformative path.* Mahwah, NJ: Paulist Press.

Kelemen, T. K., Matthews, S. H., & Breevant, K. (2020). Leading day-to-day: A review of the daily causes and consequences of leadership behaviors. *The Leadership Quarterly, 31*(1), 1–19. doi:10.1016/j.leaqua.2019.101344.

Kerr, J. (2013). *Legacy: What the all blacks can teach us about the business of life.* London: Constable.

Kotter, J. P. (1990). What leaders really do. *Harvard Business Review, 68*(11), 103–111.

Kotter, J. P. (2002). *The heart of change: Real life stories of how people change their organizations.* Boston: Harvard Business School Publishing.

Kouzes, J. M., & Posner, B. Z. (1999). *Encourage the heart: A leaders guide to rewarding and recognizing others.* San Francisco: Jossey-Bass.

Kouzes, J. M., & Posner, B. Z. (2017). *The leadership challenge: How to make extraordinary things happen in organizations* (6th ed.). Hoboken, NJ: Wiley.

Lawrence, P. R., & Pirson, M. (2015). Economist and humanistic narratives of leadership in the age of globality: Toward a renewed Darwinian theory of leadership. *Journal of Business Ethics, 128*(2), 383–394. doi:10.1007/s10 551-014-2090-2.

Nielsen, J. S. (2011). *The myth of leadership: Creating leaderless organizations.* London: John Murray Press.

Neves, P. (2009). Readiness for change: Contributions for employee's level of individual change and turnover intentions. *Journal of Change Management, 9*(2), 215–231. doi:10.1080/14697010902879178.

Padilla, A., Hogan, R., & Kaiser, R. B. (2007). The toxic triangle: Destructive leaders, susceptible followers, and conducive environments. *The Leadership Quarterly, 18*(3), 176–194. doi:10.1016/j.leaqua.2007.03.001.

Parameswar, N., & Prasad, R. (2017). Humanistic leadership, organizational culture and corporate citizenship behavior. *Purushartha: A Journal of Management Ethics and Spirituality, 9*(2), 46–53.

Petrie, N. (2014). *Future trends in leadership development* (White Paper). Center for Creative Leadership, Colorado. http://insights.ccl.org/wp-content/uploads/2015/04/futureTrends.pdf. Accessed 23 Nov 2015.

Rojek, C. (2014). Leaderless organization, world historic events, and their contradictions: The burning man city case. *Cultural Sociology, 8*(3), 351–364.

Schein, E. H. (2010). *Organizational culture and leadership.* San Francisco: Jossey-Bass.

Schyns, B., & Schilling, J. (2013). How bad are the effects of bad leaders? A meta-analysis of destructive leadership and its outcomes. *The Leadership Quarterly, 24*(1), 138–158. doi:10.1016/j.leaqua.2012.09.001.

Sergiovanni, T. (2005). The virtues of leadership. *The Educational Forum, 69*(2), 112–123. https://files.eric.ed.gov/fulltext/EJ683737.pdf.

Shaw, J. B., Erickson, A., & Harvey, M. (2011). A method of measuring destructive leadership and identifying types of destructive leaders in organizations. *The Leadership Quarterly, 22*(4), 575–590. doi:10.1016/j.leaqua.2011.05.001.

Svensson, G., & Wood, G. (2005). The serendipity of leadership effectiveness in management and business practices. *Management Decision, 43*(7-8), 1001–1009.

Tzu, L. (2021). Brainy quotes. https://www.brainyquote.com/quotes/lao_tzu_121709. Accessed 22 Mar 2021.

Wendover, R. W. (2002). *Smart hiring: The complete guide to finding and hiring the best employees* (3rd ed.). New York: Sourcebooks Inc.

World Health Organization (WHO). (2006). *Constitution of the World Health Organization* (45th ed.). Copenhagen, Denmark: World Health Organization.

Yukl, G. A. (2103). *Leadership in organizations.* Boston: Pearson.

18

The Enabling Role of Leadership in Realizing the Future

Cecile Gerwel Proches

Introduction

The global pandemic, COVID-19, has impacted the world, workforce, and the workplace in multiple, profound ways. We also find ourselves further immersed in the digital era and traversing the fourth industrial revolution, while also being cognizant of the fifth industrial revolution. Increasingly high levels of volatility, uncertainty, complexity, and ambiguity (VUCA) stemming from these events necessitate strong leadership, which will need to be task-oriented but also responsive to the needs of the people. We can see that organizations have been significantly impacted by these multiple events, which cause outcomes to not be so easily predicted, and which may also lead to unintended consequences

C. Gerwel Proches (✉)
Graduate School of Business and Leadership, University of KwaZulu-Natal, Durban, South Africa
e-mail: gerwel@ukzn.ac.za

© The Author(s), under exclusive license to Springer Nature Switzerland AG 2022
F. Hertel et al. (eds.), *Debating Leaderless Management*,
Palgrave Debates in Business and Management,
https://doi.org/10.1007/978-3-031-04593-6_18

(Angeli and Montefusco 2020; Arena and Uhl-Bien 2016; Price 2004). We also realize just how interconnected we are and how changes in one part may have an impact elsewhere (Arena and Uhl-Bien 2016; Bensley 2020; Bui 2020).

COVID-19 is an extreme example of disruptive, unplanned change, which necessitates a review of how we conceive the workplace, the nature of work, working hours, and even the very word, "*organization*" (Brammer and Clark 2020; Foss 2020; Ozimek 2020). Leadership also has to adapt and be reframed. It is suggested, for example, that leaders need to engage in continuous learning to ensure that organizations are able to face the VUCA, which characterized 2020 and continue to be so (Bensley 2020; Hynes et al. 2020; Worley and Jules 2020).

The argument presented in this chapter is that leadership is required. We need leadership that is cognizant of how valuable both leaders and followers are in navigating the complexity by engaging in sense-making processes to co-create the future for leadership. It is therefore not desirable to have leaderless management. It is argued that leadership that is centered on embracing change, developing others, not being caught up in positions or titles, and the sensible use of authority and power is needed to lead the way in driving our organizations forward to focus on both task and people.

I use the events of 2020 to argue that organizations require strong leadership that draws from personal influence rather than position power to bring people together to navigate the change and ensure capabilities to weather the storm. If we do not have strong intentional leadership, we risk slipping into a managerialist mode, which becomes primarily task-oriented and reactive and essentially more focused on crisis management and survival. The COVID-19 pandemic shapes the arguments in this chapter, as this recent crisis profoundly impacted not only the world, but also the world of work leadership. We may very well have entered a new era of leadership. A complexity and systems perspective are drawn on to shed light on the role of leadership in navigating changing conditions in the world of work.

The chapter commences with an overview of the nature of the leadership and then delves into the critical aspects of leading in VUCA. These include remote working; rapid technological advances; how leading remotely may mask the "people" side of things; and conscious leadership in the "new norm".

The Nature of Leadership

Before examining the type of leadership required to navigate the VUCA and lead the way in co-creating the future, we briefly explore what is meant by leadership. Key debates center on the idea that leadership is associated with influence, change, a shared purpose, followers, and that leadership is not about a position or title (Andersen 2016; Daft 2018; De Haan and Kasozi 2014; Northouse 2016; Shriberg and Shriberg 2011; Van Wart 2013). Leadership is also characterized by an acknowledgment of the active role that followers play in the two-way relationship (Parry and Hansen 2007). It has been further argued that there are two sides of the coin—leadership and followership. Daft (2018) in fact points to that characteristics for effective leadership and effective followership largely being the same.

Leadership scholars have pointed out that there is no magical recipe for how to become an effective leader and that it is critical to understand that different leadership styles should be applied in different situations (Daft 2018). The situation, follower, and leader are but some of the determinants which call for a particular leadership style to be applied. We are also alerted to the fact that leadership is not necessarily associated with a title or position (Parry and Hansen 2007). This aspect is especially critical as there may be individuals in leadership positions with authority, who may have very little influence and who may only achieve outcomes through fear or strict authoritarianism. Others who may not be in leadership positions could, however, be considered to have real influence. The key point is that you do not have to be in a formal leadership position to be considered a leader or display leadership qualities or characteristics.

There is also a shadow system in the organization as well as "organizational politics", which impacts leader/follower relations (Allio 2013; De Haan and Kasozi 2014).

Leadership entails influence, and thereby power which is an inherent part of the process (Shriberg and Shriberg 2011). Leaders can derive their power from a formal position, the ability to reward and punish, or softer aspects, such as possessing specialized knowledge or through personal attributes which command respect and instill awe (Daft 2018; Drew 2010; Gronn 2003). There is no simple way of conceiving or defining leadership, but leadership is something that can be developed, through both practice and introspection, as well as through textbooks, leadership development courses, mentorship, coaching, and a wealth of other resources.

Differences between leadership and management have been highlighted (Gronn 2003). Management tends to be focused on planning, command, control, and staffing and may draw on position power, thereby creating a distance between leader and followers. There may be a tendency to focus on problem-solving, goals and objectives, and budgets. Leadership, on the other hand, is concerned with a vision, the future, ensuring emotional connections, listening rather than only talking to, and challenging the status quo, as well as acknowledging the role of self (Daft 2018; De Haan and Kasozi 2014; Northouse 2016; Shriberg and Shriberg 2011; Van Wart 2013). Leadership is thus a complex phenomenon and goes far beyond job descriptions, status, titles, and positions (Marion and Uhl-Bien 2001; Price 2004).

Leading in VUCA

During the last few years, we faced major disruption, complexity, diverse challenges, loss, and transformation on multiple levels, as a result of the global pandemic, COVID-19 (Allen et al. 2020; Angeli and Montefusco 2020; Bensley 2020; El-Hani and Machado 2020; Hopman et al. 2020; Murugan et al. 2020; World Health Organisation [WHO] 2020). We also saw increased attention directed to the concept of "leading remotely", as well as "leading in a crisis". The inability of individuals and organizations to adapt would have led to the demise of the organization—this is sometimes referred to as "*adapt or die*".

Organizational life across the globe was dramatically altered as many workers suddenly found themselves having to work remotely (George 2021; Hern 2020; Kylili et al. 2020). Remote working had to be adopted by many organizations as a result of the lockdowns and social distancing restrictions pertaining to COVID-19 (Hopman et al. 2020; World Health Organisation [WHO] 2020). The experience of "working from home" has certainly changed workplace dynamics in multiple ways (Boland et al. 2020; Foss 2020; Leonardi 2020; Ozimek 2020; Sharma and Singh 2020). Many had to rearrange their homes hastily to set up a workstation, while some may have also simultaneously had to assist their children with online learning or remote learning with schools having been closed due to the pandemic (Garbe et al. 2020; O'Kane et al. 2020).

Those who could not do remote working also experienced challenges and faced more risk having to be away from the safety of their homes. This has been especially evident with frontline healthcare workers and even teachers. It is clear that the VUCA remains (Murugan et al. 2020; Worley and Jules 2020). This new setup with blurred lines has resulted in some experiencing burnout, stress, and work–life balance issues. Some organizations have chosen to continue with remote working, while others may have seen a partial or complete return to the office (Dean 2020).

Rapid Technological Advances

Many organizations had to ensure that the workforce rapidly embraced technology (Fitzpatrick et al. 2020; Molino et al. 2020). The adoption and uptake of technology certainly played a pivotal role in facilitating survival in the digital age (Fitzpatrick et al. 2020). This ensured that the workforce was able to stay connected with each other as well as with other key stakeholders. Even before COVID-19, we heard about the fourth and fifth industrial revolutions, and how these would impact workers, for example with increased automation and the emergence of jobs of the future, while some jobs that exist now, would disappear (Bangash 2020; Lee and Park 2020; Neto et al. 2020; Sarfraz et al. 2021).

It is clear that COVID-19 acted as a catalyst for change with respect to the infusion of technology in our personal and professional lives. Ironically though, while connectivity may have increased, the workforce could have become fragmented and disconnected.

How Leading Remotely May Mask the "People" Side of Things

The VUCA that we experienced with the COVID-19 pandemic (Bauer 2020; Murugan et al. 2020; Worley and Jules 2020) may have initially resulted in the focus primarily being on survival, productivity, performance, the bottom line, and efficiency. The global pandemic highlighted the fragility and paradoxes of many organizations. Many organizations found that well-formulated plans, a vision, mission, and five- or ten-year strategies suddenly had very little meaning. As the focus was on responding to the unplanned change (Brammer and Clark 2020), leaders may have consciously or unconsciously ended up mainly focusing on accomplishing tasks or goals. While all this was undeniably critical to realizing the very core purpose and survival of the organization, we may have in the process witnessed the most valuable resource, the people, fade into the background.

Remote working and technology used to connect the workforce may have further exacerbated the schism (Fitzpatrick et al. 2020; Hern 2020; Molino et al. 2020; Newman and Ford 2021; Ozimek 2020) and also contributed to mistrust from the side of management (Parker et al. 2020). Concerns about the duration of online meetings, "Zoom fatigue" and data costs, may have led to little engagement with the workforce and may instead possibly have resulted in those in formal leadership positions being most visible and primarily taking center stage.

Leaders may also have used more of an autocratic leadership style by primarily implementing and transmitting key information and messages from the top, relating to the emergency measures which had to be put in place. There may thus have been very little "real" or meaningful involvement of followers in navigating the complexity (Anderson 1999). This may have been partially justified at the time as leadership had to rapidly engage in emergency strategy formulation and execution to manage the VUCA resulting from being thrust into unknown territory (Foss 2020; Murugan et al. 2020; Worley and Jules 2020).

Conscious Leadership in the "New Norm"

COVID-19 has actualized a debate concerning the nature of leadership. I suggest that conscious leadership may be attractive as a new norm for reorganizing the leader/follower relationship. Newman and Ford (2021) have argued that followers need to be fully engaged in the "new norm" (Newman and Ford 2021). If we do not consciously lead and embrace both leader and follower in the present, we risk seeing more of a managerial-type situation dominating organizations.

I follow Gunnlaugson (2020) here in suggesting that a key consideration for leadership is to develop presencing awareness in a disconnected world and create an organizational identity given the changes to the workforce and workplace. Furthermore, he suggests that it is critical to emphasize inner leadership and the leader's state of being. As we traverse the "new norm", which may leave one asking, "what exactly is normal about it", we can see that leadership is needed. Otherwise the organization risks operating in a fragmented manner with no clear direction in achieving common goals or shared purpose.

Such leadership involves creating the right conditions to allow the workforce to thrive and contribute by drawing on the multiple strengths and diversity of the team (Angeli and Montefusco 2020; Ferdig 2007). Given the present circumstances, it may be challenging to get a holistic sense of where followers are at, especially when leaders are physically removed from employees. Workers may also have become disengaged as a result of their personal circumstances or even more compliant—perhaps in an effort to ensure job security. COVID-19 may also have created fear, mistrust, and possibly even a concern for survival.

While power is inherent and is a given (Gronn 2003), it is up to the leader to set the tone to avoid a dehumanizing situation where followers are not acknowledged as being instrumental to achieving outcomes, thereby staying "muted" and "invisible". We have probably often heard the saying, "people don't leave their emotions at home". This certainly has new meaning when considering "working from home", leading remotely, and simply experiencing the myriad emotions brought forth as we live and work through a pandemic.

We need authentic leaders who can display strong emotional and interpersonal skills. True leadership should not be afraid being vulnerable, humble, and not having all the answers. This in fact would demonstrate maturity on the part of the leader. The intrusion of work into the home, and being removed from colleagues and the workplace, have fundamentally altered organizational behavior, especially as many organizations may be considering remote or hybrid working as a permanent arrangement (Hudecheck et al. 2020; Leonardi 2020; Ozimek 2020).

Leaders need to be mindful of the well-being of the workforce, especially given the mental, emotional, and physical impact of the pandemic on individuals (Hogan 2020; O'Kane et al. 2020). The uncertainty continues and many organizations could be engaging in some form of restructuring to cut costs or reduce inefficiencies, which could be placing further strain on the already vulnerable workforce. We have seen how vulnerable groups, such as women and minority groups, have suffered tremendously over the past few years, often resulting in them losing their jobs (McLaren et al. 2020; Milliken et al. 2020; Schueller-Weidekamm and Kautzky-Willer 2012). The workforce may therefore be traumatized as a result of changing working conditions and the impact of the pandemic on self and others, such as loss of routine and support networks, and having to process more than the actual work, as well as possibly also having to deal with survivor syndrome (Hogan 2020; Werr and Wakeman 2020).

Such conditions point to the need for leadership. An organization may have the most responsible and mature followers who are able to be proactive and lead self as would be akin to Theory Y (Daft 2018), but placing suitable individuals in formal leadership positions should continue to be part of the "new norm". Even if there are experts/specialists in narrow fields or teams, someone who is capable needs to be placed in a position of authority to constantly survey the space and ensure cohesion—inside and outside, online and offline. Decisions need to be made, sometimes with limited information and during periods of uncertainty (Foss 2020).

The Character of the New Leadership

Conscious leadership requires particular characteristics. As suggested by Daft (2018), those in leadership positions must be willing to lead, demonstrate courage, drive change, and serve without being egotistical (Daft 2018). Trust and empathy are key to ensuring effective leadership, and leaders need to use their power in a responsible manner. They need to be held accountable to lead, steer the organization in a certain direction based on their ability to see the big picture, accept the risks, and provide direction, especially when it is not easy to predict the outcomes. Such leaders need to be able to respond to change, put plans in place, but also be systemic thinkers, who are able to see how diverse, multiple interactions create change (Arena and Uhl-Bien 2016; Braun 2002; Cilliers 2000; Törnblom 2018).

While it is essential that the organization has leaders in place to provide direction, enlist followers, and ensure alignment, it is also critical that leadership competencies be developed broadly. Leaders must strive to create a responsive and agile organizational culture that is not weighed down by hierarchy and bureaucracy (Angeli and Montefusco 2020; Arena and Uhl-Bien 2016; Setili 2015). It is clear that the duties and responsibilities of leadership have multiplied. Timely and meaningful communication with employees is critical.

The idea of sense-making seems especially important during these VUCA times (Angeli and Montefusco 2020; Plowman et al. 2007; Weick 1995). This implies that leaders need to be cognizant of what and how they communicate (Daft 2018), especially considering that the mode of communication has changed. Pure information transmission down the various levels is going to mean very little, and detachment may result in misinterpretation, especially if done virtually. Unintended consequences may therefore arise (Bensley 2020; Plowman et al. 2007).

The pace of change that we are seeing could result in irrelevant or outdated information being distributed, should leadership not develop an agile and responsive culture (Setili 2015). The consequences of a lack of responsiveness could be felt in customers leaving to the competitor, decreased employee job satisfaction and motivation, and even possible closure. Change leadership is necessary to ensure a change in mindset, and not only processes. Leaders and followers alike need to be resilient, flexible, and equipped with the necessary competencies to embrace change. Many traditional models of management and change, with neat steps or stages, have limitations in dealing with the VUCA (Bensley 2020; Murugan et al. 2020; Worley and Jules 2020).

Leadership during VUCA times requires leaders to be optimistic and dependable and have the necessary knowledge, judgment, decision-making skills, and interpersonal skills. They also need to be flexible, resilient, able to get people to work together, care for people and not only the task, action-oriented, innovative, able to inspire, and be open to new experiences. Leadership is about change and courage (Daft 2018). Leaders should be willing to unlearn, collaborate, and be vulnerable. Difficult decisions may need to be made, especially if leaders need to rebuild the organization, or possibly even engage in processes to reduce the workforce. This is where emotional intelligence and resilience feature strongly. The level of complexity, along with major uncertainty, may leave leaders feeling stressed (Foss 2020; Plowman et al. 2007). It is critical to know which leadership style to draw on. Leaders also need to reflect on the type of messages, whether conscious or subconscious, being sent to followers about the behaviors and characteristics required in the "new norm". Are followers truly allowed to play a role in co-creating the future or are they merely implementers?

Conclusions

Organizations need to determine what motivates leaders and followers. Changing conditions such as remote and hybrid working (Hern 2020; Hudecheck et al. 2020; Newman and Ford 2021; Ozimek 2020) may have affected those who have a strong sense of belonging and are motivated by good working relationships with colleagues. For some, lacking the support of colleagues could result in a feeling of disintegration and fragmentation. It seems that the concept of safe and secure work and lifelong careers is fading—followers should thus develop resilience and focus on developing and leading themselves. Many organizations are experiencing threats to their existence. Some industries, such as the tourism industry, for example, is under threat or already collapsing in some countries. It could be argued that leaders have an ethical and moral responsibility to assist employees in future-proofing themselves. Transformational leadership will be critical, combined with a good balance of action and vision to thrive in the "new norm" (Smith et al. 2004; Van Wart 2013). It is clear that leaders and followers require adaptability, crisis management skills, resilience, and emotional intelligence (Callan et al. 2004; Manucci 2021).

Now more than ever, followers need to be proactive, show initiative, be committed to change, learn, embrace change and technology, learn new skills, and focus on upskilling and reskilling. They should strive to be independent, critical thinkers (Daft 2018), and sense what is happening. We could also aim for open mind, will, and heart, as suggested by Scharmer (2009). True listening and dialogue are required. In going forward, leaders will need to ensure that the systems, structures, and culture enable followers to take initiative and be proactive, and that they reach a point where they do not wait for leaders and managers to provide direction. A flexible organizational culture combined with a spirit of collaboration, learning, teamwork, and humility, will be vital in navigating the VUCA (Angeli and Montefusco 2020; Bensley 2020; Bui 2020; Murugan et al. 2020). Extreme bureaucracy, hierarchies, set processes, and structure have their limitations. Distributed leadership should be encouraged, whereby an emergence of various leaders with the requisite skills and abilities can play a role in moving the organization forward. A sense of interconnectedness, along with systemic, transformational, and inspirational leadership can allow leaders and followers alike to sharpen their leadership skills.

When observing the multiple disruptive events that occurred over the past few years, and which continue to unfold, I argue for the importance of leaders in steering organizations through the VUCA. The extreme disruption has challenged our set ways of doing things and systems that we had in place. The year 2020 took organizations to levels that have not been experienced before. The COVID-19 pandemic has highlighted the need for strong leaders who can provide reassurance during high levels of VUCA and beyond.

References

Allen, M. B., Mills, M., & Mirsaeidi, M. (2020). The COVID-19 pandemic: Can open access modeling give us better answers more quickly? *Journal of Applied Clinical Medical Physics, 21*(6), 4–6.

Allio, R. J. (2013). Leaders and leadership: Many theories, but what advice is reliable? *Strategy & Leadership, 41*(1), 4–14.

Andersen, J. A. (2016). Leadership scholarship: All bridges have been burned. *Leadership & the Humanities, 4*(2), 108–125.

Anderson, P. (1999). Complexity theory and organization science. *Organization Science, 10*(3), 216–232.

Angeli, F., & Montefusco, A. (2020). Sensemaking and learning during the COVID-19 pandemic: A complex adaptive systems perspective on policy decision-making. *World Development, 136*, Article 105106.

Arena, M. J., & Uhl-Bien, M. (2016). Complexity leadership theory: Shifting from human capital to social capital. *People and Strategy, 39*(2), 22–27.

Bangash, K. K. (2020). Fourth industrial revolution and post COVID-19: Workplace implications and insight for future research. *Kardan Journal of Economics and Management Sciences, 3*(3), 1–7.

Bauer, J. (2020). COVID-19 in the VUCA world. https://www.linkedin.com/pulse/covid-19-der-vuca-welt-jan-bauer/. Accessed 26 May 2021.

Bensley, J. (2020). COVID-19: A salutary experience of VUCA. *ICCPM Newsletter.* https://iccpm.com/covid19-vuca-article/. Accessed 26 May 2021.

Boland, B., De Smet, A., Palter, R., & Sanghvi, A. (2020). Reimagining the office and work life after COVID-19. McKinsey & Company. https://www.mckinsey.com/capabilities/people-and-organizational-performance/our-insights/reimagining-the-office-and-work-life-after-covid-19?cid=other-eml-alt-mip-mck&hlkid=8778afb0af6f4f938879e2846fe15066&hctky=11396825&hdpid=4256de30-f942-4b45-948f-9a5d81ac6e68. Accessed 26 May 2021.

Brammer, S., & Clark, T. (2020). COVID-19 and management education: Reflections on challenges, opportunities, and potential futures. *British Journal of Management, 31*(3), 453–456.

Braun, W. (2002). The system archetypes. http://wwwu.uni-klu.ac.at/gossimit/pap/sd/wb_sysarch.pdf. Accessed 26 May 2021.

Bui, H. T. (2020). From the fifth discipline to the new revolution: What we have learnt from Senge's ideas over the last three decades. *The Learning Organization, 27*(6), 495–504. doi:10.1108/TLO-04-2020-0062.

Callan, V. J., Latemore, G., & Paulsen, N. (2004). The best-laid plans: Uncertainty, complexity and large-scale organisational change. *Mt. Eliza Business Review, 7*(1), 10–17.

Cilliers, P. (2000). What can we learn from a theory of complexity? *Emergence, 2*(1), 23–33.

Daft, R. L. (2018). *The leadership experience* (7th ed.). Toronto: Cengage Learning.

Dean, S. (2020). Future of work: Managing employees effectively through the COVID-19 crisis. *International Journal of Engineering Applied Sciences and Technology, 5*(6), 196–207.

De Haan, E., & Kasozi, A. (2014). *The leadership shadow: How to recognize and avoid derailment, hubris and overdrive.* London: Kogan Page Publishers.

Drew, G. M. (2010). Enabling or "real" power and influence in leadership. *Journal of Leadership Studies, 4*(1), 47–58.

El-Hani, C. N., & Machado, V. (2020). COVID-19: The need of an integrated and critical view. *Ethnobiology and Conservation, 9*(18), 1–20.

Ferdig, M. A. (2007). Sustainability leadership: Co-creating a sustainable future. *Journal of Change Management, 7*(1), 25–35.

Fitzpatrick, M., Gill, I., Libarikian, A., Smaje, K., & Zemmel, R. (2020). The digital-led recovery from COVID-19: Five questions for CEOs. McKinsey Digital. https://www.mckinsey.com/business-functions/mckinsey-digital/our-insights/the-digital-led-recovery-from-covid-19-five-questions-for-ceos. Accessed 2 July 2021.

Foss, N. J. (2020). Behavioral strategy and the COVID-19 disruption. *Journal of Management, 46*(8), 1322–1329. doi:10.1177/0149206320945015.

Garbe, A., Ogurlu, U., Logan, N., & Cook, P. (2020). COVID-19 and remote learning: Experiences of parents with children during the pandemic. *American Journal of Qualitative Research, 4*(3), 45–65.

George, B. (2021). The pros and cons of working remotely. https://fortune.com/2021/04/17/remote-work-home-hybrid-model-future/. Accessed 2 Aug 2021.

Gronn, P. (2003). Leadership: Who needs it? *School Leadership & Management, 23*(3), 267–291. doi:10.1080/1363243032000112784.

Gunnlaugson, O. (2020). *Dynamic presencing: A transformative journey into presencing mastery, leadership and flow.* Vancouver, BC: Trifoss Business Press.

Hern, A. (2020, March 13). COVID-19 could cause permanent shift towards home working. *The Guardian.* https://www.theguardian.com/technology/2020/mar/13/covid-19-could-cause-permanent-shift-towards-home-working. Accessed 26 May 2021.

Hogan, M. J. (2020). Collaborative positive psychology: Solidarity, meaning, resilience, wellbeing, and virtue in a time of crisis. *International Review of Psychiatry, 32*(7-8), 698–712.

Hopman, J., Allegranzi, B., & Mehtar, S. (2020). Managing COVID-19 in low-and middle-income countries. *Journal of the American Medical Association, 323*(16), 1549–1550.

Hudecheck, M., Sirén, C., Grichnik, D., & Wincent, J. (2020). How companies can respond to the coronavirus. *MIT Sloan Management Review.* https://sloanreview.mit.edu/article/how-companies-can-respond-to-the-coronavirus/. Accessed 26 May 2021.

Hynes, W., Trump, B., Love, P., & Linkov, I. (2020). Bouncing forward: A resilience approach to dealing with COVID-19 and future systemic shocks. *Environment Systems and Decisions, 40*(2), 174–184.

Kylili, A., Afxentiou, N., Georgiou, L., Panteli, C., Morsink-Georgalli, P. Z., Panayidou, A., Papious, C., & Fokaides, P. A. (2020). The role of remote working in smart cities: Lessons learnt from COVID-19 pandemic. *Energy Sources, Part A: Recovery, Utilization, and Environmental Effects* (Advance online publication). doi:10.1080/15567036.2020.1831108.

Lee, H. H., & Park, D. (2020). *Post-COVID Asia: Deglobalization, fourth industrial revolution, and sustainable development.* Singapore: World Scientific Publishing.

Leonardi, P. M. (2020). COVID-19 and the new technologies of organizing: Digital exhaust, digital footprints, and artificial intelligence in the wake of remote work. *Journal of Management Studies, 58*(1), 249–253.

Manucci, M. (2021). How people come back to workplaces during the pandemic: Three dimensions of intervention for new emotional performance conditions. *Human Resource Development International, 24*(4), 446–453. doi:10.1080/13678868.2021.1883937.

Marion, R., & Uhl-Bien, M. (2001). Leadership in complex organizations. *The Leadership Quarterly, 12*(4), 389–418.

McLaren, H. J., Wong, K. R., Nguyen, K. N., & Mahamadachchi, K. N. D. (2020). COVID-19 and women's triple burden: Vignettes from Sri Lanka, Malaysia, Vietnam and Australia. *Social Sciences, 9*(5), Article 87. doi:10. 3390/socsci9050087.

Milliken, F. J., Kneeland, M. K., & Flynn, E. (2020). Implications of the COVID-19 pandemic for gender equity issues at work. *Journal of Management Studies, 57*(8), 1767–1772.

Molino, M., Ingusci, E., Signore, F., Manuti, A., Giancaspro, M. L., Russo, V., Zito, M., & Cortese, C. G. (2020). Wellbeing costs of technology use during COVID-19 remote working: An investigation using the Italian translation of the technostress creators scale. *Sustainability, 12*(15), Article 5911.

Murugan, S., Rajavel, S., Aggarwal, A. K., & Singh, A. (2020). Volatility, uncertainty, complexity and ambiguity (VUCA) in context of the COVID-19 pandemic: Challenges and way forward. *International Journal of Health Systems and Implementation Research, 4*(2), 10–16.

Neto, R. D. C. S., Maia, J. S., de Silva Neiva, S., Scalia, M. D., & de Andrade, J. B. S. O. (2020). The fourth industrial revolution and the coronavirus: A new era catalyzed by a virus. *Research in Globalization, 2*, Article 100024.

Newman, S. A., & Ford, R. C. (2021). Five steps to leading your team in the virtual COVID-19 workplace. *Organizational Dynamics, 50*(1), Article 100802.

Northouse, P. G. (2016). *Leadership: Theory and practice* (7th ed.). San Francisco: Sage.

O'Kane, P., Walton, S., & Ruwhiu, D. (2020). *Remote working during COVID-19*. New Zealand National Survey: Initial Report, July 2020. Dunedin, New Zealand: Work Futures Otago. https://www.otago.ac.nz/management/research/covid-survey/otago741202.pdf. Accessed 26 May 2021.

Ozimek, A. (2020). The future of remote work. *SSRN Electronic Journal.* https://deliverypdf.ssrn.com/delivery.php?ID=283125078096 10309609511010611611406702500503308206105907407006509408 107010711207411112610600112704105800001010212408500012007 00. Accessed 26 May 2021.

Parker, S. K., Knight, C., & Keller, A. (2020). Remote managers are having trust issues. *Harvard Business Review.* https://netfamilybusiness.com/wp-content/uploads/2020/08/Remote-Managers-Are-Having-Trust-Issues.pdf. Accessed 26 May 2021.

Parry, K. W., & Hansen, H. (2007). The organizational story as leadership. *Leadership, 3*(3), 281–300.

Plowman, D. A., Solansky, S., Beck, T. E., Baker, L., Kulkarni, M., & Travis, D. V. (2007). The role of leadership in emergent, self-organization. *The Leadership Quarterly, 18*(4), 341–356.

Price, I. (2004). Complexity, complicatedness and complexity: A new science behind organizational intervention? *E:CO, 6*(1-2), 40–48.

Sarfraz, Z., Sarfraz, A., Iftikar, H., & Akhund, R. (2021). Is COVID-19 pushing us to the fifth industrial revolution (Society 5.0)? *Pakistan Journal of Medical Sciences, 37*(2), 591–594.

Scharmer, C. O. (2009). *Theory U: Leading from the future as it emerges.* San Francisco: Berrett-Koehler.

Schueller-Weidekamm, C., & Kautzky-Willer, A. (2012). Challenges of work–life balance for women physicians/mothers working in leadership positions. *Gender Medicine, 9*(4), 244–250.

Setili, A. (2015). Does your leadership style destroy agility… or supercharge it? *Leader to Leader, 78*, 56–61.

Sharma, S., & Singh, T. (2020). VUCA world and its impact on human resource function: A roadmap for HR leaders to navigate the current challenging times. *PalArch's Journal of Archaeology of Egypt/Egyptology, 17*(7), 10219–10227.

Shriberg, D., & Shriberg, A. (2011). *Practicing leadership: Principles and applications* (4th ed.). Hoboken, NJ: Wiley.

Smith, B. N., Montagno, R. V., & Kuzmenko, T. N. (2004). Transformational and servant leadership: Content and contextual comparisons. *Journal of Leadership & Organizational Studies, 10*(4), 80–91.

Törnblom, O. (2018). Managing complexity in organizations: Analyzing and discussing a managerial perspective on the nature of organizational leadership. *Behavioral Development, 23*(1), 51–62.

Van Wart, M. (2013). Lessons from leadership theory and the contemporary challenges of leaders. *Public Administration Review, 73*(40), 553–565.

Weick, K. (1995). *Sensemaking in organizations.* Thousand Oaks, CA: Sage.

Werr, A., & Wakeman, W. (2020). Dealing with "survivor syndrome". https://www.hhs.se/contentassets/08c25e73943f481a846e688becd31e43/a33.pdf. Accessed 26 May 2021.

World Health Organisation (WHO). (2020). *Coronavirus disease (COVID-19) pandemic.* https://www.who.int/emergencies/diseases/novel-coronavirus-2019. Accessed 26 June 2020.

Worley, C. G., & Jules, C. (2020). COVID-19's uncomfortable revelations about agile and sustainable organizations in a VUCA world. *The Journal of Applied Behavioral Science, 56*(3), 279–283.

Part IV
Beyond Leaderless Management

19

Organizational Management Is Paradoxically Both Leaderless and Leaderful

Jennifer L. S. Chandler and Emily Mertz

Introduction

The definition of leadership applied in this chapter is that leadership is a social process of influence that impacts the movement and direction of a group (Chandler and Kirsch 2018). This diffuse and ever-present social process impacts all human interactions because humans are social animals who rely on coordination and cooperation dynamics to maintain social cohesion that requires reciprocating between the leading and following behaviors to maintain the group (Pietraszewski 2020). Additionally, this definition allows for engaging what Jørgensen (2020) and Totschnig (2017) refer to as "new beginnings" since humans select the time boundaries that establish the beginning of a story and because

J. L. S. Chandler (✉) · E. Mertz
Leadership and Integrative Studies, Arizona State University, Tempe, AZ, USA
e-mail: jennifer.l.s.chandler@asu.edu

F. Hertel et al. (eds.), *Debating Leaderless Management*,
Palgrave Debates in Business and Management,
https://doi.org/10.1007/978-3-031-04593-6_19

action is always collective. Thus, the storyteller is vital for the actors in creating and sharing organizational understandings of leadership whether those be leaderless understandings and/or leaderful understandings.

In this chapter, leadership is understood as an emergent property of groups rather than individual actions. This reflects the understanding that "leadership is a process and not a person" (Goethals et al. 2004, p. xxxiii). Since all members of the group participate in social interactions that generate the leadership, they all can be classified as leaders and followers. This definition contrasts with the practice of referring to only a small number of group members as leaders and then considering everything they do as leadership. Understanding leadership as a social process of influence impacting the movement and direction of a group applies also to groups of organisms other than humans. Insights from research with non-human animal social cooperation and collective action is useful in broadening our understanding of the importance of both leadership and followership and contributes to a more complete conception of the evolution of leadership in humans as the social animals we are. We argue that there is a continuity between human animal and non-human animal behaviors that adds to the understanding of leadership. We do not view humans as particular animals that are separated from, or the pinnacle of, the rest of the animal kingdom but rather as integrated into a larger evolutionary scheme of adaptation where there is more overlap with the emergence of leadership than not. Further, key scholars responding to questions regarding the uniqueness of humans have demonstrated a continuity in empathy, fairness, morality, and cooperative tendencies (de Waal 2009), culture (McGrew 1998; Perry et al. 2003; Rendell and Whitehead 2001), a capacity to mediate the politics of group dynamics (de Waal 1990), complex communication (Fouts 1997), and emotion (Bekoff 2007) in non-human animals. These demonstrations support an application of non-human animal leadership behavior to the human world. In this chapter, we primarily draw connections with social non-human mammals although non-mammals such as birds, fish, and insects also demonstrate complex social cooperation and collective action relevant to this argument.

Smith et al. (2016) posit hypotheses that support for the evolution of unique leadership attributes found only in human animals remains largely untested due to a lack of comparative frameworks. In their study, Smith et al. (2016) analyzed leadership patterns within small-scale human and non-human mammalian societies, reviewing four focal areas of leadership that include: movement, food acquisition, within-group conflict mediation, and between-group interaction. The results of their research suggest that there is no clear divide regarding the emergence of leadership between human and non-human social mammals. The continuities in leadership observed in this research suggest similar underlying cognitive mechanisms influencing dominant and subordinate relationships, alliance formation, and complex decision-making between human and non-human mammals (Smith et al. 2016). The difference in leadership emergence between humans and non-human mammals found in Smith et al.'s (2016) model that is pertinent here is the scale of collective action. Humans are highly interdependent and rely on other humans who are often non-kin and an interdependent social system consisting of large groups of unrelated humans favors the emergence of mechanisms to solve complex coordination problems (Gavrilets 2015; Smith 2010; Smith et al. 2016).

Organizational Management Is Leaderless

Leaderlessness as a concept has been used in assessing individuals within organizational context for several decades. Leaderless groups are defined as "groups that exhibit the absence of formal leadership roles" (Frantz 2004, p. 834). That definition reflects the understanding of leaderless groups that was documented over seven decades ago in Bion's ([1946]1996) work testing male British army military candidates as part of an officer selection process during World War II. The objective of the leaderless group approach was to provide a method for examining and ranking the potential of men in the military to perform well as officers by comparing them in a group to reveal a man's "capacity for maintaining personal relationships in a situation of strain that tempted him to disregard the interests of his fellows for the sake of his own" (Bion [1946]1996, p. 87). In the approach used, the men knew their performance was being compared to the other candidates in the group.

However, candidates were unaware that evaluators were not examining how well they accomplished the objective provided. Rather, it was their coordinating, collaborating, and caretaking actions, labeled *leadership acts*, directed at the other participants that were evaluated and scored as either successful or unsuccessful.

Bass (1954) reviewed programs that used the leaderless group approach and defined *leadership acts* as "behavior directed toward: (a) changing the intensity and/or direction of [another person's] motivation and/or restructuring [that person's] abilities to cope with the situation and reduce [their] needs" (Bass 1954, p. 467). Leaderlessness in the leaderless group evaluations referred to the fact that the groups of men were newly formed and had no assigned hierarchy. The leaderlessness of the group was viewed as revolutionary in the 1940s as a trigger to provoke *leadership acts* among the participants because the male officer candidates "were demonstrating their skills in managing interpersonal relations on an equal footing, a dynamic that was typical of what officers needed to do in wartime conditions" (Brazaitis 2017, p. 150) and that democratic behavior contrasted with the rigid hierarchical relations among military members at the time. Therefore, the men in the candidate groups were expected to enact varying numbers of successful *leadership acts* which supported the ranking of the participants. The *leadership acts* were counted and classified as either successful or unsuccessful based on the behaviors of the other participants (Bass 1954).

Today, pieces of the leaderless group approach originally devised by Bion are still used in many educational, organizational, team building, and leadership training contexts (Brazaitis 2017) and it is no longer novel. Assessing participants' attempts as either successful or unsuccessful is something that has largely been discontinued in the use of these techniques. What has remained is that participants are aware that the exercise is supposed to trigger a set of experiences that are not part of the ostensible focus of the exercise. Then, in the discussion and reflection on the experience, participants are asked to focus on specific aspects that reveal the hidden agenda of the exercise. Consequently, what is referred to as a leaderless group might be better labeled *ambiguous group situation* because what these groups are missing is authoritarian hierarchy, not leadership. In this respect, today's groups are little different than the groups that participated in those assessment to determine who was more likely to serve effectively as a British military officer in World War II because there is plenty of leadership occurring among a group of people that do not know each other and have been thrust together for an exercise that is being evaluated, even when a specific person has not been designated as the person in command.

Within organizations, hierarchies, titles, and documented positional responsibilities abound. Contrastingly, much work is accomplished by loosely formed or ad hoc work groups. Groups of both kinds are tackling all sorts of organizational needs and challenges and there is no standard structure through which certain kinds of groups only do certain sorts of things. At times, many of these groups could be understood as leaderless groups because they share the same main feature in that they lack a designated person in charge. In those groups people participate, make collaborative decisions, support others at times, communicate, effectively solve problems, and produce deliverables. We argue that such leaderless groups are full of leadership. That is, they are "leaderful" (Raelin 2005, p. 18), as all the people in such groups impact their movement and direction. Leaderful leadership contends that leadership is situated in an activity or practice rather than exemplified through the actions and decisions of a single leader. Everyone is capable of mobilizing action and working with others despite not carrying the positional label of leader. The focus is less on the who that is offering some sort of vision and more on the where, how, and why of leadership (Raelin 2011). It is pertinent here to employ an integrated evolutionary perspective to gain insights into the evolutionary roots of leadership and provide a more holistic understanding of leaderful leadership and shared decision-making. From an evolutionary perspective, shared decision-making may be more advantageous than decisions made by single individuals due to the accuracy of collective decisions compared to a single extreme decision (Conradt and Roper 2005).

Organizational Management Is Leaderful

We argue that because humans are animals, research on leadership observed in non-human animal groups contributes to our understandings of human leadership. Thus, this section continues with an evolutionary perspective and argues for discarding the belief in a single leader and refocusing on the possibilities of leaderful leadership. Evolutionary leadership theory posits that leadership among early human ancestors was dynamic, shared, and context-specific and revolved around solving coordination problems through a decision-making process (Cook et al. 2020). In their research on leadership as behavior in teams and herds, Cook et al. (2020) link shared leadership theory and evolutionary leadership theory as important theoretical frameworks to examine interpersonal influence and coordination. Leaderful leadership also suggests that leadership be situated in an activity or practice rather than exemplified through the actions and decisions of a single individual. A theoretical and empirical synthesis of leadership in the context of the biological and social sciences is relevant in contributing to a more holistic understanding of leadership practice (Cook et al. 2020; Smith et al. 2016).

Movement Is Coordinated

Coordinated movements are a required part of group living as the group moves across space to fulfill their energy and social demands. A fundamental challenge is the capacity to move through the environment as a collective unit (Wang et al. 2016). Consequently, the necessity of collectively moving together as part of group life and its adaptive consequences has generated much attention (Boinski and Garber 2000) and tends to be the main focus of biological leadership studies (Couzin et al. 2005; Petit and Bon 2010). Investigating groups on the move is a direct way to assess consensus decision-making behaviors (Sueur and Petit 2008). By studying non-human animal group movements, a greater understanding of the collective processes of decision-making as well as some insights on the leaderful aspects of leadership can be accomplished (Conradt and Roper 2005; Couzin et al. 2005; Petit and Bon 2010).

In parallel with traditional leadership theory that emphasizes leadership be reserved for the special positional leaders that exert dominance and presence as needed to get things done, we see that there also tends to be a focus on the few individuals initiating the group move (Petit and Bon 2010). As in critical leadership studies, a critical discussion around the role of leader and follower in leadership discourse is also apparent in ethology as renewed questions have emerged concerning the full extent of the role and influence of a single leader in making decisions versus a pre-departure collective decision-making process (Petit and Bon 2010) and hence, leaderful leadership. Individual group members will most likely differ in individual characteristics (e.g., age, sex, dominance status, communicative ability), their internal state (e.g., hunger level or reproductive status such as gestation or lactation), or contextual experience with external stimuli (e.g., predation, social relationships) (Petit and Bon 2010). What this means is that a group is composed of individuals that may have different needs and therefore are differently motivated to move at any given point (Fischhoff et al. 2007; Lamprecht 1992). In this context, who makes the decision? Is there a single leader? A decision has to be made between pursuing individual interests that may in effect fracture the group or to deny one's individual needs to maintain the cohesion of the group (King and Cowlishaw 2009). How then do group members make an individual and collective decision? How much is individual decision-making modulated by the behavior of a single leader versus deliberation of conspecifics? Is the process leaderful?

Coordinated movements are considered to be the outcome of one individual's departure followed by the majority of the other group members. Among behavioral literature, the term *leader* is commonly ascribed to several different behaviors. One of those behaviors is a single animal moving in the front position during a movement bout. Research that used this understanding of leadership studied the following animals: plains zebra (*Equus burchellii*) Fischhoff et al. (2007) and chacma baboons (*Papio ursinus*) King et al. (2008). Focusing on the first departing individual and referring to that as leadership has been used in research studying white-faced capuchins (*Cebus capucinus*) Leca et al. (2003) and macaques (*Macaca* sp.) Sueur and Petit (2008). A third behavior that has been understood as leadership focused on the animal that has the capacity to recruit others due to a central position within the social network. Research that used this understanding studied mountain baboons (*Papio ursinus*) Byrne et al. (1990) and black howler monkeys (*Alouatta pigra*) Van Belle et al. (2013). The leader of movements is often presumed to hold a specific social status, i.e., social leadership (Petit and Bon 2010). Dominant individuals were classically considered as leading all or more frequently than other group members. That understanding of leadership was used in studying dwarf mongooses (*Helogale parvula*) Rasa (1987), gray wolves (*Canis lupus*) Mech (1970), and mountain gorillas (*Gorilla gorilla beringei*) Schaller (1963).

However, personal or consistent leadership where a single individual makes the decision by initiating every collective movement appears to be relatively scarce in nature or limited to a specific context (Krause et al. 2000; Petit and Bon 2010) and former long-standing research is being re-evaluated based on new behavioral studies and different interpretations of leadership. That is, distributed leadership appears to be more common among animals than personal or consistent leadership where group consensus is reached through a variety of complex pre-departure behaviors allowing for a majority of the group members to initiate a collective movement (Leca et al. 2003). For example, mountain gorilla (*Gorilla gorilla beringei*) group departures may not be limited to the decision of one individual, the silverback male (Schaller 1963), but may rather be a collective decision (Petit and Bon 2010). Stewart and Harcourt (1994) reported that the dominant male's departure was preceded by grunts emitted by group members and Watts (2000) noted double-syllabled close calls shared among group members toward the end of a nap. Stewart and Harcourt (1994) suggested that the gorillas may use these signals to assess the intentions of conspecifics and to synchronize departure from a resting site. The social leadership of the silverback male may be irrelevant in this context because the decision to move is determined by the group within the pre-departure behaviors rather than the sole decision of the silverback; a group consensus was already made before the perceived leader departs (Petit and Bon 2010).

Decision-Making Is a Collective Activity

Shared consensus-based decision-making in the pre-departure period that elicits collective movement has been reported in a number of animal taxa. For example, swans (*Cygnus cygnus, C. columbianus*) engage in a series of horizontal head-shaking or vertical head-pumping prior to the group's departure into the air (Black 1988) and African buffalo (*Syncerus caffer*) (Prins 1996) use visual signals to vote and choose when and where to move after resting. In order to initiate group movements, various primate taxa use an assortment of vocalizations in the pre-departure period. This behavior was noted in the studies of capuchins (*Cebus capucinus*) Leca et al. (2003), chacma baboons (*Papio ursinus*) Stueckle and Zinner (2008), and Verreaux's sifakas (*Propithecus verreauxi*) Trillmich et al. (2004). Pre-departure behaviors are also observed in carnivores such as golden jackals (*Canis aureus*) and Cape hunting dogs (*Lycaon pictus*) that display group greetings before moving (Holekamp et al. 2000). These examples of pre-departure behaviors demonstrate aspects of distributed leadership similar to a shared consensus where many or even all of the group members participate in the decision-making process rather than one individual consistently making all of the decisions (Conradt and Roper 2005).

Among horses, the stallion or an adult mare (Feist and McCullough 1976; Tyler 1972) are often argued to be the leader of the group (Bourjade et al. 2015). However, in research on Przewalski horses (*Equus ferus przewalskii*), no single horse was observed to qualify as the leader in two free-ranging groups (Bourjade et al. 2015). No individual, including the oldest mares and stallions, consistently moved first, elicited faster joining by group members than other first movers, or consistently traveled in the front position, suggesting distributed decision-making. The authors noted that in contrast to traditional perceptions of horse leadership, this study demonstrates that age, sex, and dominance seemed to have very limited influence on the coordination of group movements in horses. The authors also note that perhaps the discrepancy of their findings with prior research on the role of leadership in horses has to do with how leadership is defined and the data are interpreted. Closer examination of these reports (Feist and McCullough 1976; Tyler 1972) reveal that data collected did not differ much from Bourjade et al. (2015) findings. The capacity to elicit group movements or be in a front position during travel is distributed among the group members and not confined to the top-ranking/oldest members (Bourjade et al. 2015).

Also of interest in Przewalski horses are the pre-departure behaviors that involve active contributions of decision-making by several group members that signal their motivation to move in a direction by assuming peripheral positions (Bourjade et al. 2009). This primary behavior was accompanied by secondary behavior that involved joining or following a peripheral group member. The decision-making was associated with a slow subsequent joining process that suggested the horses were indecisive and reluctant to move in certain directions and that a collective decision was going to take more time. This deliberation stage takes longer and may involve more dispute when the group members are confronted with different ecological alternatives. That is, the horses seemed to need more time to resolve motivational conflicts about the direction in which to move (Bourjade et al. 2009). This study suggests the occurrence of distributed social processes between group members that contradicts the traditional idea that tends to focus on a consistent leader in horses (Bourjade et al. 2009). The authors conclude that this evidence of shared decision-making highlights that only focusing on single individuals may not be the most accurate way to describe group coordination or distributed contributions to group movement decisions. From an evolutionary perspective, shared decision-making may be advantageous because collective decisions tend to result in more accurate decision outcomes since the movement decisions become the average behavior of all the group members as opposed to a single extreme decision made by one individual (Conradt and Roper 2005).

It is more common for all group members to participate in the decision-making process and share in movement decisions across various animal taxa. Although it may seem as though a single individual initiates group movement, other group members influenced or intervened to ultimately arrive at a collective decision. It is also interesting to note the animals that initiate the movement don't always lead from the front. Research among vervet monkeys (*Chlorocebus pygerythrus*) reveal that collective group movements follow a pattern of distributed leadership and partially shared consensus decision-making and those group members that initiate the movements (i.e., the leaders) may not actually be the same individuals that maintain a position in the front of the moving group (Lee and Teichroeb 2016). Lee and Teichroeb (2016) compared their research from their study conducted in 2014 to behavioral data collected in 2012 (Teichroeb et al. 2015) and found that three of the four adult females with the highest success indices in leading group movements in 2014 did not consistently position themselves at the front of the moving group in 2012 but rather lead from the center or the back of the group. The thing that gets recognized as leadership is often celebrated without acknowledging the work and interaction, and process happening before that point. Indeed, a focus on this pre-departure period seems critical to our understanding of collective decision-making in animal groups and by extension how all the people affiliated with organizations impact the movement and direction of the organization. This movement and direction can start from the center, back, or side and does not necessarily have to be located in the front.

There Is No Neutrality

Since all individuals influence the movement and direction of a group or organization, it is important to include the behavior of individuals who remain silent or inactive. Such individuals, by doing nothing, are impacting the movement and direction of the group. In behavioral studies with non-human animals, an initiator of the group movement is not always followed (Petit and Bon 2010) and tends to give up his attempt when he is not followed by other group members (Petit et al. 2009). Individuals who do not follow the initiator are profoundly influencing how, when, and where the group moves. Similarly, non-initiating individuals influence any initial action of the group moving in the first place. By not contributing or remaining silent, individuals impact the group or organization by hindering movement and maintaining the status quo. Conversely, individuals influence the movement and direction of an organization by actively engaging and sharing individual talents, skills, and inputs.

Humans are social animals who rely on coordination and cooperation dynamics to maintain social cohesion revolving between the "information-processing roles," which is a kind of turn-taking, of leadership and followership that maintain groups (Pietraszewski 2020, p. 3). This social process of influence that impacts the movement and direction of a group also happens within groups of organisms other than humans. Motivation and knowledge tend to be distributed unevenly across groups, making distributed leadership important so that all the group members have the capacity to contribute given the situation and survival needs of the group (Conradt et al. 2009; Couzin et al. 2005). For example, among African elephants (*L. africana*), the oldest matriarch is a repository of social and ecological knowledge and her leadership may be critical during times of drought to lead her group to water sources and in assessing predatory threat (McComb et al. 2001, 2011).

Post-reproductive female killer whales (*Orcinus orca*), are more likely to lead collective group movements when food availability is scarce because of their rich ecological knowledge (Brent et al. 2015). Among fish, individuals that know the location of a foraging patch of food can lead uninformed fish to the food by initiating the group departure and swimming in a favored direction toward the food source (Reebs 2000). In parallel, individuals in human organizations have different motivations to start programs, build relationships, or initiate change moving in a new direction. It seems more adaptive to allow any group member to initiate a group movement in order to harness their individualized knowledge. The propensity of certain individuals to take the lead relates to what knowledge other group members can gain, resulting in ephemeral leadership as information becomes relevant (Collignon et al. 2019). In this context, heterogeneous leadership organically emerges as a result of different knowledge contributions individuals share promoting group collaboration and ultimately survival of groups.

Conclusion

We argue that organizations are paradoxically both leaderless and leaderful because everyone participates in leadership as we have defined it (i.e., a social process of influence that impacts the movement and direction of a group that is always there). We align with the shifting perspective that emphasizes alternate perspectives that focus on collaborative agency, moving away from the view of leadership as only an individual property emanating from a central authority. This perspective argues for the importance of valuing leadership in everyday social processes and interactions found within organizations and the contributions by all group members in the decision-making process. Based on the arguments present in this chapter, models of leadership that valorize the importance of single individuals leading all the movement of an organization are clearly out-of-step with current knowledge about animal behavior. Shared leadership models, cooperative models, and collective decision-making are prevalent among animal groups—humans included. Acknowledging that we are animals and practicing reflexivity can assist us as we embrace leaderful practice and recognize that all people affiliated with an organization impact its movement and direction.

References

Bass, B. M. (1954). The leaderless group discussion. *Psychological Bulletin, 51*(5), 465–492.

Bekoff, M. (2007). *The emotional lives of animals*. Novato, CA: New World Library.

Bion, W. R. ([1946]1996). The leaderless group project. *Therapeutic Communities, 17*(2), 87–91.

Black, J. M. (1988). Preflight signaling in swans: A mechanism for group cohesion and flock formation. *Ethology, 79*(2), 143–157. doi:10.1111/j.1439-0310.1988.tb00707.

Boinski, S., & Garber, P. A. (2000). *On the move: How and why animals travel in groups*. Chicago: University of Chicago Press.

Bourjade, M., Thierry, B., Hausberger, M., & Petit, O. (2015). Is leadership a reliable concept in animals? An empirical study in the horse. *PLoS ONE*, *10*(5), Article e0126344. doi:10.1371/journal.pone.0126344.

Bourjade, M., Thierry, B., Maumy, M., & Petit, O. (2009). Decision-making in Przewalski horses (*Equus ferus przewalskii*) is driven by the ecological contexts of collective movements. *Ethology*, *115*(4), 321–330. doi:10.1111/j.1439-0310.2009.01614.

Brazaitis, S. J. (2017). Wilfred Bion's organization change legacy: Without memory or desire. In D. B. Szabla, W. A. Pasmore, M. A. Barnes, & A. N. Gipson (Eds.), *The Palgrave handbook of organization change thinkers* (pp. 1–13). London: Palgrave Macmillan.

Brent, L. J., Franks, D. W., Foster, E. A., Balcomb, K. C., Cant, M. A., & Croft, D. P. (2015). Ecological knowledge, leadership, and the evolution of menopause in killer whales. *Current Biology*, *25*(6), 746–750. doi:10.1016/j.cub.2015.01.037.

Byrne, R. W., Whiten, A., & Henzi, S. P. (1990). Social relationships of mountain baboons: Leadership and affiliation in a non-female-bonded monkey. *American Journal of Primatolology*, *20*(4), 313–329. doi:10.1002/ajp.1350200409.

Chandler, J. L. S., & Kirsch, R. E. (2018). *Critical leadership theory: Integrating transdisciplinary perspectives*. Basingstoke, UK: Palgrave Macmillan.

Collignon, B., Séguret, A., Chemtob, Y., Cazenille, L., & Halloy, J. (2019). Collective departures and leadership in zebrafish. *PLoS ONE*, *14*(5), Article e0216798. doi:10.1371/journal.pone.0216798.

Conradt, L., Krause, J., Couzin, I. D., & Roper, T. J. (2009). "Leading according to need" on self-organizing groups. *The American Naturalist*, *173*(3), 304–312. doi:10.1086/596532.

Conradt, L., & Roper, T. J. (2005). Consensus decision making in animals. *Trends in Ecology and Evolution*, *20*(8), 449–456. doi:10.1016/j.tree.2005.05.008.

Cook, A., Zill, A., & Meyer, B. (2020). Observing leadership as behavior in teams and herds—An ethological approach to shared leadership research. *The Leadership Quarterly*, *31*(2), Article 101296. doi:10.1016/j.leaqua.2019.05.003.

Couzin, I. D., Krause, J., Franks, N. R., & Levin, S. A. (2005). Effective leadership and decision making in animal groups on the move. *Nature*, *433*(7025), 513–516. doi:10.1038/nature03236.

de Waal, F. B. (1990). *Peacemaking among primates*. Cambridge, MA: Harvard University Press.

de Waal, F. B. (2009). *The age of empathy*. New York: Three Rivers Press.

Feist, J. D., & McCullough, D. R. (1976). Behavior patterns and communication in feral horses. *Zeitschrift für Tierpsychologie, 41*(4), 337–371. doi:10.1111/j.1439-0310.1976.tb00947.x.

Fischhoff, I. R., Sundaresan, S. R., Cordingley, J., Larkin, H. M., Sellier, M. J., & Rubenstein, D. I. (2007). Social relationships and reproductive state influence leadership roles in movements of plains zebra, *Equus burchellii*. *Animal Behaviour, 73*(5), 825–831. doi:10.1016/j.anbehav.2006.10.012.

Fouts, R. (1997). *Next of kin*. New York: HarperCollins.

Frantz, D. W. (2004). Leaderless groups. In G. R. Goethals, G. J. Sorenson, & J. M. Burns (Eds.), *Encyclopedia of leadership* (pp. 834–835). Thousand Oaks, CA: Sage.

Gavrilets, S. (2015). Collective action and the collaborative brain. *Journal of the Royal Society Interface, 12*(102), Article 20141067. doi:10.1098/rsif.2014.1067.

Goethals, G., Sorenson, G. J., & Burns, J. M. (Eds.). (2004). *Encyclopedia of leadership*. Thousand Oaks, CA: Sage.

Holekamp, K. E., Boydston, E. E., & Smale, L. (2000). Collective group movement and leadership in wild black howler monkeys (*Alouatta pigra*). *Behavioral Ecology and Sociobiology, 67*, 31–41. doi:10.1007/s00265-012-1421-5.

Jørgensen, K. M. (2020). Storytelling, space and power: An Arendtian account of subjectivity in organizations. *Organization, 29*(1), 51–66. doi:10.1177/1350508420928522.

King, A. J., & Cowlishaw, G. (2009). Leaders, followers and group decision-making. *Communicative & Integrative Biology, 2*(2), 147–150. doi:10.4161/cib.7562.

King, A. J., Douglas, C. M. S., Huchard, E., Isaac, N. J. B., & Cowlishaw, G. (2008). Dominance and affiliation mediate despotism in a social primate. *Current Biology, 18*(23), 1833–1838. doi:10.1016/j.cub.2008.10.048.

Krause, J., Hoare, D. J., Krause, S., Hemelrijk, C. K., & Rubenstein, D. I. (2000). Leadership in fish shoals. *Fish Fisheries, 1*(1), 82–89. doi:10.1111/j.1467-2979.2000.tb00001.

Lamprecht, J. (1992). Variable leadership in bar-headed geese (*Anser indicus*)—An analysis of pair and family departures. *Behaviour, 122*(1-2), 105–120. doi:10.1163/156853992X00336.

Leca, J. B., Gunst, N., Thierry, B., & Petit, O. (2003). Distributed leadership in semifree-ranging white-faced capuchin monkeys. *Animal Behaviour, 66*(6), 1045–1052. doi:10.1006/anbe.2003.2276.

Lee, H. C., & Teichroeb, J. A. (2016). Partially shared consensus decision making and distributed leadership in vervet monkeys: Older females lead the group to forage. *American Journal of Physical Anthropology*, *161*(4), 580–590. doi:10.1002/ajpa.23058.

McComb, K., Moss, C., Durant, S. M., Baker, L., & Sayialel, S. (2001). Matriarchs as repositories of social knowledge in African elephants. *Science*, *292*(5516), 491–494. doi:10.1126/science.1057895.

McComb, K., Shannon, G., Durant, S. M., Sayialel, K., Slotow, R., Poole, J., & Moss, C. (2011). Leadership in elephants: The adaptive value of age. *Proceedings of the Royal Society B*, *278*(1722), 3270–3276. doi:10.1098/rspb.2011.0168.

Mech, L. D. (1970). *The wolf*. New York: Natural History Press.

McGrew, W. C. (1998). Culture in nonhuman primates? *Annual Review of Anthropology*, *27*, 301–328.

Perry, S., Baker, M., Fedigan, L., Gros-louis, J., Jack, K., MacKinnon, K., Manson, J., Panger, M., Pyle, K., & Rose, L. (2003). Social conventions in wild white-faced capuchin monkeys. *Current Anthropology*, *44*(2), 241–258.

Petit, O., & Bon, R. (2010). Decision-making processes: The case of collective movements. *Behavioural Processes*, *84*(3), 635–647. doi:10.1016/j.beproc.2010.04.009.

Petit, O., Gautrais, J., Leca, J. B., Theraulaz, G., & Deneubourg, J. L. (2009). Collective decision-making in white-faced capuchin monkeys. *Proceedings of the Royal Society B*, *276*(1672), 3495–3503. doi:10.1098/rspb.2009.0983.

Pietraszewski, D. (2020). The evolution of leadership: Leadership and followership as a solution to the problem of creating and executing successful coordination and cooperation enterprises. *The Leadership Quarterly*, *31*(2), Article 101299. doi:10.1016/j.leaqua.2019.05.006.

Prins, H. (1996). *Ecology and behaviour of the African buffalo: Social inequality and decision-making*. London: Chapman & Hall.

Raelin, J. (2005). We the leaders: In order to form a leaderful organization. *Journal of Leadership and Organizational Studies*, *12*(2), 18–30. doi:10.1177/107179190501200202.

Raelin, J. (2011). From leadership-as-practice to leaderful practice. *Leadership*, *7*(2), 195–211. doi:10.1177/1742715010394808.

Rasa, O. A. E. (1987). The dwarf mongoose: A study of behavior and social structure in relation to ecology in a small social carnivore. *Advances in the Study of Behavior*, *17*, 121–163. doi:10.1016/S0065-3454(08)60178-3.

Reebs, S. G. (2000). Can a minority of informed leaders determine the foraging movements of a fish shoal? *Animal Behaviour*, *59*(2), 403–409. doi:10. 1006/anbe.1999.1314.

Rendell, L., & Whitehead, H. (2001). Culture in whales and dolphins. *Behavioral and Brain Sciences*, *24*(2), 309–382.

Schaller, G. B. (1963). *The mountain gorilla: Ecology and behaviour*. Chicago: University of Chicago Press.

Smith, E. A. (2010). Communication and collective action: Language and the evolution of human cooperation. *Evolution and Human Behavior*, *31*(4), 231–245.

Smith, J. E., Gavrilets, S., Borgerhoff Mulder, M., Hooper, P. L., Moudon, C., Nettle, D., Hauert, C., Hill, K., Perry, S., Pusey, A. E., & van Vugt, M. (2016). Leadership in mammalian societies: Emergence, distribution, power, and payoff. *Trends in Ecology & Evolution*, *31*(1), 54–66. doi:10.1016/j.tree. 2015.09.013.

Stewart, K. J., & Harcourt, A. H. (1994). Gorillas' vocalizations during rest periods: Signals of impending departure? *Behaviour*, *130*(1-2), 29–40. doi:10.1163/156853994X00127.

Stueckle, S., & Zinner, D. (2008). To follow or not to follow: Decision making and leadership during the morning departure in chacma baboons. *Animal Behaviour*, *75*(6), 1995–2004. doi:10.1016/j.anbehav.2007.12.012.

Sueur, C., & Petit, O. (2008). Shared or unshared consensus decision in macaques? *Behavioural Processes*, *78*(1), 84–92. doi:10.1016/j.beproc.2008. 01.004.

Teichroeb, J. A., White, M. M. J., & Chapman, C. A. (2015). Vervet monkey (*Chlorocebus pygerythrus*) intragroup spatial positioning: Dominants trade-off predation risk for increased food acquisition. *International Journal of Primatology*, *36*, 154–176. doi:10.1007/s10764-015-9818-4.

Totschnig, W. (2017). Arendt's notion of natality: An attempt at clarification. *Ideas y Valores*, *66*(165), 327–346. doi:10.15446/ideasyvalores.v66n165. 55202.

Trillmich, J., Fichtel, C., & Kappeler, P. M. (2004). Coordination of group movements in wild Verreaux's Sifakas (*Propithecus verreauxi*). *Behaviour*, *141*(9), 1103–1120. doi:10.1007/s10764-011-9549-0.

Tyler, S. J. (1972). The behaviour and social organization of the New Forest ponies. *Animal Behaviour Monographs*, *5*(Part 2), 87–196.

Van Belle, S., Estrada, A., & Garber, P. A. (2013). Collective group movement and leadership in wild black howler monkeys (*Alouatta pigra*). *Behavioral Ecology and Sociobiology*, *67*, 31–41. doi:10.1007/s00265-012-1421-5.

Wang, X., Sun, L., Sheeran, L., Sun, B., Zhang, Q., Zhang, D., Xia, D., & Li, J. (2016). Social rank versus affiliation: Which is more closely related to leadership of group movements in Tibetan macaques (*Macaca thibetana*)? *American Journal of Primatology, 78*(8), 816–824. doi:10.1002/ajp.22546.

Watts, D. (2000). Mountain gorilla habitat use strategies and group movements. In S. Boinski & P. A. Garber (Eds.), *On the move: How and why animals travel in groups* (pp. 351–374). Chicago: University of Chicago Press.

Epilogue

Gabriele Lakomski

Introduction

The diversity of views regarding leaderless management represented in this volume is astounding, complex, and challenging. Writing an Epilogue or Afterword presents a challenge of its own. On the one hand, it is not possible in a relatively short piece to discuss the diversity of perspectives in anywhere near the depth that would be required to do them justice. On the other hand, the opportunity to reflect and comment upon the debate presented here allows me to offer some thoughts on what emerged as central elements and common theoretical themes. It also allows for comment on what may not be there, and how the leadership debate could be advanced further.

A quick glance at the organization of this volume tells the reader that the weight of the argument is fairly evenly distributed between those

G. Lakomski
The University of Melbourne, Melbourne, VIC, Australia
e-mail: lakomski@unimelb.edu.au

who argue that we need leaderless management and those who argue that leaders are indispensable. The three chapters that make up Part II take up positions that locate them between these opposing camps, while the final chapter points to perspectives that are said to lie beyond leaderless management.

There could be no better Leitmotiv for the discussions of leaderless management than Nielsen's (Chapter 2 in this volume) astute observation that "Our belief in the need for leaders has so completely captured our imagination that we have a difficult time thinking organizationally without it". Indeed, this belief is implicit or explicit in the discussions of leadership in this volume, whether of the leaderless or leader*ful* kind. We may have a difficult time thinking organizationally without reference to leadership but it is not impossible. Indeed, one radical solution is proposed by Hertel and Sparre (Chapter 9 in this volume) who advocate that the whole box and dice of leadership must be rejected before we can contemplate managing without leaders. I think they are right. (The title of my 2005 book, *Managing Without Leadership*, is a bit of a give-away.)

My reasons for sharing Hertel and Sparre's conclusion, however, have less to do with the utopian vision of anarchism the authors advocate but more with the theoretical assumptions of leadership theories, especially *leader-centric* views (Evers and Lakomski 2022). The core of such views is the assumption that leaders by virtue of their exceptional qualities are responsible for organizational functioning. The supporting principle of such views is the doctrine of *Methodological Individualism*. As this doctrine is fundamental for *leader-centric* views, and even those that oppose them but still believe in the importance of leaders, its validity is essential to uphold the claim. In the following, I will canvass some reasons for why this principle is invalid, what consequences follow from its demise, and how we can steer the leadership debate into more productive directions.

Overview of Themes

The discussion in favor of *leaderless management* in Part I offers a variety of solutions that arrange themselves around fundamental concerns for moral and ethical leadership, presumed lacking in leader*ful* approaches. It places much emphasis on the creation of equal power relationships that support the values of cooperation, trust, and collaboration, and supports democratic leadership and practices in the service of the greater good (Borchmann and Pedersen, Chapter 4 in this volume; Hsu and Sun, Chapter 6 in this volume). An example of such values Selberg and Mulinari (Chapter 5 in this volume) argue, on the basis of a feminist-Marxist framework, can be seen in the work of ward nurses who are said to be the moral center of the healthcare organization. The concept of *Autonomist Leadership* inspired by Bakunin's anarchist philosophy, Hsu and Sun (Chapter 6 in this volume) suggest, is a radical version of democratic leadership where the main idea is its generation in and by networks of followers and not from a hierarchical structure. *Co-leadership* is another example of leaderless management, so Martins and Martins (Chapter 7 in this volume) suggest, following Mary Parker Follett's thinking and the anarchists' rejection of western growth philosophy and surplus value, can make way for restoring an emphasis on Heidegger's essence of being. *Leaderless Leadership* (Jørgensen and Ingman, Chapter 8 in this volume), influenced by Arendt's distinction between work and action, is a kind of workplace democracy that requires public spaces such as the "agora" and comes about when people come together, meet as equals, and initiate collective action. It does not rely on the Great Man idea or any thought of individualist leadership.

It is interesting that only one chapter (Borchmann and Pedersen, Chapter 4 in this volume) directly addresses the question of the adequacy of leaders, especially in relation to managing and maintaining the psycho-social work environment that, the authors note, they do poorly. This is due in part to exaggerating their actual abilities in addition to the role political, psychological, and practical constraints play that shape their functioning. Importantly, the authors understand the psychological constraints to be ones where leaders have stereotypical views of subordinates. Potential shortcomings of leaders' psyches or mental/cognitive abilities are not raised. This issue will be taken up again later.

Creating the kinds of radical, relational, moral collectives advocated in Part I requires commitment and engagement, and above all, as Garvey and Fatien Diochon (Chapter 3 in this volume) rightly stress, different forms of learning and development. They suggest learning informed coaching, and community of discoveries, based on the concept of *situated learning* with the associated notion of *legitimate peripheral participation*, made popular by Lave and Wenger (1991). Importantly, then, leaderless management needs to be learnt, a critical point often overlooked.

The three "in-between" chapters take very different directions. Flanigan (Chapter 10 in this volume) does not argue for or against leaderless management, but rightly points out that context needs to be taken into account to determine whether leaderless management is in fact beneficial for workers. There may be circumstances where it is not. Respecting workers' autonomy and their independence might be more important than emphasizing workers' participation. Leaderless management can be successful only insofar as it leads to improving workers' material conditions and reduces subordination. Siltaoja and Heikkinen (Chapter 11 in this volume) examine an issue that has not been discussed elsewhere in this volume, the role of passion that is advocated by some theorists as leading to leaderless management. The authors suspect that "passion" as the successor concept to "charisma" is applied more to leaders than employees. Rather than emphasizing "passionate" employees as more motivated and/or innovative, the idea of *shared leadership* may do more to motivate employees and get them involved than appeal to passion. Taking yet another approach, McKayle (Chapter 12 in this volume) compares leaderless management with creative leadership and argues that there is overlap between the desired output of a creative leadership approach, and the desired outcomes for a leaderless or peer-based approach to organizations. What is required in her view is the creation of an environment for creativity which is best brought about by a *deliberate creative leadership approach*.

Part III, against leaderless management, might be placed under the heading of "leaders are good for us". Thus, Sidani and Kaissi (Chapter 13 in this volume) claim that leaders are not only necessary for proper organizational performance but indispensable. There is an organizational need for a leader in terms of their emotional, ethical, inspirational, and values-driven roles as shapers of organizational cultures, a role that goes beyond organizational performance. Leadership in the end is not substitutable. In any case, the notion of leaderless management, so Auvinen et al. (Chapter 14 in this volume) argue, has turned out to be a mere myth. On the basis of a Finnish case study in the high-tech sector, the authors claim that a certain kind of leader always exists—the non-corporeal ghost leader conjured up or "narrated into existence" by organization members.

Commenting from within the South African context, Gobind (Chapter 15 in this volume) decries the absence of leadership by which she means "ethical leadership" in the face of the current leadership that is self-interested, corrupt, and squanders the nation's resources. In this context, leaderless management, based on the Anarchists' philosophy, is in her view, unrealistic. The development of *shared leadership* is a goal that should be worked toward.

Declaring leaderless management a "misnomer", Blank (Chapter 16 in this volume) argues that the reality of organizational, goal-directed, action depends on the collaboration of many interdependent actors, so what is required is "leadership at all levels". Talk of leaderless management also obscures the distinction between leader and manager roles.

As suggested by Kenny-Blanchard (Chapter 17 in this volume), leaderless management is neither practical nor sustainable. The case for leadership, she claims, consists in the fact that people need boundaries, structures, and frameworks and that leaderless management leads to stagnation. The antidote to this is the *principled leader* who has vision, is innovative, leads efficaciously, and is entrepreneurial. If this is the case, leaderless management is superfluous. In a similar vein, Gerwel Proches (Chapter 18 in this volume) argues that leaders are required who are focused on task and people. *Transformational leadership* is best able to deal with the complexities of an uncertain future, which also means that followers need to be committed to change. But to deal with volatility, uncertainty, complexity, and ambiguity (VUCA), *distributed leadership* is also of value as various leaders can emerge with requisite skills at a given point in time. Leaders and followers alike need to sharpen their leadership skills to deal with VUCA successfully.

Garvey and Fatien Diochon's (Chapter 3 in this volume) observation that "The led organization promotes individualism and hierarchy. The leaderless organization relies on the collective" is a succinct summation of the essence of both perspectives and could serve as a suitable conclusion.

In their discussion of how we go beyond leaderless management, Chandler and Mertz (Chapter 19 in this volume) argue that, paradoxically, organizational management is both leader*less* and leader*ful*. Defining leadership broadly as a social process of influence that impacts the movement and direction of a group that is always there, the authors move away from the idea of a central authority toward collaborative agency. Drawing on an evolutionary perspective, they argue that human organizational functioning also depends on shared or cooperative leadership and collective decision-making. The authors' observation that restricting leadership to a single heroic, positional individual creates an idealized illusion is one I share, as argued in the following.

Leader Centrism and Methodological Individualism

In these final pages, I would like to focus on the central idea of *leader centrism*. It is this concept that is accepted as either necessary and good, or that is rejected, to be replaced by versions of leaderless management. As noted earlier, at the core of leader-centric views it is the concept of *Methodological Individualism* that shores up these perspectives. But before I canvass some of the central problems of this concept, it is useful to remind ourselves that the predominance of leadership as an explanation for organizational functioning is a relatively recent phenomenon. It was not always so. Orchestras indeed performed well in the absence of a conductor, as noted in Chapter 2 in this volume (authored by Nielsen) and Chapter 16 in this volume (authored by Blank).

Early debates in organizational theory critical of the Great Man theory pointed out that effective leadership can only work when situational factors are considered. Although the importance of the leader was not challenged in any substantial way, the perspective of *situational contingency* blurred the distinction between leader influence and context (e.g., Perrow 1973; Salancik and Pfeffer 1977). Organizational and structural factors were considered to be highly influential, complex, and changing, and it was near impossible to determine where one set of influences began or ended. On this account, the leader is embedded in the whole organization, neither less nor more important in the explanation of organizational effectiveness. Why a situational approach to organizational functioning did not become prominent is a question without a satisfactory answer to date. But at least one answer is found in the Western belief of Individualism and individual agency based on the notion of the autonomous self.

The rise of, say, transformational, authentic, or charismatic leadership, or in short, of leader centrism in all types of organizations, social, educational, or commercial, is a turn away from potential structural explanations of organizational functioning and a move toward the category that locates explanation in the actions of individuals, here the individual leader. In social science, this is known as the doctrine of *Methodological Individualism* (Arrow 1994; Elster 2007; Lukes 1968). It claims that an organization can be reduced to the individuals who comprise it (ontological thesis), and secondly, that an organization and its activity can be fully explained in terms of the individuals that make it up; that is, in terms of their beliefs and desires. There are a number of reasons why this doctrine fails. (1) It is not possible to describe individual action *without* recourse to structures; (2) leadership may be attributed where none exists due to the *centralized mind*, and (3) leaders are not omniscient and *cognition is distributed* (see Evers and Lakomski 2022, for extended discussion).

Consider the first problem. Much discussed in the education literature is the question why schools in Finland seem to have achieved such good student outcomes as shown in PISA (e.g., Evers and Lakomski 2022, Chapter 2; Sahlberg and Hargreaves 2011), and what we (in Australia) could learn from the Finnish example. If we adopt an individualist market-oriented approach, we look for possible rewards or penalties, including national standardized tests all students have to undergo, and whose results are published by schools; we would also link teacher employment conditions including salary increments or retrenchments to the learning outcomes. Finland, however, does not appear to have taken this, individualist, road but a more structural one. Finnish teachers (unlike Australian ones in the government sector) get high salaries and entry requirements for teacher education courses are also high. Perhaps more importantly, teaching is held in high esteem and teachers enjoy a considerable degree of professional autonomy. Furthermore, Finland has high levels of income equality, and we know that there is a strong relationship between educational achievement and equality of income (Wilkinson and Pickett 2010, pp. 103–117). Although it is undoubtedly true that individuals have an impact on the quality of education, to base an account of good (or poor) education outcomes entirely on the actions of individuals (individualist explanation) is to miss the broader picture that involves structures at many levels, all of which have a part to play in the delivery of education and its outcomes. It is one thing for a country to "borrow" certain techniques to improve teacher education from another country, but it is quite another to "borrow" its culture with all that goes with it, including income distribution!

The second problem, known as the "*centralized mindset*" (Resnick 2000), refers to the apparently in-built human bias toward centralized thinking that attributes a single cause to observed patterns. According to this bias, any patterns observed are assumed to have been created by someone or something. When we watch a flock of birds flying in formation it always seems to be "led" by one bird, just as ants are "led" by their queen. It is observations like these that make us believe that "leadership" is a natural phenomenon. This seems initially a plausible assumption because the many patterns and regularities we detect around us appear to be caused by a planner or designer. We run into problems, however, when we assume that all observed patterns *must* have been designed or created by a central controller. We know from the study of emergence and complex systems that regularities, patterns, as well as artifacts may be better understood as the result of initial, low-level coordination and collaboration. Reynolds's (1987) simulation of the flocking behavior of birds is a classic example of emergent behavior (Holland 1998 and Johnson 2001 provide excellent discussions of emergence). In other words, regularities may be said to have emerged rather than come about as a result of planning by a central controller.

The third problem relates to the claim that leaders, especially of the transformational and/or charismatic kind, are supposed to provide *cognitive* leadership (e.g., the four "Is" of Transformational Leadership, a classic source is Bass and Avolio 1993), in terms of intellectual stimulation, creating culture, and generally solving problems. This brings us to the matter of human cognition that naturally includes leader cognition. The assumption of "leader knows best" locates all important knowledge in the leader's head. But brains are biological entities that carry out computations in parallel distributed fashion rather than by centralized processing. Although they are awe-inspiring computational machines, brains are nevertheless limited in their computational powers. For this reason, they rely in large part on the resources and artifacts of the external environment that act as *cognitive scaffolding*. The two theories that explain this best are the theory of *distributed cognition* and the *extended mind* (Clark 1997, 2008; Clark and Chalmers 1998; Hollan et al. 2000). It follows that cognition is neither confined to the human skull nor is it the property of a single individual. Our reliance on "smart" devices such as iPhones well exemplifies this complex interplay between brain and (technological) world.

Beyond "Beyond ..."

The interdependence of brain/mind and world has many consequences, the most fundamental being that *cognition is always context-bound*. So if cognition extends beyond the skull, necessarily drawing on and being shaped by the resources of the external world, the explanatory frame of reference for social-organizational phenomena significantly expands. Therefore, when it comes to attributing organizational failure or success to a leader linear causality literally misses the point as it does not map onto the much more fluid and changing interrelationships that characterize cognition in context. Organizationally speaking, what gets the work done and accounts for organizational effectiveness is the interaction and collaboration of many actors and their brains. This insight is present in most of the chapters in the leaderless management section (Part III), although it tends to be seen as a feature of various forms of distributed or shared *leadership*, or in Blank's assessment (Chapter 16 in this volume), as "leadership at all levels". Just to emphasize this important point: it is not leadership in whatever form that gets organizational work done but the combined and collective brain power of the many who make up the organization. To what extent *leadership* figures in this account, if it figures at all, is an open question that requires investigation and cannot be decided before the event.

A further consequence of distributed cognition is that the presumed autonomy of the Self that "owns" its knowledge also comes under threat. In fact, it too, is a myth.

Given the mutual interdependence of brain and world, it should come as no surprise that our conception of ourselves as autonomous selves is also "constructed". The idea of the autonomous self has a long and venerable history, and we customarily refer to Descartes and his famous dictum "*I think, therefore I am*" (Descartes [1637]1998, p. 18, italics in source text) to anchor it. For present purposes, the most important point here is that Descartes' dualism, the splitting of brain/mind from body, is the root cause of our current conception of the autonomous self or "I". Like the rest of our cognitive apparatus, "self" is the product of a very long evolutionary chain of development. It is a process that emerges from the coordinated efforts of the body and through many distributed brain structures over at least three evolutionary stages, according to Damasio (2010). Self is neither a disembodied nor metaphysical entity (Descartes' view) but is the product of biological evolution; secondly, as brains operate in a distributed manner, there is no central controller in our heads that coordinates mental activity; third, there is no one brain center or location that produces the "self" (LeDoux 2002 is a good source for this discussion). This means for leaders that they cannot be assumed to be the a priori (cognitive) centers for all contexts and purposes. This conclusion further undercuts the central assumption of *leader-centric* views. Add to this that most organizational tasks and solutions are distributed in any case, different cognitive centers are drawn on. Such cognitive collaboration and coordination is always shaped by structural constraints—think of the ward nurses in Chapter 5 in this volume (authored by Selberg and Mulinari) for one example—and these are beyond the control of any one individual.

I have spent much time on discussing the various problems encountered by *Methodological Individualism* because it is so enshrined in our Western culture and permeates all discussions of leadership, especially *leader-centric* approaches. In this context, the emergence of a "noncorporeal ghost leader" discussed in Chapter 14 in this volume (authored by Auvinen et al.) may just be an expression of such deeply embedded, nonconscious views.

Although the details of the philosophical-theoretical machinery that does the work in this analysis have largely remained hidden, let me just note that it is philosophically *naturalist* and a version of *scientific realism*. In its simplest form, this means that claims are only as good as the evidence provided to defend them. And the evidence is constrained both by coherence, a common virtue of good theories, as well as by what we as biological agents are able to do, including how we think (Evers and Lakomski 2022 and Lakomski 2005, provide source material for the theoretical-philosophical machinery employed here). The view of cognition as distributed glimpsed here goes deep and has far-reaching consequences. From the perspective of cognition and what we know about how human brains function, the "leader knows best" attitude turns out to be a dangerous myth not based in empirical reality.

Although there are many differences and shifts in emphases between the various accounts of the leaderless management section (Part III), what many seem to share is a belief in the superiority of *de-centeredness* despite continuous use of the term "leader". My brief account of distributed cognition tilts us "naturally" toward de-centeredness and provides a compelling account for why leaderless management might better accord with our cognitive natures. This is not to claim that leaders are superfluous, only that they are part and parcel of the organizational fabric and that their (usually formal) status as leaders or CEOs does not bestow extraordinary cognitive powers a priori.

If de-centeredness seems a better account of organizations, what organizational-structural forms such de-centeredness might take differs between authors and raises important issues. It is an open question whether leaderless management in the forms discussed here leads to the goals many desire: equal power relationships that support the values of cooperation, trust, and collaboration, and support democratic leadership and practices in the service of the greater good. No doubt these are valid and valuable goals, but they need to be enshrined in cultural-organizational practices that reinforce the values of democracy and critical open debate, more important now than it ever was. These practices need to be learnt and entrained, and as was remarked by Garvey and Fatien Diochon (Chapter 3 in this volume), *situated learning* is key here as we need to pay much more attention to the contexts in which learning occurs. Leaders have their part to play in these processes, but they neither cause them nor control them, despite claims to the contrary that wish to maintain the myth of leadership (Pfeffer's 1977 article is an early and excellent discussion). Perceptions of leadership are just that, attributions that have no base in empirical reality (see Nisbett 2015 on the fundamental attribution error).

Furthermore, all organizations and their members exist in specific cultural, social, political, and geographical *contexts* that determine what is or is not possible to do, and what resources are available to solve organizational problems. The explanation of organizational performance and/or problem-solving is not determined by fiat, that is, the a priori assumption of leadership. Rather, what is required is fine-grained, ground-up, empirical investigation of what contextual factors, including individual and structural, might have contributed to whatever organizational problem has been solved, or is to be solved. Such a broadening of perspective refocuses the study of leadership that not only lets us question leadership but also has the potential to break the stranglehold *leader-centric* thinking has had for too long as a purported explanation for how organizations function. Most importantly, a shift to context undercuts the assumption that *leader centrism* is the *default or go-to option* in the explanation of organizational performance and functioning.

Finally, collaborative agency and collective decision-making, advocated by Chandler and Mertz (Chapter 19 in this volume), are important concepts that also raise specific questions: How do we avoid confirmation bias (or Groupthink in an older terminology); how can groups make rational decisions that are not only fair to all members but also further the common good? And how do we take account of organizational actors' *emotions* (rather than passion) that are integral to the decision-making process? Emotions, what they are, and what role they play in decision-making are still under-researched topics. It is clear that we will not run out of things to discuss in the leadership debate, but in my view, we should re-focus it. Instead of asking "what do leaders do?" or "what is leadership?", let us ask instead, "what is the organizational problem we need to solve?". Change your glasses, and you will see differently!

References

Arrow, K. J. (1994). Methodological individualism and social knowledge. *The American Economic Review, 84*(2), 1–9.

Bass, B. M., & Avolio, B. J. (1993). Transformational leadership: A response to critics. In M. M. Chemers & R. Ayman (Eds.), *Leadership theory and research: Perspectives and directions* (pp. 49–80). San Diego, CA: Academic Press.

Clark, A. (1997). *Being there: Putting brain, body, and world together again.* Cambridge, MA: MIT Press.

Clark, A. (2008). *Supersizing the mind.* Oxford: Oxford University Press.

Clark, D., & Chalmers, D. (1998). The extended mind. *Analysis, 58*(1), 7–19.

Damasio, A. R. (2010). *Self comes to mind: Constructing the conscious brain.* New York: Pantheon Books.

Descartes, R. ([1637]1998). *Discourse on method and meditations on first philosophy* (trans: Cress, D. A.). Indianapolis, IN: Hackett.

Elster, J. (2007). *Explaining social behavior: More nuts and bolts for the social sciences.* Cambridge, UK: Cambridge University Press.

Evers, C. W., & Lakomski, G. (2022). *Why context matters in educational leadership: A new theoretical understanding.* London and New York: Routledge.

Hollan, J., Hutchins, E., & Kirsh, D. (2000). Distributed cognition: Toward a new foundation for human–computer interaction research. *ACM Transactions on Computer–Human Interaction, 7*(2), 174–196.

Holland, J. H. (1998). *Emergence: From chaos to order.* Cambridge, MA: Perseus.

Johnson, S. (2001). *Emergence: The connected lives of ants, brains, cities, and software.* New York: Simon and Schuster.

Lakomski, G. (2005). *Managing without leadership.* Oxford: Elsevier.

Lave, J., & Wenger, E. (1991). *Situated learning: Legitimate peripheral participation.* Cambridge, UK: Cambridge University Press.

LeDoux, J. (2002). *Synaptic self.* New York: Penguin Putnam.

Lukes, S. (1968). Methodological individualism reconsidered. *The British Journal of Sociology, 19*(2), 119–129.

Nisbett, R. E. (2015). *Mindware: Tools for smart thinking.* New York: Farrar, Straus and Giroux.

Perrow, C. (1973). The short and glorious history of organizational theory. *Organizational Dynamics, 2*(1), 2–15.

Pfeffer, J. (1977). The ambiguity of leadership. *The Academy of Management Review, 2*(1), 104–112.

Resnick, M. (2000). *Turtles, termites, and traffic jams: Explorations in massively parallel microworlds.* Cambridge, MA: MIT Press.

Reynolds, C. (1987). Flocks, herds and schools: A distributed behavioral model. *Computer Graphics, 21*(4), 25–34.

Sahlberg, P., & Hargreaves, A. (2011). *Finnish lessons: What can the world learn from educational change in Finland?* New York and London: Teachers College Press.

Salancik, G. R., & Pfeffer, J. (1977). Constraints on administrator discretion: The limited influence of mayors on city budgets. *Urban Affairs Quarterly, 12*(4), 457–498.

Wilkinson, R., & Pickett, K. (2010). *The spirit level: Why equality is better for everyone.* London: Penguin.

Appendix

Table A.1 An overview of the chapters in the book

Position	Chapter	Perception of LLM	Key-arguments	Authors inclusion of overall key-concept included in the book							
				Ethics	Sociality (order, equality [gender and economic] belonging)	Democracy (decision-making, empowerment)	Ecology	Politics (anarchism),	Economy	Binary logic	Practice (work as action, quality of work), probability, desirability
PART I. For LLM	2. The moral necessity of leaderless organizations	Organization LLM as a peer-based management council system. No leaders or managers but rotational stewardship positions, and mentors	ensure basic human dignity and autonomy. Empower people to involve in decision-making affecting own lives. Mutual, equal, and reciprocal obligation to speak and listen	Ethical (respect for human dignity and autonomy)	Mutual, equal, and reciprocal obligation to speak and listen	Empower people		Ideology (people embedded in contemporary discourse believe leaders/ managers are needed). Leaders and managers will oppose LLM			Practice (realistic, desirability, efficiency)

Position	Chapter	Perception of LLM	Key-arguments	Authors inclusion of overall key-concept included in the book							
				Ethics	Sociality (order, equality [gender and economic] belonging)	Democracy (decision-making, empowerment)	Ecology	Politics (anarchism),	Economy	Binary logic	Practice (work as action, quality of work), probability, desirability
	3. Developing for leaderless organizations: two eco-friendly coaching practices	LLM as self-led democratic communities offering people participation and mutual responsibility to the common entity. Realistic but requires fundamentally different organizational technologies to work	Collaboration in communities based on self-organization, self-led democratic communities weaving people together around a common horizon	Ethics (opposite leadership),	Weaving people together around a common horizon	Democracy (decision-making, empowerment),	Ecology (eco-friendly)	Contemporary hierarchies as arbitrarily constructs			Practice (realistic, attractive),

(continued)

Table A.1 (continued)

Position	Chapter	Perception of LLM	Key-arguments	Authors inclusion of overall key-concept included in the book							
				Ethics	Sociality (order, equality [gender and economic] belonging)	Democracy (decision-making, empowerment)	Ecology	Politics (anarchism),	Economy	Binary logic	Practice (work as action, quality of work), probability, desirability
	4. When matters are too important to be left to leaders and better left to democratic control	LLM e.g., self-management peer-regulated practices, democratic decision-making, and democratic governance/control	LLM in the form of democratic practices	Ethics	Sociality (equality)	Democracy (decision-making, empowerment)	Echology				Practice (possible, attractive)

Position	Chapter	Perception of LLM	Key-arguments	Authors inclusion of overall key-concept included in the book								
				Ethics	Sociality (order, equality [gender and economic] belonging)	Democracy (decision-making, empowerment)	Ecology	Politics (anarchism),	Economy	Binary logic	Practice (work as action, quality of work), probability, desirability
	5. Leaderless management as the solution to struggles over the moral center of healthcare? Ward nurses' critique of management as "real utopias" in the public sector	LLM as a way of locating power and the moral center with workers, rather than managers	LLM based on a feminist-Marxist approach inspired by Fraser, Wright. Employees may need managerial tasks performed by managers, but they do not need managers to "lead"	Ethics	Sociality (equality - gender)	Empowerment					Practice (possible but need for *management*). Focus on content and improve quality of health-work

(continued)

Table A.1 (continued)

Position	Chapter	Perception of LLM	Key-arguments	Authors inclusion of overall key-concept included in the book							
				Ethics	Sociality (order, equality [gender and economic] belonging)	Democracy (decision-making, empower-ment)	Ecology	Politics (anar-chism),	Economy	Binary logic	Practice (work as action, quality of work), probability, desirability
6. Dissolving the leader-follower schism: autonomist leadership and the case of word of warcraft	LLM is "manage-ment without fixed leader-ship in the center". Self-organizing and nonhier-ar-chical	Introduce autonomist leader-ship to solve the leader-follower schism. LLM intro-duce manage-ment without fixed leader-ship in the center			Co-players	Democracy (non-hierarchical, empow-er-ment—cf. including silent people)		Politics (Anar-chism)		Binary logic (rebel against the binary logic of leaders/followers)	Practice (desirable)

Position	Chapter	Perception of LLM	Key-arguments	Authors inclusion of overall key-concept included in the book							
				Ethics	Sociality (order, equality [gender and economic] belonging)	Democracy (decision-making, empowerment)	Ecology	Politics (anarchism)	Economy	Binary logic	Practice (work as action, quality of work, probability, desirability)
	7. In favor of leaderless management: perspective of co-leadership	LLM as group-based or shared-leadership. Collaboration and shared purpose. The principle of authority is based on knowledge and not on position	Leaderless management is inherent in and shared by the group. Besides, LLM promotes an auspicious learning culture	Ethical	Sociality (inequality, justice, realization of human potential)	Democracy (Co-leadership, peer, flat-structure, mutuality—balance between individual and collective needs, dialogue)		Politics (anarchism)	Economy (surplus-value)		Practice (effectivity)

(continued)

Table A.1 (continued)

Position	Chapter	Perception of LLM	Key-arguments	Authors inclusion of overall key-concept included in the book							
				Ethics	Sociality (order, equality [gender and economic] belonging)	Democracy (decision-making, empowerment)	Ecology	Politics (anarchism)	Economy	Binary logic	Practice (work as action, quality of work), probability, desirability)
	8. Leaderless leadership: implications of the "agora" and the "public library"	LLM (leaderless leadership) as collective action based on equality (democratic participation in decision-making) enabling all to step forward and partake in actions	Due to the creation of democratic participation imbedded in LLM by the authors named Leaderless leadership		Sociality (belonging, equality, common aim. All can step forward and partake in actions)	Democratic (empowerment, non-hierarchical, control of activities)					Practice ('authentic work', professional pride, dedication, collective actions)

Position	Chapter	Perception of LLM	Key-arguments	Authors inclusion of overall key-concept included in the book							
				Ethics	Sociality (order, equality [gender and economic] belonging)	Democracy (decision-making, empowerment)	Ecology	Politics (anarchism),	Economy	Binary logic	Practice (work as action, quality of work), probability, desirability
	9. Beyond leaderlessness: Even less than nothing is way too much	LLM as self-created, and non-surplus hunting organizations	Beyond LLM to realize Proudhon's watchword: "The government of the none"	Ethical (nobody as mean)	Sociality (free associations, non-hierarchy, anti-authority)	Democracy (empowerment)	The inner, external, and others inner nature	Politics (Anarchism)	Economy (surplus-value)		Practice (latently confirmation)

(continued)

Table A.1 (continued)

Position	Chapter	Perception of LLM	Key-arguments	Authors inclusion of overall key-concept included in the book							
				Ethics	Sociality (order, equality [gender and economic] belonging)	Democracy (decision-making, empowerment)	Ecology	Politics (anarchism),	Economy	Binary logic	Practice (work as action, quality of work), probability, desirability
PART II. In between for and against LLM	10. Leaderless work and workplace participation	LLM is an egalitarian approach focusing on workplace democracy or more worker participation by distribute power and authority among employees	In Between: change from LLM to workplace participation and applying values from LLM to encouraging workers independence rather than their participation								Practice (workplace participation, workers independence (from the power of others))

Position	Chapter	Perception of LLM	Key-arguments	Authors inclusion of overall key-concept included in the book							
				Ethics	Sociality (order, equality [gender and economic] belonging)	Democracy (decision-making, empowerment)	Ecology	Politics (anarchism),	Economy	Binary logic	Practice (work as action, quality of work), probability, desirability
	11. Who sustains whose passion?	LLM is perceived as individual's self-managementtion. and leaderless orga-nizing, making leader-figures unnec-essary	In between: neither LLM nor its opposi-tion. Suggest targeting the latently imbedded "pas-sion" discus-sion. The demand for passion somehow passed from leaders to employees								Practice (Passionate employees become leaders, discourse on passion)

(continued)

Table A.1 (continued)

Position	Chapter	Perception of LLM	Key-arguments	Authors inclusion of overall key-concept included in the book							
				Ethics	Sociality (order, equality [gender and economic] belonging)	Democracy (decision-making, empowerment)	Ecology	Politics (anarchism),	Economy	Binary logic	Practice (work as action, quality of work), probability, desirability
	12. Leaderless organization versus leading for creativity: the case for creative leadership	LLM means flat hierarchy, and decentralized decision-making. LLM is obtained by self-management and participatory democracy	Against LLM since it is less effective and predictable in realization innovative outcomes								Practice (creativity, innovation, creative leadership, effectivity, predictability, innovative outcomes)

Position	Chapter	Perception of LLM	Key arguments	Authors inclusion of overall key-concept included in the book							
				Ethics	Sociality (order, equality [gender and economic] belonging)	Ecology	Democracy (decision-making, empowerment)	Politics (anarchism)	Economy	Binary logic	Practice
											Practice (work as action, quality of work, probability, desirability)
PART III. Against LLM	13. Why leaders are necessary	LLM as mature employees e.g., in self-managing groups not needing or wanting leaders	Rejects LLM since organizations risk of losing values, identity and basically direction								Practice (emotionally inspiration, essential values, and identity)
	14. Ghostbusters! On the narrative creation of (absent) leader characters	LLM as self-governance and local autonomy either based on self-organized work-groups or whole organizations	LLM is a fata morgana. Leadership always presents even when a leader is physical absent				Democracy (authority, hierarchy)	LLM is a fata morgana			Practice (functionalities embedded in the leader)

(continued)

Table A.1 (continued)

Position	Chapter	Perception of LLM	Key-arguments	Authors inclusion of overall key-concept included in the book							
				Ethics	Sociality (order, equality [gender and economic] belonging)	Democracy (decision-making, empowerment)	Ecology	Politics (anarchism),	Economy	Binary logic	Practice (work as action, quality of work), probability, desirability
	15. Against leaderless management: what leaderless means in South Africa	LLM perceived as the Anarchist's rebel against authority, hierarchy, and order. Organizations as cooperatives based on bottom-up democracy, self-management, and self-organization	Against LLM due to the SA a need of ethical leaders able to avoid the contemporary waste of resources	Ethics (need f. ethical leaders)							Practice (suffering - waisted resources, urgent social, cultural and health issues)

Position	Chapter	Perception of LLM	Key-arguments	Authors inclusion of overall key-concept included in the book							
				Ethics	Sociality (order, equality [gender and economic] belonging)	Democracy (decision-making, empowerment)	Ecology	Politics (anarchism),	Economy	Binary logic	Practice (work as action, quality of work), probability, desirability
	16. Leaderless management: no! Leaders at all levels: yes!	LLM within the contemporary situation. LLM reduce authority and formal hierarchy in everyday work	Against LLM – since it is a misnomer, wrong and inaccurate use of a name			Democracy (IT flattering hierarchies)					Practice ("real" LLM unrealistic, modern organizations requires leadership)

(continued)

Table A.1 (continued)

Position	Chapter	Perception of LLM	Key-arguments	Authors inclusion of overall key-concept included in the book							
				Ethics	Sociality (order, equality [gender and economic] belonging)	Democracy (decision-making, empowerment)	Ecology	Politics (anarchism)	Economy	Binary logic	Practice (work as action, quality of work), probability, desirability
	17. Principled leadership: the antidote to leaderless management	LLM means individuals working collectively to obtain organizational aims and goals without formal leadership	Against LLM since it led to status quo + a lack of direction, support, and responsibility result in chaos								Practice (effectivity, improbability, inability, necessarily, changeability, responsibility, responsivity, evidential)

Appendix 359

Position	Chapter	Perception of LLM	Key-arguments	Authors inclusion of overall key-concept included in the book							
				Ethics	Sociality (order, equality [gender and economic] belonging)	Democracy (decision-making, empowerment)	Ecology	Politics (anarchism),	Economy	Binary logic	Practice (work as action, quality of work), probability, desirability
	18. The enabling role of leadership in realizing the future	LLM remains undefined	Against LLM due to VUCA (volatility, uncertainty, complexity, and ambiguity)								Practice (reframing, navigability, complexity, strength, sense-making, co-created future, undesirability, personal influence, intentionality, VUCA)

(continued)

Table A.1 (continued)

Position	Chapter	Perception of LLM	Key-arguments	Authors inclusion of overall key-concept included in the book							
				Ethics	Sociality (order, equality [gender and economic] belonging)	Democracy (decision-making, empowerment)	Ecology	Politics (anarchism)	Economy	Binary logic	Practice (work as action, quality of work), probability, desirability
PART IV. Beyond LLM	19. Organizational Management is Paradoxically both Leaderless and Leaderful	LLM based on Bion and perceived as groups without formal leaders. LLM established to expose potential leaders in a group	Leadership as a process not a person. Since all participate in generating leadership – all could become considered (potential) leaders		Sociality (disembodiment, group-based, non-human animals)					Cross the binary logic	
Epilogue (5)	Epilogue: Reflections and comments on leaderless management										

Index

Printed by Printforce, United Kingdom